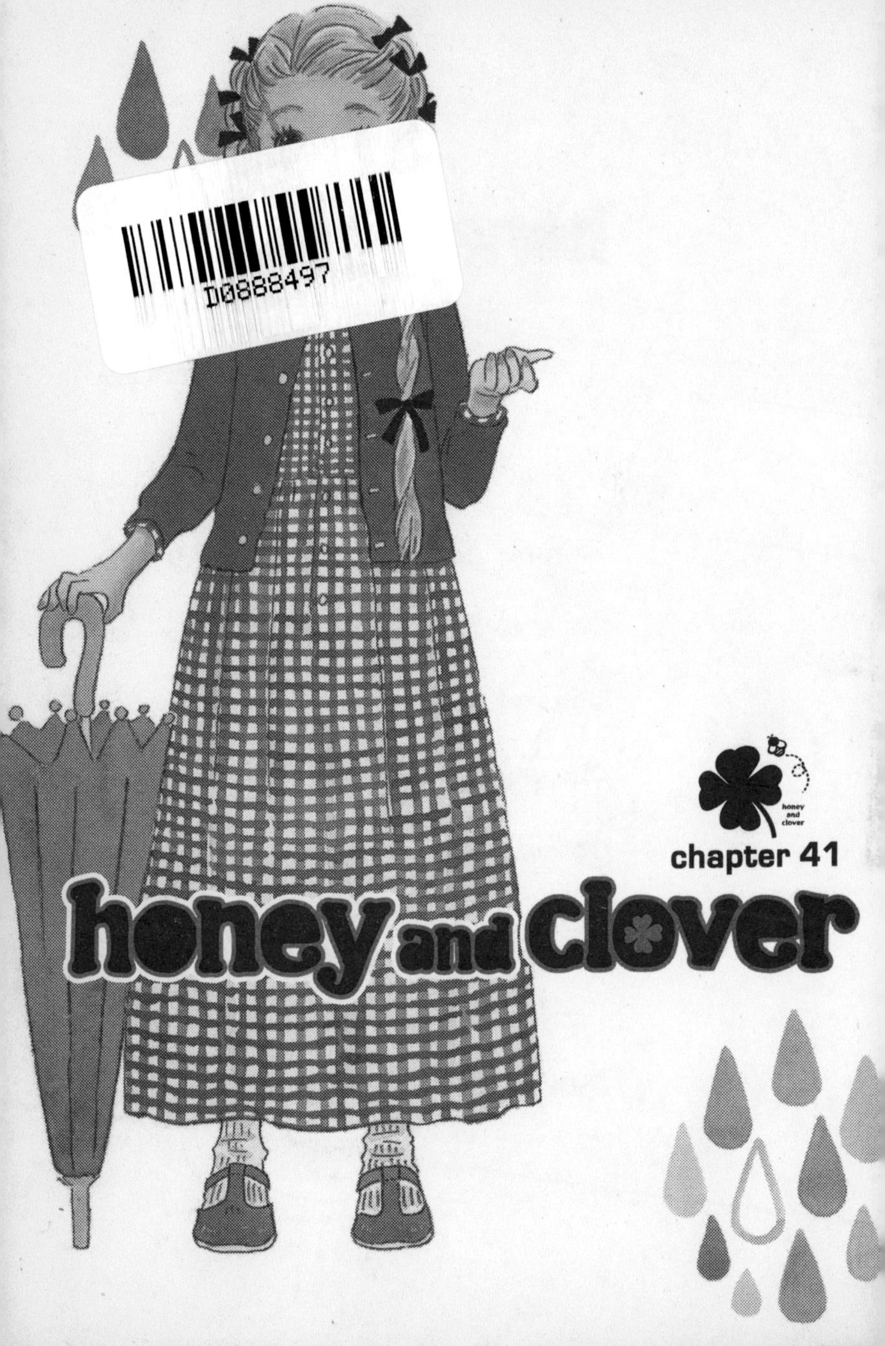

chapter 41

honey and clover

☆ For this volume, I've picked out various sketches from my "Idea Notebook."

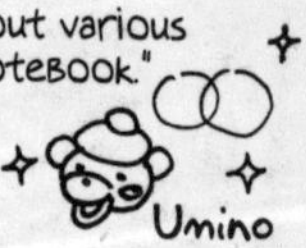

Umino

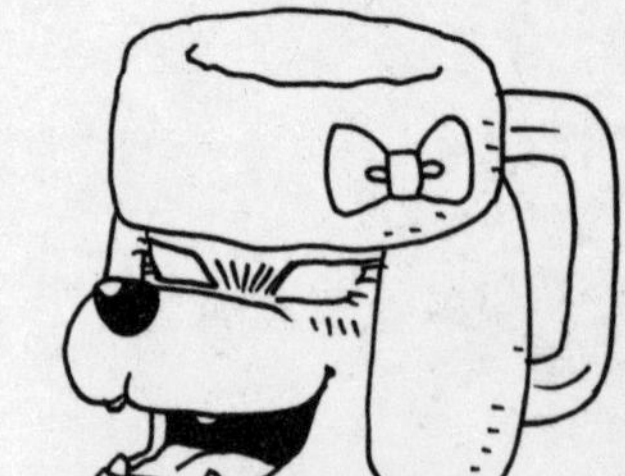

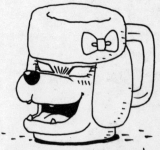

#1: Midori-chan Mug

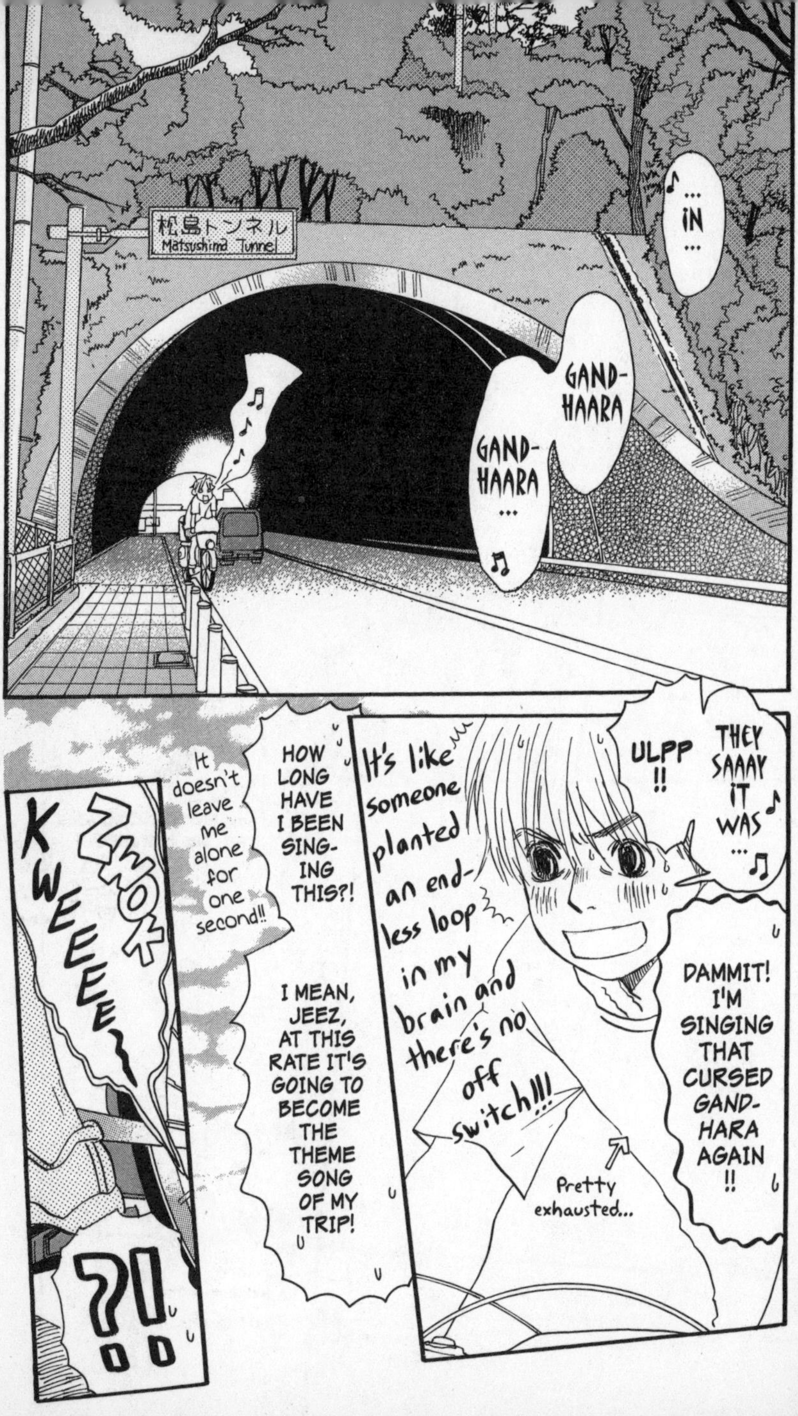
♪ ...IN...
GANDHAARA
GANDHAARA... ♪
松島トンネル
Matsushima Tunnel
THEY SAAAY IT WAS... ♪
ULPP!!
DAMMIT! I'M SINGING THAT CURSED GANDHARA AGAIN!!
It's like someone planted an endless loop in my brain and there's no off switch!!!
Pretty exhausted...
HOW LONG HAVE I BEEN SINGING THIS?!
It doesn't leave me alone for one second!!
I MEAN, JEEZ, AT THIS RATE IT'S GOING TO BECOME THE THEME SONG OF MY TRIP!
KWEEEE~
ZWOK
?!!

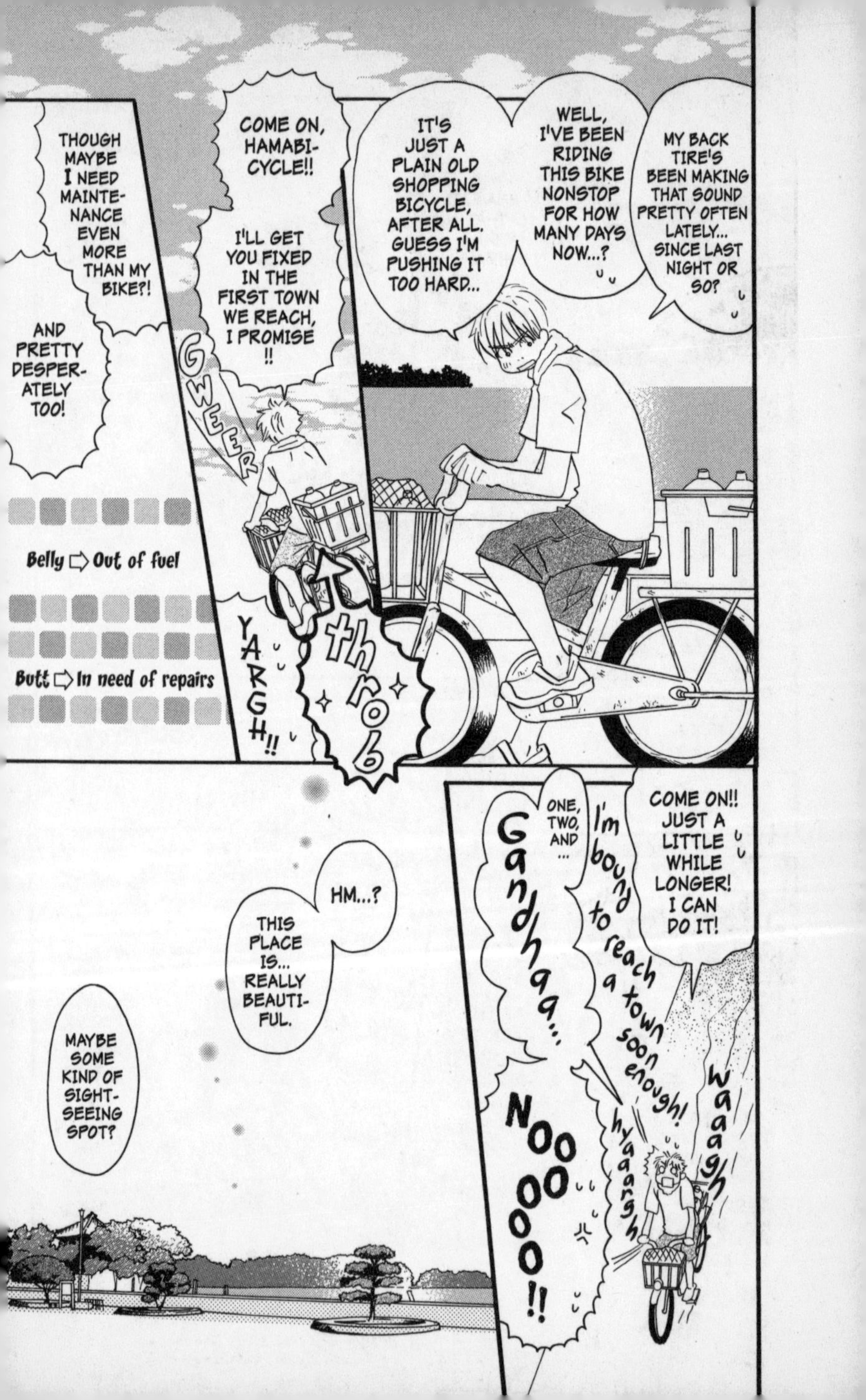
MY BACK TIRE'S BEEN MAKING THAT SOUND PRETTY OFTEN LATELY... SINCE LAST NIGHT OR SO?
WELL, I'VE BEEN RIDING THIS BIKE NONSTOP FOR HOW MANY DAYS NOW...?
IT'S JUST A PLAIN OLD SHOPPING BICYCLE, AFTER ALL. GUESS I'M PUSHING IT TOO HARD...
COME ON, HAMABI-CYCLE!!
I'LL GET YOU FIXED IN THE FIRST TOWN WE REACH, I PROMISE !!
GWEER
throb
YARGH!!
THOUGH MAYBE I NEED MAINTE-NANCE EVEN MORE THAN MY BIKE?!
AND PRETTY DESPER-ATELY TOO!
Belly ⇨ Out of fuel
Butt ⇨ In need of repairs
COME ON!! JUST A LITTLE WHILE LONGER! I CAN DO IT!
I'm bound to reach a town soon enough!
ONE, TWO, AND ...
Gandhaa...
Waaagh
hyaaargh
NOOOOOOO!!
HM...?
THIS PLACE IS... REALLY BEAUTI-FUL.
MAYBE SOME KIND OF SIGHT-SEEING SPOT?

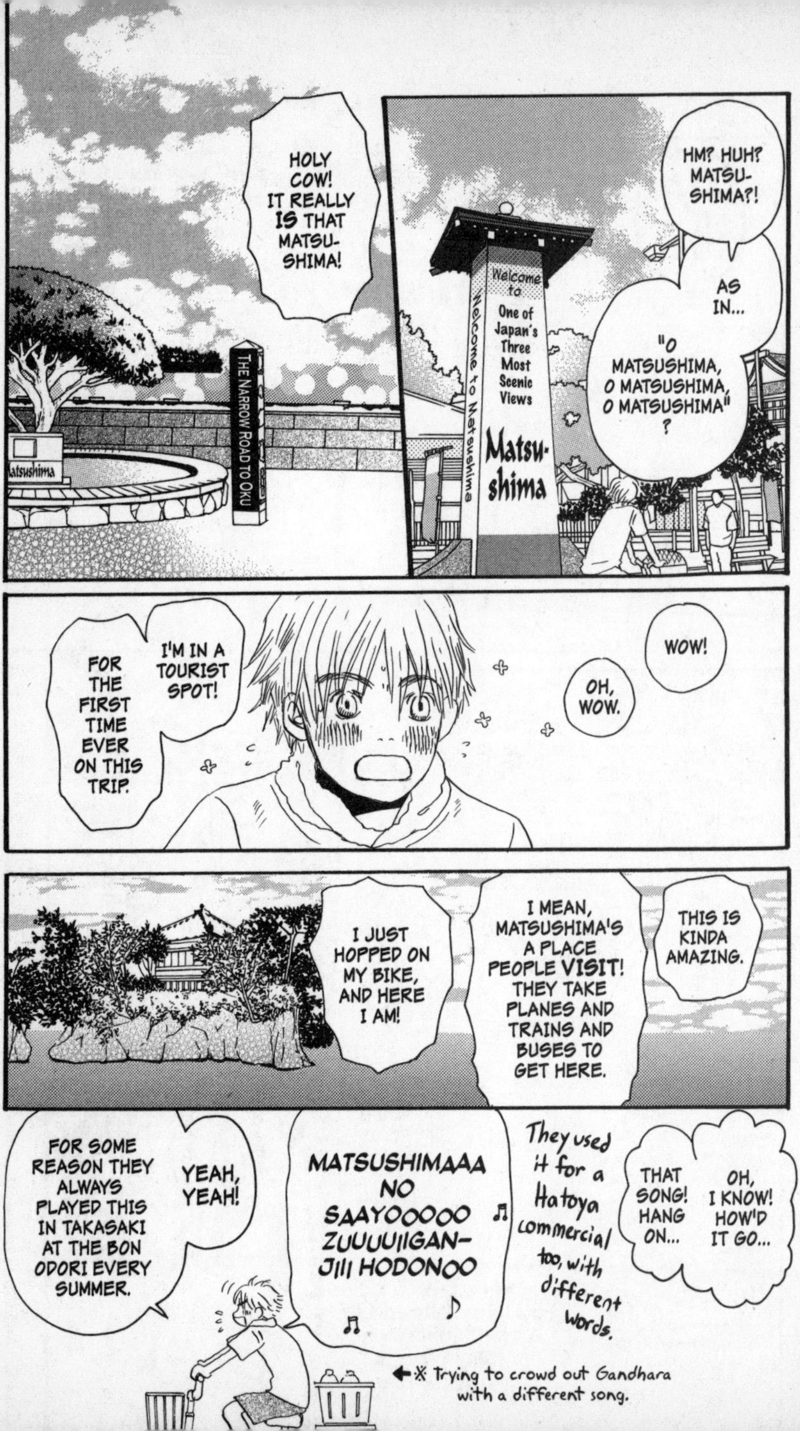
HM? HUH? MATSU-SHIMA?!
AS IN...
"O MATSUSHIMA, O MATSUSHIMA, O MATSUSHIMA"?
Welcome to One of Japan's Three Most Scenic Views Matsu-shima
Welcome to Matsushima
HOLY COW! IT REALLY IS THAT MATSU-SHIMA!
THE NARROW ROAD TO OKU
Matsushima
WOW!
OH, WOW.
I'M IN A TOURIST SPOT!
FOR THE FIRST TIME EVER ON THIS TRIP.
THIS IS KINDA AMAZING.
I MEAN, MATSUSHIMA'S A PLACE PEOPLE VISIT! THEY TAKE PLANES AND TRAINS AND BUSES TO GET HERE.
I JUST HOPPED ON MY BIKE, AND HERE I AM!
OH, I KNOW! HOW'D IT GO...
THAT SONG! HANG ON...
They used it for a Hatoya commercial too, with different words.
MATSUSHIMAAA NO SAAYOOOOO ZUUUUIIGAN-JIII HODONOO
YEAH, YEAH!
FOR SOME REASON THEY ALWAYS PLAYED THIS IN TAKASAKI AT THE BON ODORI EVERY SUMMER.
←※ Trying to crowd out Gandhara with a different song.

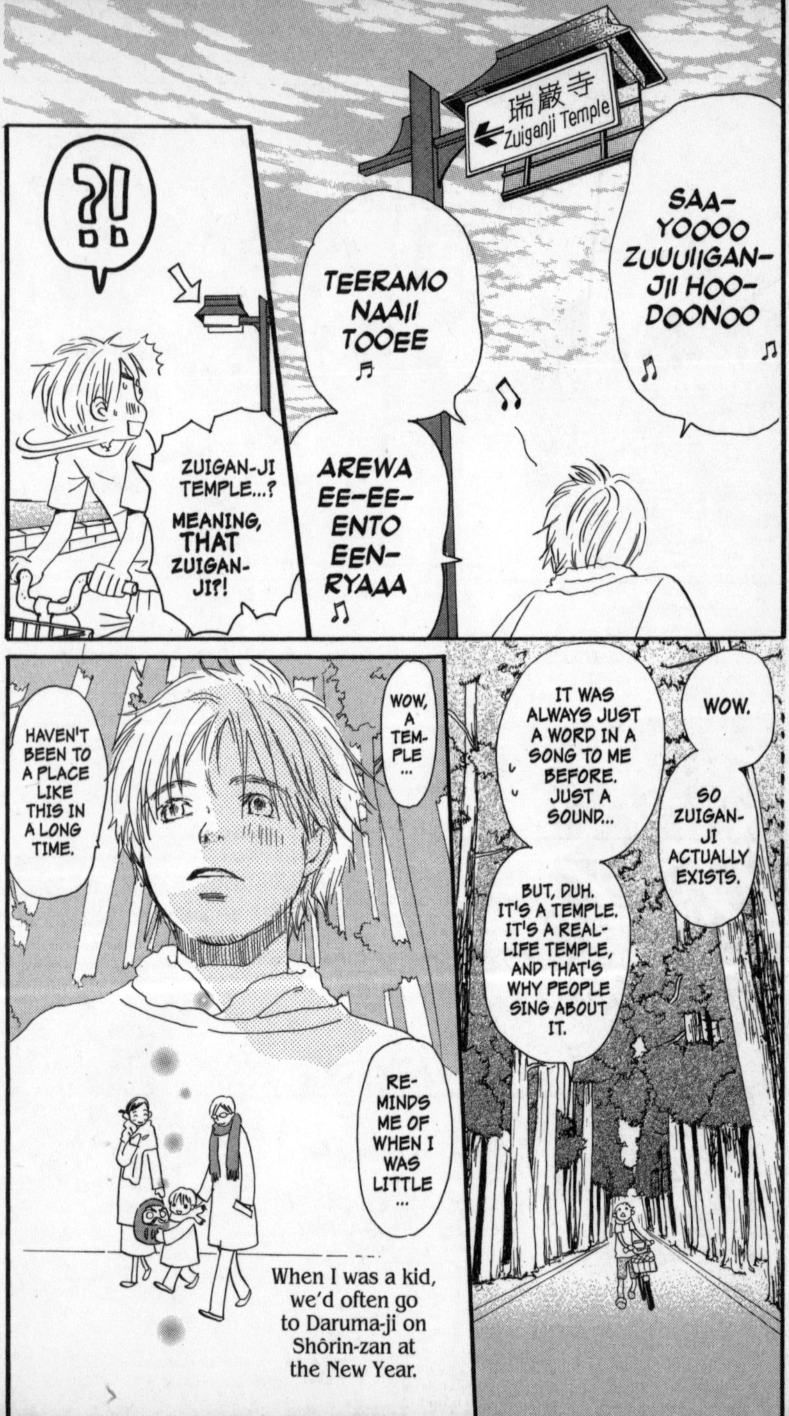
瑞巌寺
Zuiganji Temple
SAA-YOOOO ZUUUIIGAN-JII HOO-DOONOO ♫
TEERAMO NAAII TOOEE ♫
AREWA EE-EE-ENTO EEN-RYAAA ♫
?!
ZUIGAN-JI TEMPLE...?
MEANING, THAT ZUIGAN-JI?!
WOW.
SO ZUIGAN-JI ACTUALLY EXISTS.
IT WAS ALWAYS JUST A WORD IN A SONG TO ME BEFORE. JUST A SOUND...
BUT, DUH. IT'S A TEMPLE. IT'S A REAL-LIFE TEMPLE, AND THAT'S WHY PEOPLE SING ABOUT IT.
WOW, A TEMPLE...
HAVEN'T BEEN TO A PLACE LIKE THIS IN A LONG TIME.
REMINDS ME OF WHEN I WAS LITTLE...
When I was a kid, we'd often go to Daruma-ji on Shôrin-zan at the New Year.

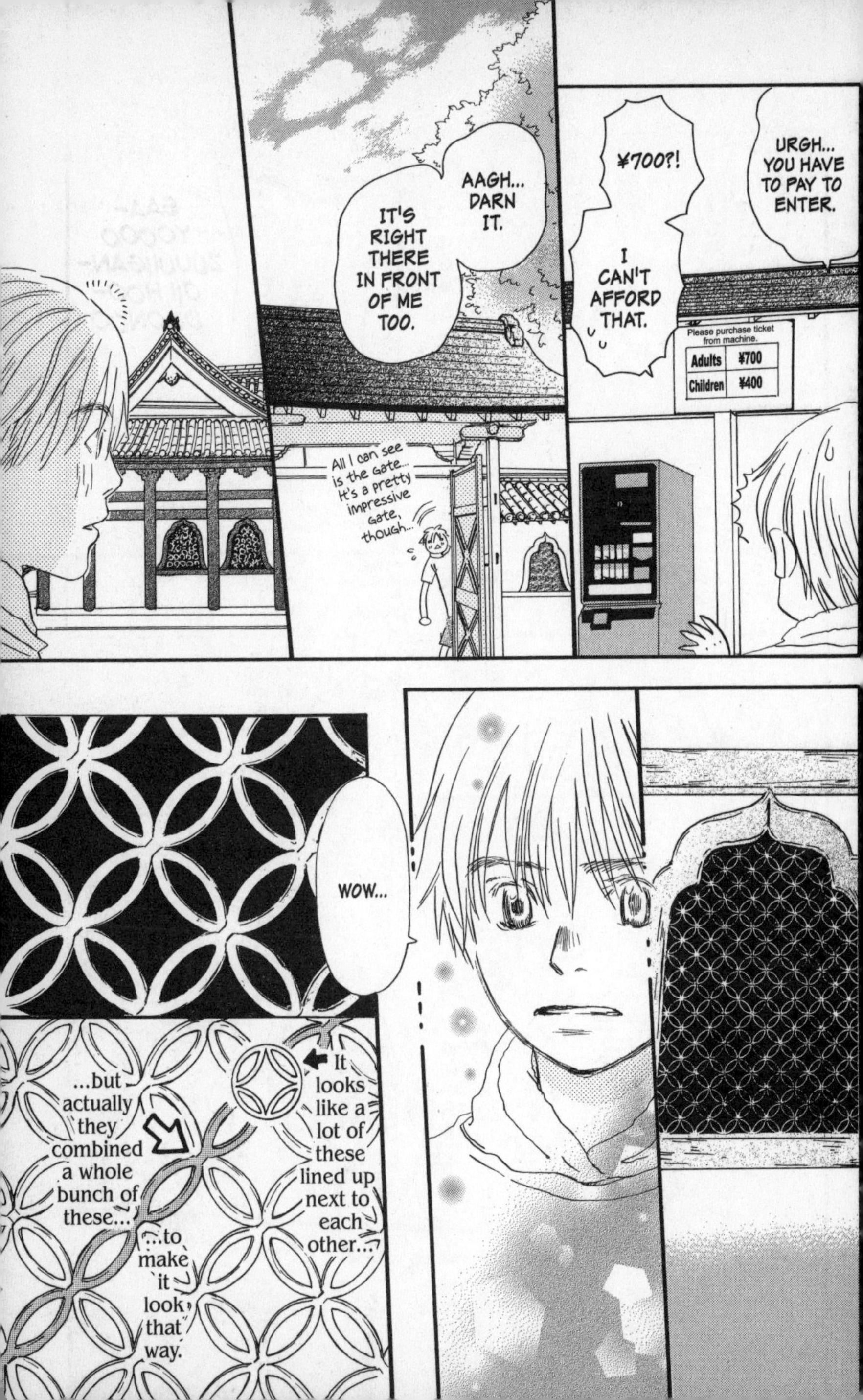
URGH... YOU HAVE TO PAY TO ENTER.
¥700?!
I CAN'T AFFORD THAT.
Please purchase ticket from machine.
Adults ¥700
Children ¥400
AAGH... DARN IT.
IT'S RIGHT THERE IN FRONT OF ME TOO.
All I can see is the Gate... It's a pretty impressive Gate, though...
WOW...
It looks like a lot of these lined up next to each other...
...but actually they combined a whole bunch of these...
...to make it look that way.

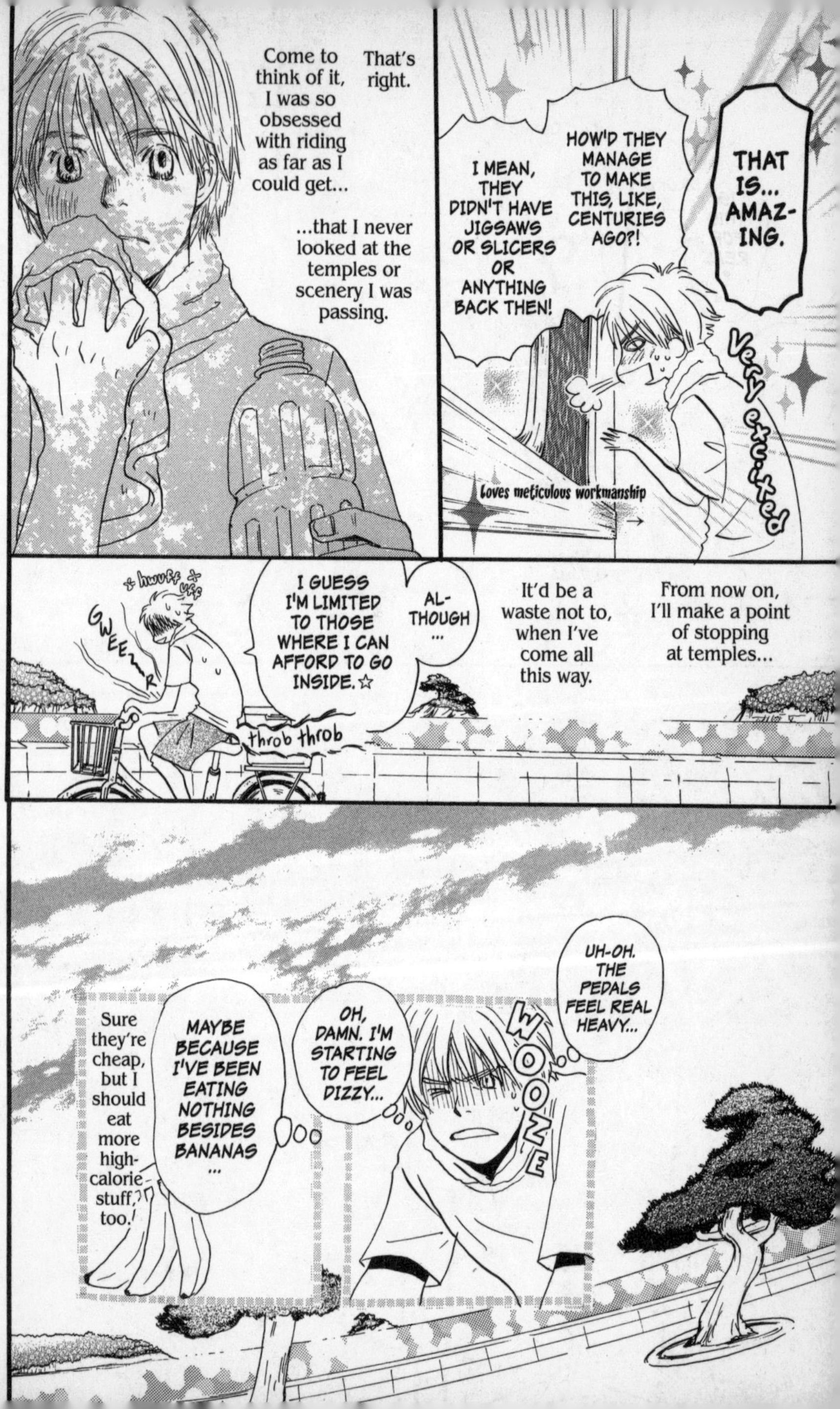
THAT IS... AMAZ-ING.
HOW'D THEY MANAGE TO MAKE THIS, LIKE, CENTURIES AGO?!
I MEAN, THEY DIDN'T HAVE JIGSAWS OR SLICERS OR ANYTHING BACK THEN!
Very excited
Loves meticulous workmanship →
That's right.
Come to think of it, I was so obsessed with riding as far as I could get...
...that I never looked at the temples or scenery I was passing.
From now on, I'll make a point of stopping at temples...
It'd be a waste not to, when I've come all this way.
AL-THOUGH...
I GUESS I'M LIMITED TO THOSE WHERE I CAN AFFORD TO GO INSIDE.☆
throb throb
hwuff uff
GWEEZR
UH-OH. THE PEDALS FEEL REAL HEAVY...
WOOZE
OH, DAMN. I'M STARTING TO FEEL DIZZY...
MAYBE BECAUSE I'VE BEEN EATING NOTHING BESIDES BANANAS...
Sure they're cheap, but I should eat more high-calorie stuff, too.

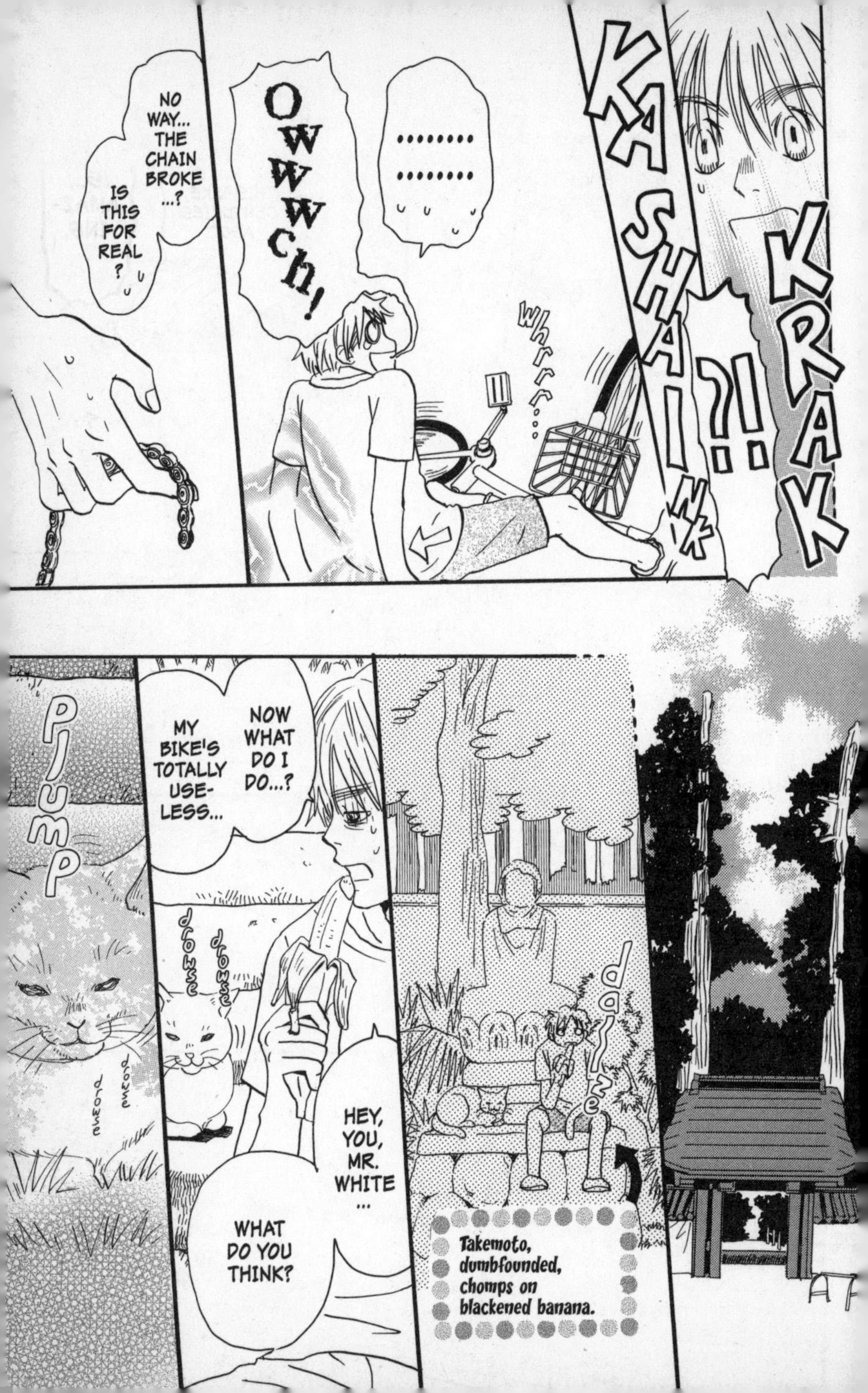
KRAK
?!!
KASHAINK
whrrr...
....
OWWWCh!
NO WAY... THE CHAIN BROKE ...?
IS THIS FOR REAL?
daze
Takemoto, dumbfounded, chomps on blackened banana.
NOW WHAT DO I DO...?
MY BIKE'S TOTALLY USE-LESS...
drowse drowse
HEY, YOU, MR. WHITE...
WHAT DO YOU THINK?
PLUMP
drowse drowse

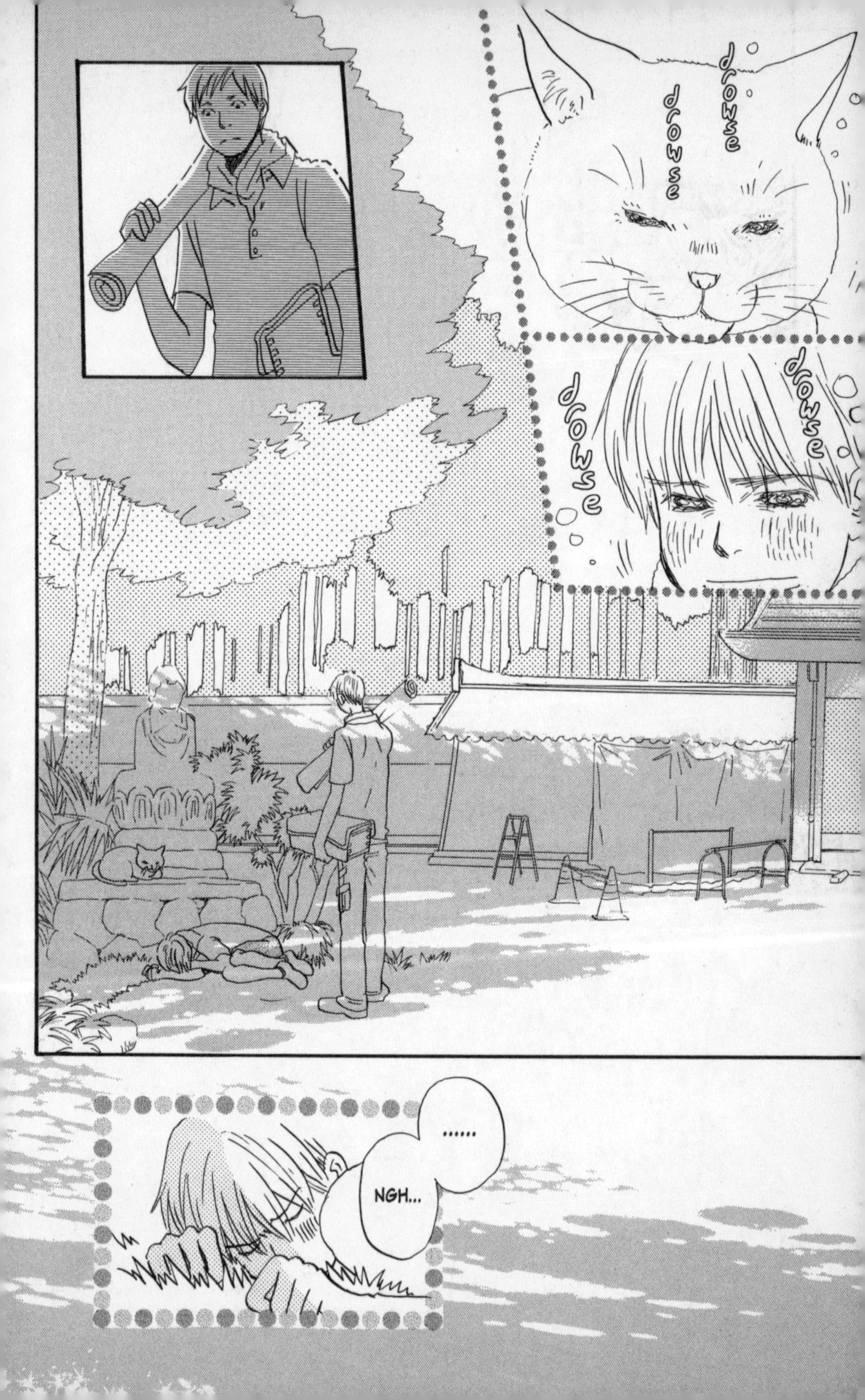
drowse
drowse
drowse
drowse
......
NGH...

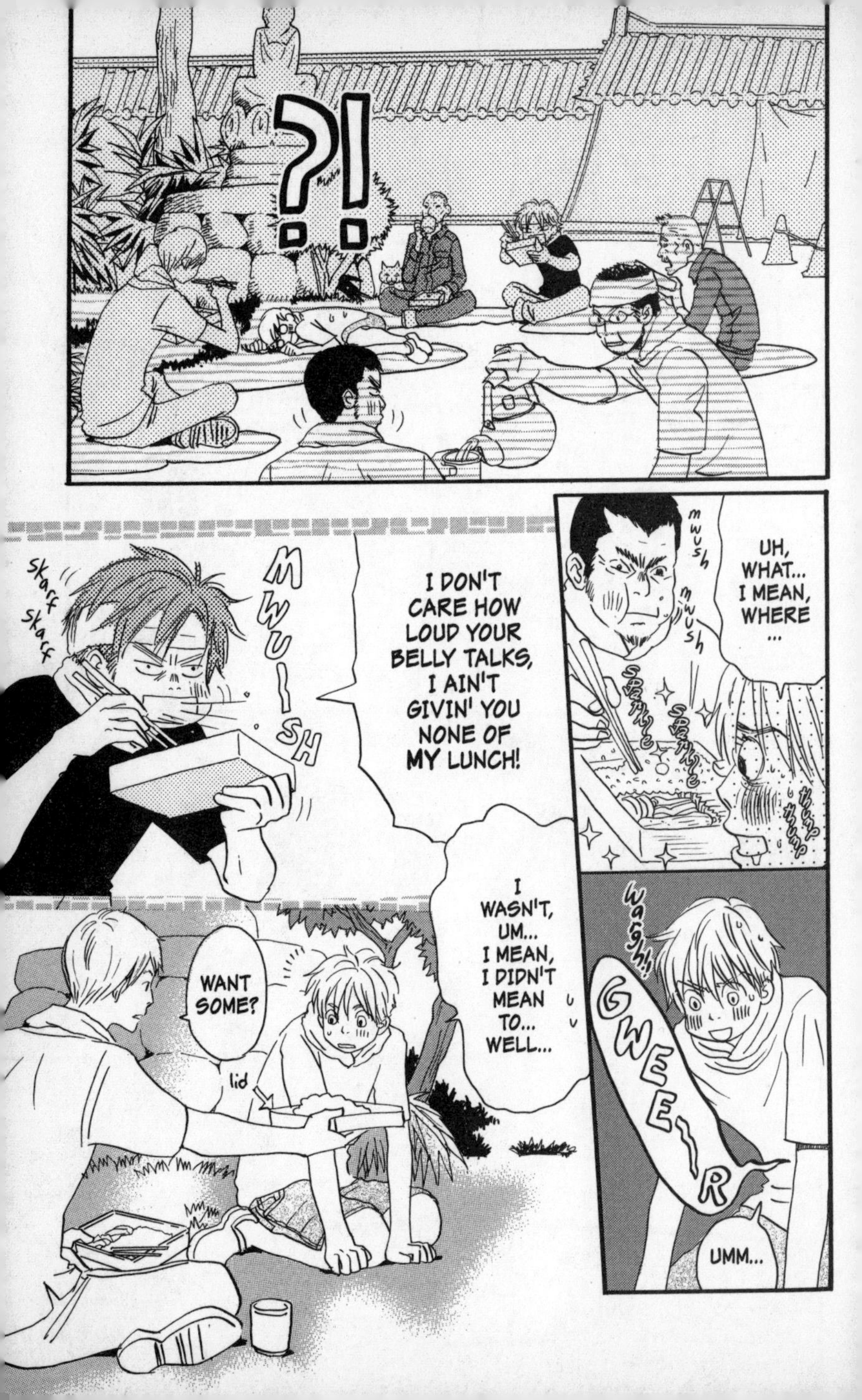
?!
mwush
mwush
UH, WHAT... I MEAN, WHERE ...
sparkle
sparkle
thump thump
Skarf skarf
MWUISH
I DON'T CARE HOW LOUD YOUR BELLY TALKS, I AIN'T GIVIN' YOU NONE OF MY LUNCH!
Wargh!!
GWEE-R
UMM...
I WASN'T, UM... I MEAN, I DIDN'T MEAN TO... WELL...
WANT SOME?
lid

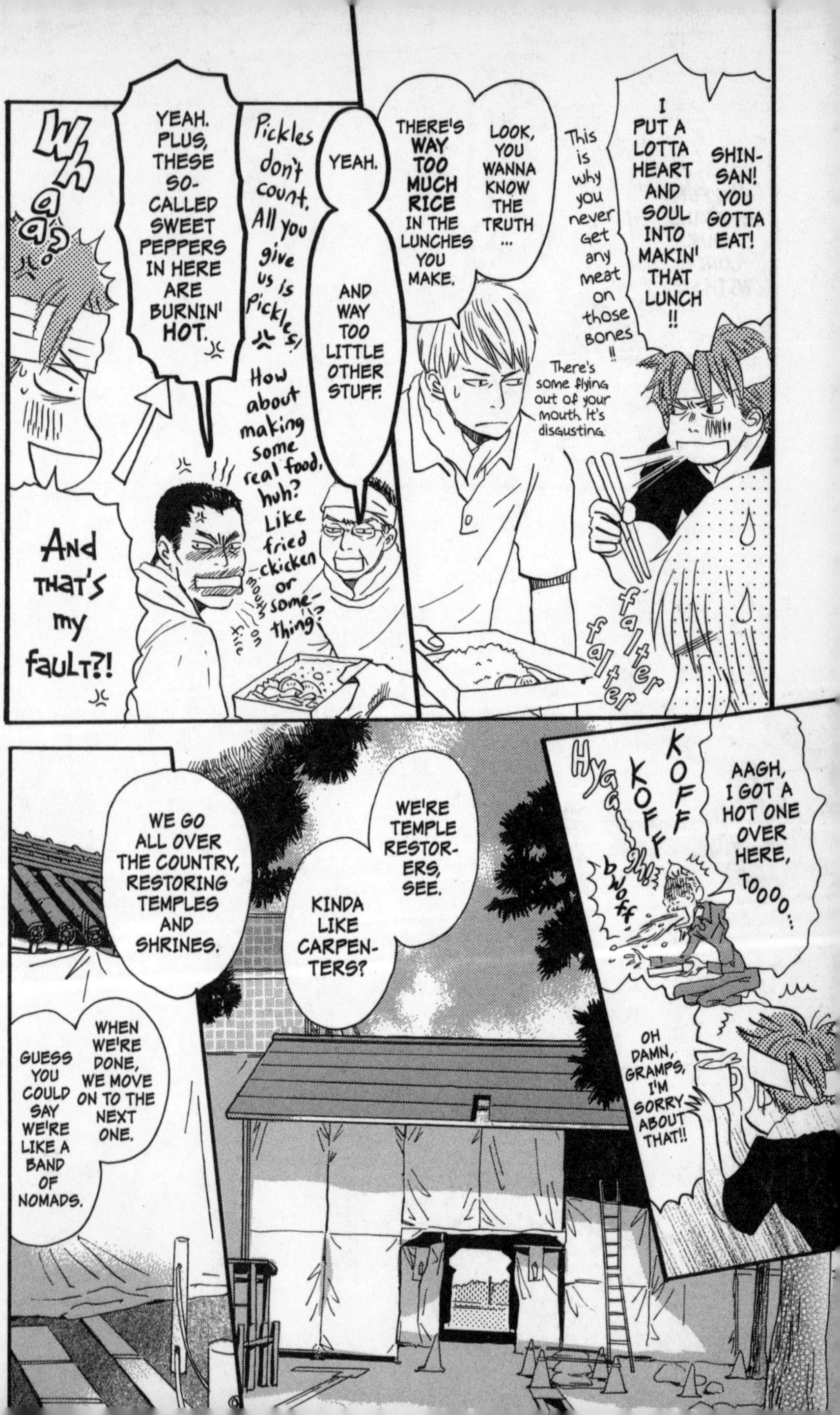
SHIN-SAN! YOU GOTTA EAT!
I PUT A LOTTA HEART AND SOUL INTO MAKIN' THAT LUNCH!!
This is why you never get any meat on those bones!!
LOOK, YOU WANNA KNOW THE TRUTH...
THERE'S WAY TOO MUCH RICE IN THE LUNCHES YOU MAKE.
There's some flying out of your mouth. It's disgusting.
falter falter
YEAH.
AND WAY TOO LITTLE OTHER STUFF.
Pickles don't count. All you give us is pickles!
How about making some real food, huh? Like fried ckicken or some-thing?
mouth's on fire
YEAH. PLUS, THESE SO-CALLED SWEET PEPPERS IN HERE ARE BURNIN' HOT.
Whaa?
And THAT's my fauLT?!
KOFF KOFF
Hyaa—gh!!
bwoff
AAGH, I GOT A HOT ONE OVER HERE, TOOOO...
OH DAMN, GRAMPS, I'M SORRY ABOUT THAT!!
WE'RE TEMPLE RESTORERS, SEE.
KINDA LIKE CARPENTERS?
WE GO ALL OVER THE COUNTRY, RESTORING TEMPLES AND SHRINES.
WHEN WE'RE DONE, WE MOVE ON TO THE NEXT ONE.
GUESS YOU COULD SAY WE'RE LIKE A BAND OF NOMADS.

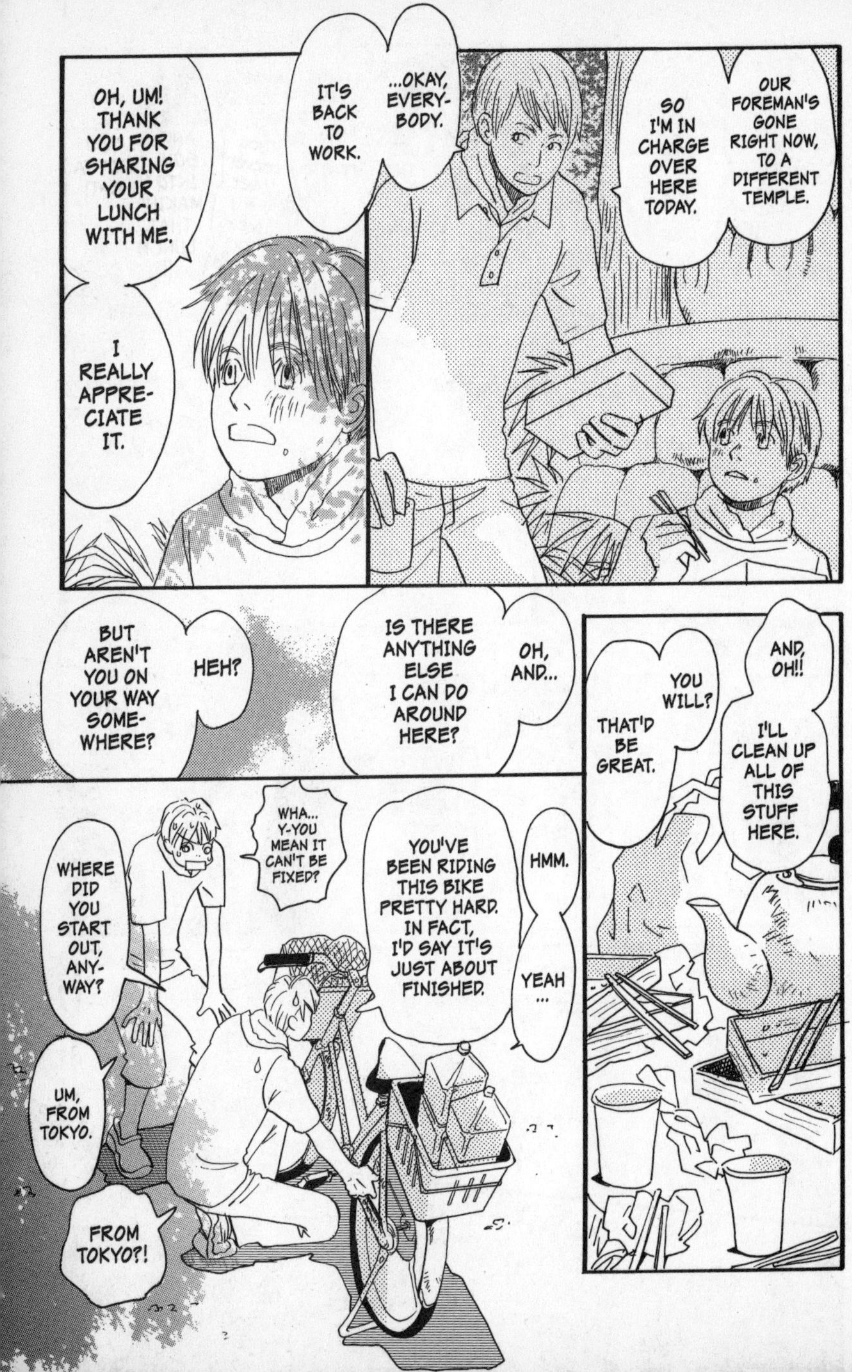
OUR FOREMAN'S GONE RIGHT NOW, TO A DIFFERENT TEMPLE.
SO I'M IN CHARGE OVER HERE TODAY.
...OKAY, EVERYBODY.
IT'S BACK TO WORK.
OH, UM! THANK YOU FOR SHARING YOUR LUNCH WITH ME.
I REALLY APPRECIATE IT.
AND, OH!!
I'LL CLEAN UP ALL OF THIS STUFF HERE.
YOU WILL?
THAT'D BE GREAT.
OH, AND...
IS THERE ANYTHING ELSE I CAN DO AROUND HERE?
HEH?
BUT AREN'T YOU ON YOUR WAY SOMEWHERE?
HMM.
YEAH...
YOU'VE BEEN RIDING THIS BIKE PRETTY HARD. IN FACT, I'D SAY IT'S JUST ABOUT FINISHED.
WHA... Y-YOU MEAN IT CAN'T BE FIXED?
WHERE DID YOU START OUT, ANYWAY?
UM, FROM TOKYO.
FROM TOKYO?!

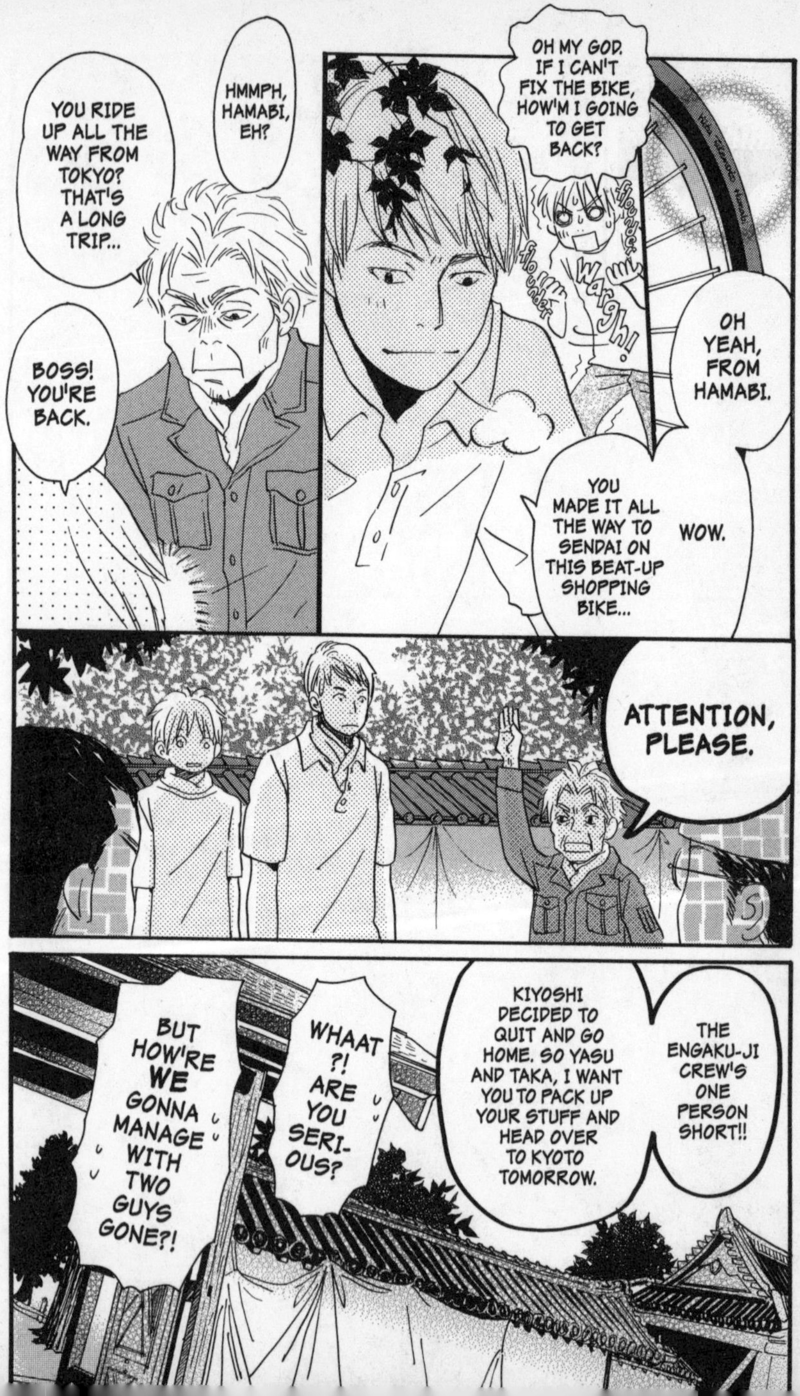
OH MY GOD. IF I CAN'T FIX THE BIKE, HOW'M I GOING TO GET BACK?
flounder
flounder
Wargh!
OH YEAH, FROM HAMABI.
WOW.
YOU MADE IT ALL THE WAY TO SENDAI ON THIS BEAT-UP SHOPPING BIKE...
HMMPH, HAMABI, EH?
YOU RIDE UP ALL THE WAY FROM TOKYO? THAT'S A LONG TRIP...
BOSS! YOU'RE BACK.
ATTENTION, PLEASE.
THE ENGAKU-JI CREW'S ONE PERSON SHORT!!
KIYOSHI DECIDED TO QUIT AND GO HOME. SO YASU AND TAKA, I WANT YOU TO PACK UP YOUR STUFF AND HEAD OVER TO KYOTO TOMORROW.
WHAAT?! ARE YOU SERI-OUS?
BUT HOW'RE WE GONNA MANAGE WITH TWO GUYS GONE?!

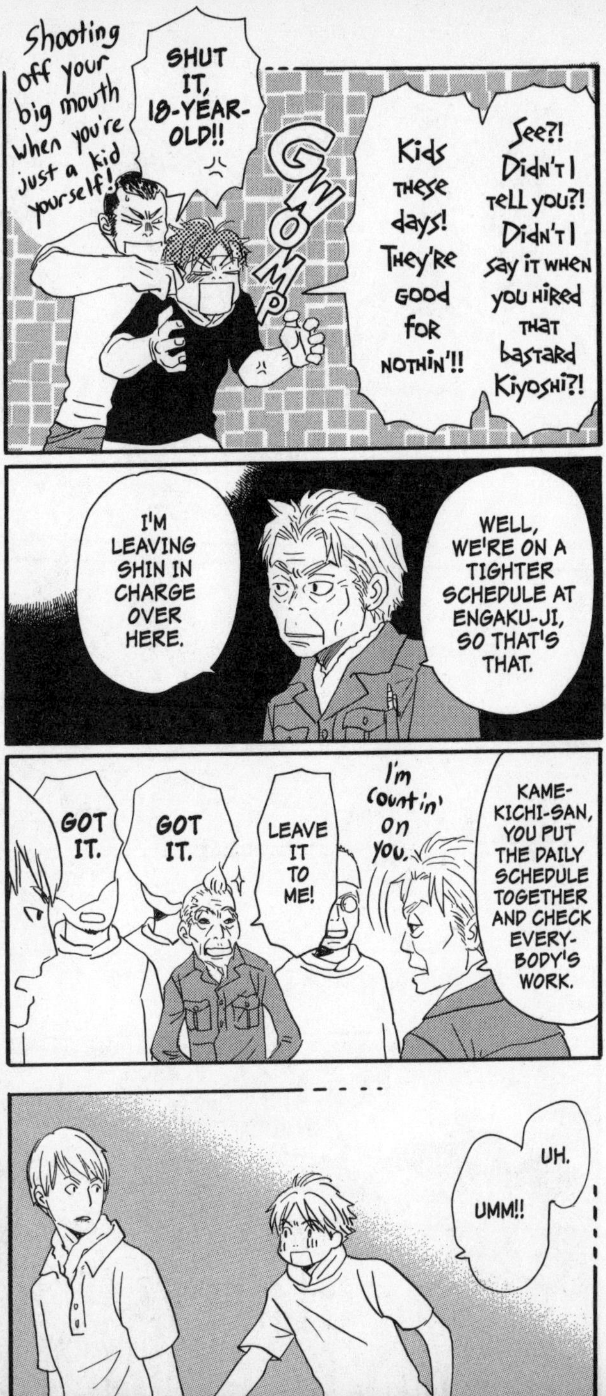
See?! Didn't I tell you?! Didn't I say it when you hired that bastard Kiyoshi?!
Kids these days! They're good for nothin'!!
GWOMP
SHUT IT, 18-YEAR-OLD!!
Shooting off your big mouth when you're just a kid yourself!
WELL, WE'RE ON A TIGHTER SCHEDULE AT ENGAKU-JI, SO THAT'S THAT.
I'M LEAVING SHIN IN CHARGE OVER HERE.
KAME-KICHI-SAN, YOU PUT THE DAILY SCHEDULE TOGETHER AND CHECK EVERY-BODY'S WORK.
I'm countin' on you.
LEAVE IT TO ME!
GOT IT.
GOT IT.
UH.
UMM!!

I love umbrellas!

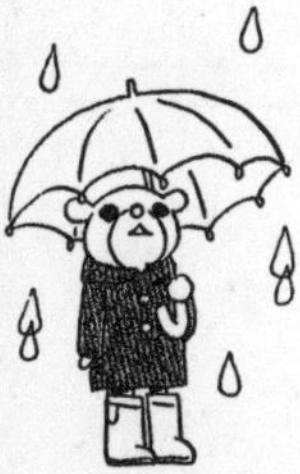

My favorite umbrellas are those clear plastic ones, because you see the sky through them. Even on rainy days, the sky seems bright if you have one of those.

Chica Umino

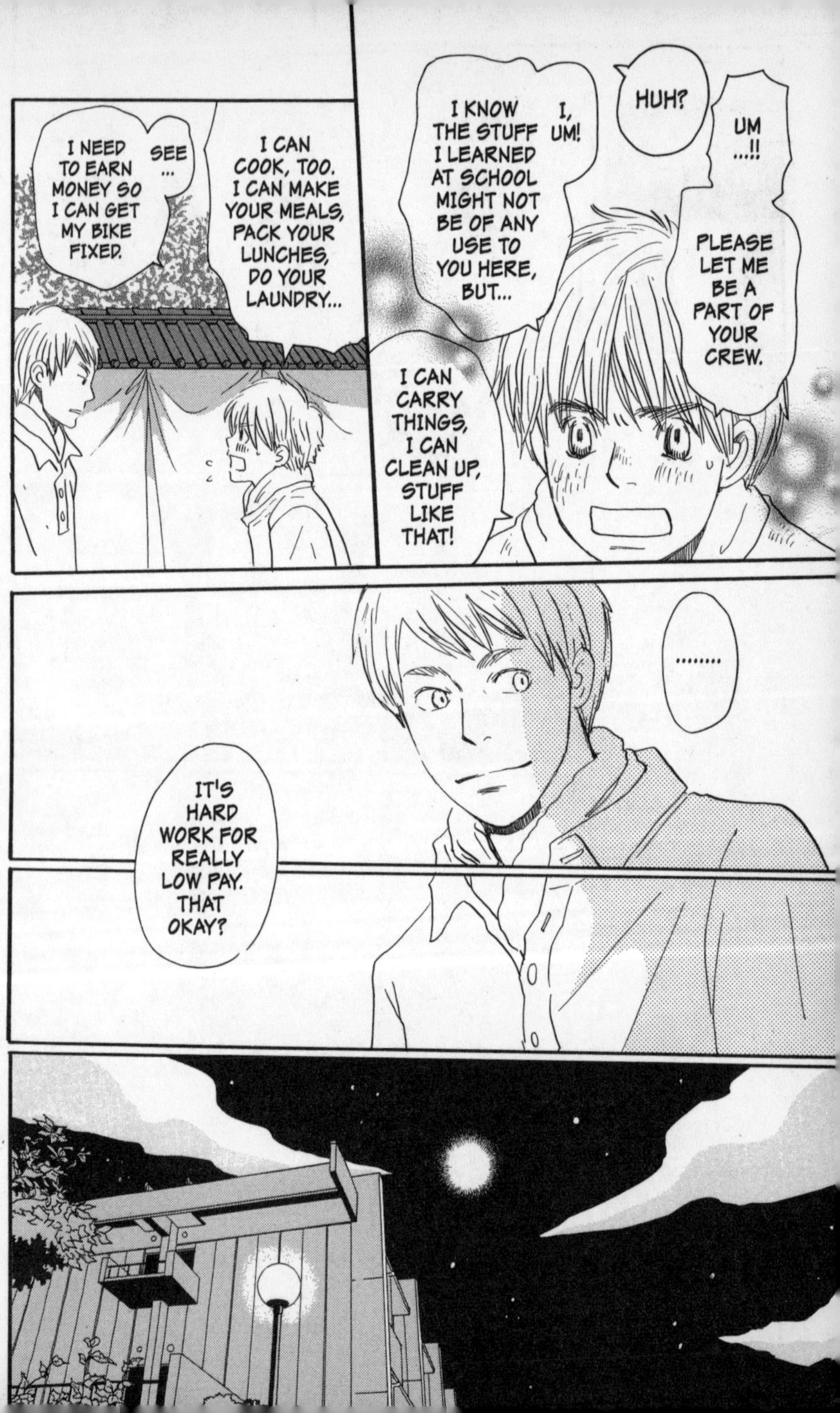
HUH?
UM ...!!
PLEASE LET ME BE A PART OF YOUR CREW.
I, UM!
I KNOW THE STUFF I LEARNED AT SCHOOL MIGHT NOT BE OF ANY USE TO YOU HERE, BUT...
I CAN CARRY THINGS, I CAN CLEAN UP, STUFF LIKE THAT!
I CAN COOK, TOO. I CAN MAKE YOUR MEALS, PACK YOUR LUNCHES, DO YOUR LAUNDRY...
SEE ...
I NEED TO EARN MONEY SO I CAN GET MY BIKE FIXED.
....
IT'S HARD WORK FOR REALLY LOW PAY. THAT OKAY?

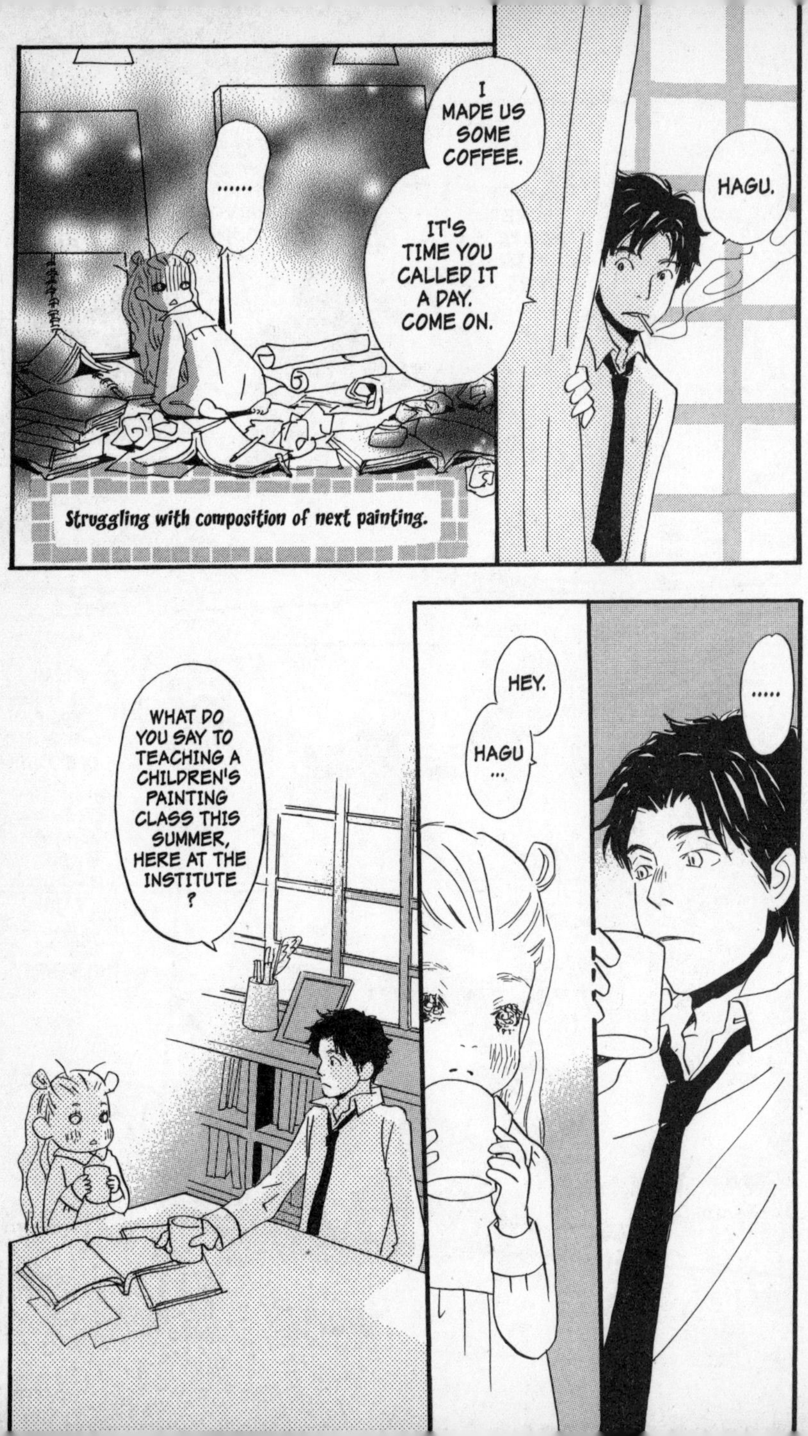
HAGU.
I MADE US SOME COFFEE.
IT'S TIME YOU CALLED IT A DAY. COME ON.
......
Struggling with composition of next painting.
......
HEY.
HAGU ...
WHAT DO YOU SAY TO TEACHING A CHILDREN'S PAINTING CLASS THIS SUMMER, HERE AT THE INSTITUTE ?

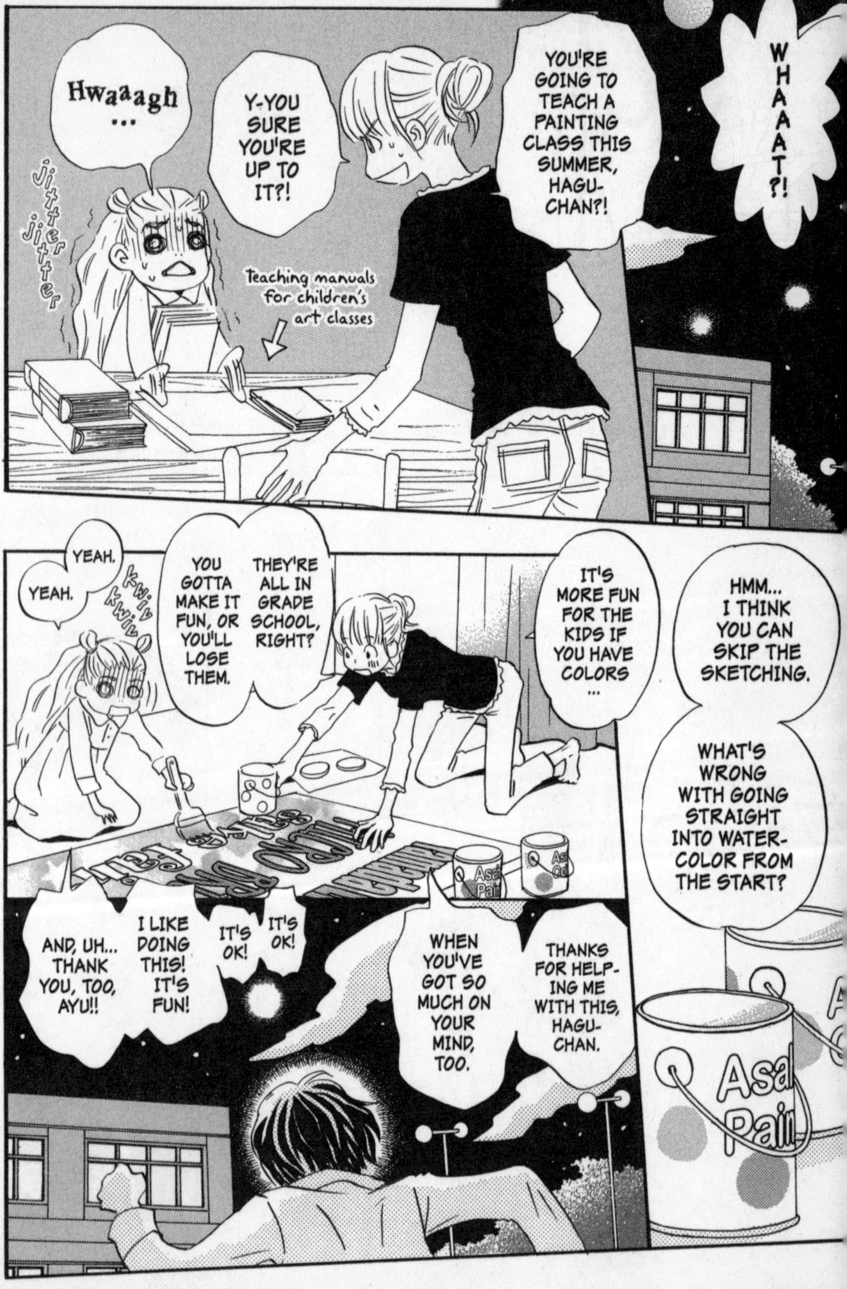
WHAAAT?!
YOU'RE GOING TO TEACH A PAINTING CLASS THIS SUMMER, HAGU-CHAN?!
Y-YOU SURE YOU'RE UP TO IT?!
Hwaaagh ...
jitter jitter
teaching manuals for children's art classes
HMM... I THINK YOU CAN SKIP THE SKETCHING.
WHAT'S WRONG WITH GOING STRAIGHT INTO WATER-COLOR FROM THE START?
IT'S MORE FUN FOR THE KIDS IF YOU HAVE COLORS ...
THEY'RE ALL IN GRADE SCHOOL, RIGHT?
YOU GOTTA MAKE IT FUN, OR YOU'LL LOSE THEM.
kwiv kwiv
YEAH.
YEAH.
THANKS FOR HELP-ING ME WITH THIS, HAGU-CHAN.
WHEN YOU'VE GOT SO MUCH ON YOUR MIND, TOO.
IT'S OK!
IT'S OK!
I LIKE DOING THIS! IT'S FUN!
AND, UH... THANK YOU, TOO, AYU!!

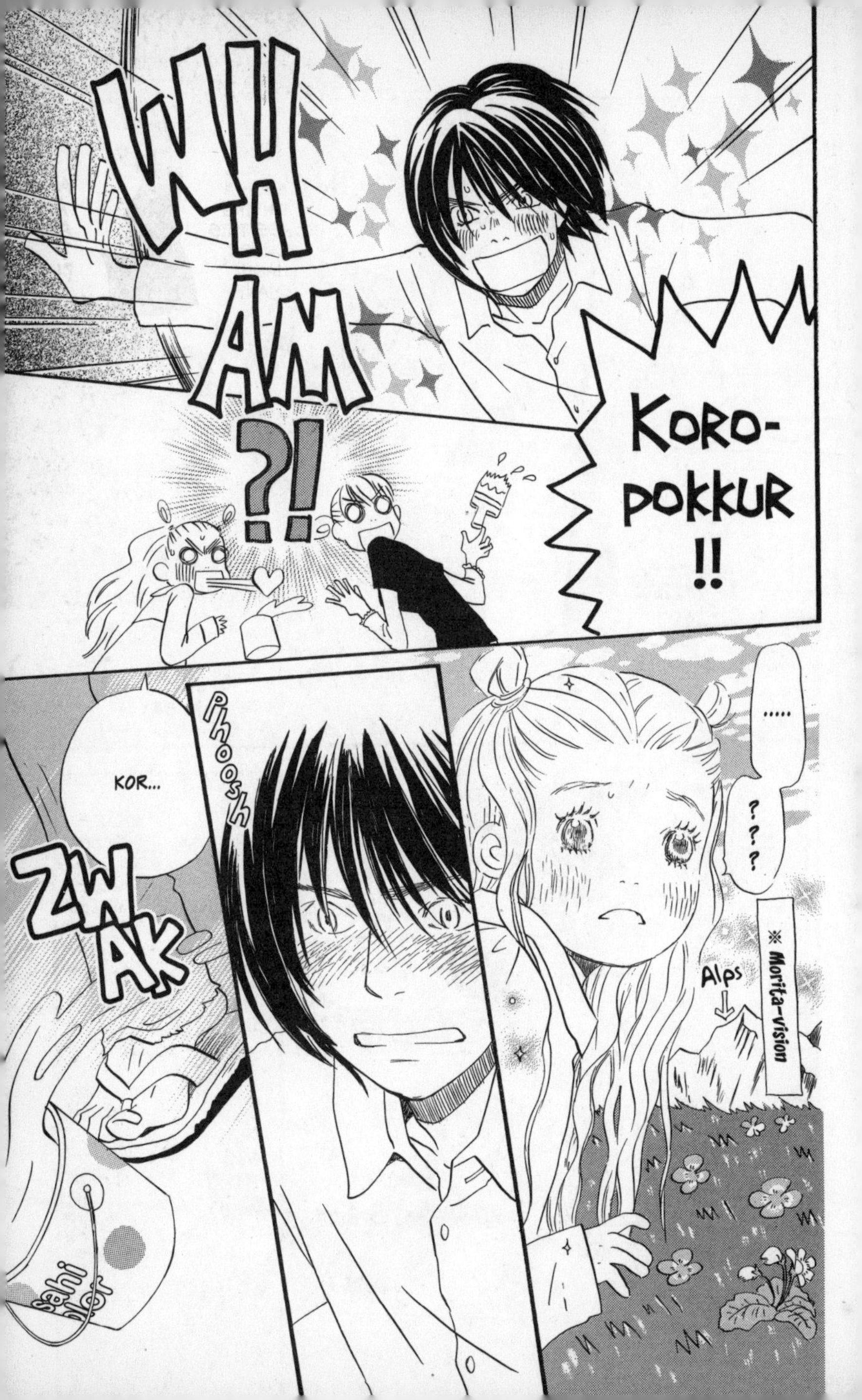
KORO-POKKUR!!
WHAM
?!
.....
???
※ Morita-vision
Alps
Phoosh
KOR...
ZWAK

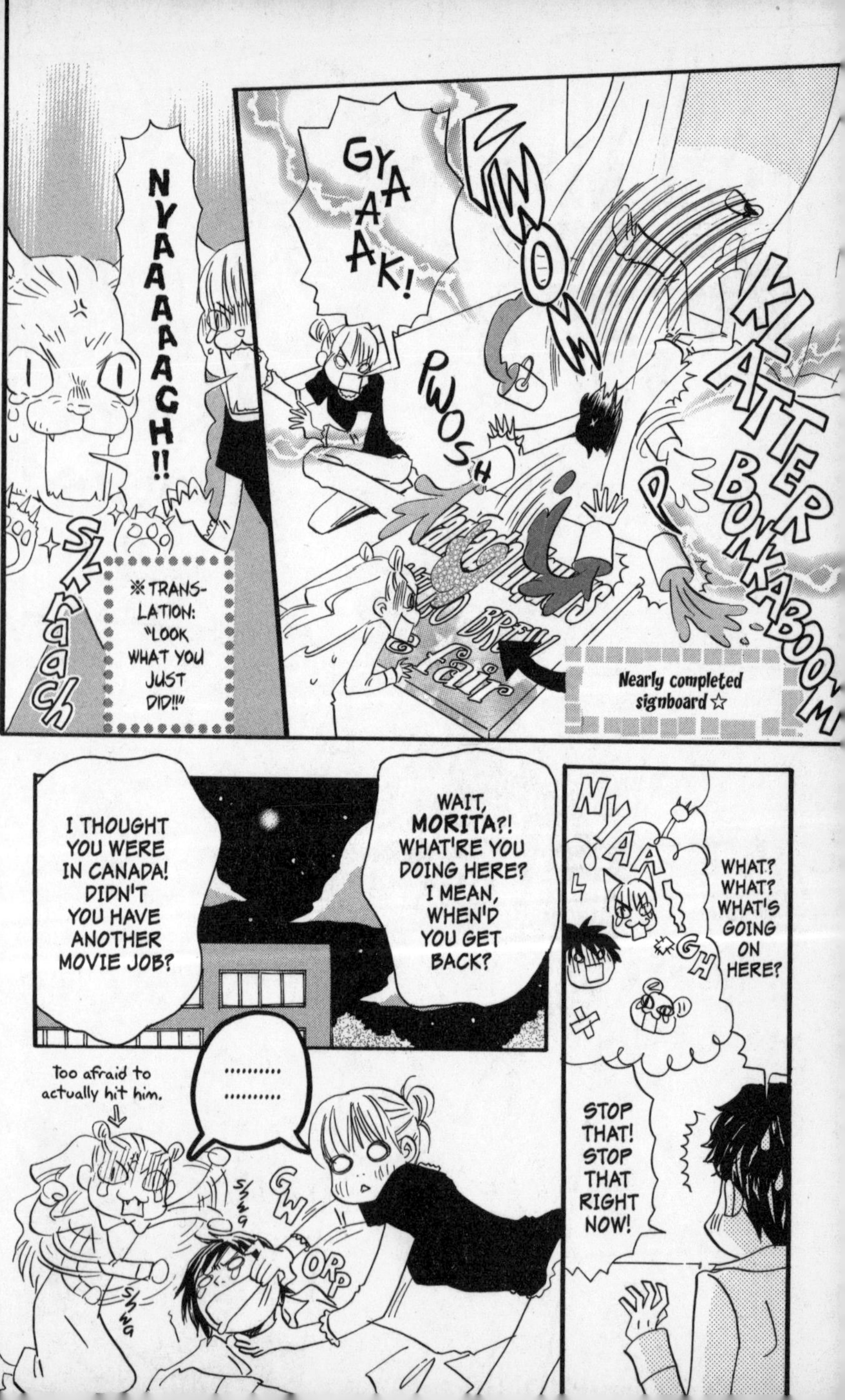
GYAAAK!
PWOSH
KLATTER
BONKABOOM
Nearly completed signboard ☆
NYAAAAAGH!!
※TRANSLATION: "LOOK WHAT YOU JUST DID!!"
NYAAAGH
WHAT? WHAT? WHAT'S GOING ON HERE?
WAIT, MORITA?! WHAT'RE YOU DOING HERE? I MEAN, WHEN'D YOU GET BACK?
I THOUGHT YOU WERE IN CANADA! DIDN'T YOU HAVE ANOTHER MOVIE JOB?
STOP THAT! STOP THAT RIGHT NOW!
....
....
GWORP
Too afraid to actually hit him.

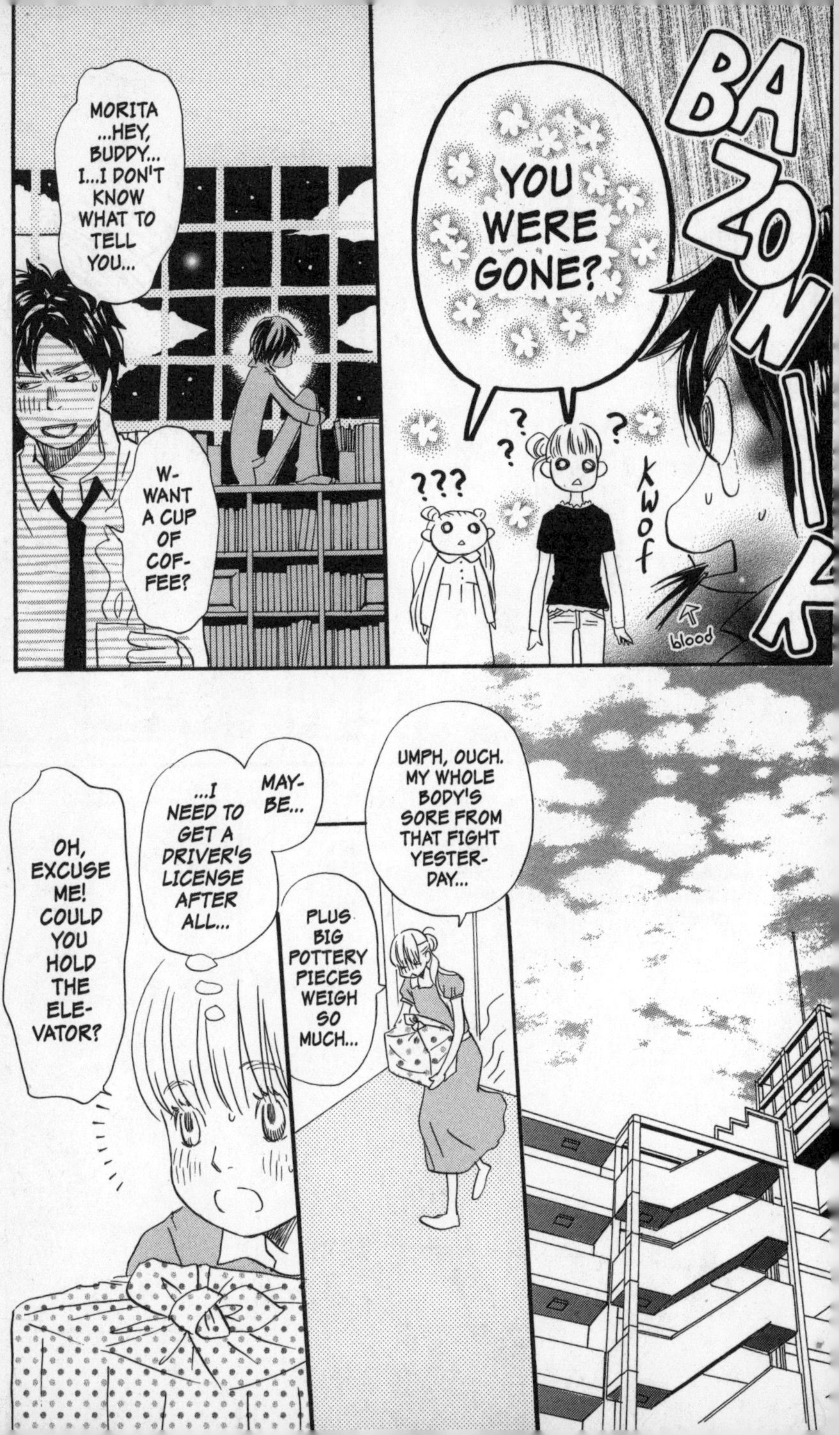
BAZONK
YOU WERE GONE?
?
?
?
???
KWOF
blood
MORITA ...HEY, BUDDY... I...I DON'T KNOW WHAT TO TELL YOU...
W-WANT A CUP OF COF-FEE?
UMPH, OUCH. MY WHOLE BODY'S SORE FROM THAT FIGHT YESTER-DAY...
PLUS BIG POTTERY PIECES WEIGH SO MUCH...
MAY-BE...
...I NEED TO GET A DRIVER'S LICENSE AFTER ALL...
OH, EXCUSE ME! COULD YOU HOLD THE ELE-VATOR?

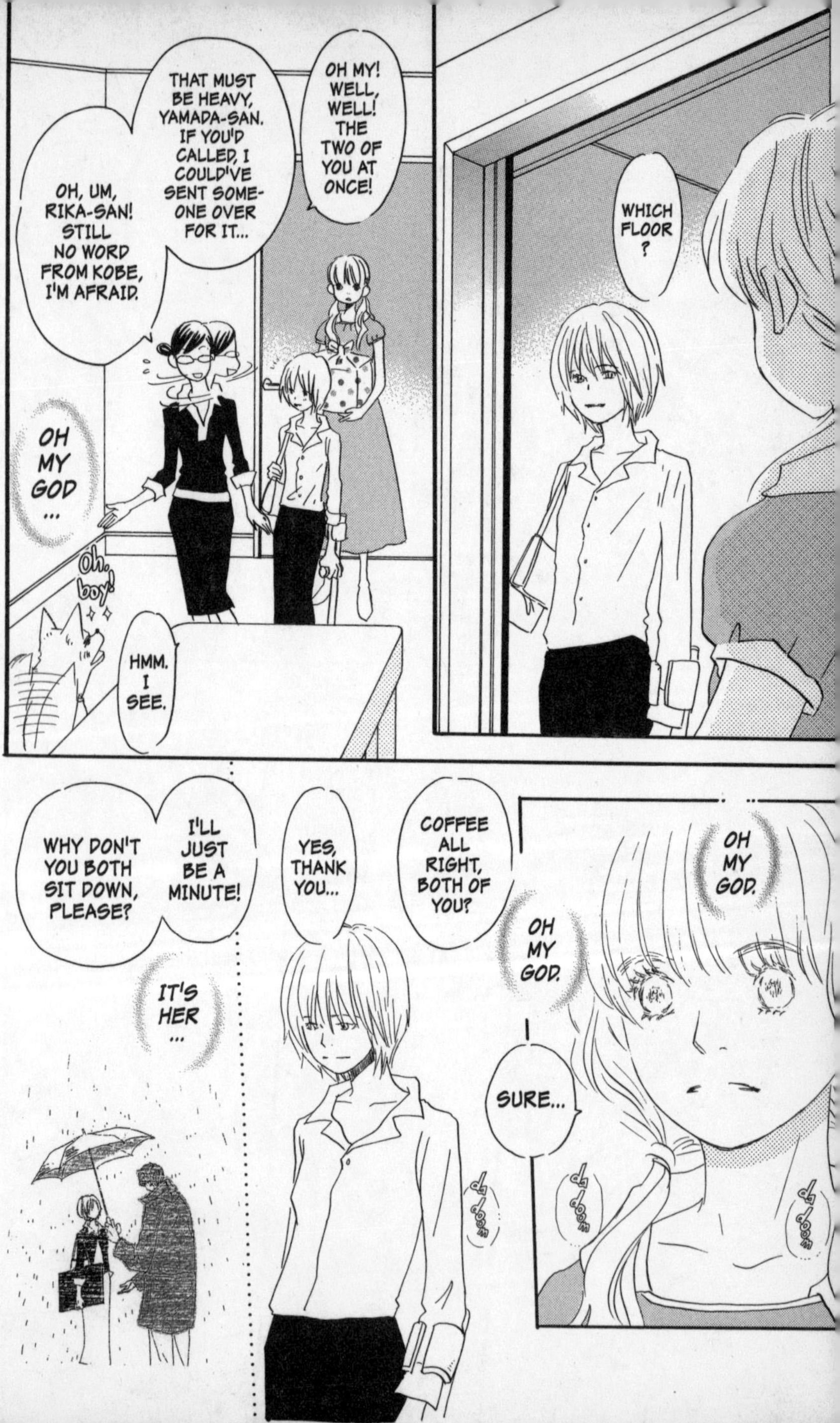
WHICH FLOOR?
OH MY! WELL, WELL! THE TWO OF YOU AT ONCE!
THAT MUST BE HEAVY, YAMADA-SAN. IF YOU'D CALLED, I COULD'VE SENT SOME-ONE OVER FOR IT...
OH, UM, RIKA-SAN! STILL NO WORD FROM KOBE, I'M AFRAID.
OH MY GOD...
Oh, boy!
HMM. I SEE.
OH MY GOD.
OH MY GOD.
SURE...
da doom
da doom
COFFEE ALL RIGHT, BOTH OF YOU?
YES, THANK YOU...
da doom
I'LL JUST BE A MINUTE!
WHY DON'T YOU BOTH SIT DOWN, PLEASE?
IT'S HER...

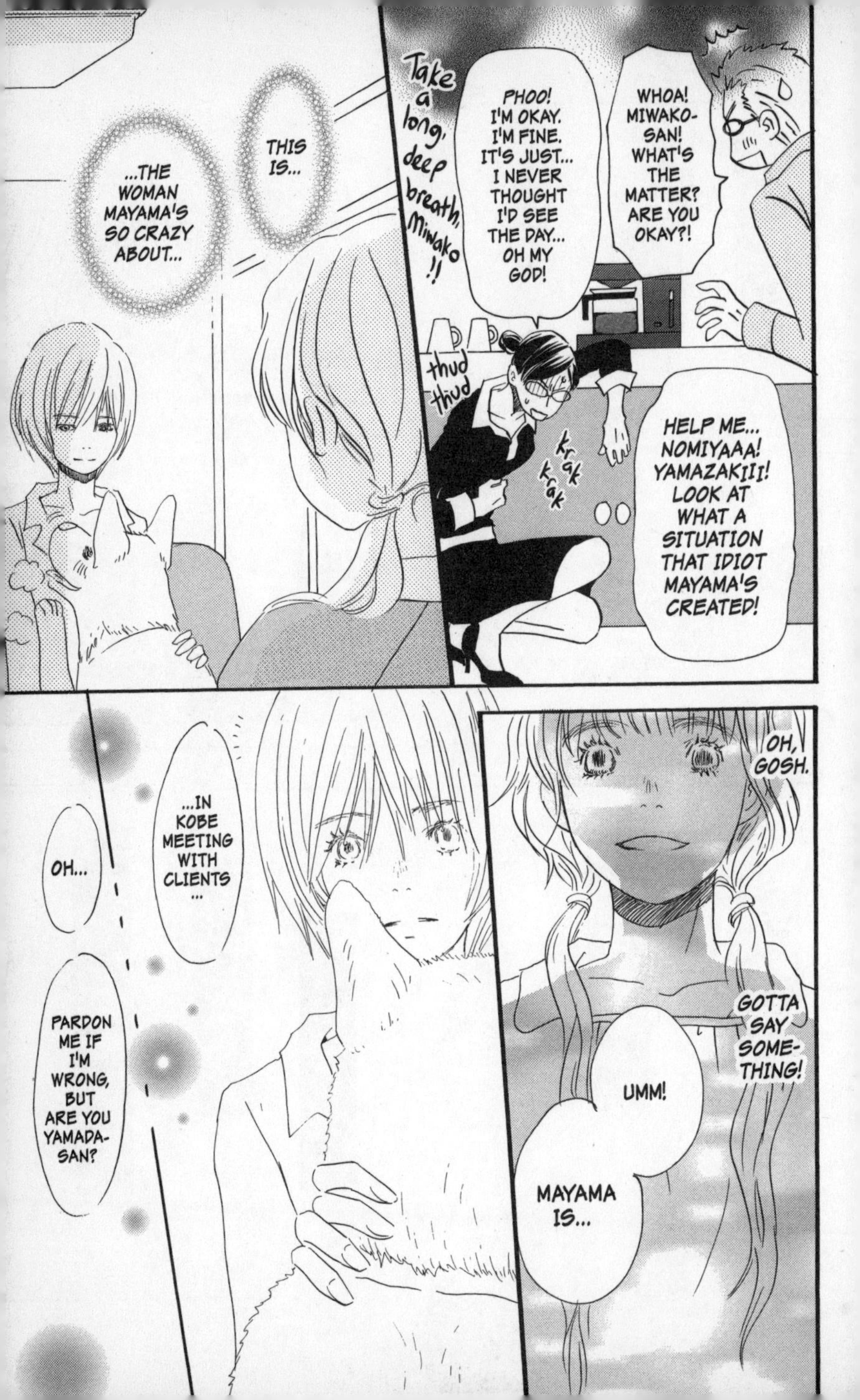
WHOA! MIWAKO-SAN! WHAT'S THE MATTER? ARE YOU OKAY?!
PHOO! I'M OKAY. I'M FINE. IT'S JUST... I NEVER THOUGHT I'D SEE THE DAY... OH MY GOD!
Take a long, deep breath, Miwako!!
HELP ME... NOMIYAAA! YAMAZAKIII! LOOK AT WHAT A SITUATION THAT IDIOT MAYAMA'S CREATED!
krak krak
thud thud
THIS IS...
...THE WOMAN MAYAMA'S SO CRAZY ABOUT...
OH, GOSH.
GOTTA SAY SOME-THING!
UMM!
MAYAMA IS...
...IN KOBE MEETING WITH CLIENTS...
OH...
PARDON ME IF I'M WRONG, BUT ARE YOU YAMADA-SAN?

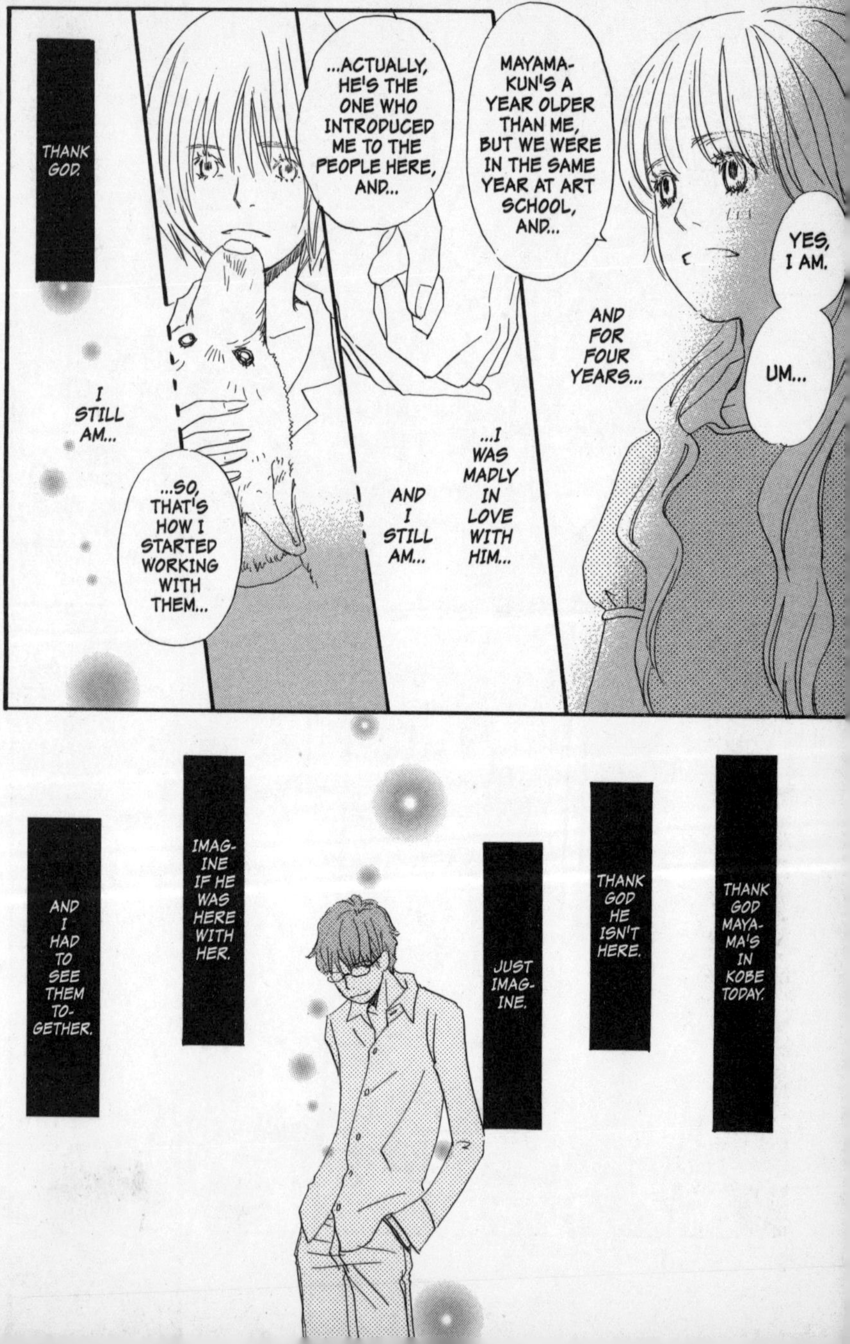
YES, I AM.
UM...
AND FOR FOUR YEARS...
MAYAMA-KUN'S A YEAR OLDER THAN ME, BUT WE WERE IN THE SAME YEAR AT ART SCHOOL, AND...
...I WAS MADLY IN LOVE WITH HIM...
AND I STILL AM...
...ACTUALLY, HE'S THE ONE WHO INTRODUCED ME TO THE PEOPLE HERE, AND...
...SO, THAT'S HOW I STARTED WORKING WITH THEM...
THANK GOD.
I STILL AM...
THANK GOD MAYAMA'S IN KOBE TODAY.
THANK GOD HE ISN'T HERE.
JUST IMAGINE.
IMAGINE IF HE WAS HERE WITH HER.
AND I HAD TO SEE THEM TOGETHER.

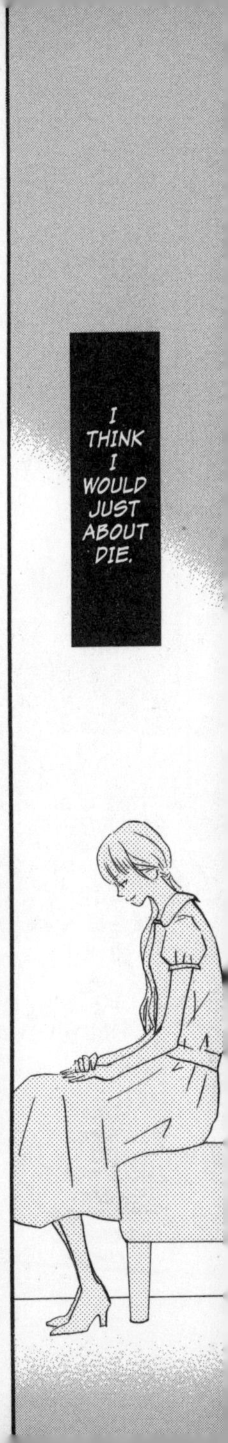
I THINK I WOULD JUST ABOUT DIE.

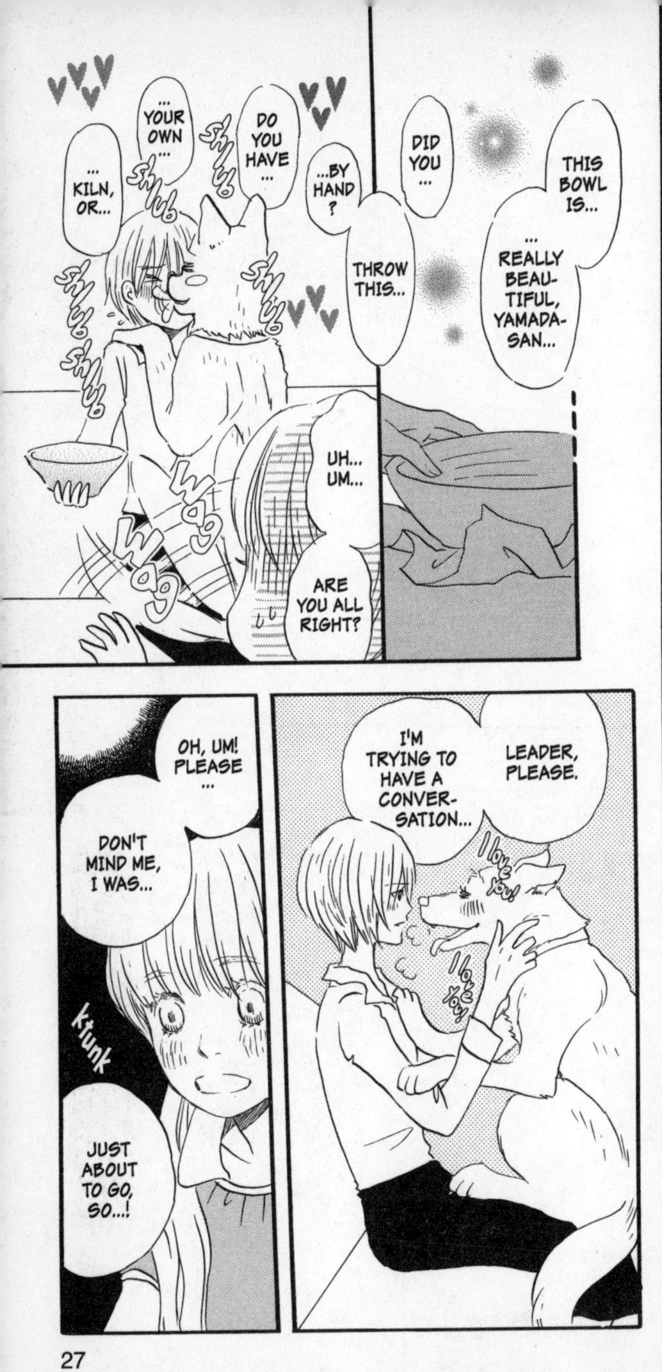
THIS BOWL IS...
... REALLY BEAUTIFUL, YAMADA-SAN...
DID YOU ...
THROW THIS...
...BY HAND?
DO YOU HAVE ...
... YOUR OWN ...
... KILN, OR...
shlub shlub
shlub shlub shlub shlub
wag wag
UH... UM...
ARE YOU ALL RIGHT?
LEADER, PLEASE.
I'M TRYING TO HAVE A CONVERSATION...
I love you!
I love you!
OH, UM! PLEASE ...
DON'T MIND ME, I WAS...
ktunk
JUST ABOUT TO GO, SO...!

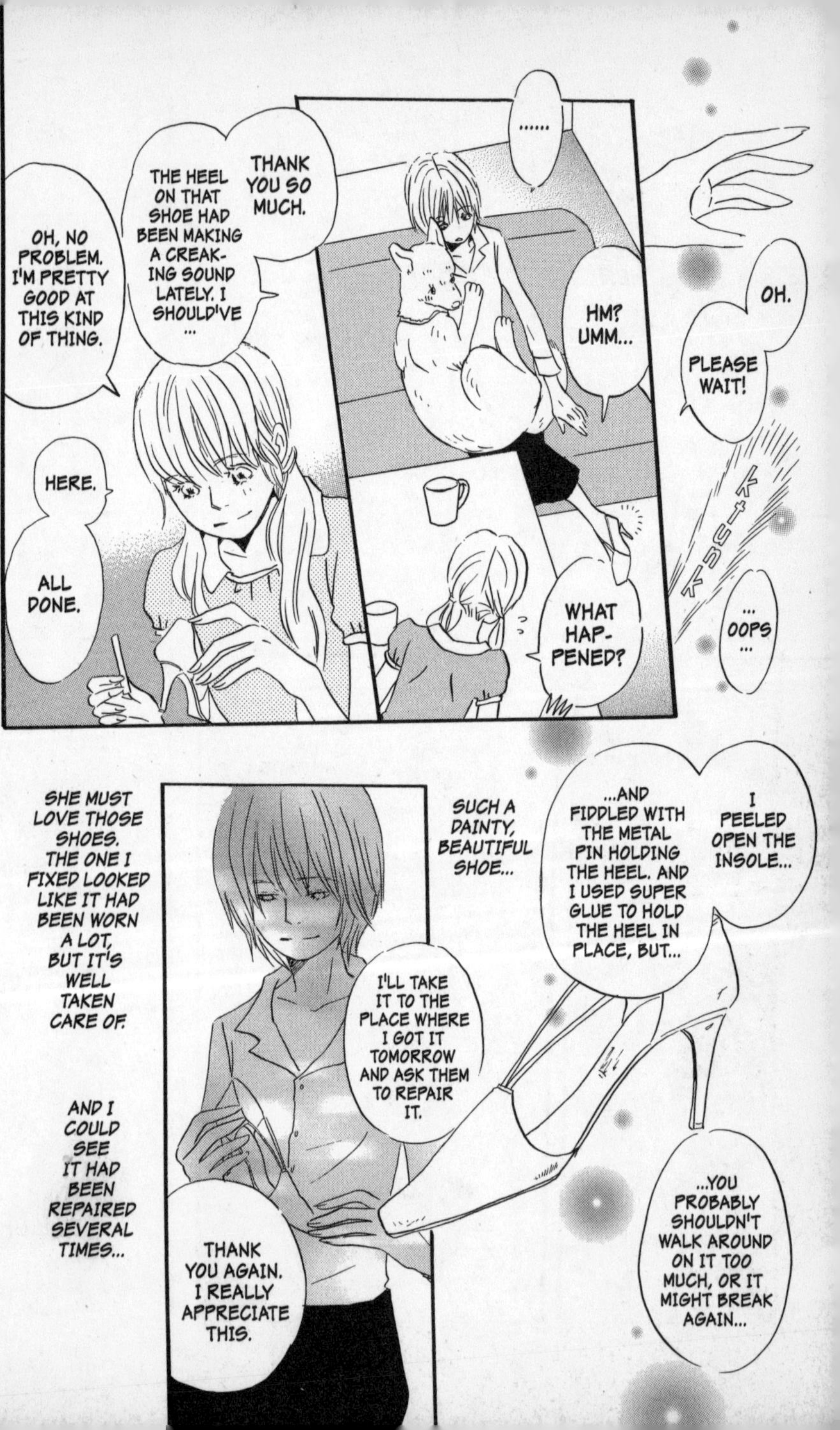
OH.
PLEASE WAIT!
...OOPS...
......
HM? UMM...
WHAT HAPPENED?
THANK YOU SO MUCH.
THE HEEL ON THAT SHOE HAD BEEN MAKING A CREAK-ING SOUND LATELY. I SHOULD'VE ...
OH, NO PROBLEM. I'M PRETTY GOOD AT THIS KIND OF THING.
HERE.
ALL DONE.
I PEELED OPEN THE INSOLE...
...AND FIDDLED WITH THE METAL PIN HOLDING THE HEEL. AND I USED SUPER GLUE TO HOLD THE HEEL IN PLACE, BUT...
SUCH A DAINTY, BEAUTIFUL SHOE...
...YOU PROBABLY SHOULDN'T WALK AROUND ON IT TOO MUCH, OR IT MIGHT BREAK AGAIN...
I'LL TAKE IT TO THE PLACE WHERE I GOT IT TOMORROW AND ASK THEM TO REPAIR IT.
THANK YOU AGAIN. I REALLY APPRECIATE THIS.
SHE MUST LOVE THOSE SHOES. THE ONE I FIXED LOOKED LIKE IT HAD BEEN WORN A LOT, BUT IT'S WELL TAKEN CARE OF.
AND I COULD SEE IT HAD BEEN REPAIRED SEVERAL TIMES...

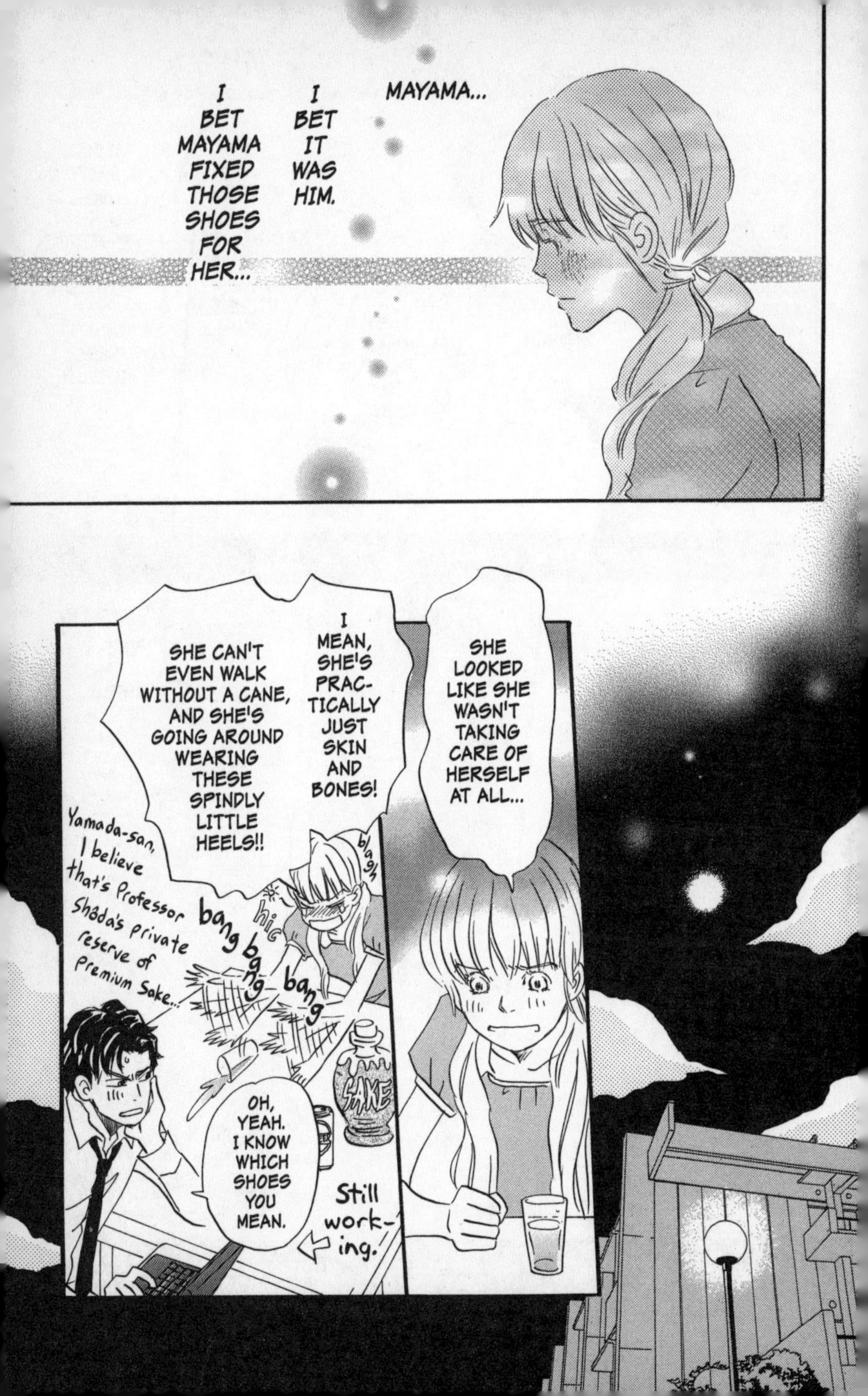
MAYAMA...
I BET IT WAS HIM.
I BET MAYAMA FIXED THOSE SHOES FOR HER...
SHE LOOKED LIKE SHE WASN'T TAKING CARE OF HERSELF AT ALL...
I MEAN, SHE'S PRAC-TICALLY JUST SKIN AND BONES!
SHE CAN'T EVEN WALK WITHOUT A CANE, AND SHE'S GOING AROUND WEARING THESE SPINDLY LITTLE HEELS!!
blagh
hic
bang bang bang
Yamada-san, I believe that's Professor Shōda's private reserve of Premium Sake...
SAKE
OH, YEAH. I KNOW WHICH SHOES YOU MEAN.
Still work-ing.

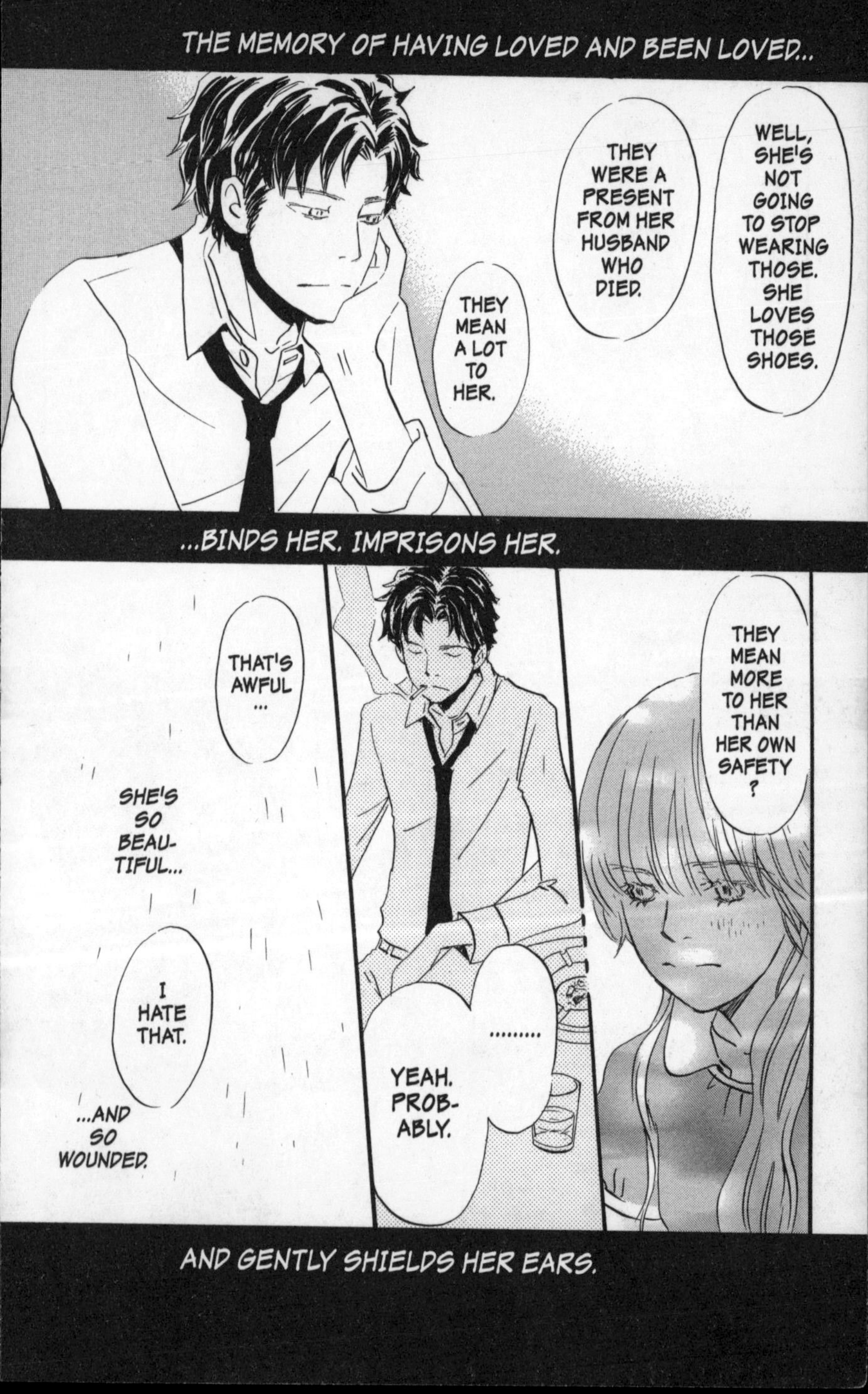
THE MEMORY OF HAVING LOVED AND BEEN LOVED...
WELL, SHE'S NOT GOING TO STOP WEARING THOSE. SHE LOVES THOSE SHOES.
THEY WERE A PRESENT FROM HER HUSBAND WHO DIED.
THEY MEAN A LOT TO HER.
...BINDS HER. IMPRISONS HER.
THEY MEAN MORE TO HER THAN HER OWN SAFETY?
....
YEAH. PROBABLY.
THAT'S AWFUL...
SHE'S SO BEAU-TIFUL...
I HATE THAT.
...AND SO WOUNDED.
AND GENTLY SHIELDS HER EARS.

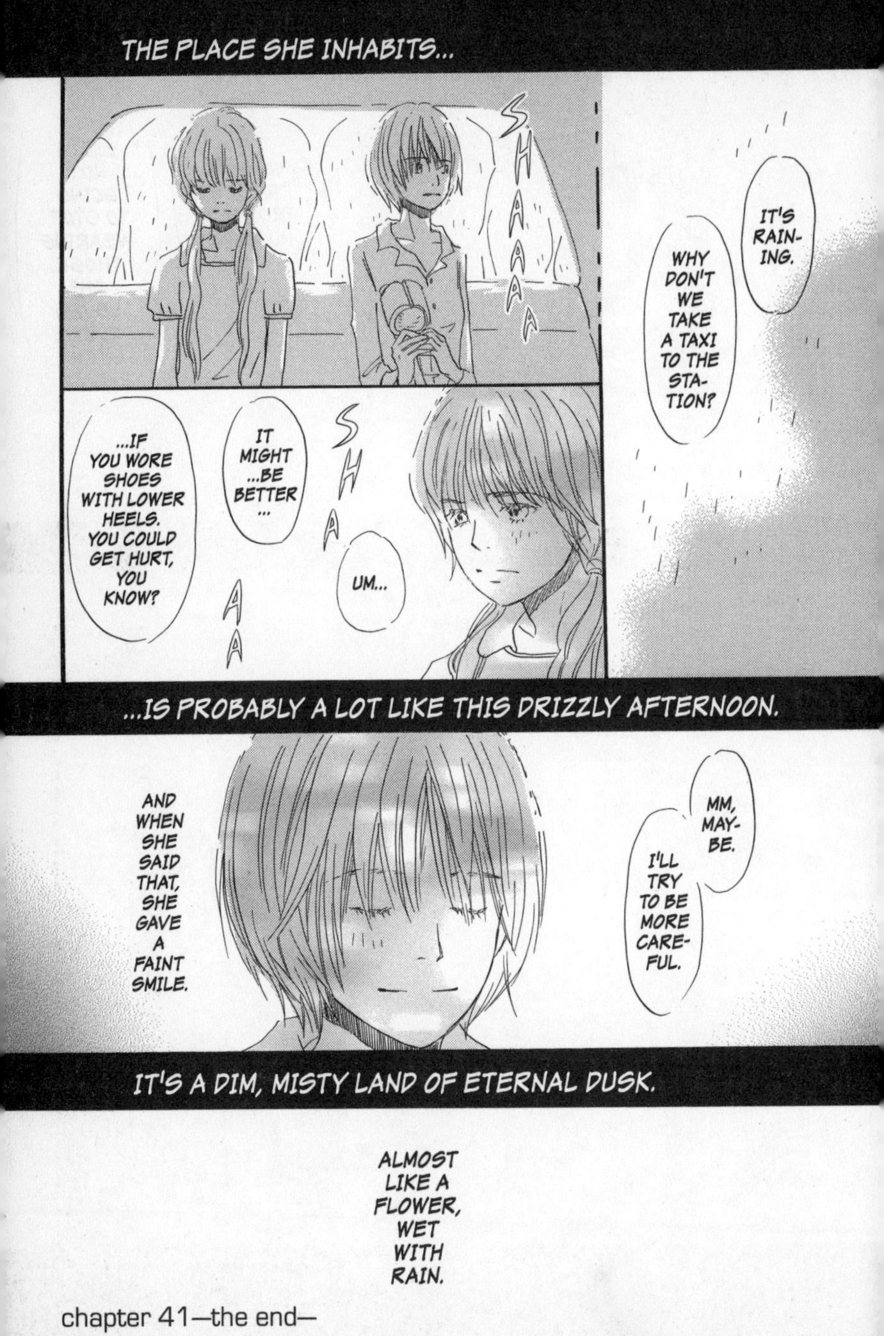
THE PLACE SHE INHABITS...
IT'S RAINING.
WHY DON'T WE TAKE A TAXI TO THE STATION?
SHAAAAA
SHAAA
UM...
IT MIGHT ...BE BETTER...
...IF YOU WORE SHOES WITH LOWER HEELS. YOU COULD GET HURT, YOU KNOW?
...IS PROBABLY A LOT LIKE THIS DRIZZLY AFTERNOON.
MM, MAYBE.
I'LL TRY TO BE MORE CAREFUL.
AND WHEN SHE SAID THAT, SHE GAVE A FAINT SMILE.
IT'S A DIM, MISTY LAND OF ETERNAL DUSK.
ALMOST LIKE A FLOWER, WET WITH RAIN.

chapter 41—the end—

#2: Rough sketch for a
coming next issue illustration

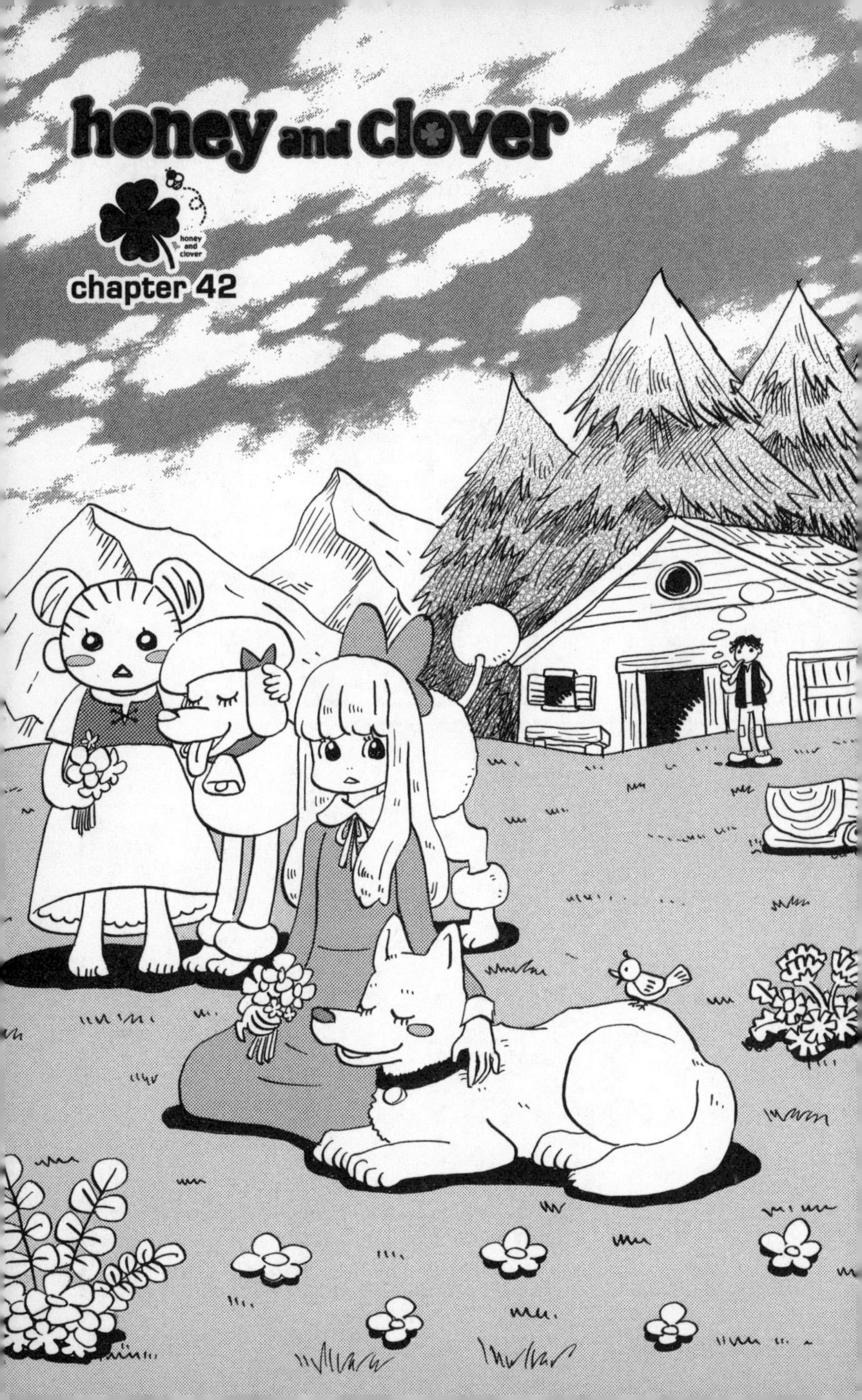
honey and clover
honey and clover
chapter 42

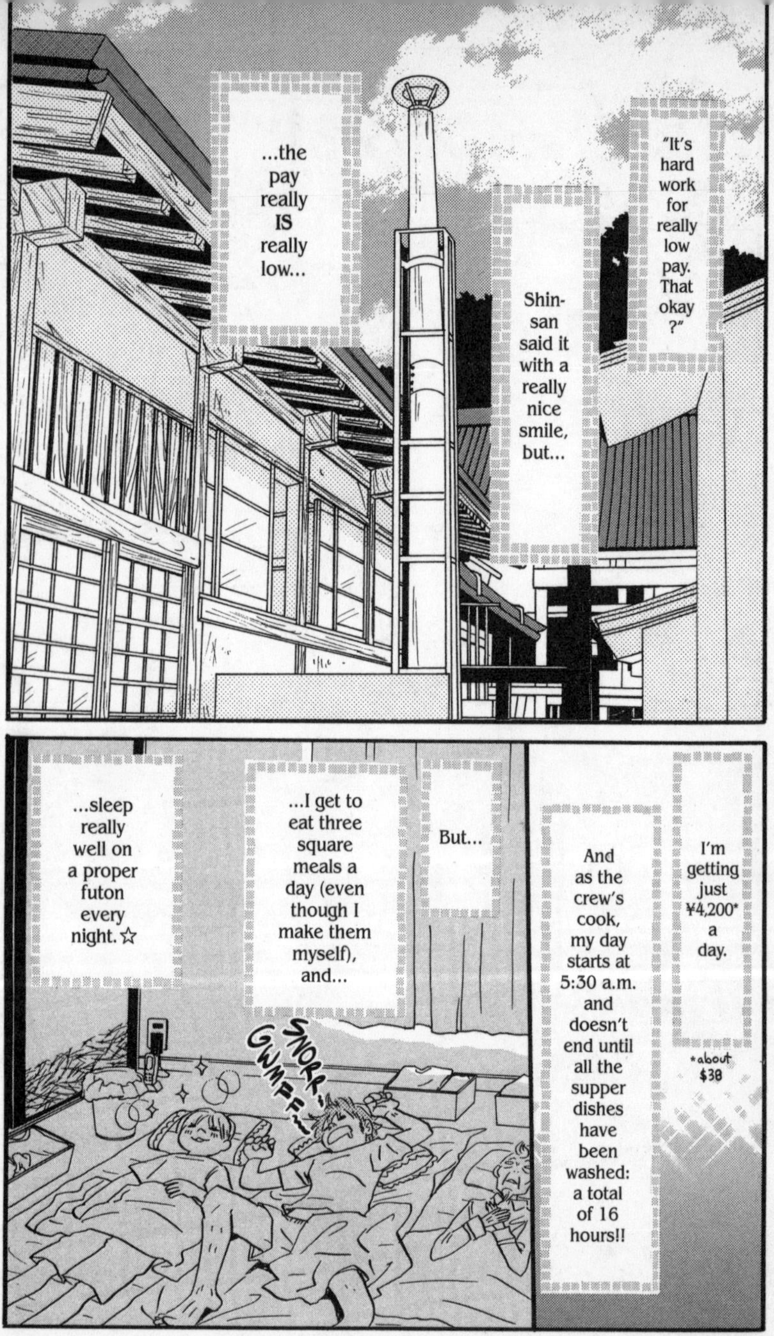
"It's hard work for really low pay. That okay?"
Shin-san said it with a really nice smile, but...
...the pay really IS really low...
I'm getting just ¥4,200* a day.
*about $38
And as the crew's cook, my day starts at 5:30 a.m. and doesn't end until all the supper dishes have been washed: a total of 16 hours!!
But...
...I get to eat three square meals a day (even though I make them myself), and...
...sleep really well on a proper futon every night.☆
SNORR
GWMPF~

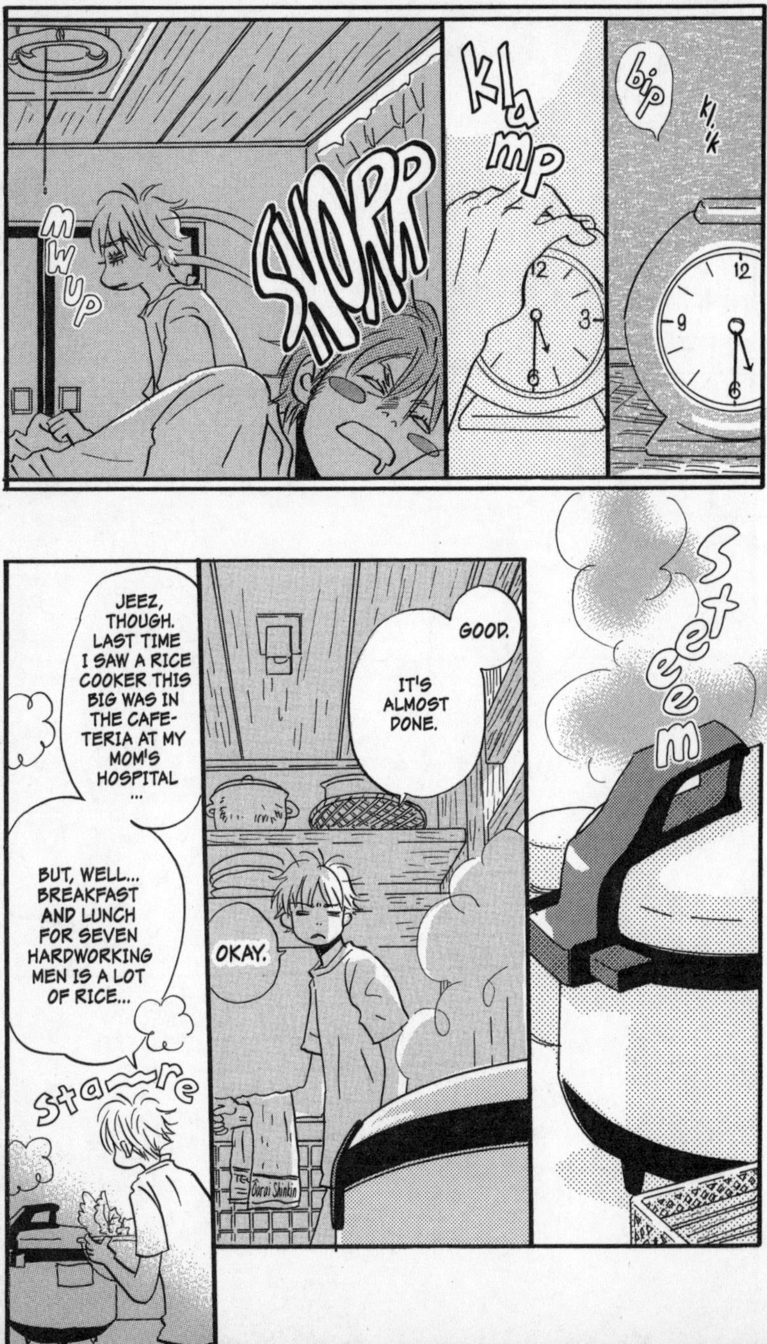
bip
klik
klamp
SNORR
MWUP
steeem
GOOD.
IT'S ALMOST DONE.
OKAY.
JEEZ, THOUGH. LAST TIME I SAW A RICE COOKER THIS BIG WAS IN THE CAFETERIA AT MY MOM'S HOSPITAL...
BUT, WELL... BREAKFAST AND LUNCH FOR SEVEN HARDWORKING MEN IS A LOT OF RICE...
sta—re

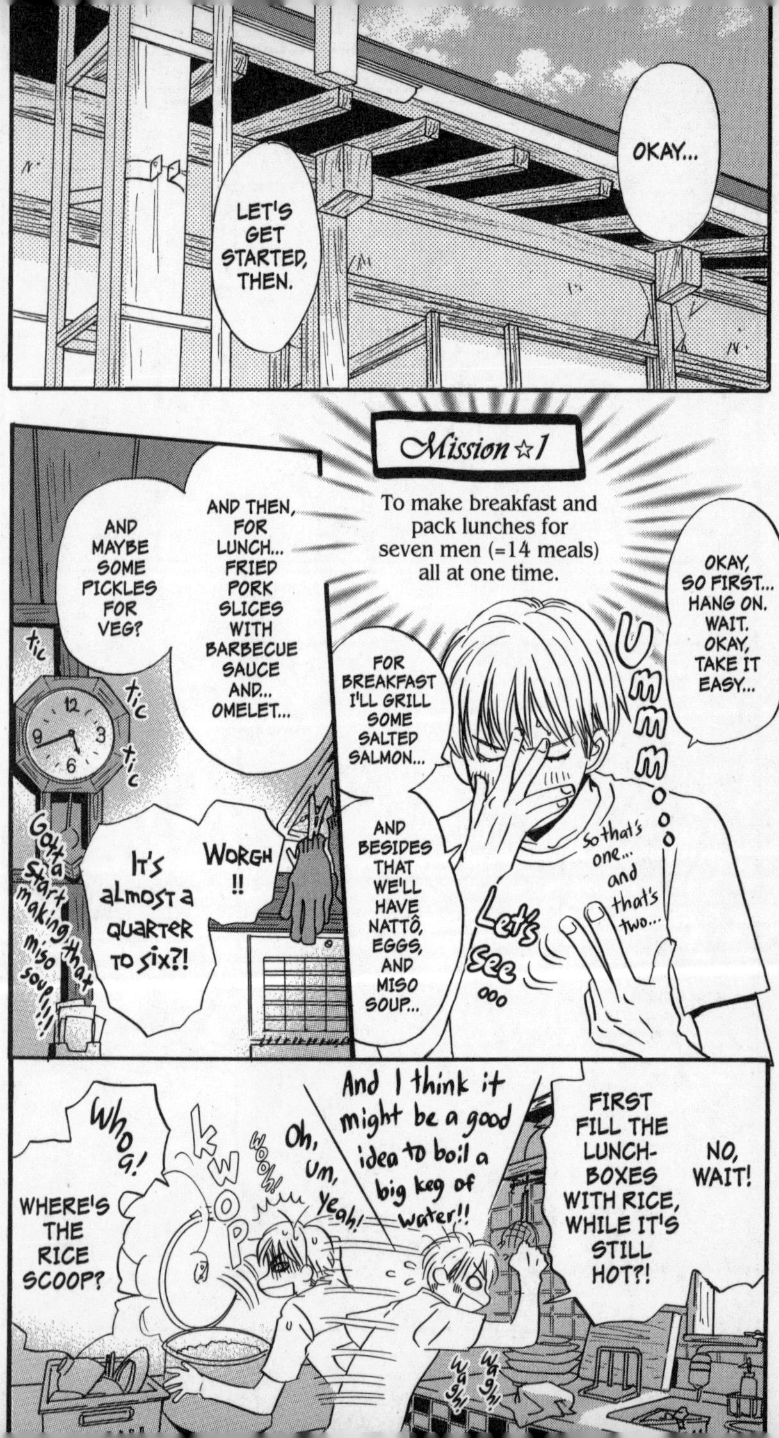
OKAY...
LET'S GET STARTED, THEN.
Mission☆1
To make breakfast and pack lunches for seven men (=14 meals) all at one time.
OKAY, SO FIRST... HANG ON. WAIT. OKAY, TAKE IT EASY...
Ummmmooo
So that's one... and that's two...
Let's see ooo
FOR BREAKFAST I'LL GRILL SOME SALTED SALMON...
AND BESIDES THAT WE'LL HAVE NATTÔ, EGGS, AND MISO SOUP...
AND THEN, FOR LUNCH... FRIED PORK SLICES WITH BARBECUE SAUCE AND... OMELET...
AND MAYBE SOME PICKLES FOR VEG?
tic
tic
tic
WORGH!!
It's almost a quarter to six?!
Gotta start making that miso soup!!!!
NO, WAIT!
FIRST FILL THE LUNCH-BOXES WITH RICE, WHILE IT'S STILL HOT?!
And I think it might be a good idea to boil a big keg of water!!
Oh, um, yeah!
Wooh!
KWOP
Whoa!
WHERE'S THE RICE SCOOP?
Wagh!
Wagh!

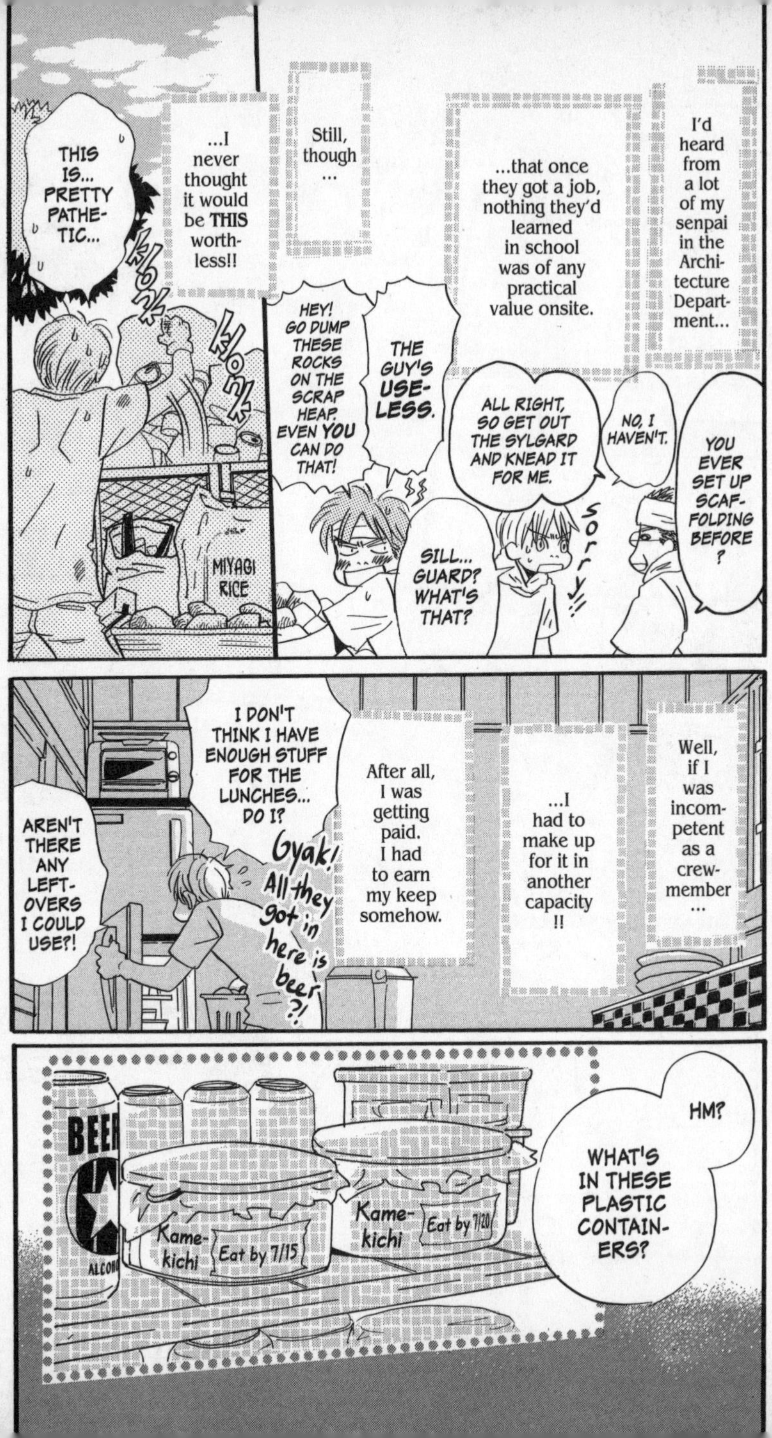
I'd heard from a lot of my senpai in the Architecture Department...
...that once they got a job, nothing they'd learned in school was of any practical value onsite.
Still, though...
YOU EVER SET UP SCAFFOLDING BEFORE?
NO, I HAVEN'T.
ALL RIGHT, SO GET OUT THE SYLGARD AND KNEAD IT FOR ME.
Sorry...!!
SILL... GUARD? WHAT'S THAT?
THE GUY'S USELESS.
HEY! GO DUMP THESE ROCKS ON THE SCRAP HEAP. EVEN YOU CAN DO THAT!
...I never thought it would be THIS worthless!!
THIS IS... PRETTY PATHETIC...
klonk
klonk
MIYAGI RICE
Well, if I was incompetent as a crewmember...
...I had to make up for it in another capacity!!
After all, I was getting paid. I had to earn my keep somehow.
I DON'T THINK I HAVE ENOUGH STUFF FOR THE LUNCHES... DO I?
AREN'T THERE ANY LEFTOVERS I COULD USE?!
Gyak! All they got in here is beer?!
HM?
WHAT'S IN THESE PLASTIC CONTAINERS?
Kame-kichi
Eat by 7/20
Kame-kichi
Eat by 7/15
BEER

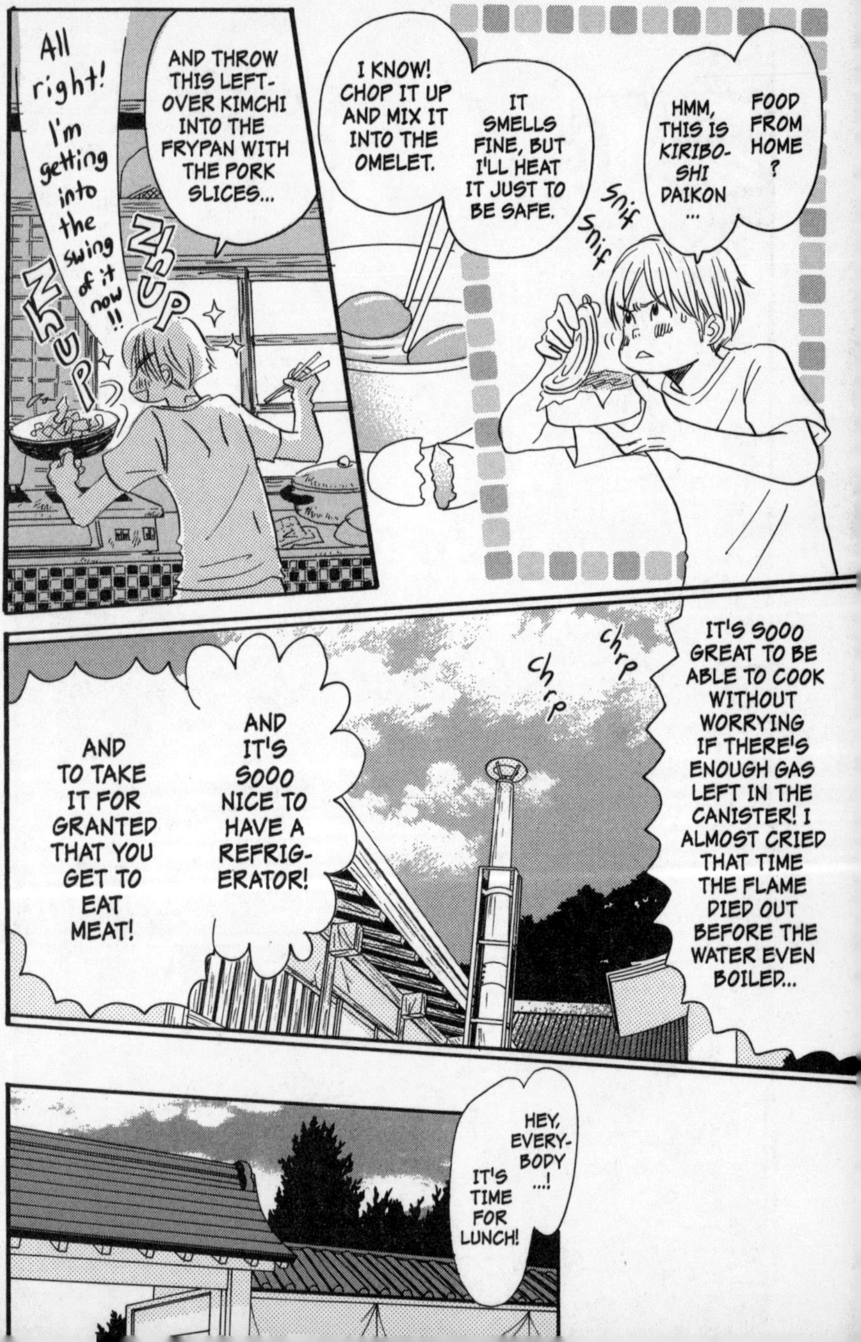
FOOD FROM HOME?
HMM, THIS IS KIRIBOSHI DAIKON...
Snif Snif
IT SMELLS FINE, BUT I'LL HEAT IT JUST TO BE SAFE.
I KNOW! CHOP IT UP AND MIX IT INTO THE OMELET.
AND THROW THIS LEFT-OVER KIMCHI INTO THE FRYPAN WITH THE PORK SLICES...
ZhUP ZhUP
All right! I'm getting into the swing of it now!!
IT'S SOOO GREAT TO BE ABLE TO COOK WITHOUT WORRYING IF THERE'S ENOUGH GAS LEFT IN THE CANISTER! I ALMOST CRIED THAT TIME THE FLAME DIED OUT BEFORE THE WATER EVEN BOILED...
chrp chrp
AND IT'S SOOO NICE TO HAVE A REFRIGERATOR!
AND TO TAKE IT FOR GRANTED THAT YOU GET TO EAT MEAT!
HEY, EVERYBODY...!
IT'S TIME FOR LUNCH!

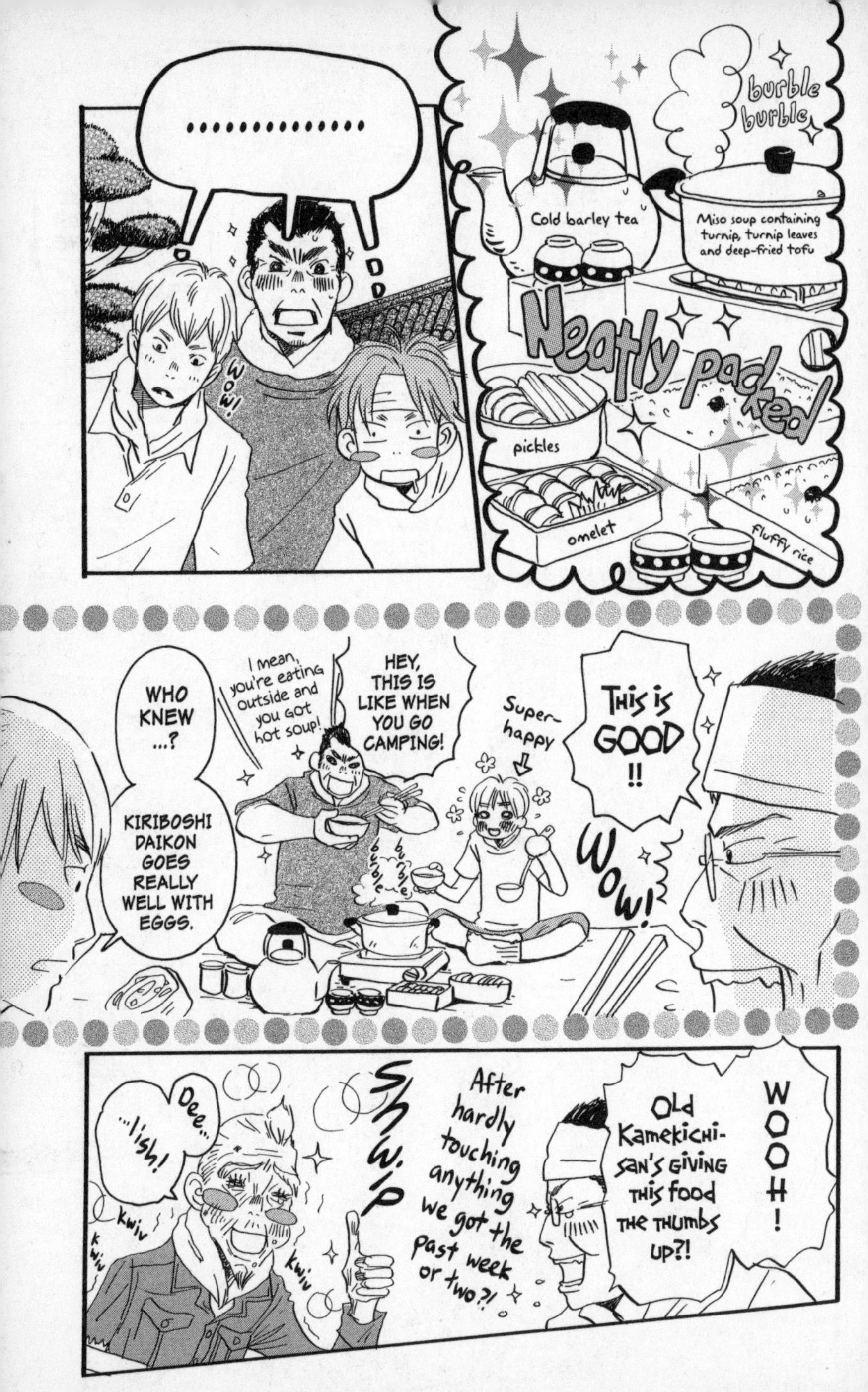
burble burble
Cold barley tea
Miso soup containing turnip, turnip leaves and deep-fried tofu
Neatly packed
pickles
omelet
fluffy rice
....
WOW!
THIS is GOOD!!
WOW!
Super-happy
HEY, THIS IS LIKE WHEN YOU GO CAMPING!
I mean, you're eating outside and you got hot soup!
burble burble
WHO KNEW ...?
KIRIBOSHI DAIKON GOES REALLY WELL WITH EGGS.
WOOOH!
Old Kamekichi-san's giving this food the thumbs up?!
After hardly touching anything we got the past week or two?!
SHWIP
Dee...
...lish!
kwiv
kwiv
kwiv

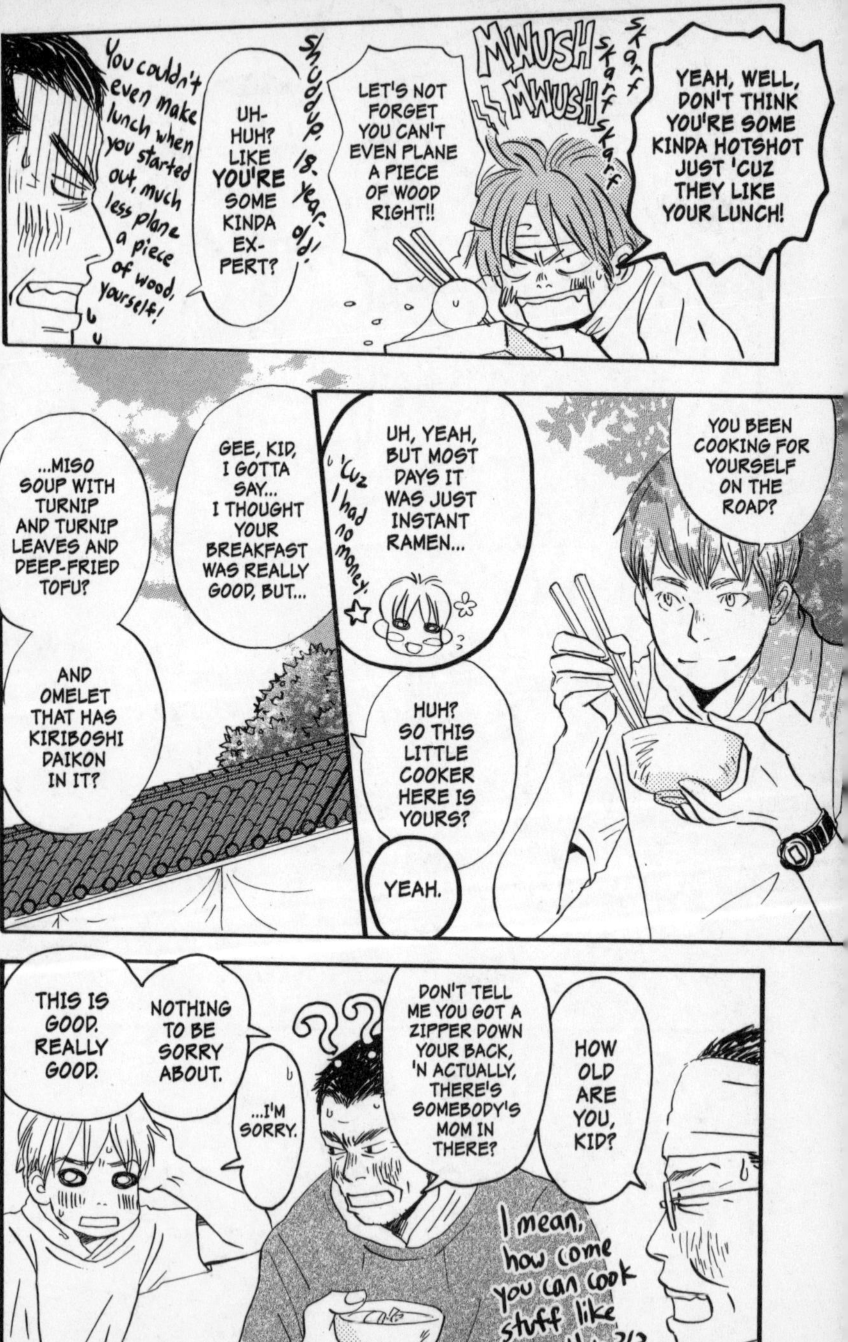
YEAH, WELL, DON'T THINK YOU'RE SOME KINDA HOTSHOT JUST 'CUZ THEY LIKE YOUR LUNCH!
skarf skarf skarf
MWUSH MWUSH
LET'S NOT FORGET YOU CAN'T EVEN PLANE A PIECE OF WOOD RIGHT!!
Shuddup, 18-year-old!
UH-HUH? LIKE YOU'RE SOME KINDA EXPERT?
You couldn't even make lunch when you started out, much less plane a piece of wood yourself!
YOU BEEN COOKING FOR YOURSELF ON THE ROAD?
UH, YEAH, BUT MOST DAYS IT WAS JUST INSTANT RAMEN...
'Cuz I had no money.
HUH? SO THIS LITTLE COOKER HERE IS YOURS?
YEAH.
GEE, KID, I GOTTA SAY... I THOUGHT YOUR BREAKFAST WAS REALLY GOOD, BUT...
...MISO SOUP WITH TURNIP AND TURNIP LEAVES AND DEEP-FRIED TOFU?
AND OMELET THAT HAS KIRIBOSHI DAIKON IN IT?
HOW OLD ARE YOU, KID?
I mean, how come you can cook stuff like this?!?
DON'T TELL ME YOU GOT A ZIPPER DOWN YOUR BACK, 'N ACTUALLY, THERE'S SOMEBODY'S MOM IN THERE?
...I'M SORRY.
NOTHING TO BE SORRY ABOUT.
THIS IS GOOD. REALLY GOOD.

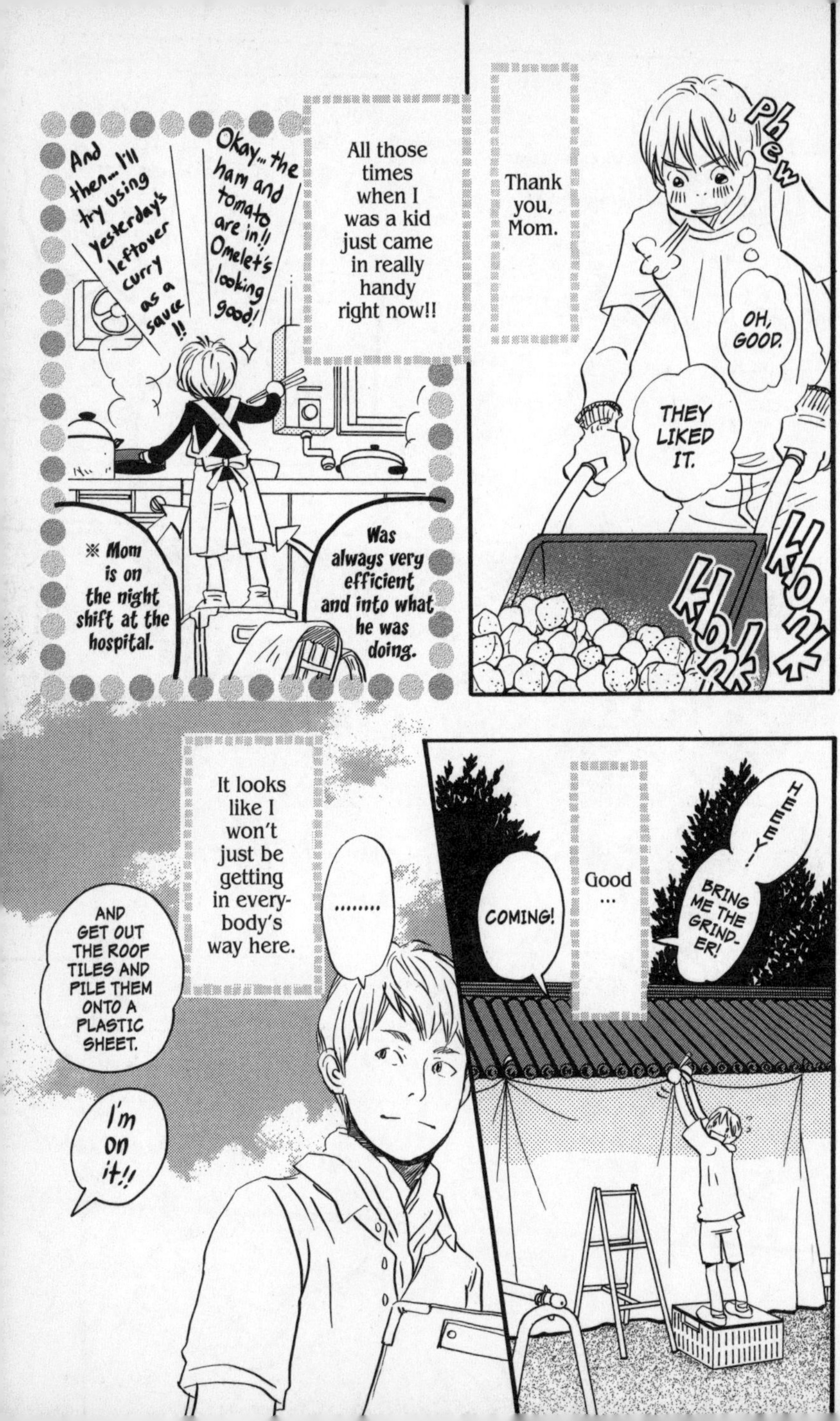
Thank you, Mom.
Phew
OH, GOOD.
THEY LIKED IT.
kbonk
kbonk
All those times when I was a kid just came in really handy right now!!
Okay... the ham and tomato are in!! Omelet's looking good!
And then... I'll try using yesterday's leftover curry as a sauce!!
Was always very efficient and into what he was doing.
※ Mom is on the night shift at the hospital.
HEEEY! BRING ME THE GRINDER!
Good...
COMING!
It looks like I won't just be getting in everybody's way here.
....
AND GET OUT THE ROOF TILES AND PILE THEM ONTO A PLASTIC SHEET.
I'm on it!!

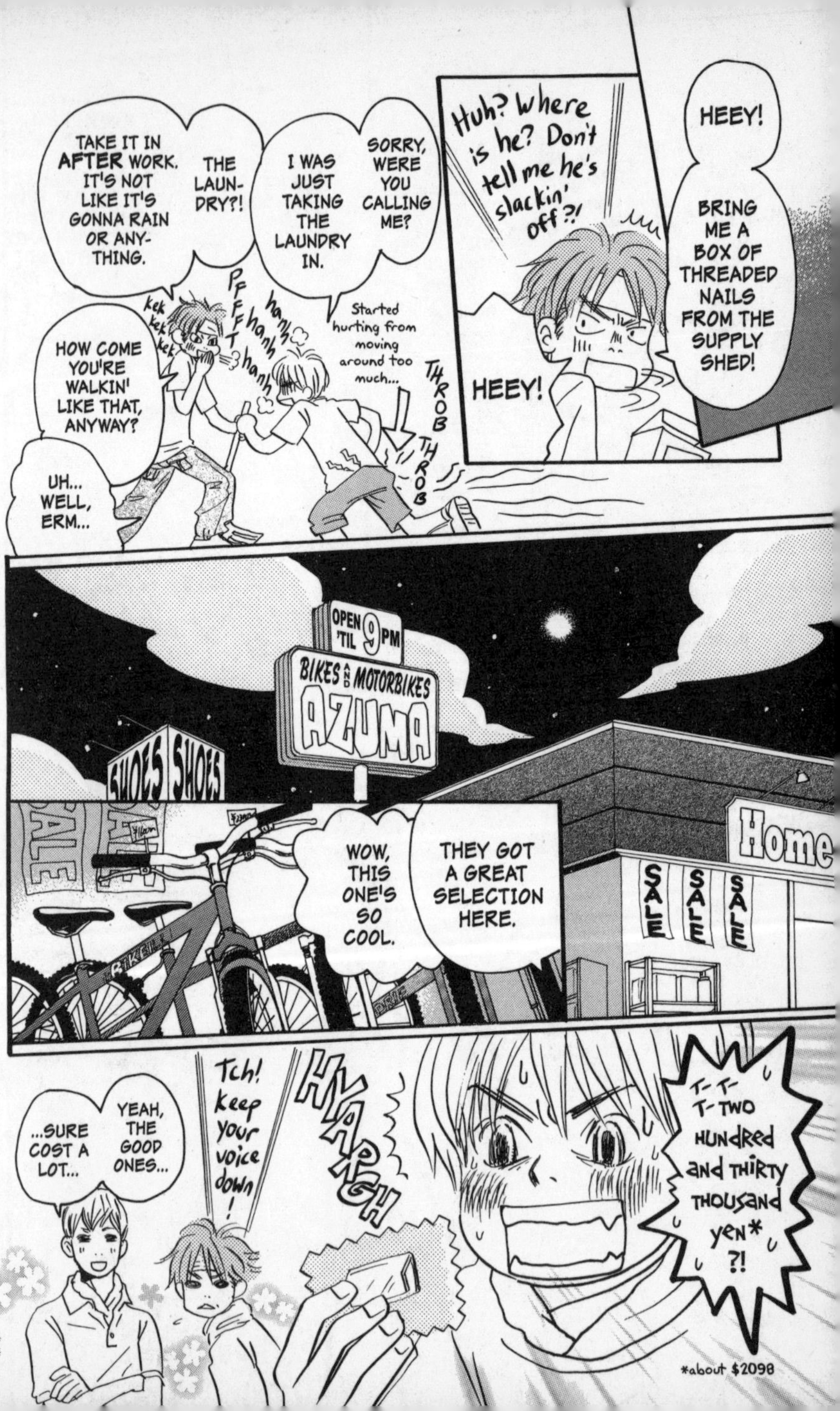
HEEY!
BRING ME A BOX OF THREADED NAILS FROM THE SUPPLY SHED!
Huh? Where is he? Don't tell me he's slackin' off?!
HEEY!
SORRY, WERE YOU CALLING ME?
I WAS JUST TAKING THE LAUNDRY IN.
THE LAUN-DRY?!
TAKE IT IN AFTER WORK. IT'S NOT LIKE IT'S GONNA RAIN OR ANY-THING.
Started hurting from moving around too much...
THROB THROB
PFFFT
hanh hanh hanh
kek kek kek
HOW COME YOU'RE WALKIN' LIKE THAT, ANYWAY?
UH... WELL, ERM...
OPEN 'TIL 9 PM
BIKES AND MOTORBIKES AZUMA
SHOES SHOES
Home
SALE SALE SALE
THEY GOT A GREAT SELECTION HERE.
WOW, THIS ONE'S SO COOL.
T-T-T-TWO HUNDRED AND THIRTY THOUSAND YEN* ?!
HYAARGH
Tch! Keep your voice down!
YEAH, THE GOOD ONES...
...SURE COST A LOT...

*about $2098

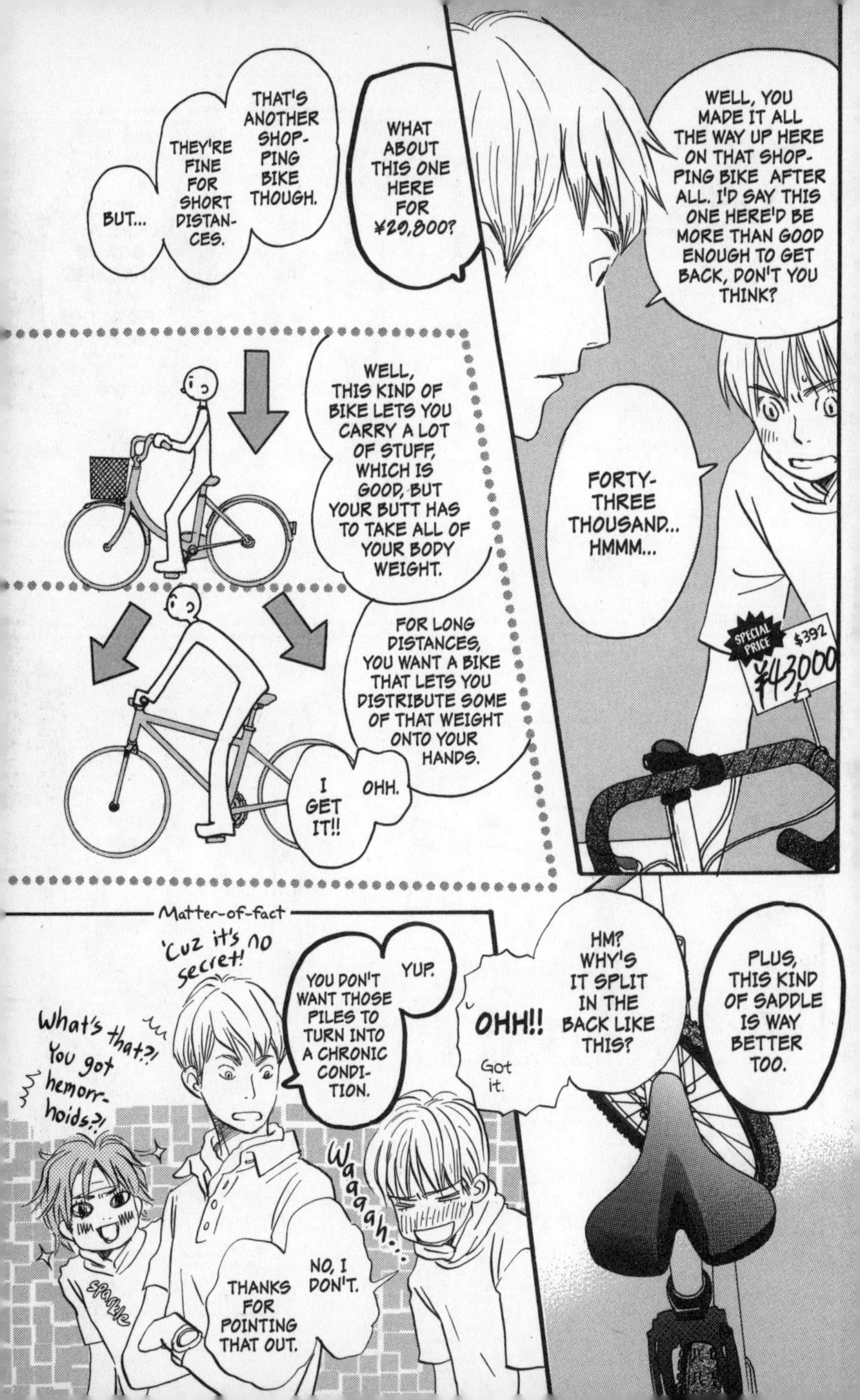
WELL, YOU MADE IT ALL THE WAY UP HERE ON THAT SHOPPING BIKE AFTER ALL. I'D SAY THIS ONE HERE'D BE MORE THAN GOOD ENOUGH TO GET BACK, DON'T YOU THINK?
FORTY-THREE THOUSAND... HMMM...
SPECIAL PRICE
$392
¥43000
WHAT ABOUT THIS ONE HERE FOR ¥29,800?
THAT'S ANOTHER SHOPPING BIKE THOUGH.
THEY'RE FINE FOR SHORT DISTANCES.
BUT...
WELL, THIS KIND OF BIKE LETS YOU CARRY A LOT OF STUFF, WHICH IS GOOD, BUT YOUR BUTT HAS TO TAKE ALL OF YOUR BODY WEIGHT.
FOR LONG DISTANCES, YOU WANT A BIKE THAT LETS YOU DISTRIBUTE SOME OF THAT WEIGHT ONTO YOUR HANDS.
OHH.
I GET IT!!
PLUS, THIS KIND OF SADDLE IS WAY BETTER TOO.
HM? WHY'S IT SPLIT IN THE BACK LIKE THIS?
OHH!!
Got it.
Matter-of-fact
YUP.
YOU DON'T WANT THOSE PILES TO TURN INTO A CHRONIC CONDITION.
'Cuz it's no secret!
What's that?! You got hemorrhoids?!
sparkle
Waaaah...
NO, I DON'T.
THANKS FOR POINTING THAT OUT.

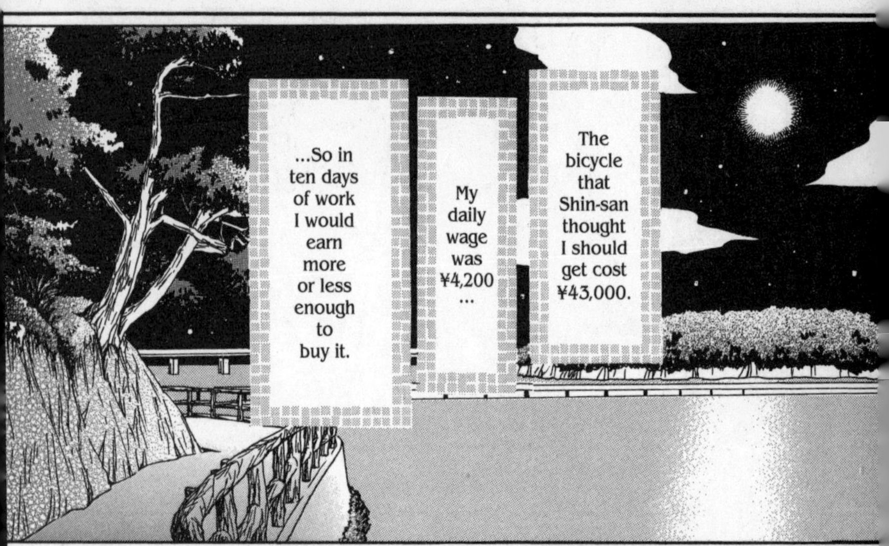
The bicycle that Shin-san thought I should get cost ¥43,000.
My daily wage was ¥4,200 ...
...So in ten days of work I would earn more or less enough to buy it.
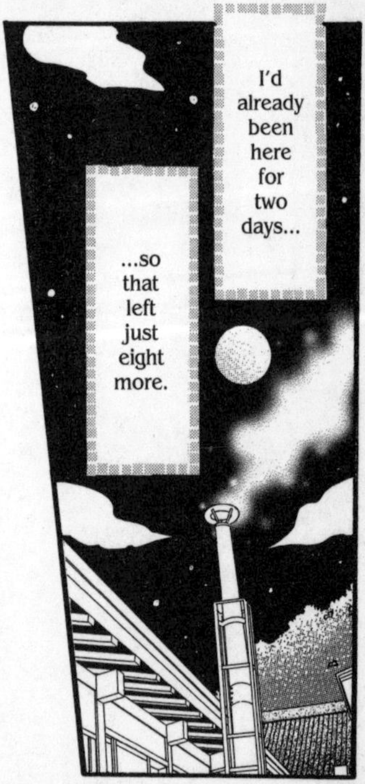
I'd already been here for two days...
...so that left just eight more.
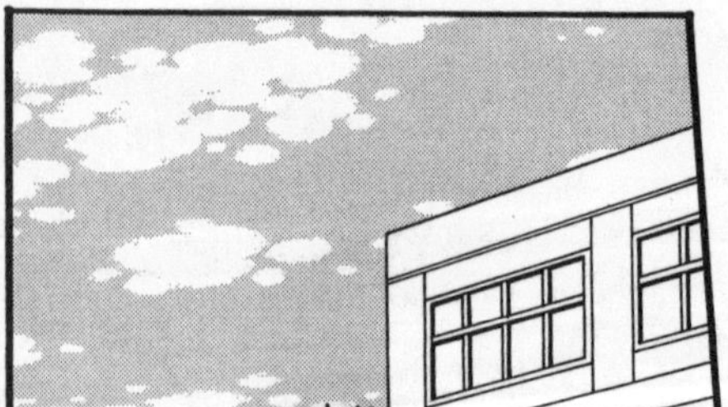
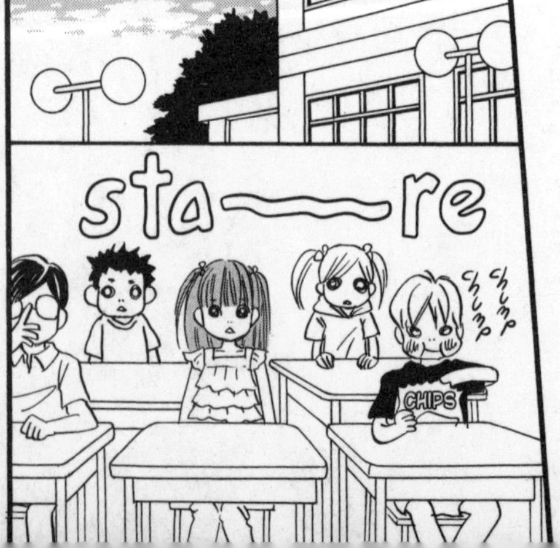
sta——re
chump chump
CHIPS

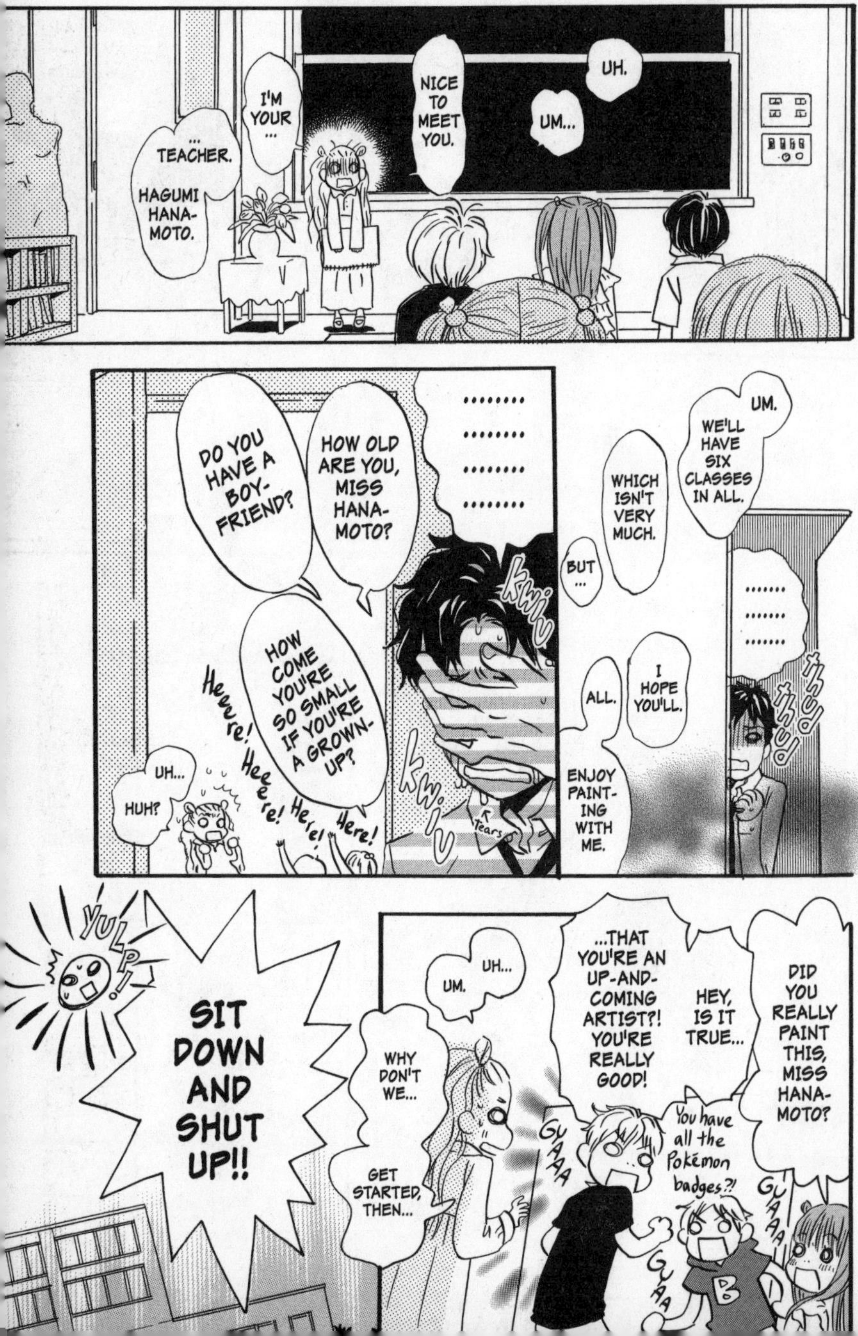
UH.
UM...
NICE TO MEET YOU.
I'M YOUR ...
... TEACHER.
HAGUMI HANAMOTO.
UM.
WE'LL HAVE SIX CLASSES IN ALL.
WHICH ISN'T VERY MUCH.
BUT ...
....
thud thud
I HOPE YOU'LL.
ALL.
ENJOY PAINTING WITH ME.
....
kwiu
kwiu
Tears
HOW OLD ARE YOU, MISS HANAMOTO?
DO YOU HAVE A BOYFRIEND?
HOW COME YOU'RE SO SMALL IF YOU'RE A GROWN-UP?
Heeere! Heeere! Here! Here!
UH...
HUH?
DID YOU REALLY PAINT THIS, MISS HANAMOTO?
HEY, IS IT TRUE...
...THAT YOU'RE AN UP-AND-COMING ARTIST?! YOU'RE REALLY GOOD!
You have all the Pokémon badges?!
GUAAA
GUAAA
GUAAA
UH...
UM.
WHY DON'T WE...
GET STARTED, THEN...
YULP!
SIT DOWN AND SHUT UP!!

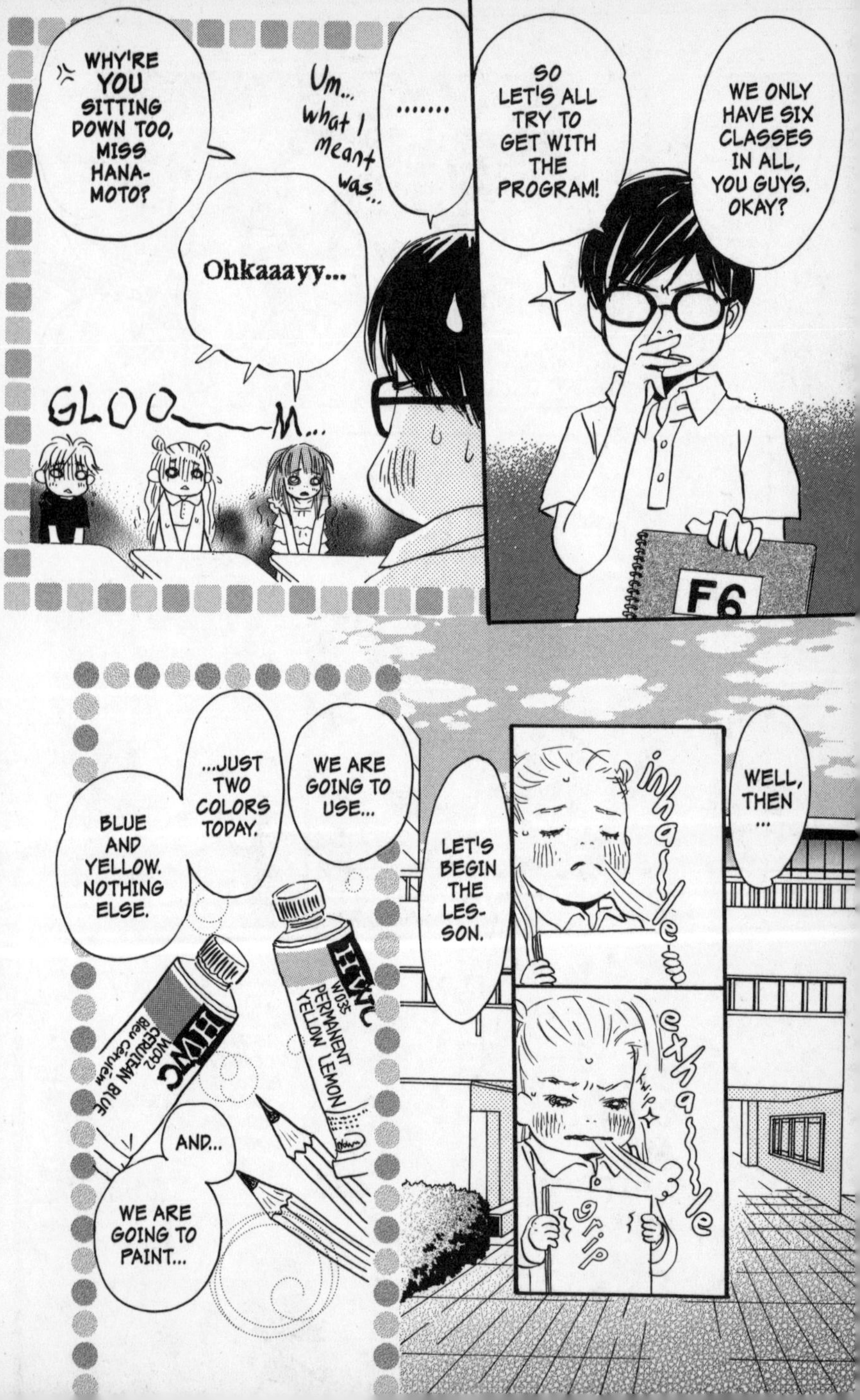
WE ONLY HAVE SIX CLASSES IN ALL, YOU GUYS. OKAY?
SO LET'S ALL TRY TO GET WITH THE PROGRAM!
F6
....
Um... what I meant was...
WHY'RE YOU SITTING DOWN TOO, MISS HANA-MOTO?
Ohkaaayy...
GLOO___M...
WELL, THEN...
LET'S BEGIN THE LES-SON.
inha~le~
exha~le
grip
WE ARE GOING TO USE...
...JUST TWO COLORS TODAY.
BLUE AND YELLOW. NOTHING ELSE.
HWC W035 PERMANENT YELLOW LEMON
HWC W092 CERULEAN BLUE Bleu céruléum
AND...
WE ARE GOING TO PAINT...

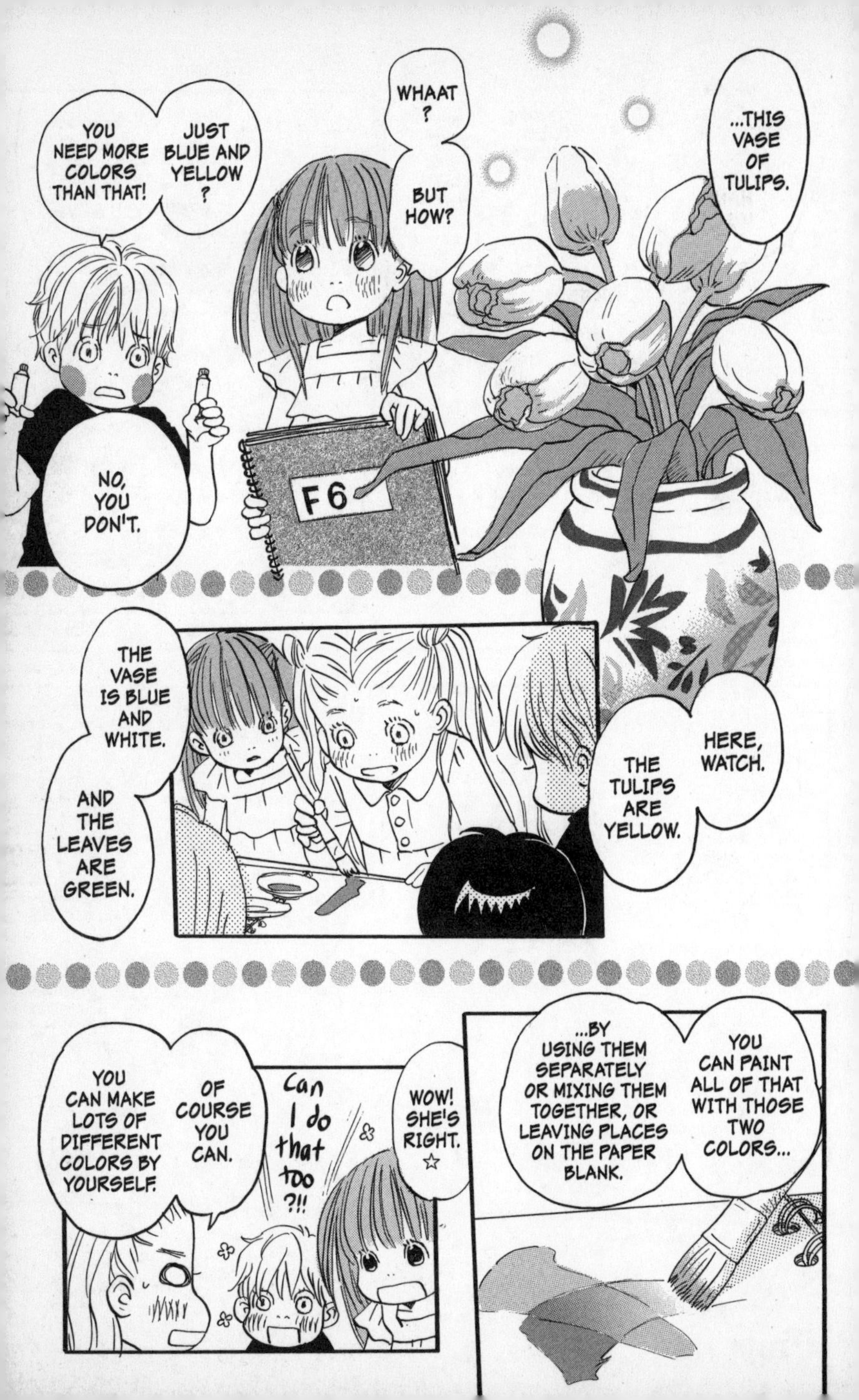
...THIS VASE OF TULIPS.
WHAAT?
BUT HOW?
JUST BLUE AND YELLOW?
YOU NEED MORE COLORS THAN THAT!
F6
NO, YOU DON'T.
HERE, WATCH.
THE TULIPS ARE YELLOW.
THE VASE IS BLUE AND WHITE.
AND THE LEAVES ARE GREEN.
YOU CAN PAINT ALL OF THAT WITH THOSE TWO COLORS...
...BY USING THEM SEPARATELY OR MIXING THEM TOGETHER, OR LEAVING PLACES ON THE PAPER BLANK.
WOW! SHE'S RIGHT. ☆
Can I do that too?!!
OF COURSE YOU CAN.
YOU CAN MAKE LOTS OF DIFFERENT COLORS BY YOURSELF.

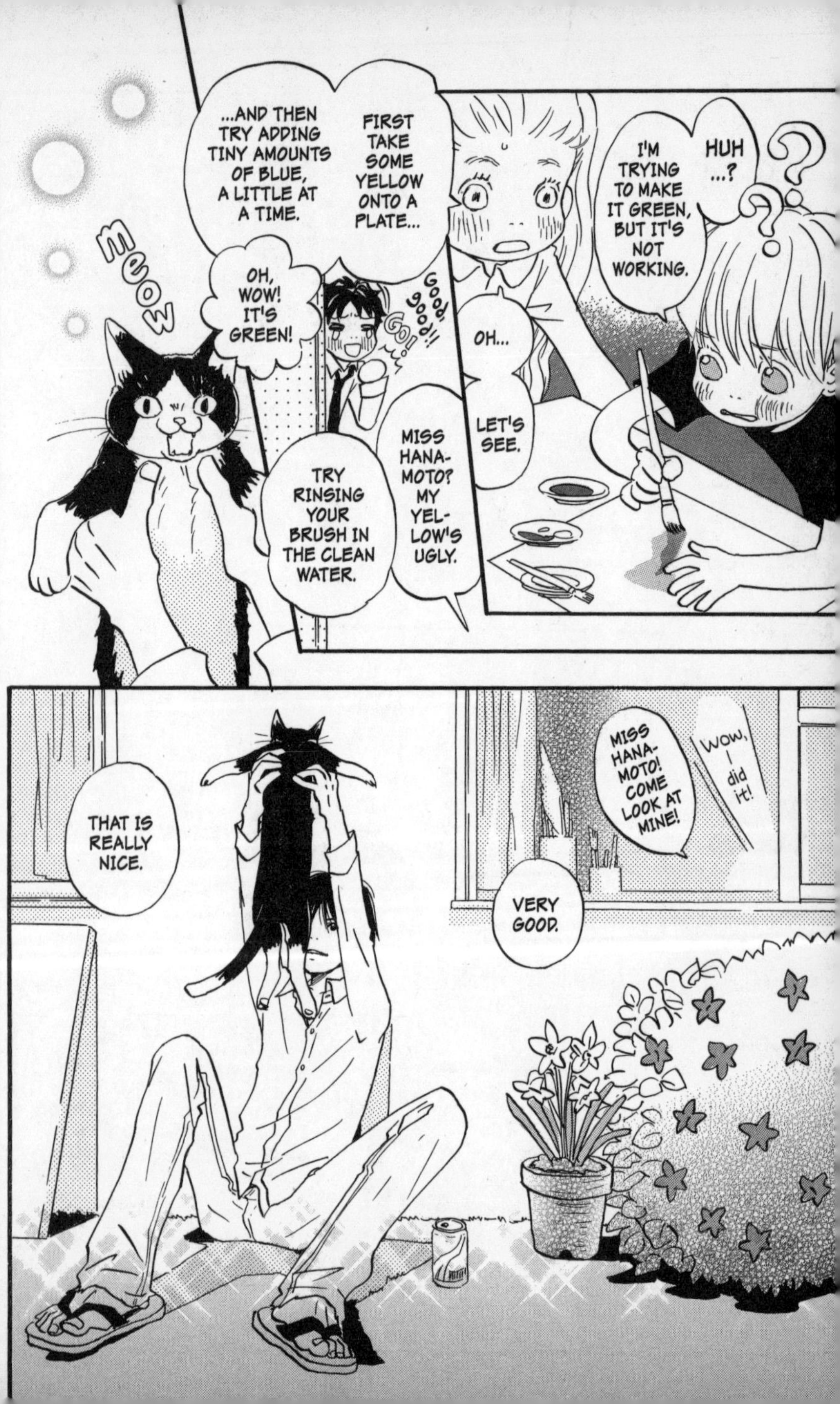
HUH ...?
I'M TRYING TO MAKE IT GREEN, BUT IT'S NOT WORKING.
OH...
LET'S SEE.
FIRST TAKE SOME YELLOW ONTO A PLATE...
...AND THEN TRY ADDING TINY AMOUNTS OF BLUE, A LITTLE AT A TIME.
MISS HANA-MOTO? MY YEL-LOW'S UGLY.
TRY RINSING YOUR BRUSH IN THE CLEAN WATER.
Good, good!!
GO!
OH, WOW! IT'S GREEN!
meow
Wow, I did it!
MISS HANA-MOTO! COME LOOK AT MINE!
VERY GOOD.
THAT IS REALLY NICE.

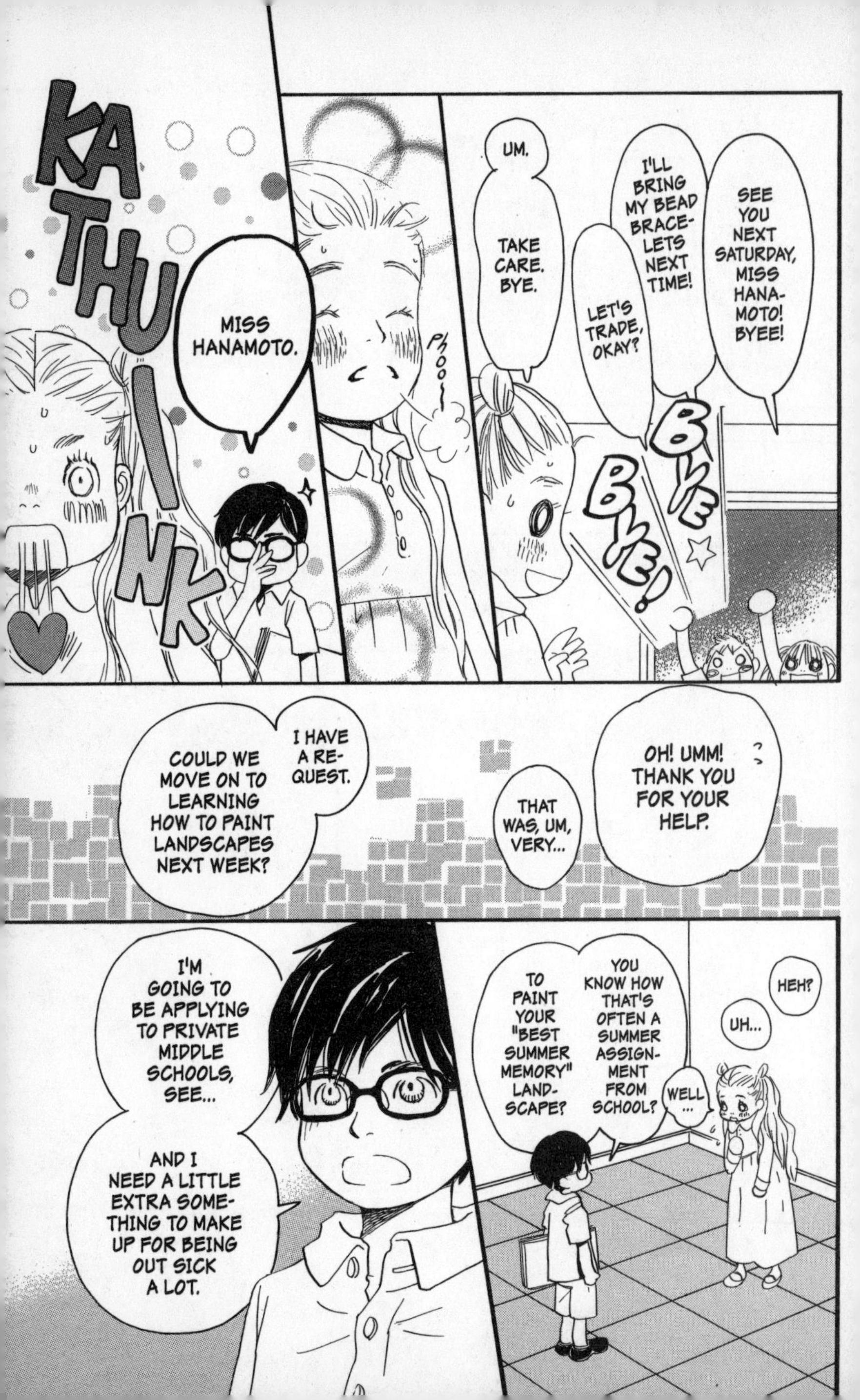
SEE YOU NEXT SATURDAY, MISS HANAMOTO! BYEE!
I'LL BRING MY BEAD BRACELETS NEXT TIME!
LET'S TRADE, OKAY?
UM.
TAKE CARE. BYE.
BYE BYE!
MISS HANAMOTO.
KATHUNK
OH! UMM! THANK YOU FOR YOUR HELP.
THAT WAS, UM, VERY...
I HAVE A REQUEST.
COULD WE MOVE ON TO LEARNING HOW TO PAINT LANDSCAPES NEXT WEEK?
HEH?
UH...
WELL ...
YOU KNOW HOW THAT'S OFTEN A SUMMER ASSIGNMENT FROM SCHOOL?
TO PAINT YOUR "BEST SUMMER MEMORY" LANDSCAPE?
I'M GOING TO BE APPLYING TO PRIVATE MIDDLE SCHOOLS, SEE...
AND I NEED A LITTLE EXTRA SOMETHING TO MAKE UP FOR BEING OUT SICK A LOT.

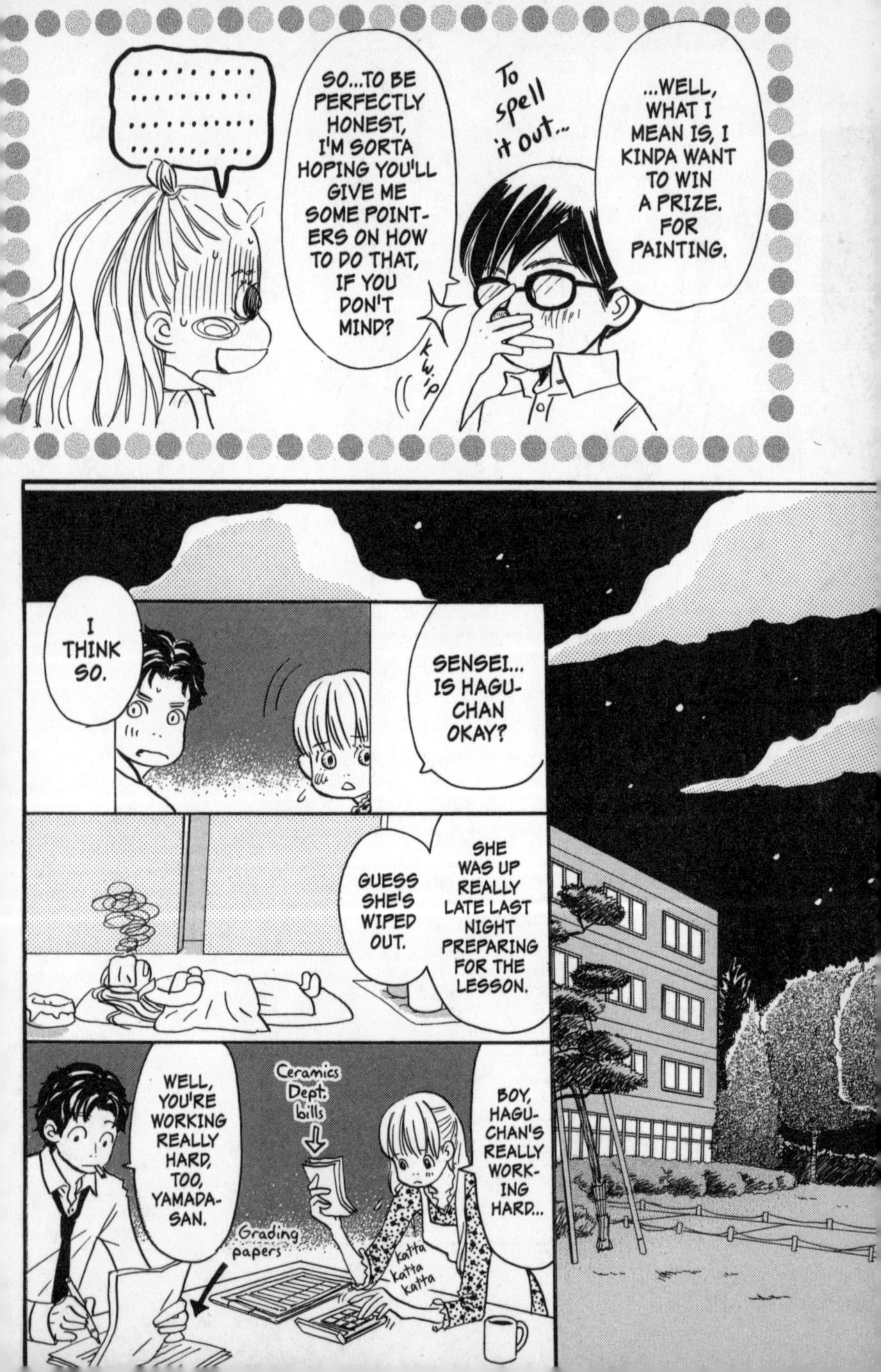
...WELL, WHAT I MEAN IS, I KINDA WANT TO WIN A PRIZE. FOR PAINTING.
To spell it out...
SO...TO BE PERFECTLY HONEST, I'M SORTA HOPING YOU'LL GIVE ME SOME POINTERS ON HOW TO DO THAT, IF YOU DON'T MIND?
Kwip
....
....
....
....
SENSEI... IS HAGU-CHAN OKAY?
I THINK SO.
SHE WAS UP REALLY LATE LAST NIGHT PREPARING FOR THE LESSON.
GUESS SHE'S WIPED OUT.
BOY, HAGU-CHAN'S REALLY WORKING HARD...
Ceramics Dept. bills
katta katta katta
WELL, YOU'RE WORKING REALLY HARD, TOO, YAMADA-SAN.
Grading papers

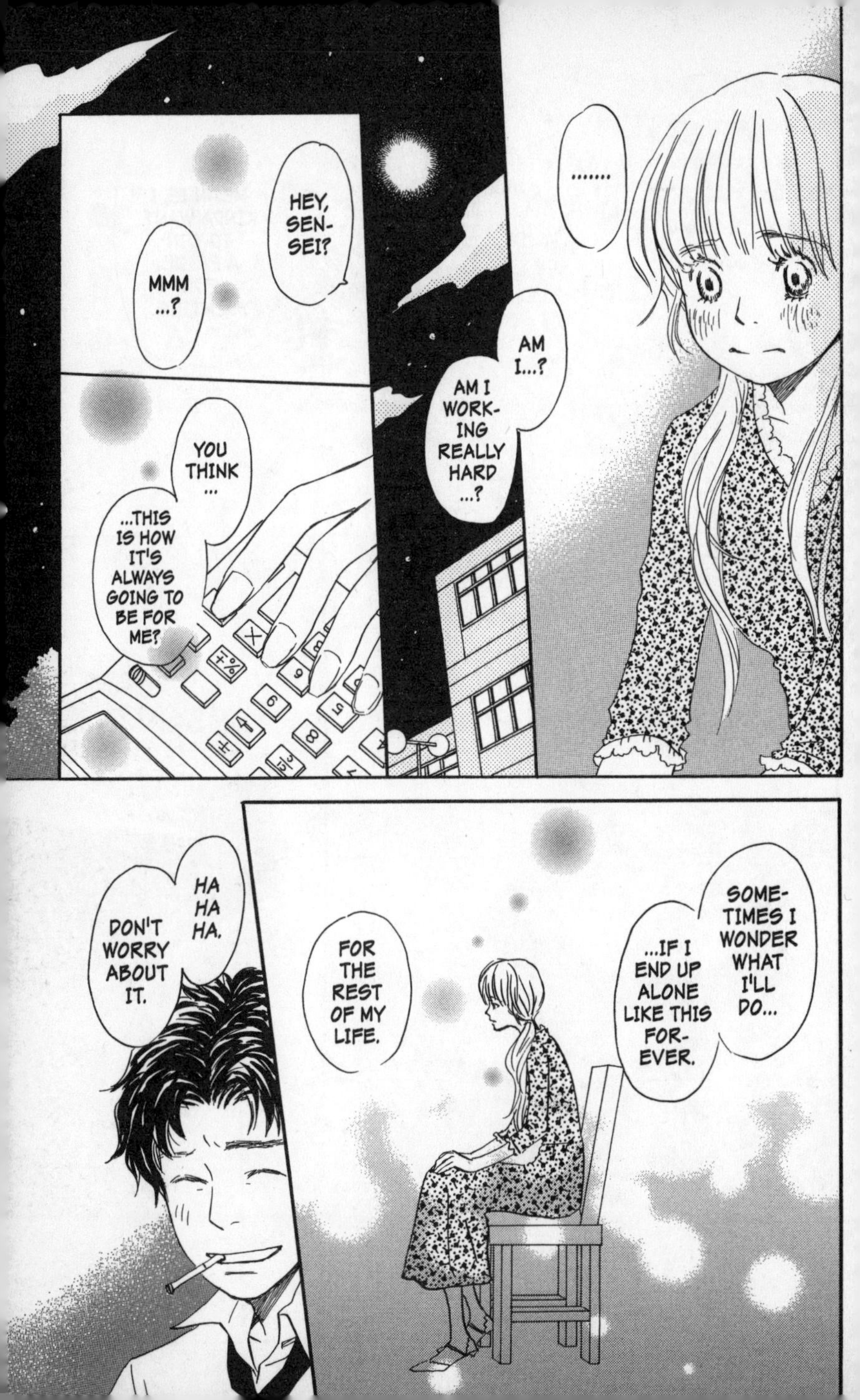
......
AM I...?
AM I WORKING REALLY HARD...?
HEY, SENSEI?
MMM...?
YOU THINK...
...THIS IS HOW IT'S ALWAYS GOING TO BE FOR ME?
SOMETIMES I WONDER WHAT I'LL DO...
...IF I END UP ALONE LIKE THIS FOREVER.
FOR THE REST OF MY LIFE.
HA HA HA.
DON'T WORRY ABOUT IT.

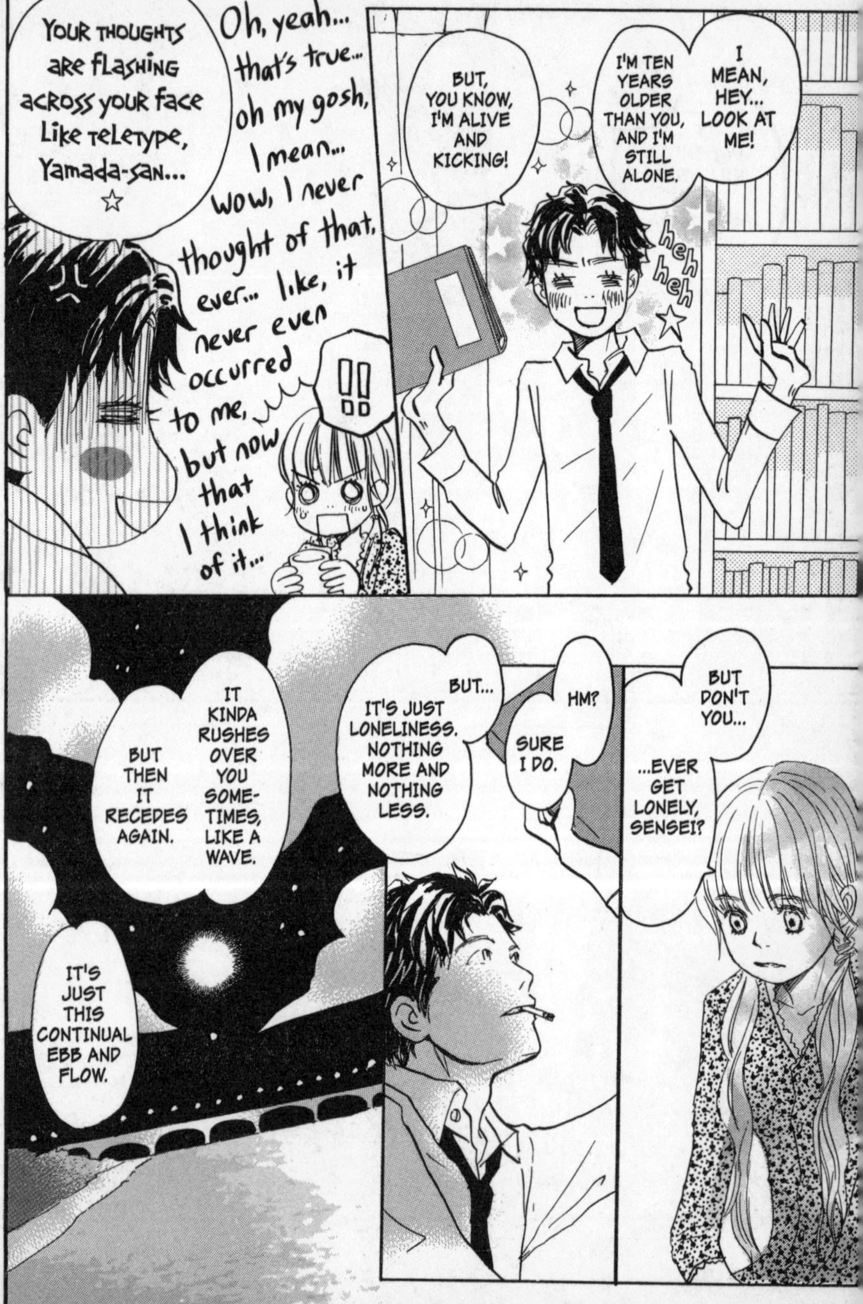
I MEAN, HEY... LOOK AT ME!
I'M TEN YEARS OLDER THAN YOU, AND I'M STILL ALONE.
heh heh
BUT, YOU KNOW, I'M ALIVE AND KICKING!
Oh, yeah... that's true... oh my gosh, I mean... wow, I never thought of that, ever... like, it never even occurred to me, but now that I think of it...
!!
YOUR THOUGHTS are flashing across your face Like teletype, Yamada-san... ☆
BUT DON'T YOU...
...EVER GET LONELY, SENSEI?
HM?
SURE I DO.
BUT...
IT'S JUST LONELINESS. NOTHING MORE AND NOTHING LESS.
IT KINDA RUSHES OVER YOU SOMETIMES, LIKE A WAVE.
BUT THEN IT RECEDES AGAIN.
IT'S JUST THIS CONTINUAL EBB AND FLOW.

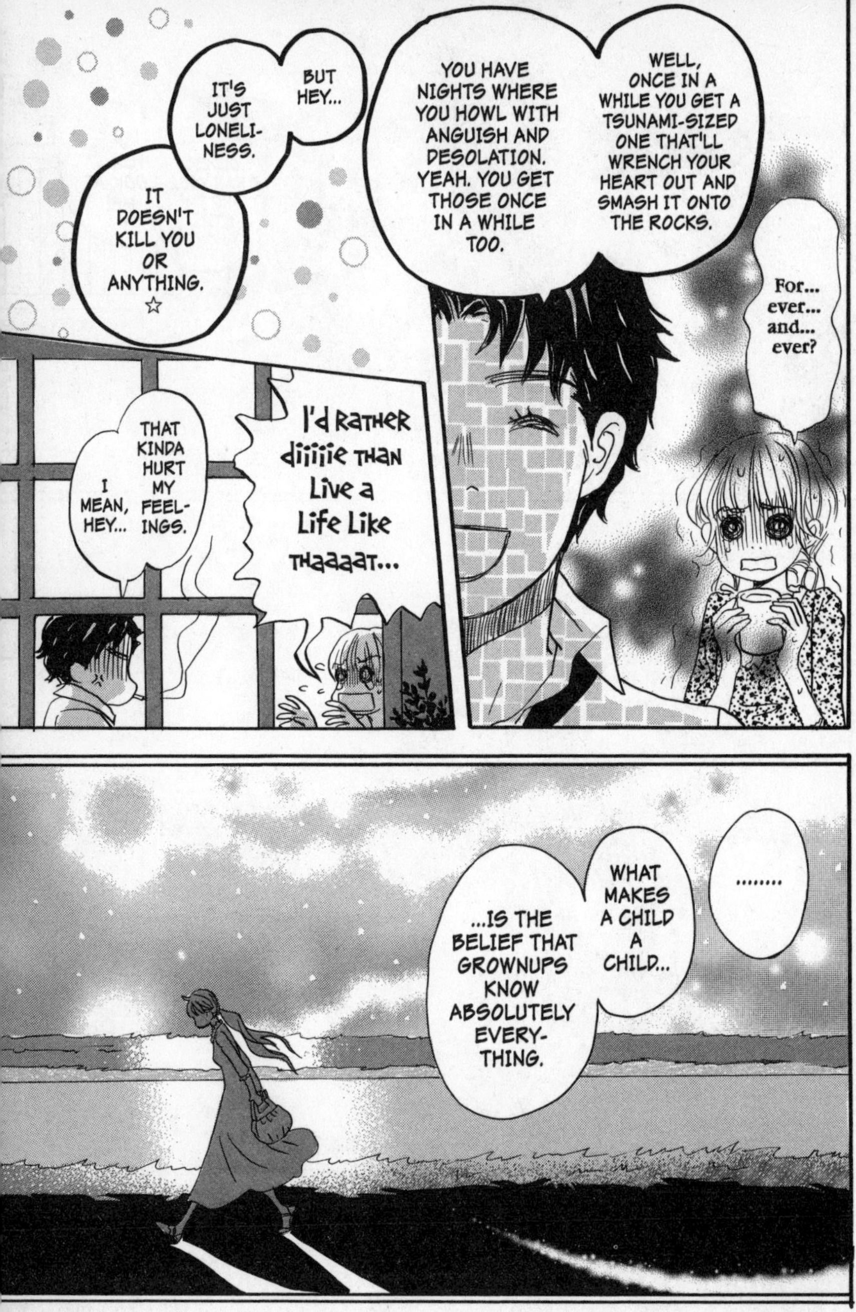
WELL, ONCE IN A WHILE YOU GET A TSUNAMI-SIZED ONE THAT'LL WRENCH YOUR HEART OUT AND SMASH IT ONTO THE ROCKS.
YOU HAVE NIGHTS WHERE YOU HOWL WITH ANGUISH AND DESOLATION. YEAH. YOU GET THOSE ONCE IN A WHILE TOO.
BUT HEY...
IT'S JUST LONELINESS.
IT DOESN'T KILL YOU OR ANYTHING. ☆
For... ever... and... ever?
I'd rather diiiie than live a life like thaaaat...
THAT KINDA HURT MY FEELINGS. I MEAN, HEY...
....
WHAT MAKES A CHILD A CHILD...
...IS THE BELIEF THAT GROWNUPS KNOW ABSOLUTELY EVERYTHING.

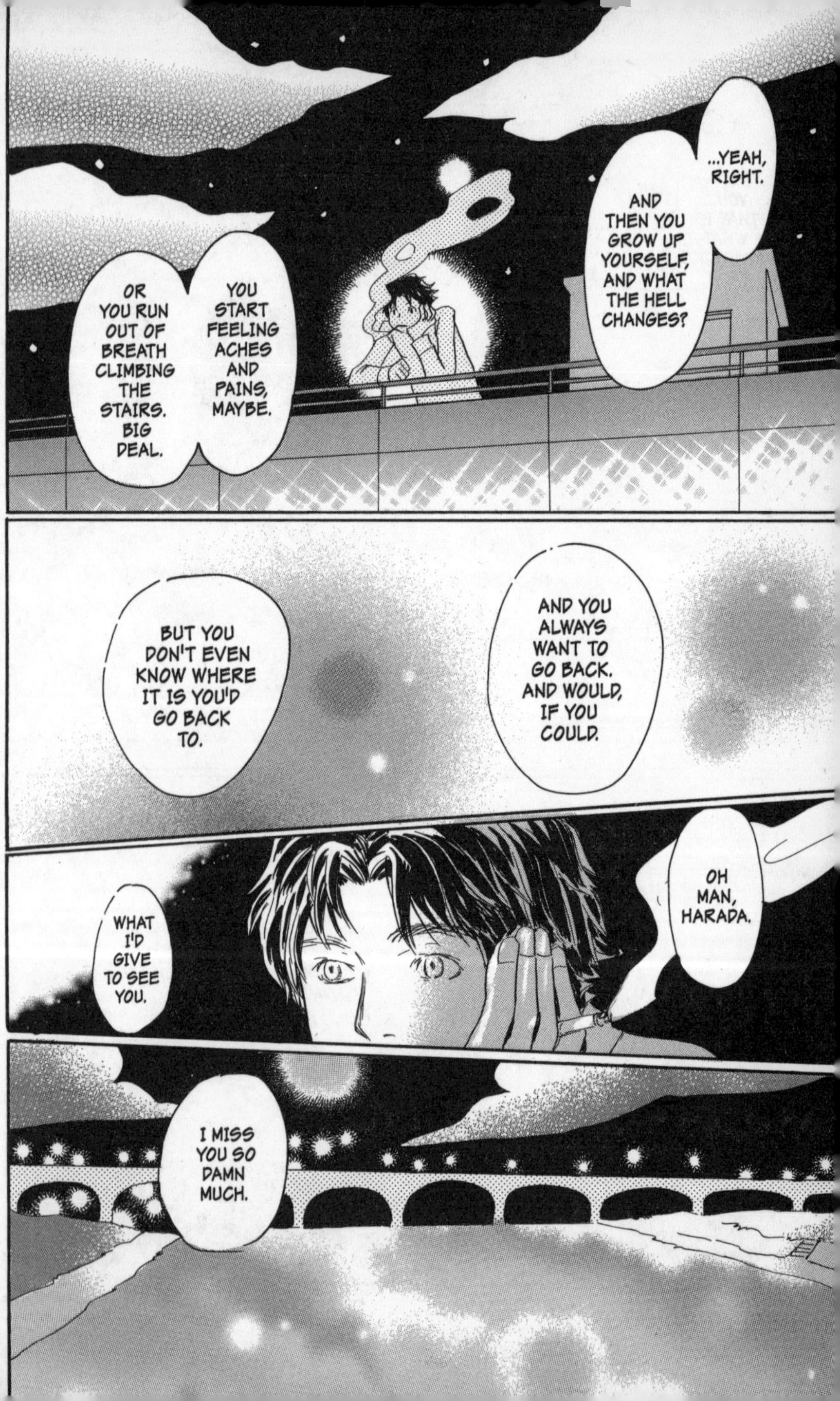
...YEAH, RIGHT.
AND THEN YOU GROW UP YOURSELF, AND WHAT THE HELL CHANGES?
YOU START FEELING ACHES AND PAINS, MAYBE.
OR YOU RUN OUT OF BREATH CLIMBING THE STAIRS. BIG DEAL.
AND YOU ALWAYS WANT TO GO BACK. AND WOULD, IF YOU COULD.
BUT YOU DON'T EVEN KNOW WHERE IT IS YOU'D GO BACK TO.
OH MAN, HARADA.
WHAT I'D GIVE TO SEE YOU.
I MISS YOU SO DAMN MUCH.

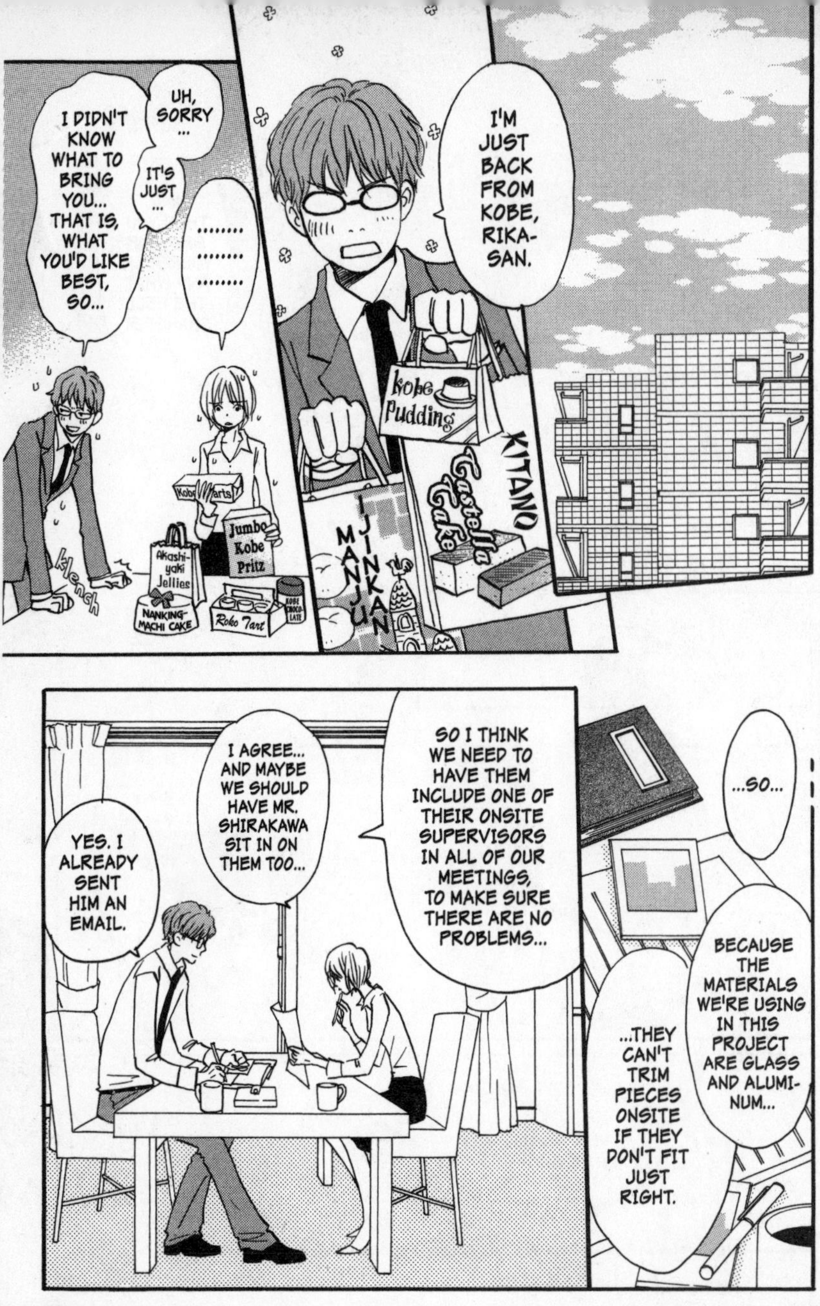
I'M JUST BACK FROM KOBE, RIKA-SAN.
Kobe Pudding
KITANO
Castella Cake
IJINKAN
MANJU
....
....
....
UH, SORRY ...
IT'S JUST ...
I DIDN'T KNOW WHAT TO BRING YOU... THAT IS, WHAT YOU'D LIKE BEST, SO...
Jumbo Kobe Pritz
Akashi-yaki Jellies
NANKING-MACHI CAKE
Roko Tart
KOBE CHOCOLATE
klench
...SO...
BECAUSE THE MATERIALS WE'RE USING IN THIS PROJECT ARE GLASS AND ALUMI-NUM...
...THEY CAN'T TRIM PIECES ONSITE IF THEY DON'T FIT JUST RIGHT.
SO I THINK WE NEED TO HAVE THEM INCLUDE ONE OF THEIR ONSITE SUPERVISORS IN ALL OF OUR MEETINGS, TO MAKE SURE THERE ARE NO PROBLEMS...
I AGREE... AND MAYBE WE SHOULD HAVE MR. SHIRAKAWA SIT IN ON THEM TOO...
YES. I ALREADY SENT HIM AN EMAIL.

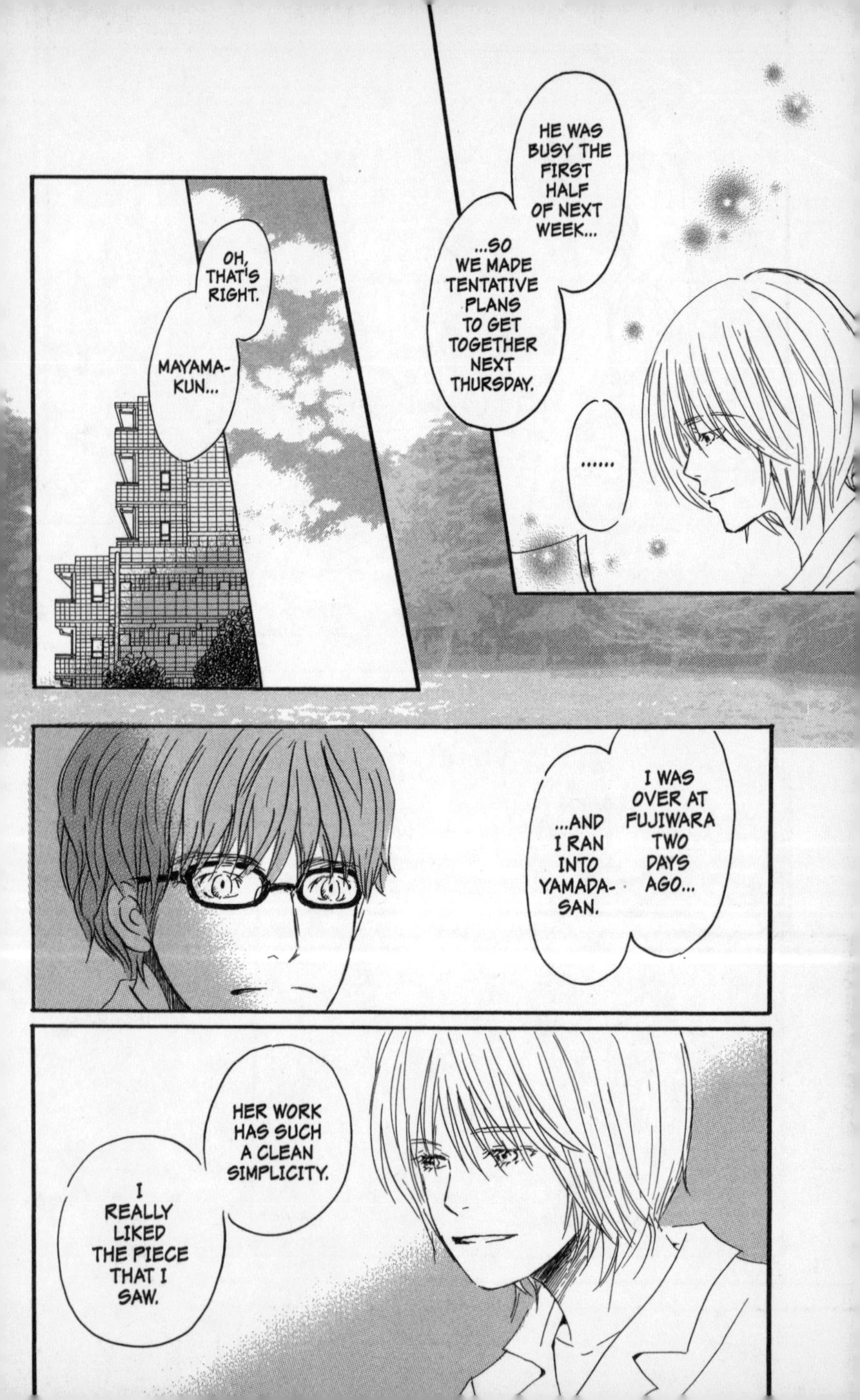
HE WAS BUSY THE FIRST HALF OF NEXT WEEK...
...SO WE MADE TENTATIVE PLANS TO GET TOGETHER NEXT THURSDAY.
......
OH, THAT'S RIGHT.
MAYAMA-KUN...
I WAS OVER AT FUJIWARA TWO DAYS AGO...
...AND I RAN INTO YAMADA-SAN.
HER WORK HAS SUCH A CLEAN SIMPLICITY.
I REALLY LIKED THE PIECE THAT I SAW.

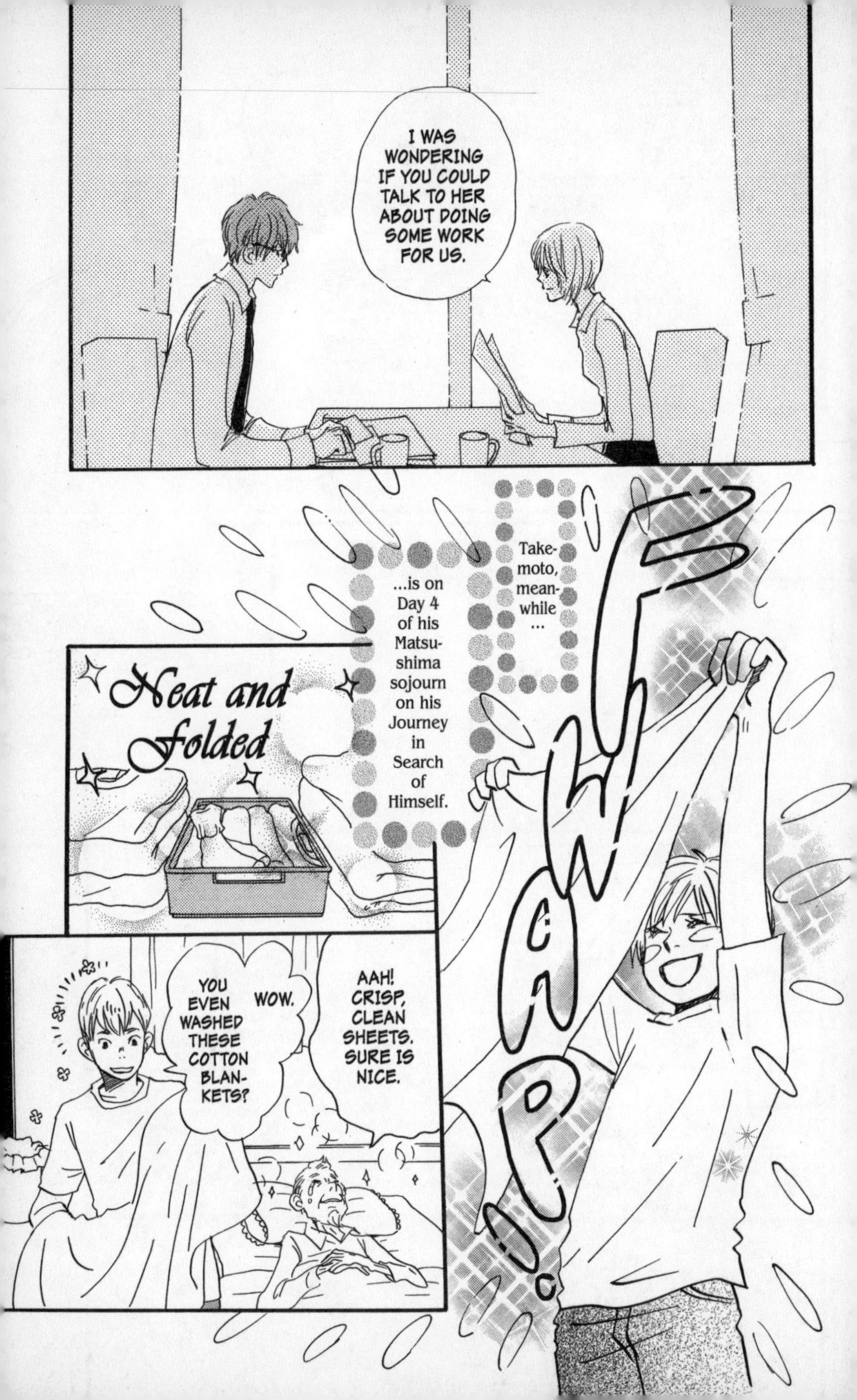
I WAS WONDERING IF YOU COULD TALK TO HER ABOUT DOING SOME WORK FOR US.
Take-moto, mean-while ...
...is on Day 4 of his Matsu-shima sojourn on his Journey in Search of Himself.
Neat and folded
AAH! CRISP, CLEAN SHEETS. SURE IS NICE.
WOW.
YOU EVEN WASHED THESE COTTON BLAN-KETS?

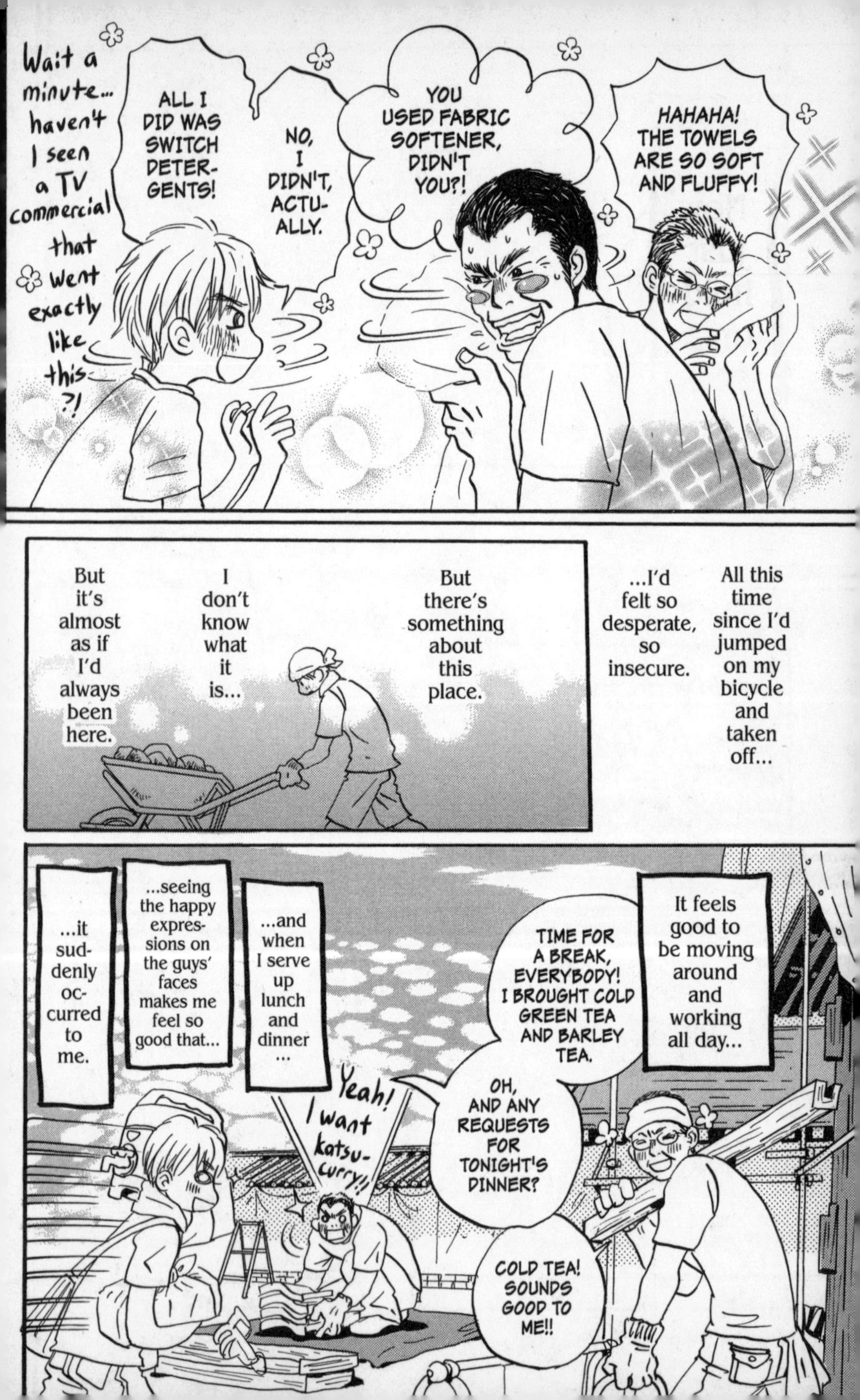
HAHAHA! THE TOWELS ARE SO SOFT AND FLUFFY!
YOU USED FABRIC SOFTENER, DIDN'T YOU?!
NO, I DIDN'T, ACTUALLY.
ALL I DID WAS SWITCH DETERGENTS!
Wait a minute... haven't I seen a TV commercial that went exactly like this?!
All this time since I'd jumped on my bicycle and taken off...
...I'd felt so desperate, so insecure.
But there's something about this place.
I don't know what it is...
But it's almost as if I'd always been here.
It feels good to be moving around and working all day...
TIME FOR A BREAK, EVERYBODY! I BROUGHT COLD GREEN TEA AND BARLEY TEA.
OH, AND ANY REQUESTS FOR TONIGHT'S DINNER?
COLD TEA! SOUNDS GOOD TO ME!!
Yeah! I want katsu-curry!!
...and when I serve up lunch and dinner...
...seeing the happy expressions on the guys' faces makes me feel so good that...
...it suddenly occurred to me.

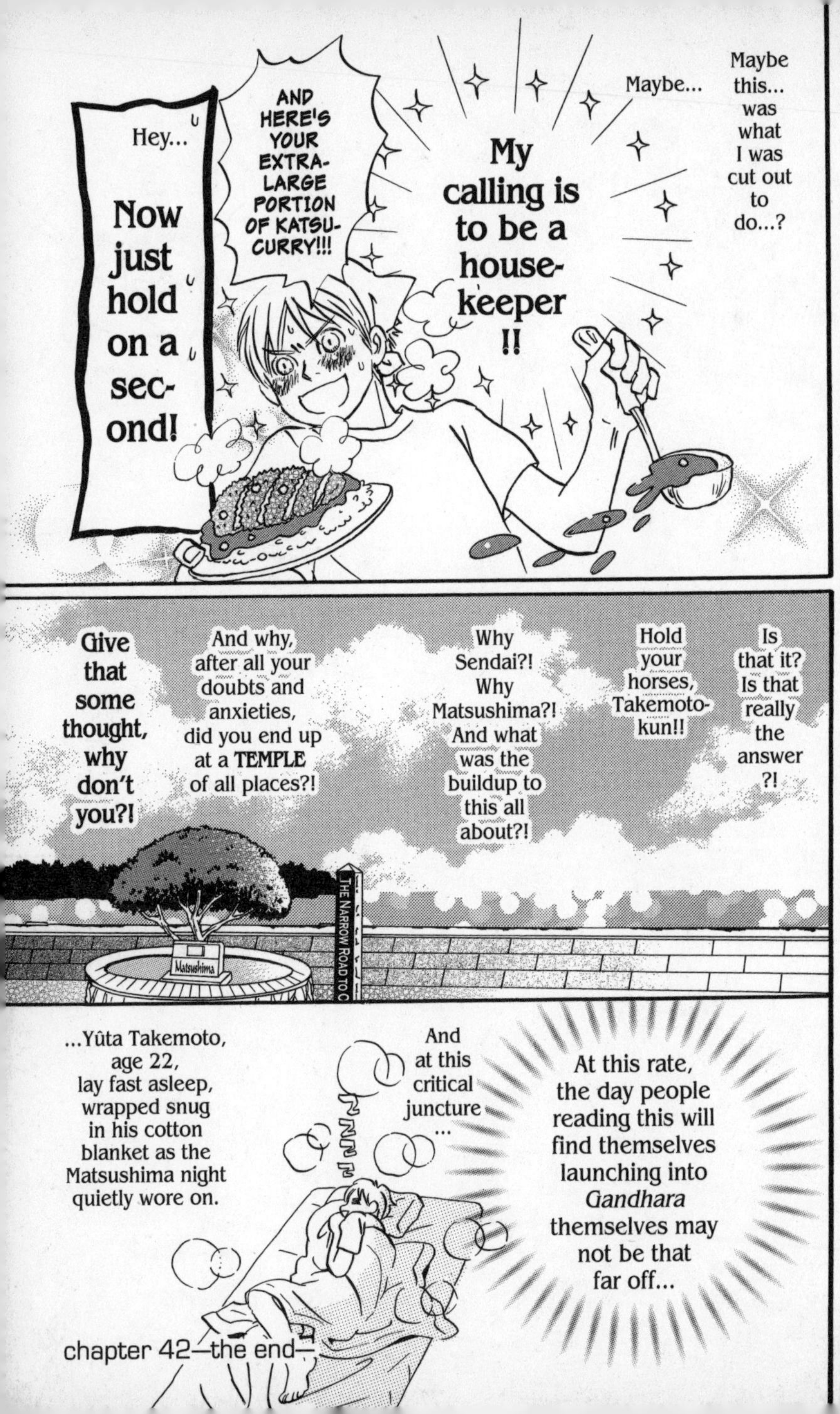
Maybe this... was what I was cut out to do...?
Maybe...
My calling is to be a house-keeper!!
AND HERE'S YOUR EXTRA-LARGE PORTION OF KATSU-CURRY!!!
Hey...
Now just hold on a sec-ond!
Is that it? Is that really the answer?!
Hold your horses, Takemoto-kun!!
Why Sendai?! Why Matsushima?! And what was the buildup to this all about?!
And why, after all your doubts and anxieties, did you end up at a TEMPLE of all places?!
Give that some thought, why don't you?!
THE NARROW ROAD TO C
Matsushima
At this rate, the day people reading this will find themselves launching into *Gandhara* themselves may not be that far off...
And at this critical juncture...
...Yûta Takemoto, age 22, lay fast asleep, wrapped snug in his cotton blanket as the Matsushima night quietly wore on.
chapter 42—the end—

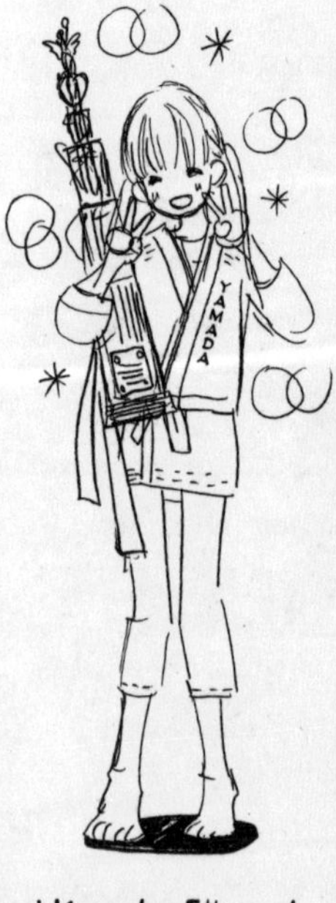
YAMADA

#3: Ayumi Yamada, 5th grade

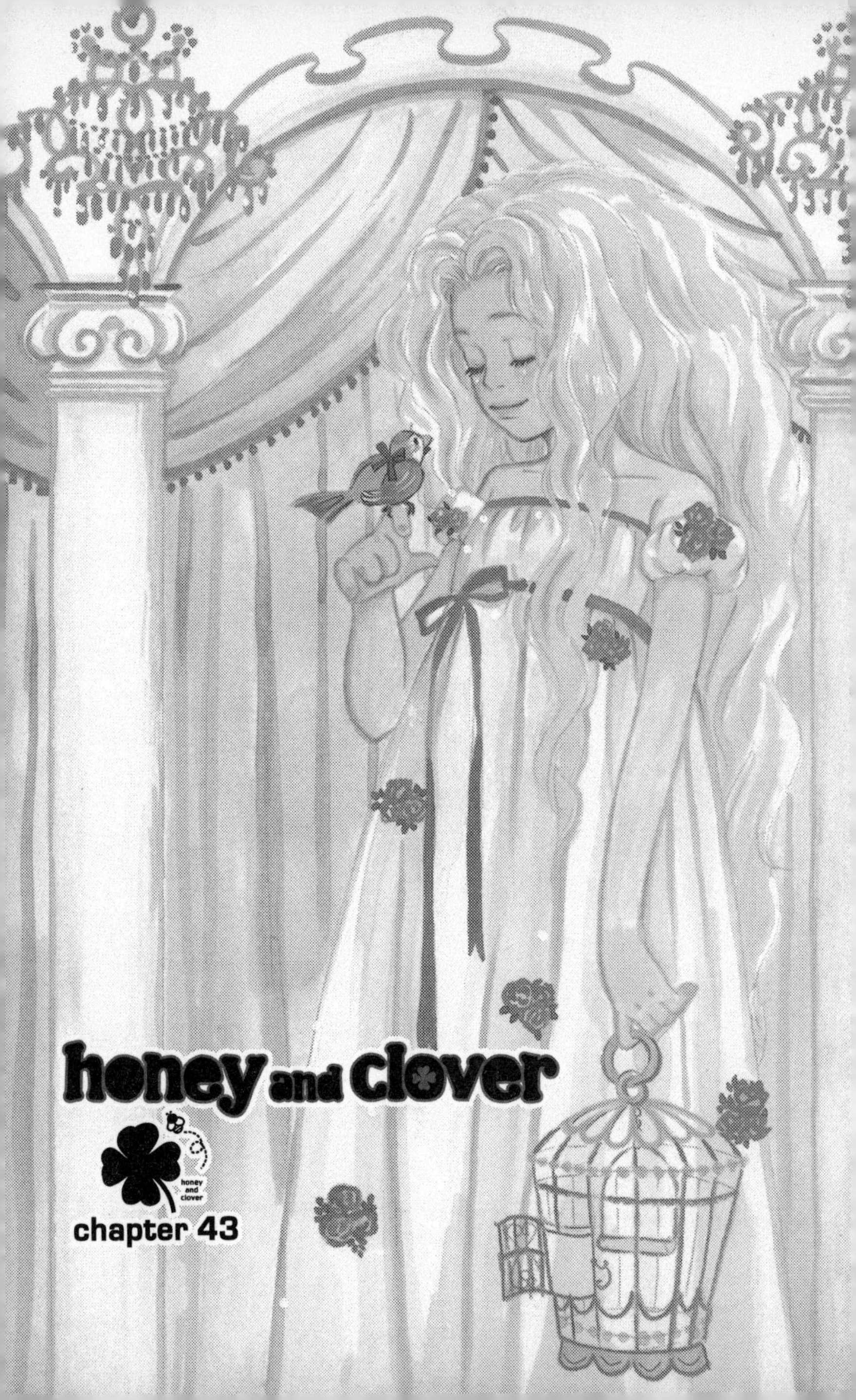
honey and clover
honey and clover
chapter 43

#4 cluster:

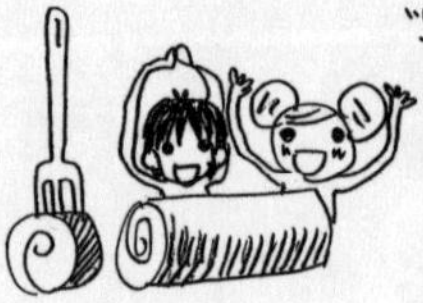

"Yaaay!
It's a Swiss roll!"

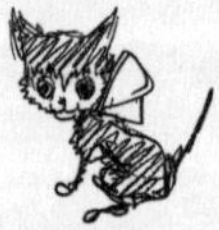

"Kittens are quivery."

I
want
an
iPod...

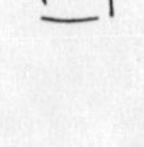

← doodled in the margins;
I must've been super-sleepy
at the time...

← ?!
Aghast at my own pathetic
lameness...

(Ai = love. Ai pot = ipod)

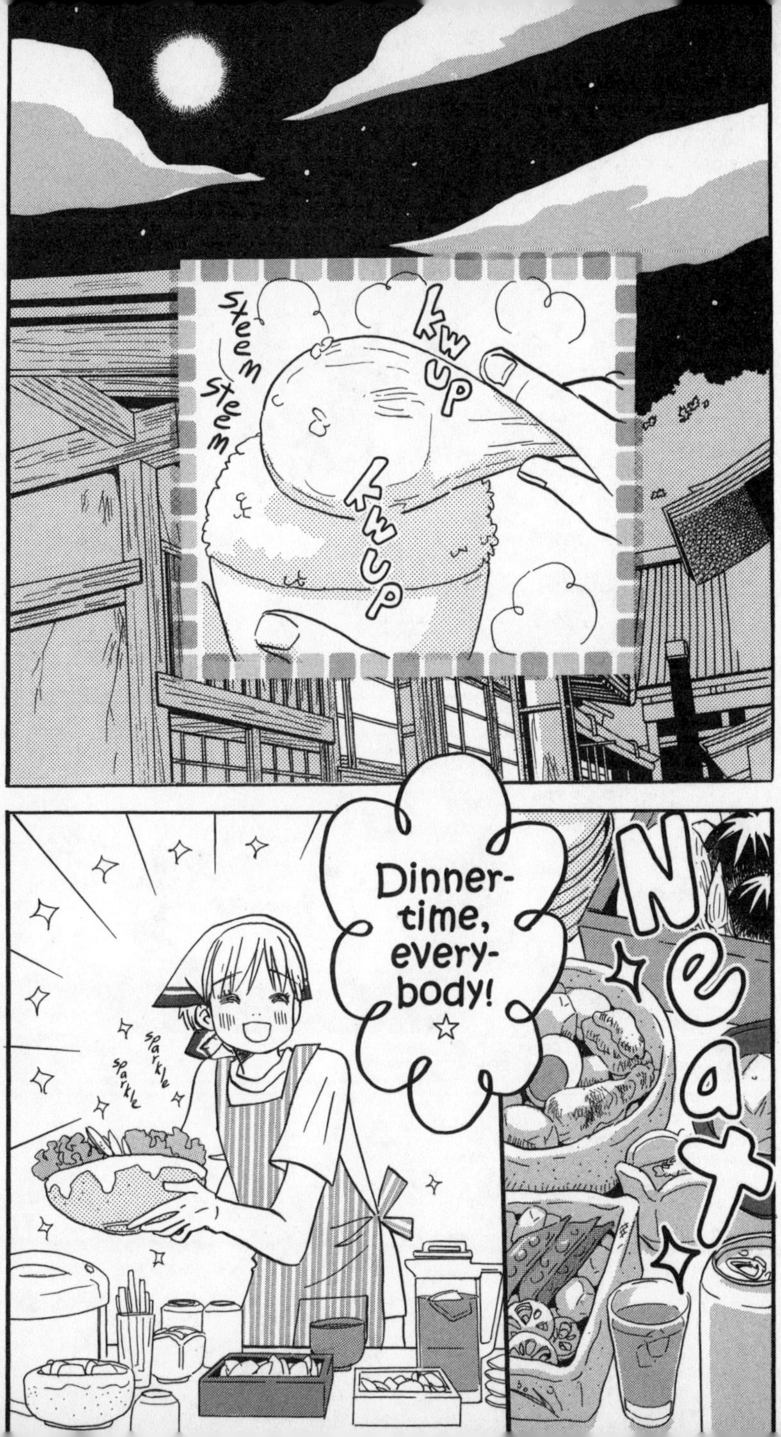
kwup kwup
steem steem
Neat
Dinner-time, everybody! ☆
sparkle sparkle

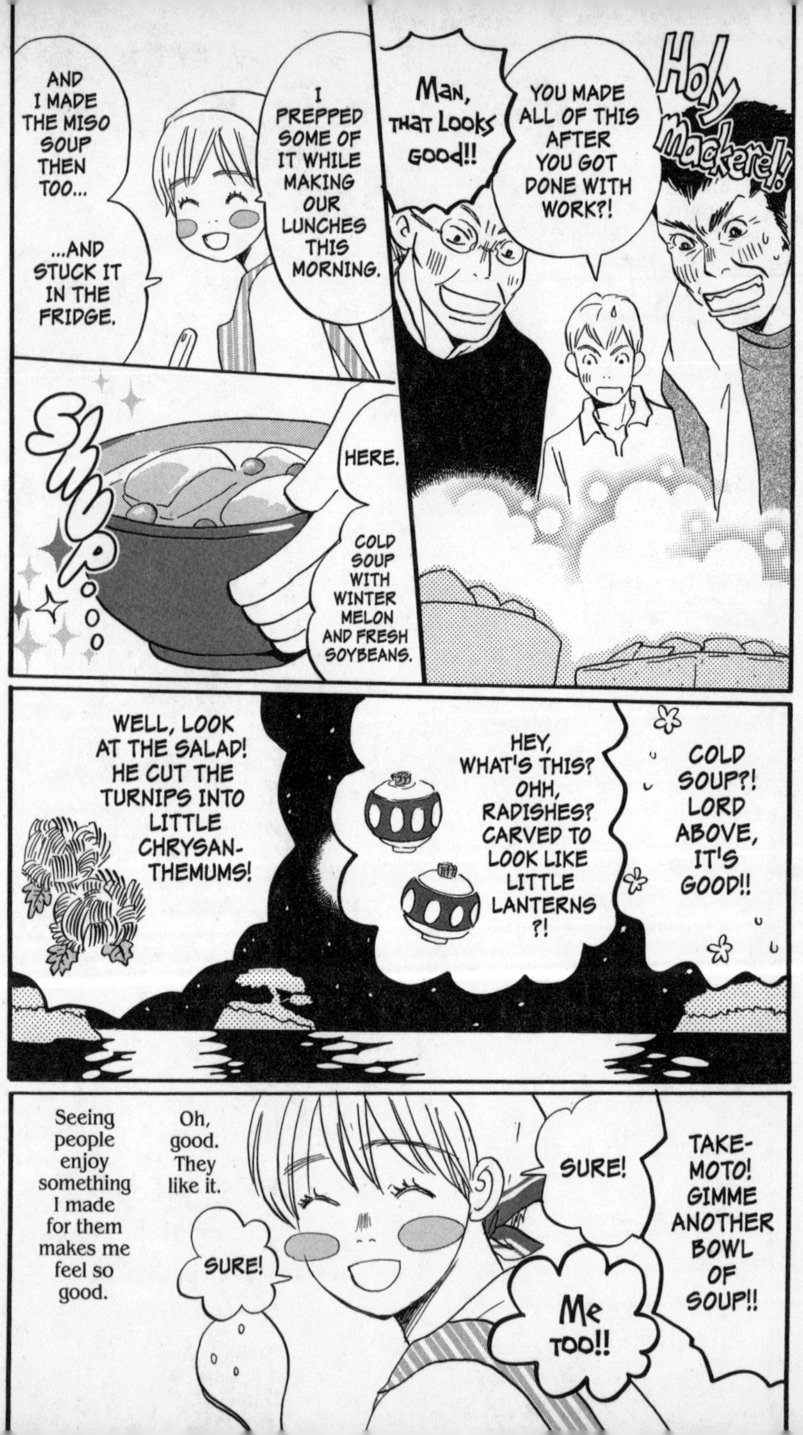
Holy mackerel!!
YOU MADE ALL OF THIS AFTER YOU GOT DONE WITH WORK?!
Man, THAT LOOKS GOOD!!
I PREPPED SOME OF IT WHILE MAKING OUR LUNCHES THIS MORNING.
AND I MADE THE MISO SOUP THEN TOO...
...AND STUCK IT IN THE FRIDGE.
HERE.
COLD SOUP WITH WINTER MELON AND FRESH SOYBEANS.
SHUPOOOO
COLD SOUP?! LORD ABOVE, IT'S GOOD!!
HEY, WHAT'S THIS? OHH, RADISHES? CARVED TO LOOK LIKE LITTLE LANTERNS ?!
WELL, LOOK AT THE SALAD! HE CUT THE TURNIPS INTO LITTLE CHRYSAN-THEMUMS!
TAKE-MOTO! GIMME ANOTHER BOWL OF SOUP!!
SURE!
Me TOO!!
SURE!
Oh, good. They like it.
Seeing people enjoy something I made for them makes me feel so good.

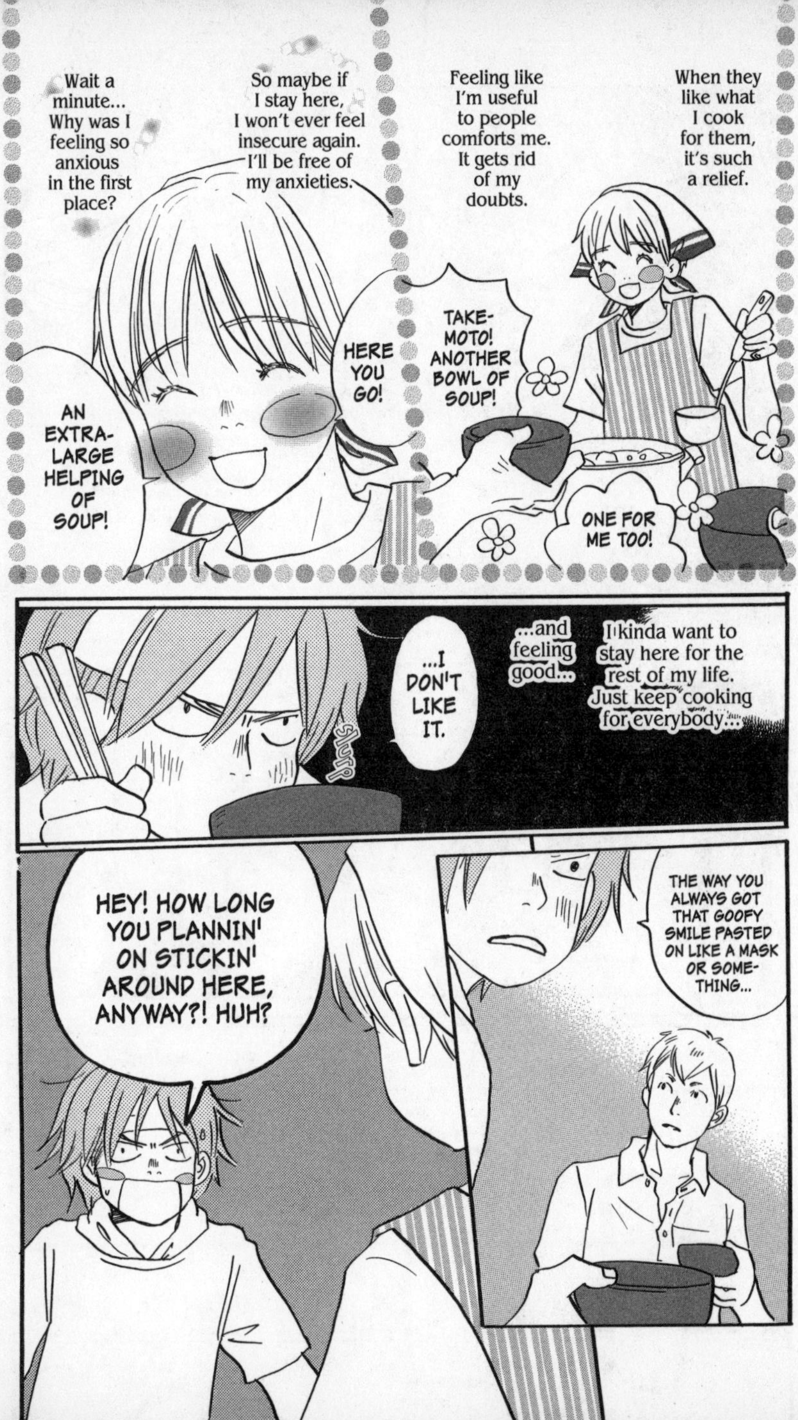
When they like what I cook for them, it's such a relief.
Feeling like I'm useful to people comforts me. It gets rid of my doubts.
TAKE-MOTO! ANOTHER BOWL OF SOUP!
ONE FOR ME TOO!
So maybe if I stay here, I won't ever feel insecure again. I'll be free of my anxieties.
Wait a minute... Why was I feeling so anxious in the first place?
HERE YOU GO!
AN EXTRA-LARGE HELPING OF SOUP!
I kinda want to stay here for the rest of my life. Just keep cooking for everybody...
...and feeling good...
...I DON'T LIKE IT.
slurp
THE WAY YOU ALWAYS GOT THAT GOOFY SMILE PASTED ON LIKE A MASK OR SOME-THING...
HEY! HOW LONG YOU PLANNIN' ON STICKIN' AROUND HERE, ANYWAY?! HUH?

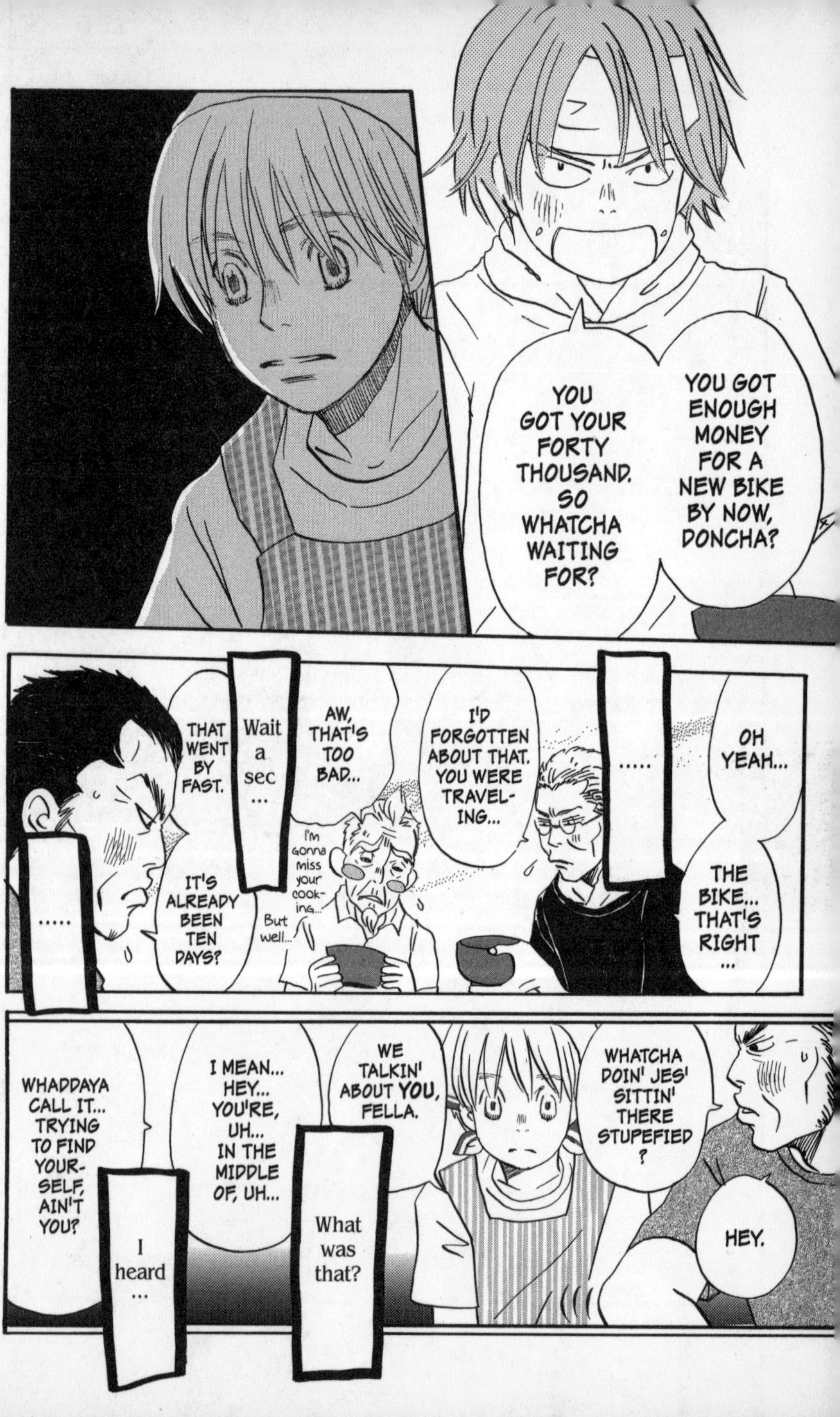
YOU GOT ENOUGH MONEY FOR A NEW BIKE BY NOW, DONCHA?
YOU GOT YOUR FORTY THOUSAND. SO WHATCHA WAITING FOR?
OH YEAH...
THE BIKE... THAT'S RIGHT...
.....
I'D FORGOTTEN ABOUT THAT. YOU WERE TRAVEL-ING...
AW, THAT'S TOO BAD...
I'm gonna miss your cook-ing...
But well...
Wait a sec...
THAT WENT BY FAST.
IT'S ALREADY BEEN TEN DAYS?
.....
HEY.
WHATCHA DOIN' JES' SITTIN' THERE STUPEFIED?
WE TALKIN' ABOUT YOU, FELLA.
What was that?
I MEAN... HEY... YOU'RE, UH... IN THE MIDDLE OF, UH...
WHADDAYA CALL IT... TRYING TO FIND YOUR-SELF, AIN'T YOU?
I heard...

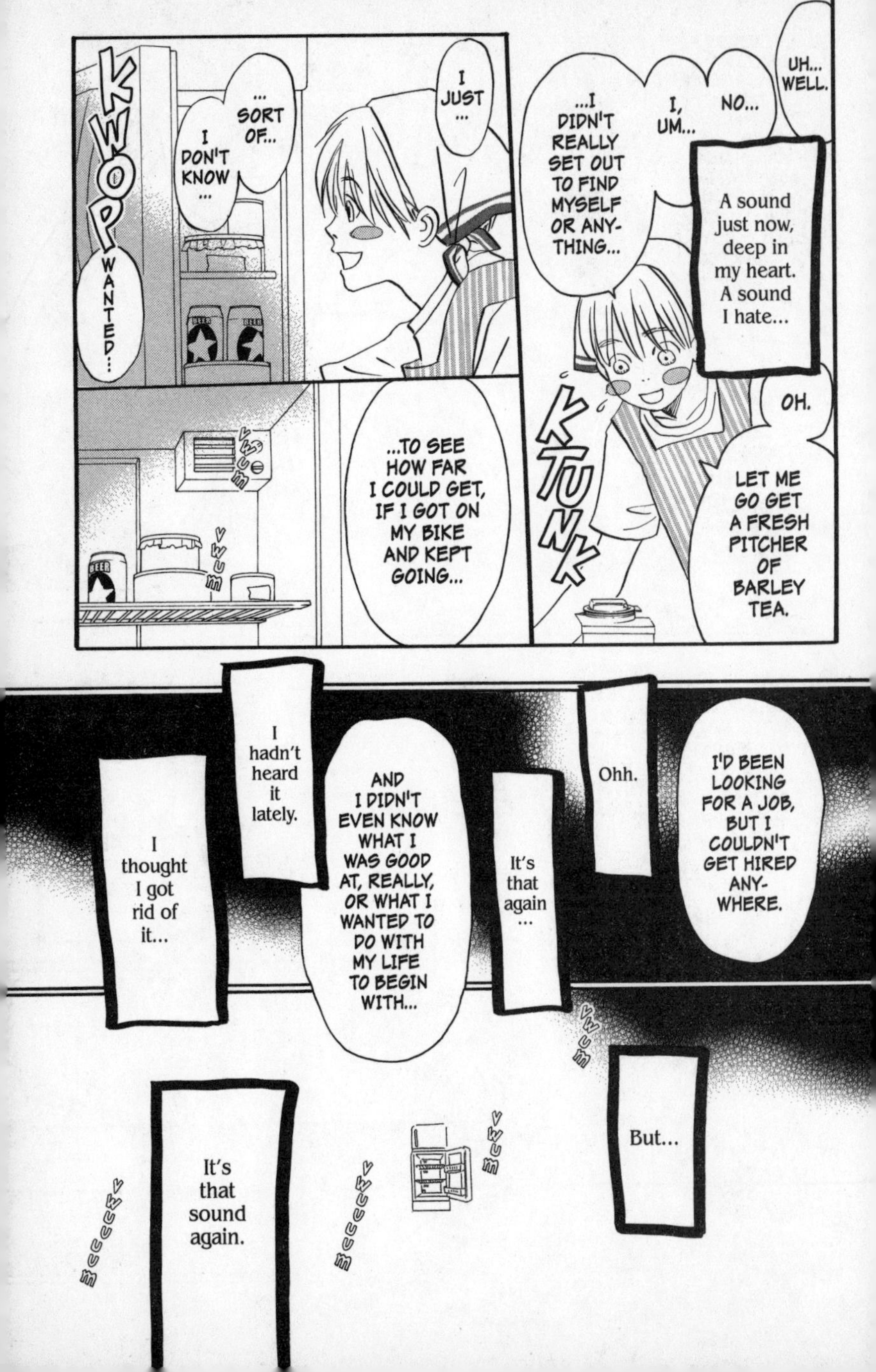
UH... WELL.
NO...
I, UM...
...I DIDN'T REALLY SET OUT TO FIND MYSELF OR ANYTHING...
A sound just now, deep in my heart. A sound I hate...
KTUNK
OH.
LET ME GO GET A FRESH PITCHER OF BARLEY TEA.
I JUST ...
... SORT OF...
I DON'T KNOW ...
KWOP
WANTED...
...TO SEE HOW FAR I COULD GET, IF I GOT ON MY BIKE AND KEPT GOING...
VWUM
VWUM
I'D BEEN LOOKING FOR A JOB, BUT I COULDN'T GET HIRED ANY-WHERE.
Ohh.
It's that again ...
AND I DIDN'T EVEN KNOW WHAT I WAS GOOD AT, REALLY, OR WHAT I WANTED TO DO WITH MY LIFE TO BEGIN WITH...
I hadn't heard it lately.
I thought I got rid of it...
VWUM
But...
VWUM
VWUUUUM
It's that sound again.
VWUUUUM

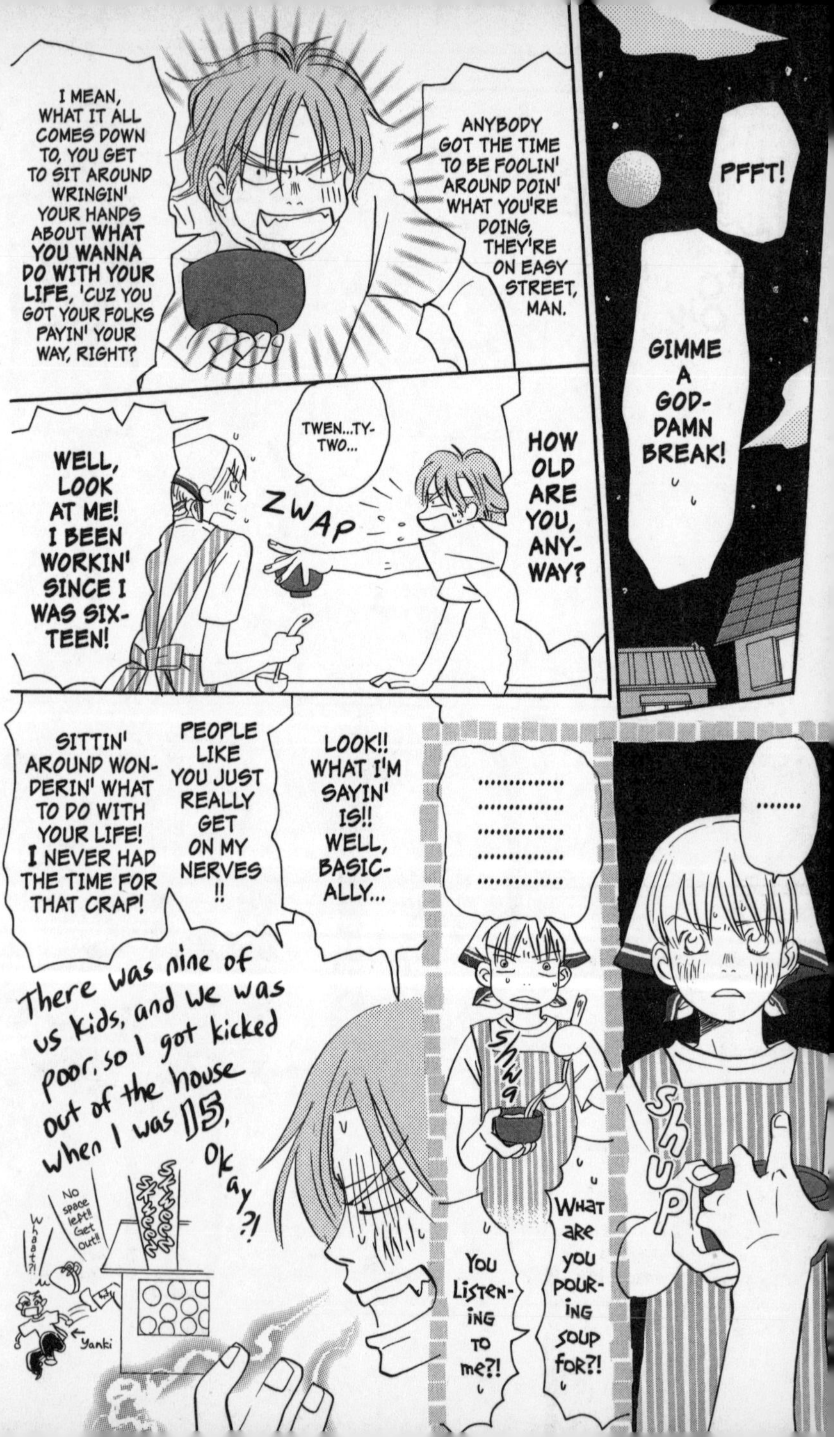
PFFT!
GIMME A GOD-DAMN BREAK!
ANYBODY GOT THE TIME TO BE FOOLIN' AROUND DOIN' WHAT YOU'RE DOING, THEY'RE ON EASY STREET, MAN.
I MEAN, WHAT IT ALL COMES DOWN TO, YOU GET TO SIT AROUND WRINGIN' YOUR HANDS ABOUT WHAT YOU WANNA DO WITH YOUR LIFE, 'CUZ YOU GOT YOUR FOLKS PAYIN' YOUR WAY, RIGHT?
HOW OLD ARE YOU, ANY-WAY?
TWEN...TY-TWO...
ZWAP
WELL, LOOK AT ME! I BEEN WORKIN' SINCE I WAS SIX-TEEN!
....
SHUP
....
....
....
....
....
What are you pour-ing soup for?!
You listen-ing to me?!
SHWA
LOOK!! WHAT I'M SAYIN' IS!! WELL, BASIC-ALLY...
PEOPLE LIKE YOU JUST REALLY GET ON MY NERVES!!
SITTIN' AROUND WON-DERIN' WHAT TO DO WITH YOUR LIFE! I NEVER HAD THE TIME FOR THAT CRAP!
There was nine of us kids, and we was poor, so I got kicked out of the house when I was 15, okay?!
No space left!! Get out!!
Sweet Sweet
Whaaat?!
Yanki

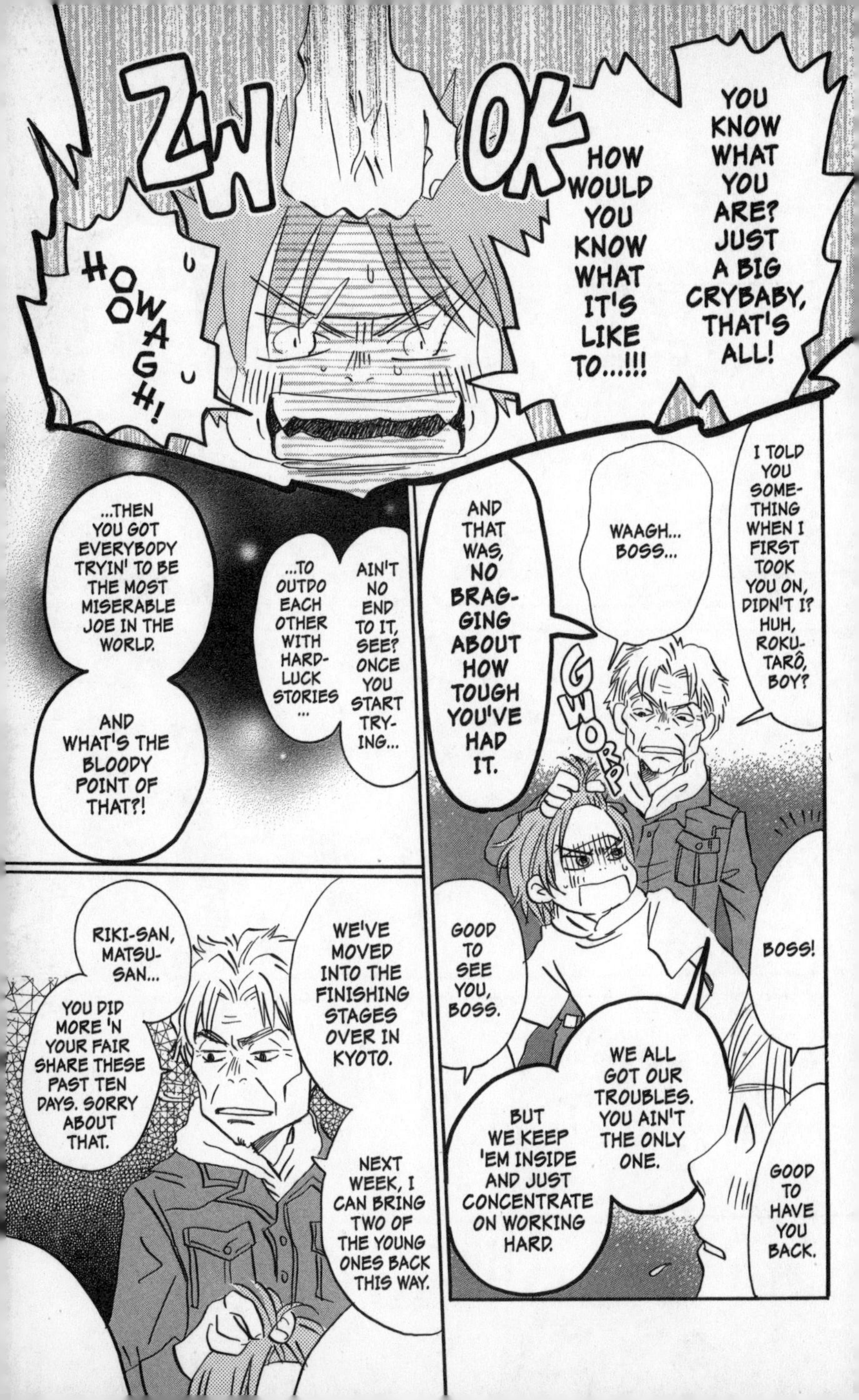
ZW
OK
YOU KNOW WHAT YOU ARE? JUST A BIG CRYBABY, THAT'S ALL!
HOW WOULD YOU KNOW WHAT IT'S LIKE TO...!!!
HOOWAGH!
I TOLD YOU SOMETHING WHEN I FIRST TOOK YOU ON, DIDN'T I? HUH, ROKUTARÔ, BOY?
WAAGH... BOSS...
AND THAT WAS, NO BRAGGING ABOUT HOW TOUGH YOU'VE HAD IT.
GWORP
BOSS!
GOOD TO HAVE YOU BACK.
GOOD TO SEE YOU, BOSS.
WE ALL GOT OUR TROUBLES. YOU AIN'T THE ONLY ONE.
BUT WE KEEP 'EM INSIDE AND JUST CONCENTRATE ON WORKING HARD.
AIN'T NO END TO IT, SEE? ONCE YOU START TRYING...
...TO OUTDO EACH OTHER WITH HARD-LUCK STORIES...
...THEN YOU GOT EVERYBODY TRYIN' TO BE THE MOST MISERABLE JOE IN THE WORLD.
AND WHAT'S THE BLOODY POINT OF THAT?!
WE'VE MOVED INTO THE FINISHING STAGES OVER IN KYOTO.
RIKI-SAN, MATSU-SAN...
YOU DID MORE 'N YOUR FAIR SHARE THESE PAST TEN DAYS. SORRY ABOUT THAT.
NEXT WEEK, I CAN BRING TWO OF THE YOUNG ONES BACK THIS WAY.

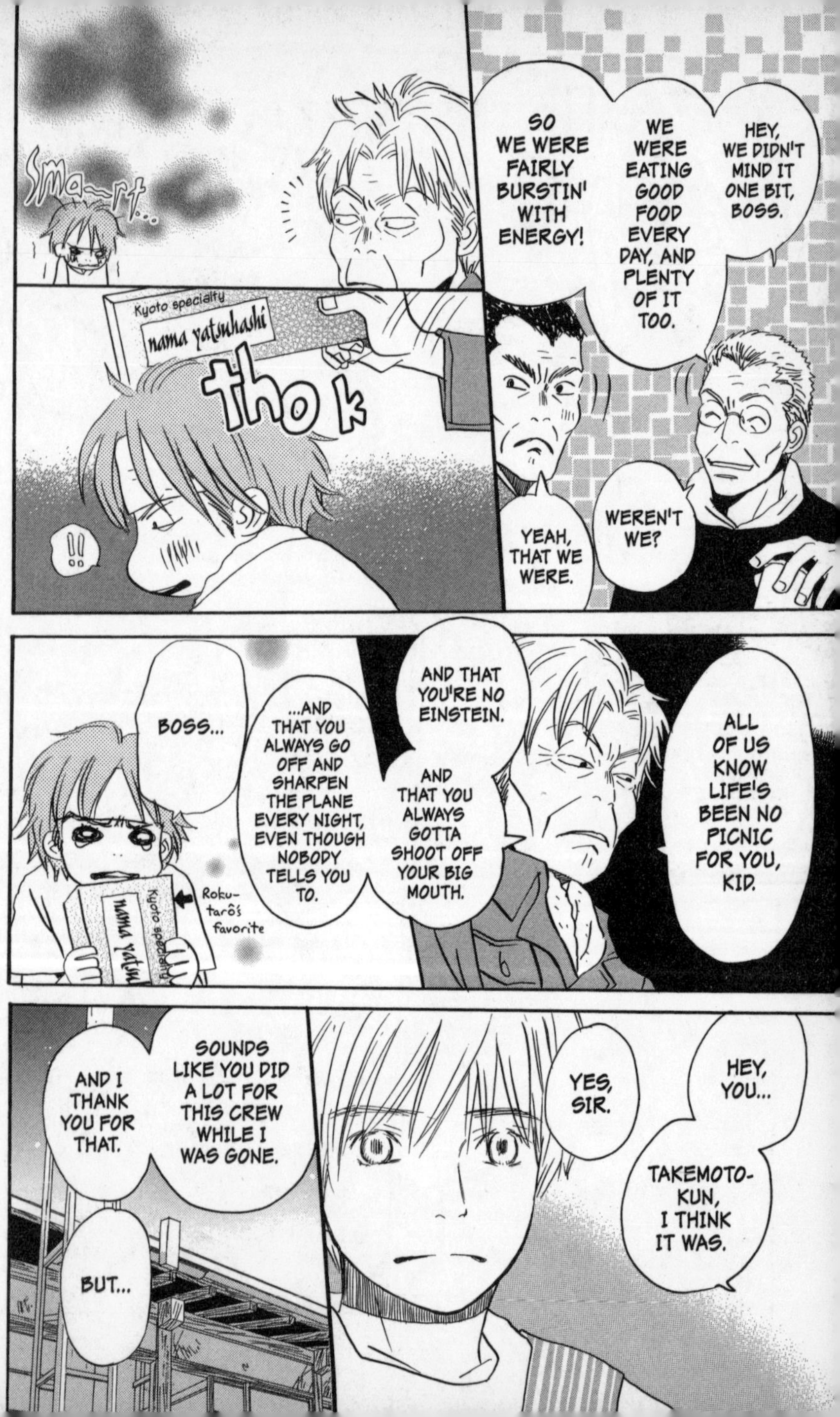
HEY, WE DIDN'T MIND IT ONE BIT, BOSS.
WE WERE EATING GOOD FOOD EVERY DAY, AND PLENTY OF IT TOO.
SO WE WERE FAIRLY BURSTIN' WITH ENERGY!
WEREN'T WE?
YEAH, THAT WE WERE.
Sma~rt...
Kyoto specialty
nama yatsuhashi
thok
!!
ALL OF US KNOW LIFE'S BEEN NO PICNIC FOR YOU, KID.
AND THAT YOU'RE NO EINSTEIN.
AND THAT YOU ALWAYS GOTTA SHOOT OFF YOUR BIG MOUTH.
...AND THAT YOU ALWAYS GO OFF AND SHARPEN THE PLANE EVERY NIGHT, EVEN THOUGH NOBODY TELLS YOU TO.
BOSS...
Kyoto specialty
nama yatsu
Roku-tarô's favorite
HEY, YOU...
TAKEMOTO-KUN, I THINK IT WAS.
YES, SIR.
SOUNDS LIKE YOU DID A LOT FOR THIS CREW WHILE I WAS GONE.
AND I THANK YOU FOR THAT.
BUT...

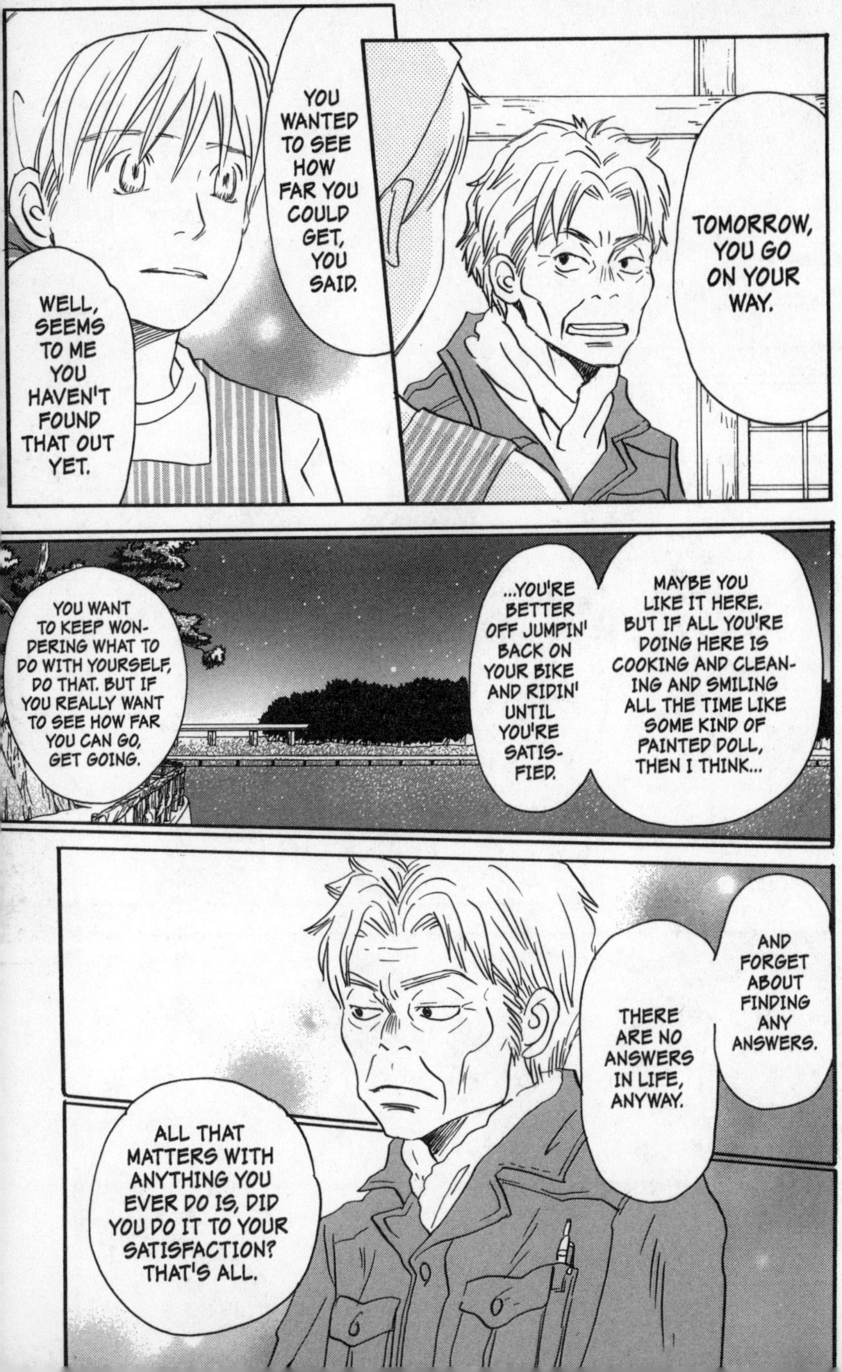
TOMORROW, YOU GO ON YOUR WAY.
YOU WANTED TO SEE HOW FAR YOU COULD GET, YOU SAID.
WELL, SEEMS TO ME YOU HAVEN'T FOUND THAT OUT YET.
MAYBE YOU LIKE IT HERE. BUT IF ALL YOU'RE DOING HERE IS COOKING AND CLEANING AND SMILING ALL THE TIME LIKE SOME KIND OF PAINTED DOLL, THEN I THINK...
...YOU'RE BETTER OFF JUMPIN' BACK ON YOUR BIKE AND RIDIN' UNTIL YOU'RE SATISFIED.
YOU WANT TO KEEP WONDERING WHAT TO DO WITH YOURSELF, DO THAT. BUT IF YOU REALLY WANT TO SEE HOW FAR YOU CAN GO, GET GOING.
AND FORGET ABOUT FINDING ANY ANSWERS.
THERE ARE NO ANSWERS IN LIFE, ANYWAY.
ALL THAT MATTERS WITH ANYTHING YOU EVER DO IS, DID YOU DO IT TO YOUR SATISFACTION? THAT'S ALL.

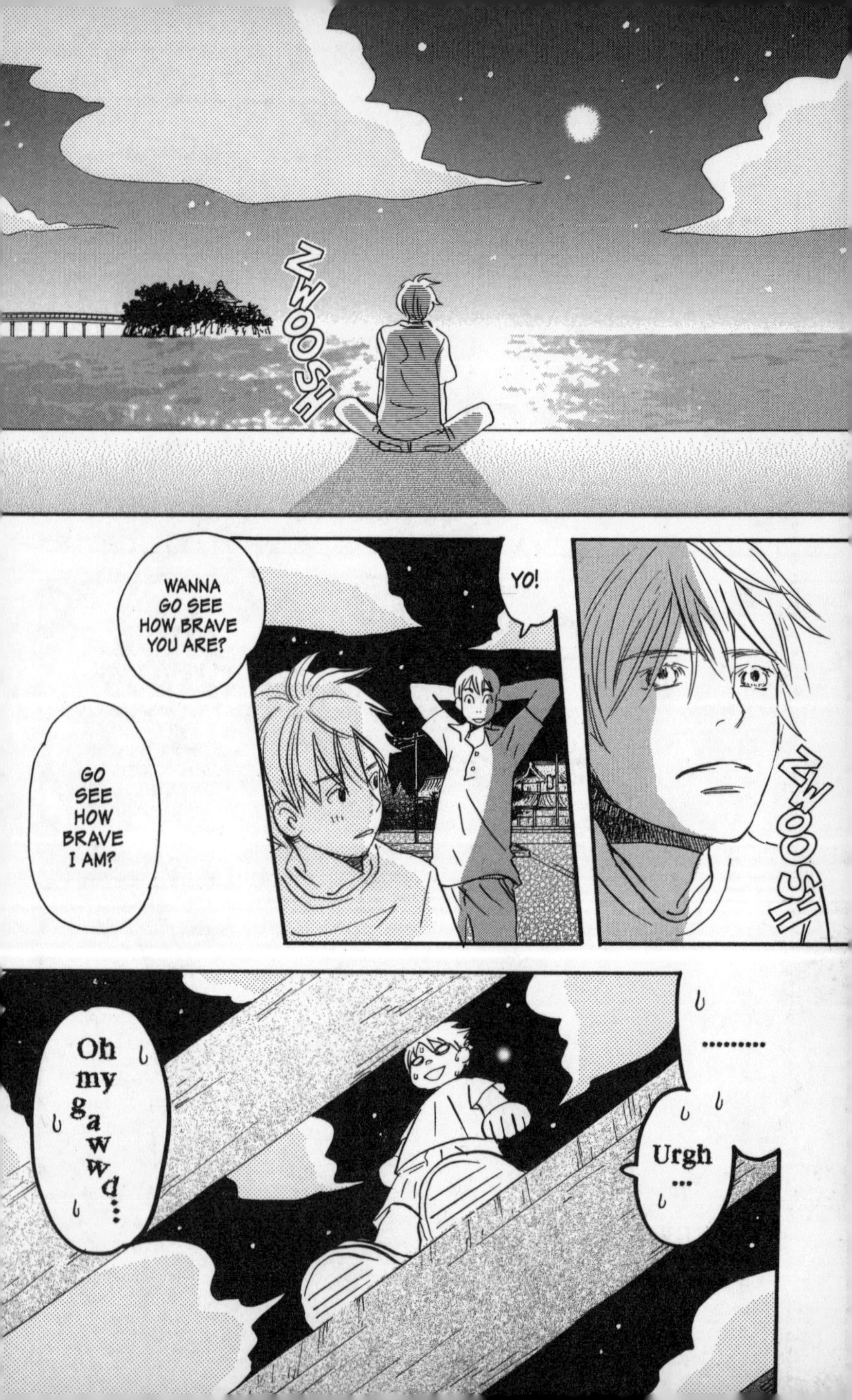
ZWOOSH
ZWOOSH
YO!
WANNA GO SEE HOW BRAVE YOU ARE?
GO SEE HOW BRAVE I AM?
....
Urgh...
Oh my gawwd...

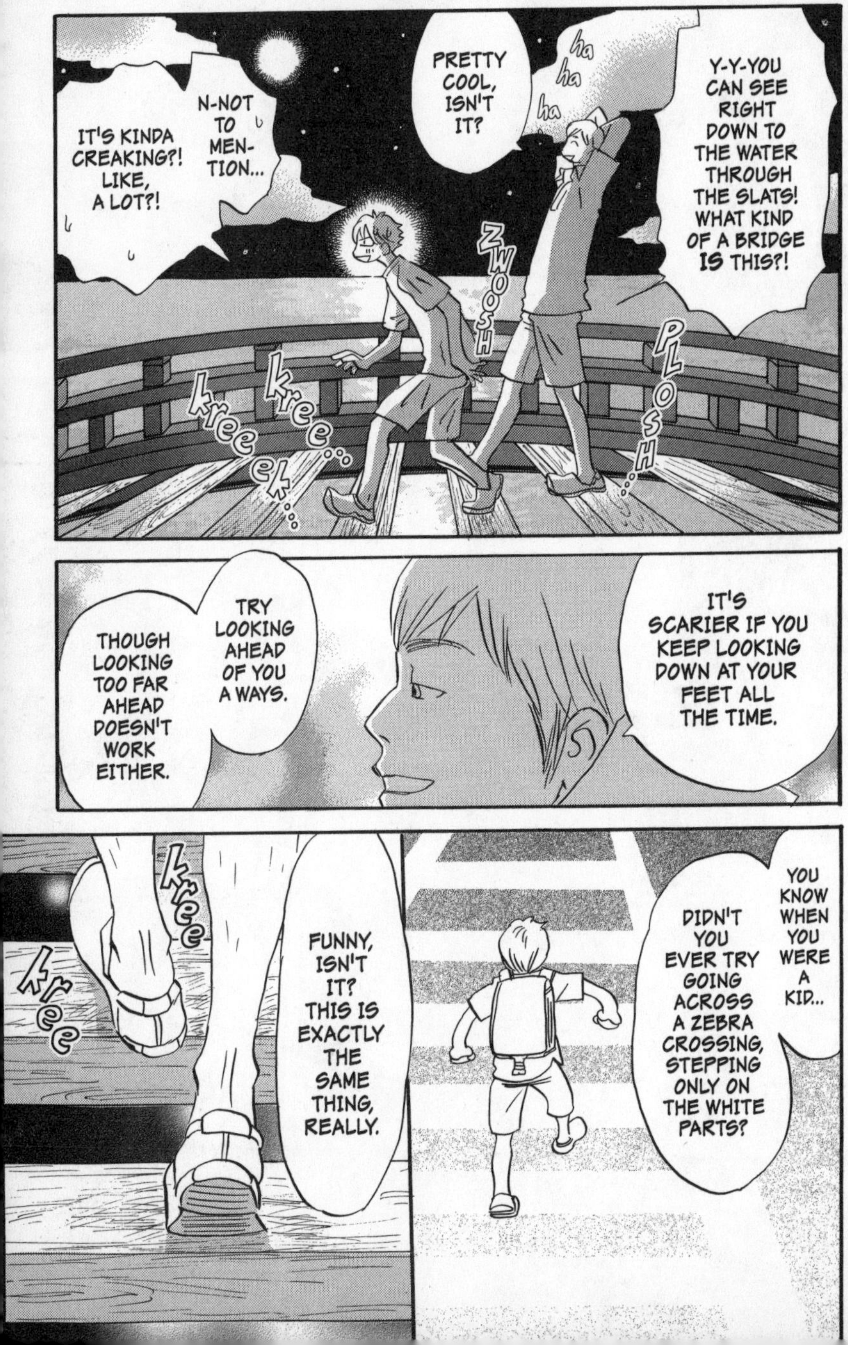
Y-Y-YOU CAN SEE RIGHT DOWN TO THE WATER THROUGH THE SLATS! WHAT KIND OF A BRIDGE IS THIS?!
ha ha ha
PRETTY COOL, ISN'T IT?
N-NOT TO MENTION...
IT'S KINDA CREAKING?! LIKE, A LOT?!
ZWOOSH
PLOSH...
kree...
kreeek...
IT'S SCARIER IF YOU KEEP LOOKING DOWN AT YOUR FEET ALL THE TIME.
TRY LOOKING AHEAD OF YOU A WAYS.
THOUGH LOOKING TOO FAR AHEAD DOESN'T WORK EITHER.
YOU KNOW WHEN YOU WERE A KID...
DIDN'T YOU EVER TRY GOING ACROSS A ZEBRA CROSSING, STEPPING ONLY ON THE WHITE PARTS?
FUNNY, ISN'T IT? THIS IS EXACTLY THE SAME THING, REALLY.
kree
kree

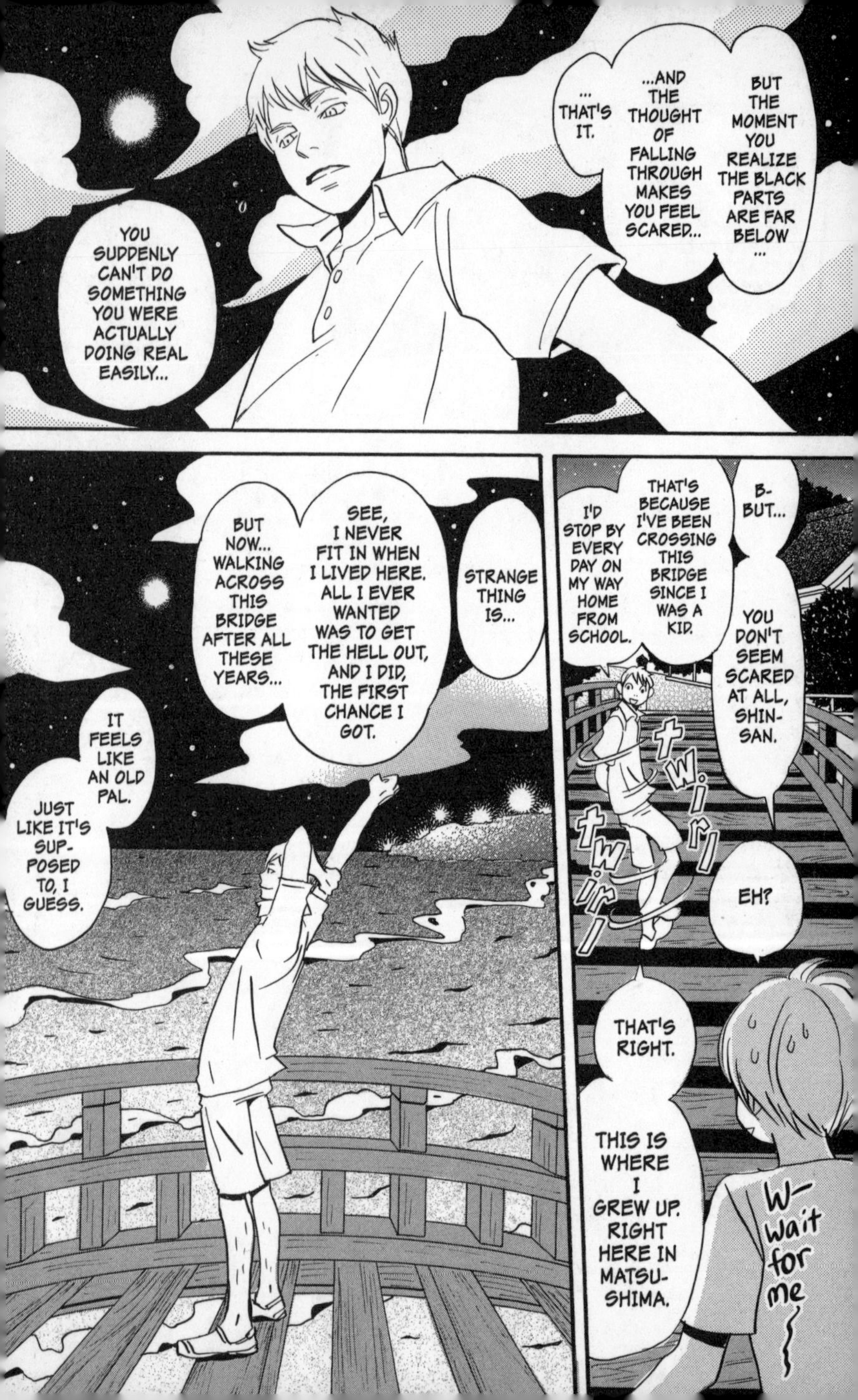
BUT THE MOMENT YOU REALIZE THE BLACK PARTS ARE FAR BELOW ...
...AND THE THOUGHT OF FALLING THROUGH MAKES YOU FEEL SCARED...
... THAT'S IT.
YOU SUDDENLY CAN'T DO SOMETHING YOU WERE ACTUALLY DOING REAL EASILY...
B-BUT...
YOU DON'T SEEM SCARED AT ALL, SHIN-SAN.
THAT'S BECAUSE I'VE BEEN CROSSING THIS BRIDGE SINCE I WAS A KID.
I'D STOP BY EVERY DAY ON MY WAY HOME FROM SCHOOL.
twirl
twirl
EH?
THAT'S RIGHT.
THIS IS WHERE I GREW UP. RIGHT HERE IN MATSU-SHIMA.
W-wait for me~
STRANGE THING IS...
SEE, I NEVER FIT IN WHEN I LIVED HERE. ALL I EVER WANTED WAS TO GET THE HELL OUT, AND I DID, THE FIRST CHANCE I GOT.
BUT NOW... WALKING ACROSS THIS BRIDGE AFTER ALL THESE YEARS...
IT FEELS LIKE AN OLD PAL.
JUST LIKE IT'S SUP-POSED TO, I GUESS.

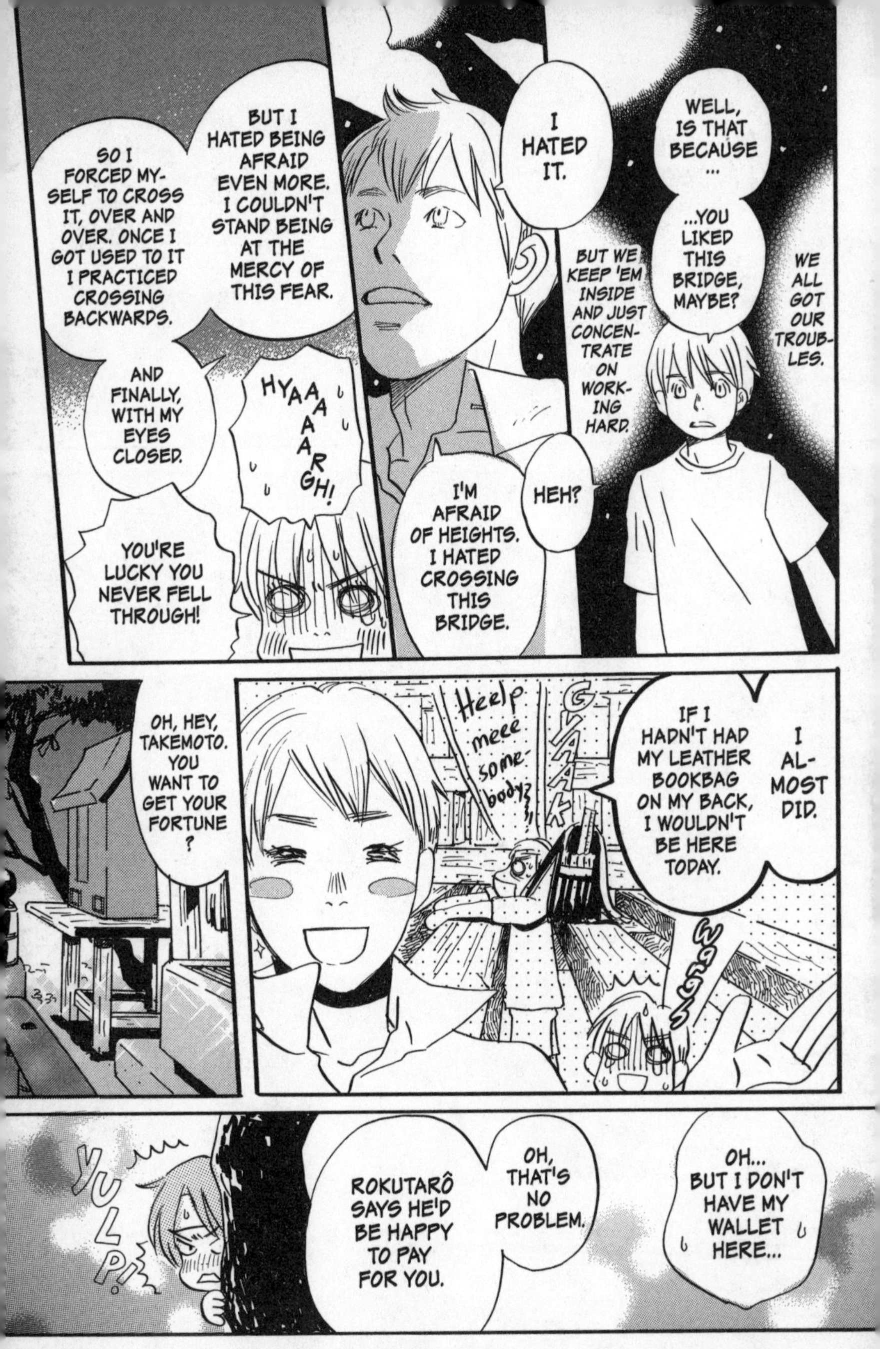
WELL, IS THAT BECAUSE ...
...YOU LIKED THIS BRIDGE, MAYBE?
WE ALL GOT OUR TROUBLES.
BUT WE KEEP 'EM INSIDE AND JUST CONCENTRATE ON WORKING HARD.
I HATED IT.
HEH?
I'M AFRAID OF HEIGHTS. I HATED CROSSING THIS BRIDGE.
BUT I HATED BEING AFRAID EVEN MORE. I COULDN'T STAND BEING AT THE MERCY OF THIS FEAR.
SO I FORCED MYSELF TO CROSS IT, OVER AND OVER. ONCE I GOT USED TO IT I PRACTICED CROSSING BACKWARDS.
AND FINALLY, WITH MY EYES CLOSED.
HYAAAAARGH!
YOU'RE LUCKY YOU NEVER FELL THROUGH!
I ALMOST DID.
IF I HADN'T HAD MY LEATHER BOOKBAG ON MY BACK, I WOULDN'T BE HERE TODAY.
GYAAAK
Heerlp meee somebody?!
OH, HEY, TAKEMOTO. YOU WANT TO GET YOUR FORTUNE?
OH... BUT I DON'T HAVE MY WALLET HERE...
OH, THAT'S NO PROBLEM.
ROKUTARÔ SAYS HE'D BE HAPPY TO PAY FOR YOU.
YULP!

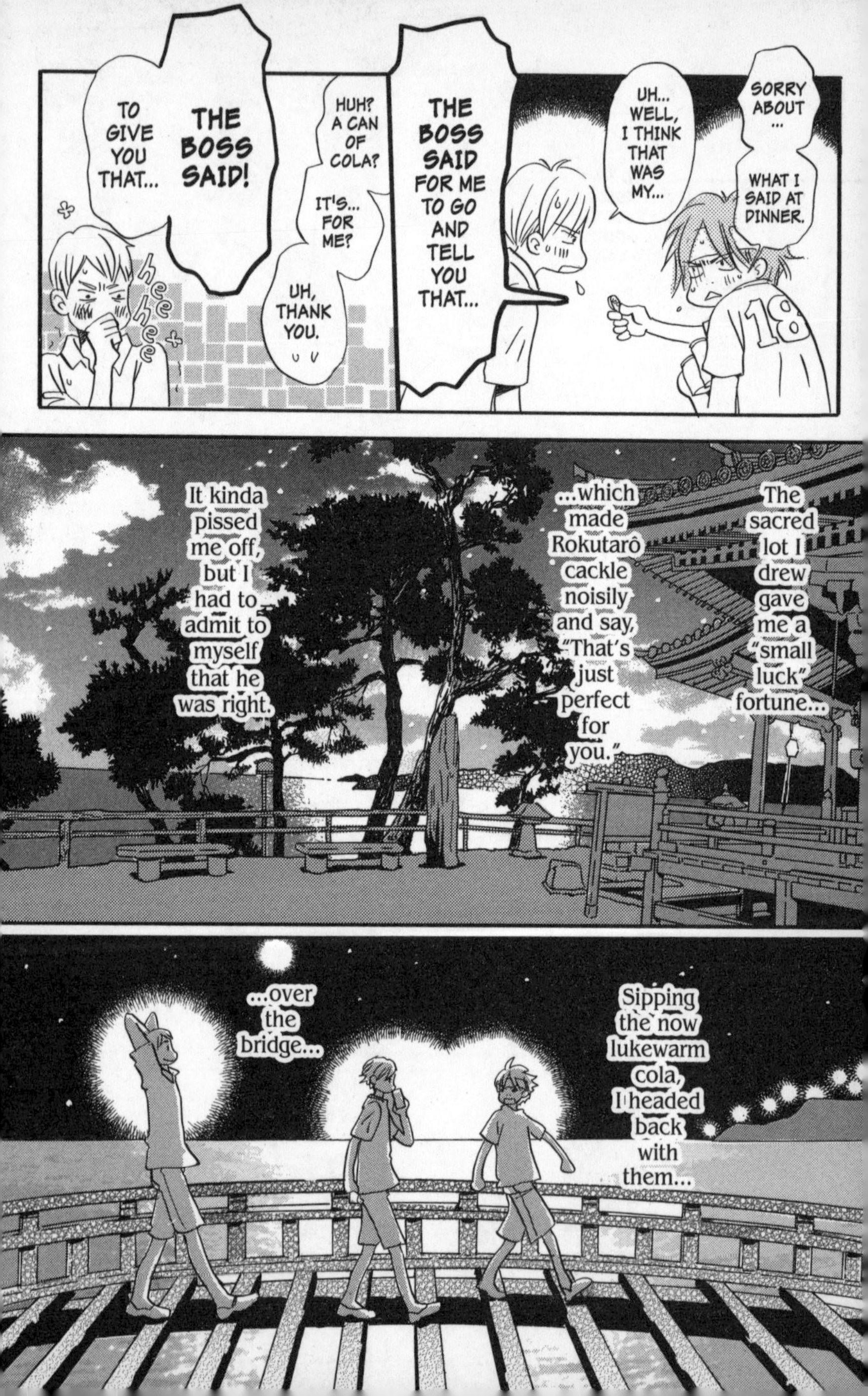
SORRY ABOUT... WHAT I SAID AT DINNER.
UH... WELL, I THINK THAT WAS MY...
THE BOSS SAID FOR ME TO GO AND TELL YOU THAT...
HUH? A CAN OF COLA?
IT'S... FOR ME?
UH, THANK YOU.
THE BOSS SAID!
TO GIVE YOU THAT...
hee hee
The sacred lot I drew gave me a "small luck" fortune...
...which made Rokutarô cackle noisily and say, "That's just perfect for you."
It kinda pissed me off, but I had to admit to myself that he was right.
Sipping the now lukewarm cola, I headed back with them...
...over the bridge...

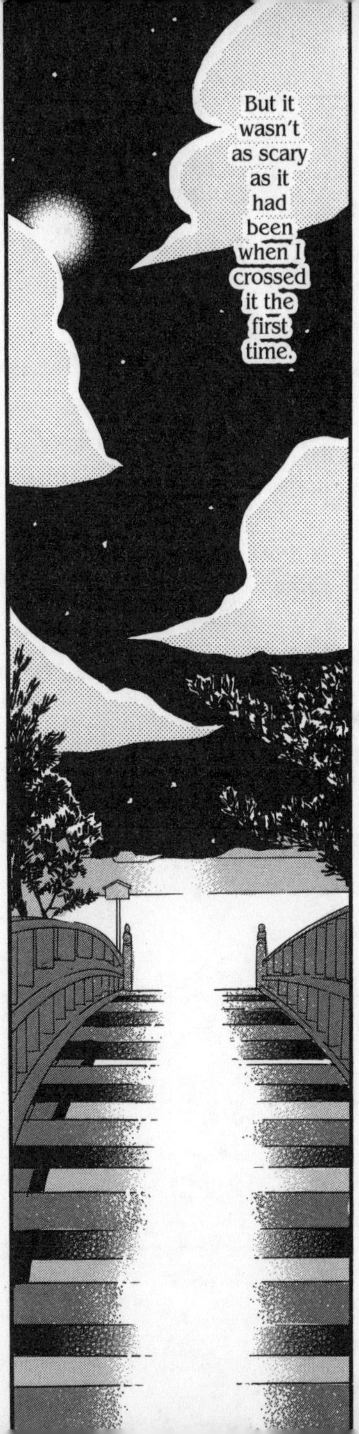
But it wasn't as scary as it had been when I crossed it the first time.

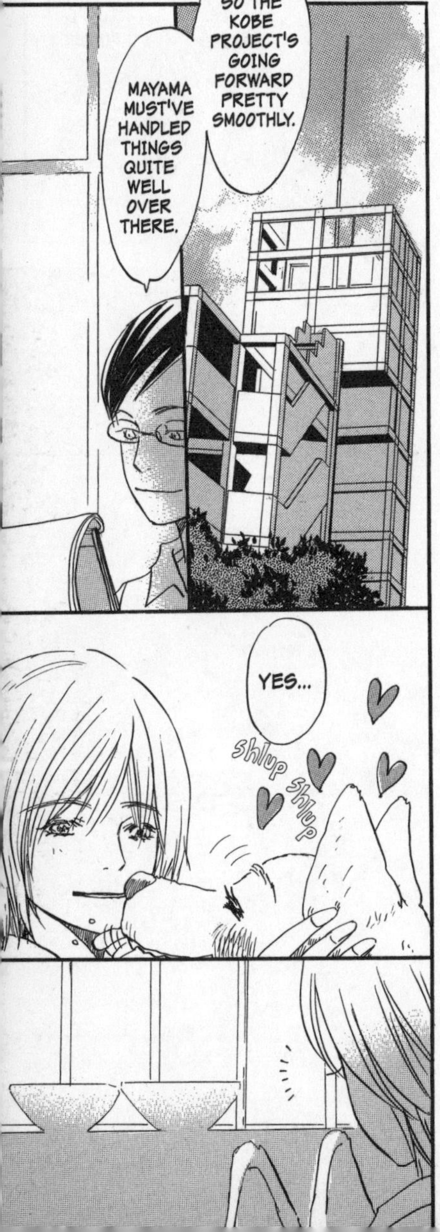
SO THE KOBE PROJECT'S GOING FORWARD PRETTY SMOOTHLY.
MAYAMA MUST'VE HANDLED THINGS QUITE WELL OVER THERE.
YES...
shlup shlup

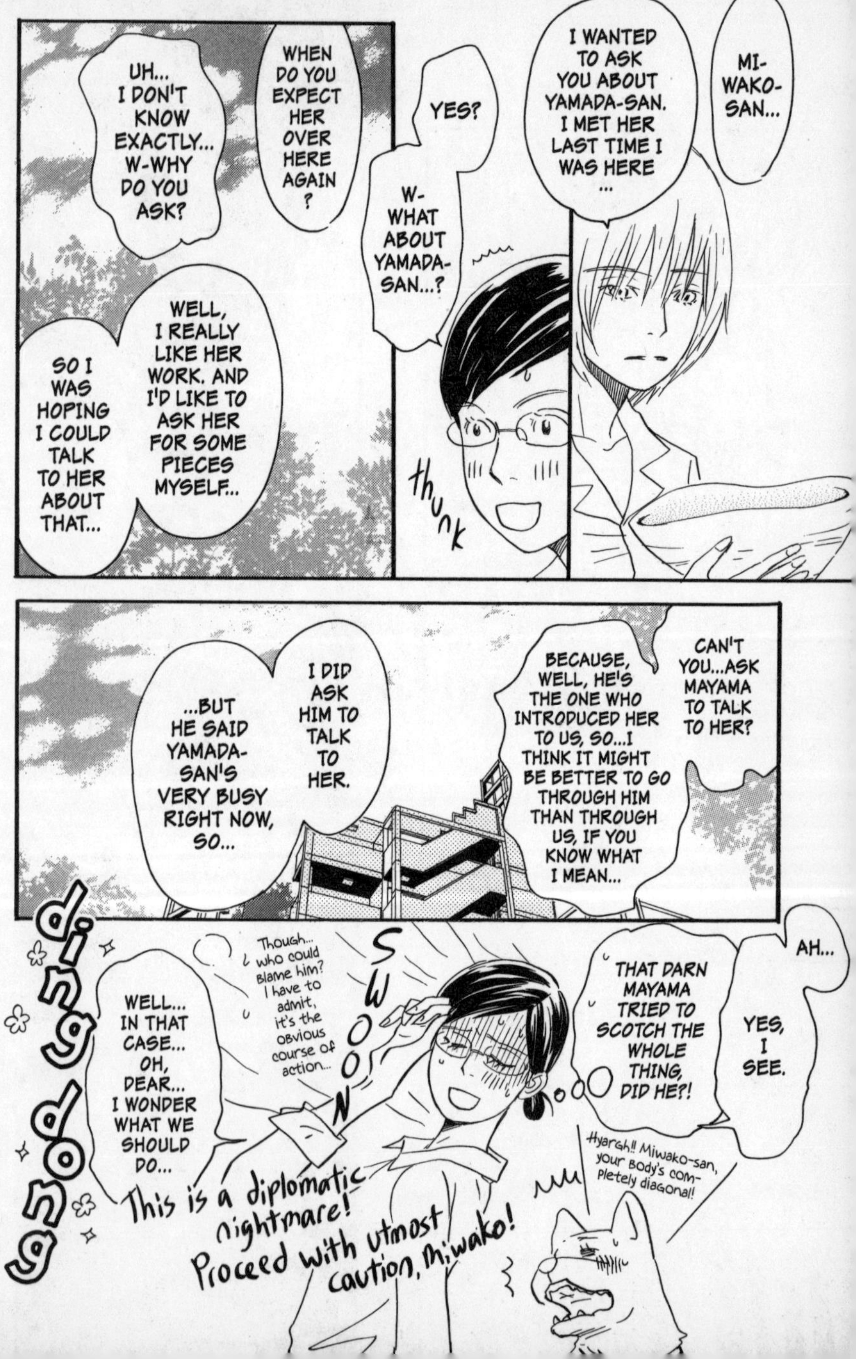
MI-WAKO-SAN...
I WANTED TO ASK YOU ABOUT YAMADA-SAN. I MET HER LAST TIME I WAS HERE ...
YES?
W-WHAT ABOUT YAMADA-SAN...?
thunk
WHEN DO YOU EXPECT HER OVER HERE AGAIN?
UH... I DON'T KNOW EXACTLY... W-WHY DO YOU ASK?
WELL, I REALLY LIKE HER WORK. AND I'D LIKE TO ASK HER FOR SOME PIECES MYSELF...
SO I WAS HOPING I COULD TALK TO HER ABOUT THAT...
CAN'T YOU...ASK MAYAMA TO TALK TO HER?
BECAUSE, WELL, HE'S THE ONE WHO INTRODUCED HER TO US, SO...I THINK IT MIGHT BE BETTER TO GO THROUGH HIM THAN THROUGH US, IF YOU KNOW WHAT I MEAN...
I DID ASK HIM TO TALK TO HER.
...BUT HE SAID YAMADA-SAN'S VERY BUSY RIGHT NOW, SO...
AH...
YES, I SEE.
THAT DARN MAYAMA TRIED TO SCOTCH THE WHOLE THING, DID HE?!
Hyargh!! Miwako-san, your body's completely diagonal!
Though... who could blame him? I have to admit, it's the obvious course of action...
SWOON
WELL... IN THAT CASE... OH, DEAR... I WONDER WHAT WE SHOULD DO...
This is a diplomatic nightmare! Proceed with utmost caution, Miwako!

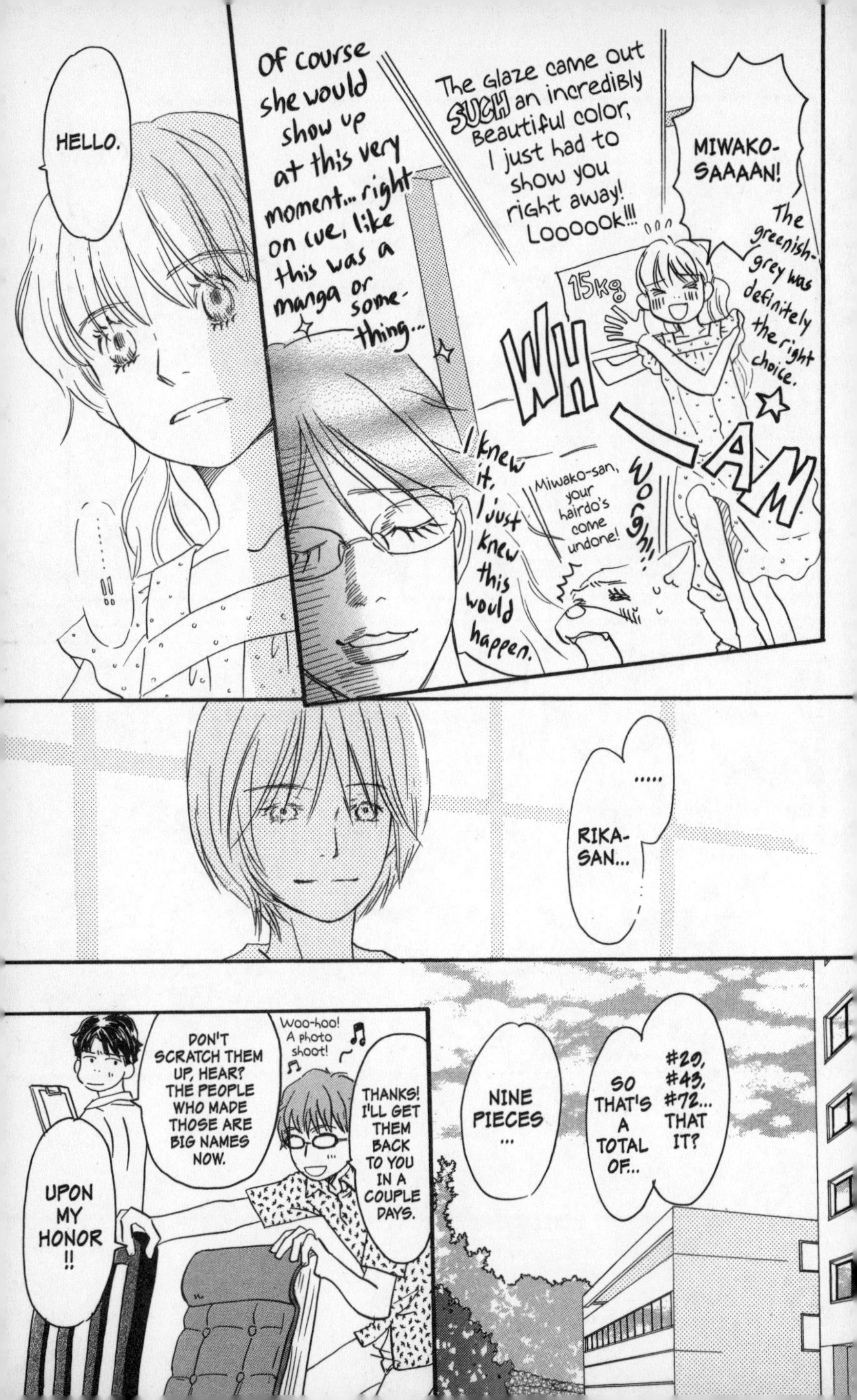
MIWAKO-SAAAAN!
The glaze came out SUCH an incredibly beautiful color, I just had to show you right away! Looooook!!!
The greenish-grey was definitely the right choice.
15kg
WH—AM
Of course she would show up at this very moment... right on cue, like this was a manga or some-thing...
Miwako-san, your hairdo's come undone!
Woogh!!
I knew it, I just knew this would happen.
HELLO.
......!!
..... RIKA-SAN...
#29, #43, #72... THAT IT?
SO THAT'S A TOTAL OF...
NINE PIECES ...
THANKS! I'LL GET THEM BACK TO YOU IN A COUPLE DAYS.
Woo-hoo! A photo shoot!
DON'T SCRATCH THEM UP, HEAR? THE PEOPLE WHO MADE THOSE ARE BIG NAMES NOW.
UPON MY HONOR !!

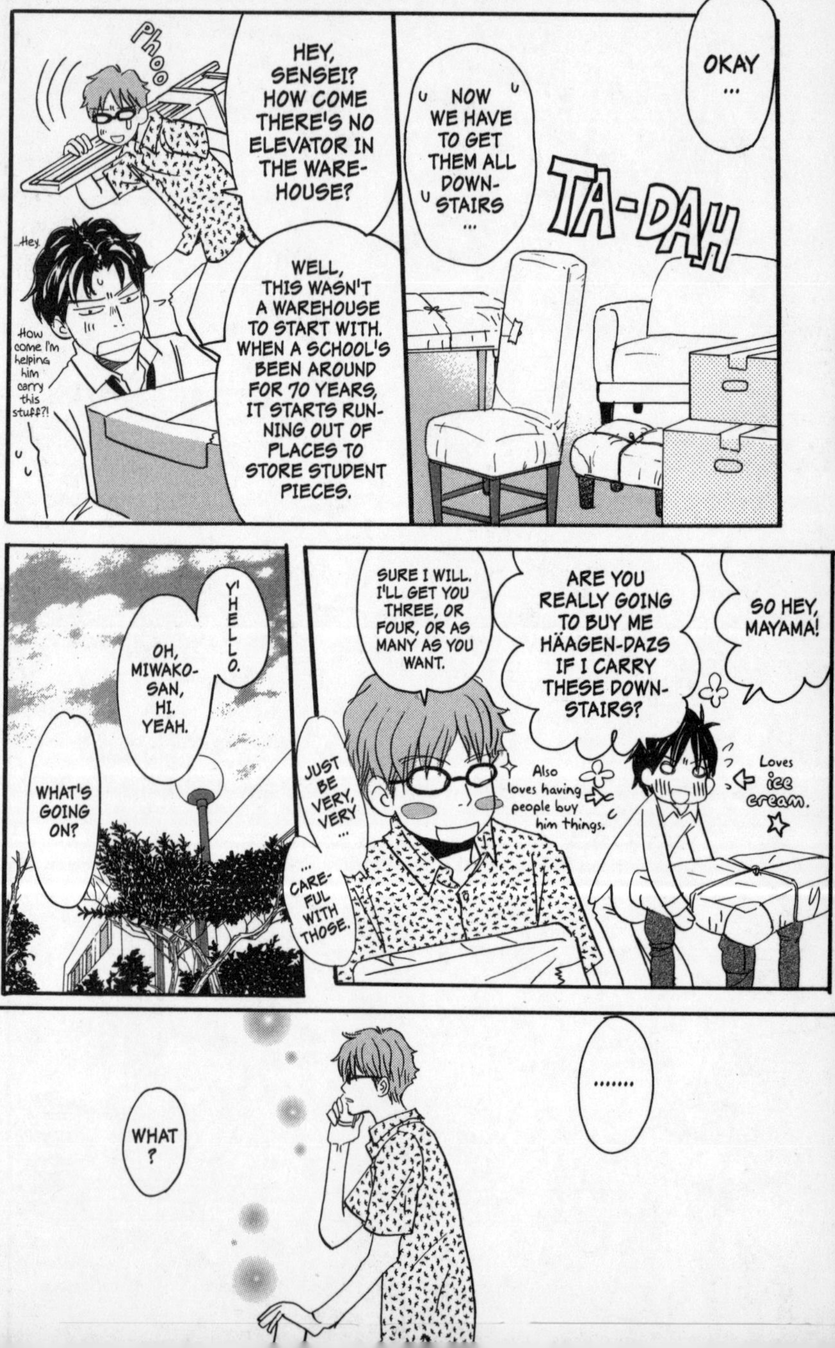
OKAY ...
NOW WE HAVE TO GET THEM ALL DOWN-STAIRS ...
TA-DAH
HEY, SENSEI? HOW COME THERE'S NO ELEVATOR IN THE WARE-HOUSE?
Phoo
WELL, THIS WASN'T A WAREHOUSE TO START WITH. WHEN A SCHOOL'S BEEN AROUND FOR 70 YEARS, IT STARTS RUN-NING OUT OF PLACES TO STORE STUDENT PIECES.
...Hey.
How come I'm helping him carry this stuff?!
SO HEY, MAYAMA!
ARE YOU REALLY GOING TO BUY ME HÄAGEN-DAZS IF I CARRY THESE DOWN-STAIRS?
SURE I WILL. I'LL GET YOU THREE, OR FOUR, OR AS MANY AS YOU WANT.
Loves ice cream.
Also loves having people buy him things.
JUST BE VERY, VERY ...
... CARE-FUL WITH THOSE.
Y'HELLO.
OH, MIWAKO-SAN, HI. YEAH.
WHAT'S GOING ON?
....
WHAT?

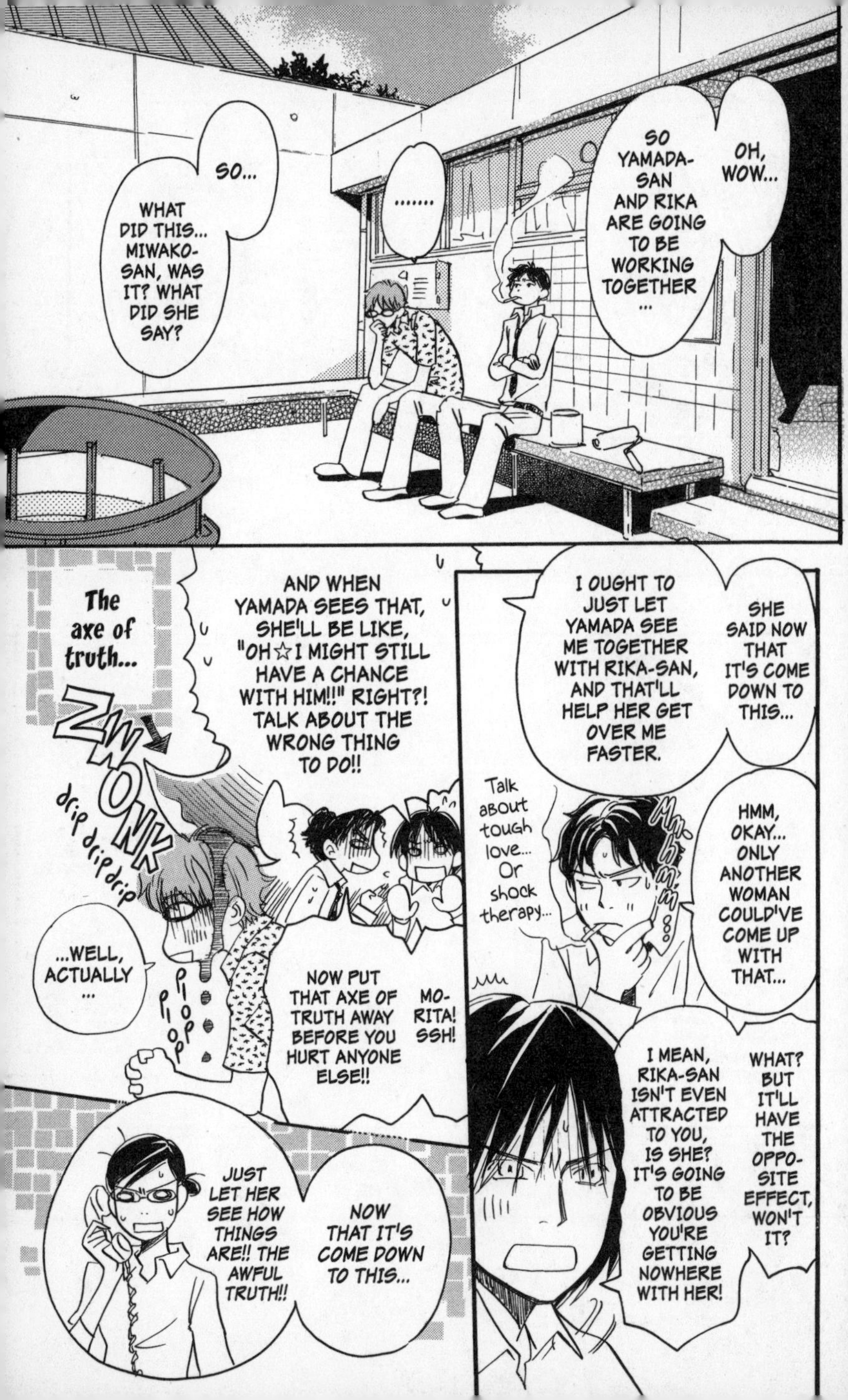
OH, WOW...
SO YAMADA-SAN AND RIKA ARE GOING TO BE WORKING TOGETHER...
....
SO...
WHAT DID THIS... MIWAKO-SAN, WAS IT? WHAT DID SHE SAY?
SHE SAID NOW THAT IT'S COME DOWN TO THIS...
I OUGHT TO JUST LET YAMADA SEE ME TOGETHER WITH RIKA-SAN, AND THAT'LL HELP HER GET OVER ME FASTER.
HMM, OKAY... ONLY ANOTHER WOMAN COULD'VE COME UP WITH THAT...
Mm-hmm...
Talk about tough love... Or shock therapy...
WHAT? BUT IT'LL HAVE THE OPPO-SITE EFFECT, WON'T IT?
I MEAN, RIKA-SAN ISN'T EVEN ATTRACTED TO YOU, IS SHE? IT'S GOING TO BE OBVIOUS YOU'RE GETTING NOWHERE WITH HER!
AND WHEN YAMADA SEES THAT, SHE'LL BE LIKE, "OH☆I MIGHT STILL HAVE A CHANCE WITH HIM!!" RIGHT?! TALK ABOUT THE WRONG THING TO DO!!
The axe of truth...
ZWONK
drip drip drip
...WELL, ACTUALLY...
MO-RITA! SSH!
NOW PUT THAT AXE OF TRUTH AWAY BEFORE YOU HURT ANYONE ELSE!!
NOW THAT IT'S COME DOWN TO THIS...
JUST LET HER SEE HOW THINGS ARE!! THE AWFUL TRUTH!!

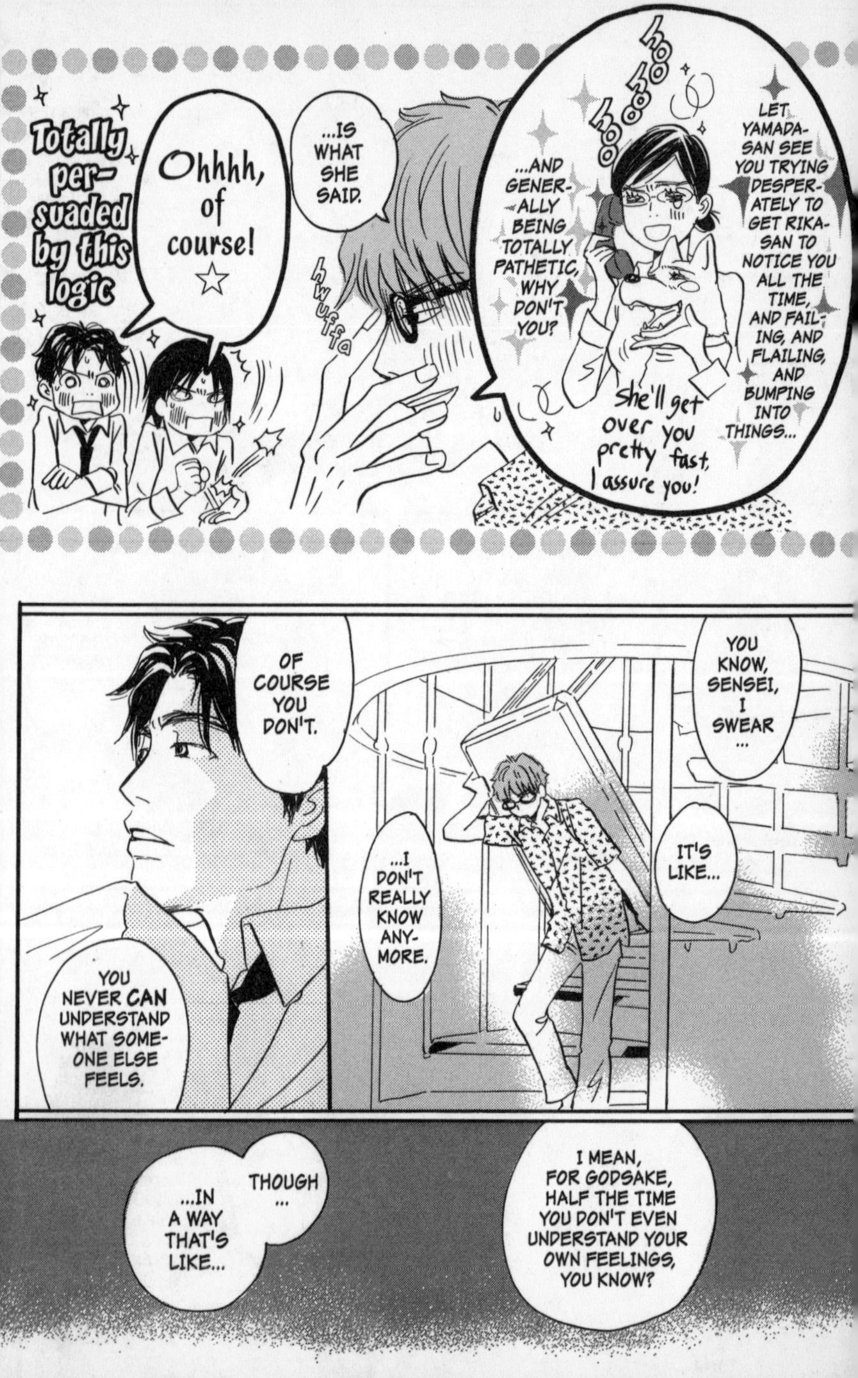
LET YAMADA-SAN SEE YOU TRYING DESPERATELY TO GET RIKA-SAN TO NOTICE YOU ALL THE TIME, AND FAILING, AND FLAILING, AND BUMPING INTO THINGS...
...AND GENERALLY BEING TOTALLY PATHETIC, WHY DON'T YOU?
hoo hoo hoo hoo
She'll get over you pretty fast, I assure you!
...IS WHAT SHE SAID.
hwuffa
Ohhhh, of course! ☆
Totally persuaded by this logic
YOU KNOW, SENSEI, I SWEAR...
IT'S LIKE...
...I DON'T REALLY KNOW ANYMORE.
OF COURSE YOU DON'T.
YOU NEVER CAN UNDERSTAND WHAT SOMEONE ELSE FEELS.
I MEAN, FOR GODSAKE, HALF THE TIME YOU DON'T EVEN UNDERSTAND YOUR OWN FEELINGS, YOU KNOW?
THOUGH...
...IN A WAY THAT'S LIKE...

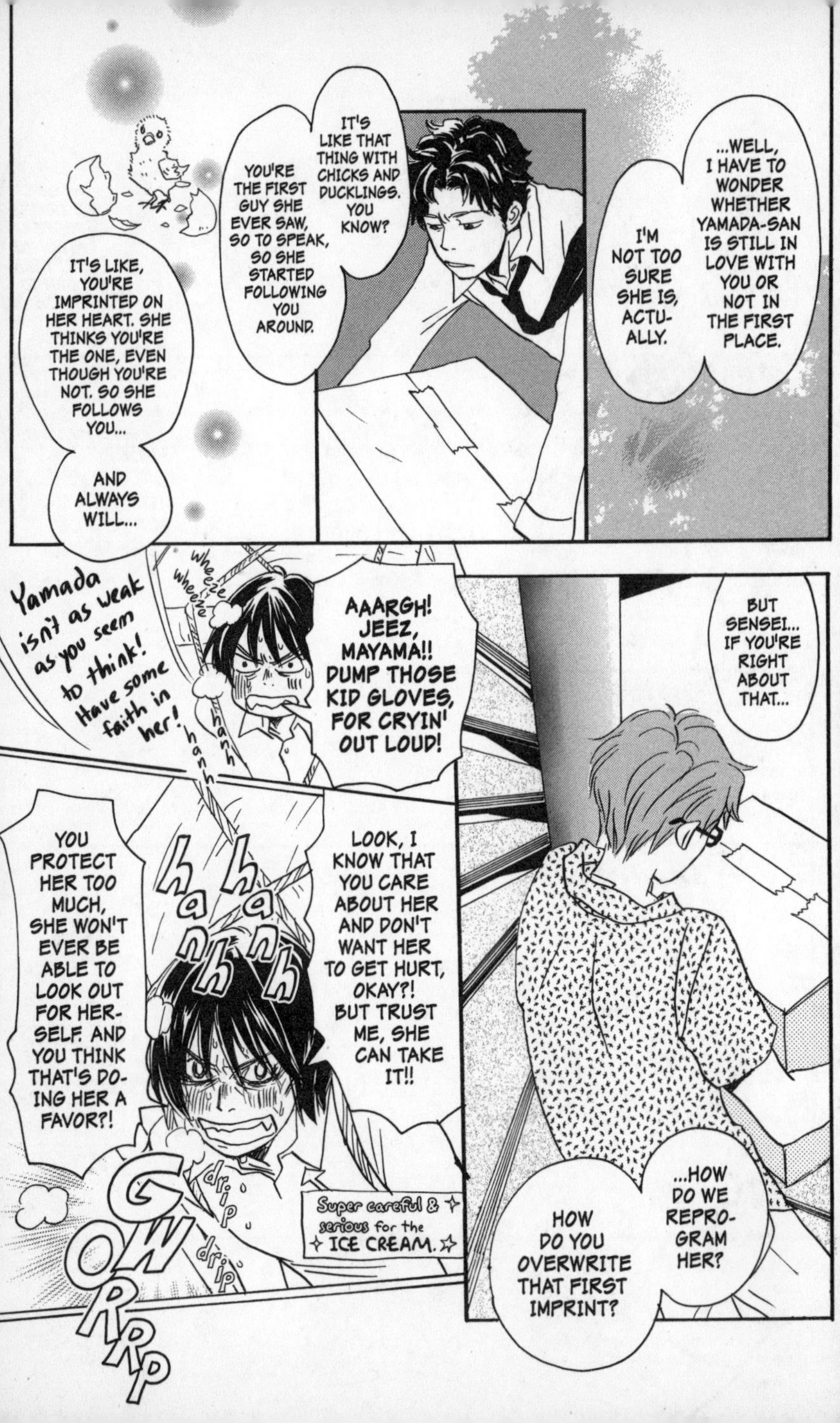
...WELL, I HAVE TO WONDER WHETHER YAMADA-SAN IS STILL IN LOVE WITH YOU OR NOT IN THE FIRST PLACE.
I'M NOT TOO SURE SHE IS, ACTU-ALLY.
IT'S LIKE THAT THING WITH CHICKS AND DUCKLINGS. YOU KNOW?
YOU'RE THE FIRST GUY SHE EVER SAW, SO TO SPEAK, SO SHE STARTED FOLLOWING YOU AROUND.
IT'S LIKE, YOU'RE IMPRINTED ON HER HEART. SHE THINKS YOU'RE THE ONE, EVEN THOUGH YOU'RE NOT. SO SHE FOLLOWS YOU...
AND ALWAYS WILL...
BUT SENSEI... IF YOU'RE RIGHT ABOUT THAT...
...HOW DO WE REPRO-GRAM HER?
HOW DO YOU OVERWRITE THAT FIRST IMPRINT?
wheeze wheeze
AAARGH! JEEZ, MAYAMA!! DUMP THOSE KID GLOVES, FOR CRYIN' OUT LOUD!
Yamada isn't as weak as you seem to think! Have some faith in her!
hanh hanh
LOOK, I KNOW THAT YOU CARE ABOUT HER AND DON'T WANT HER TO GET HURT, OKAY?! BUT TRUST ME, SHE CAN TAKE IT!!
YOU PROTECT HER TOO MUCH, SHE WON'T EVER BE ABLE TO LOOK OUT FOR HER-SELF. AND YOU THINK THAT'S DO-ING HER A FAVOR?!
hanh hanh
drip drip
Super careful & serious for the ICE CREAM.
GWORRP

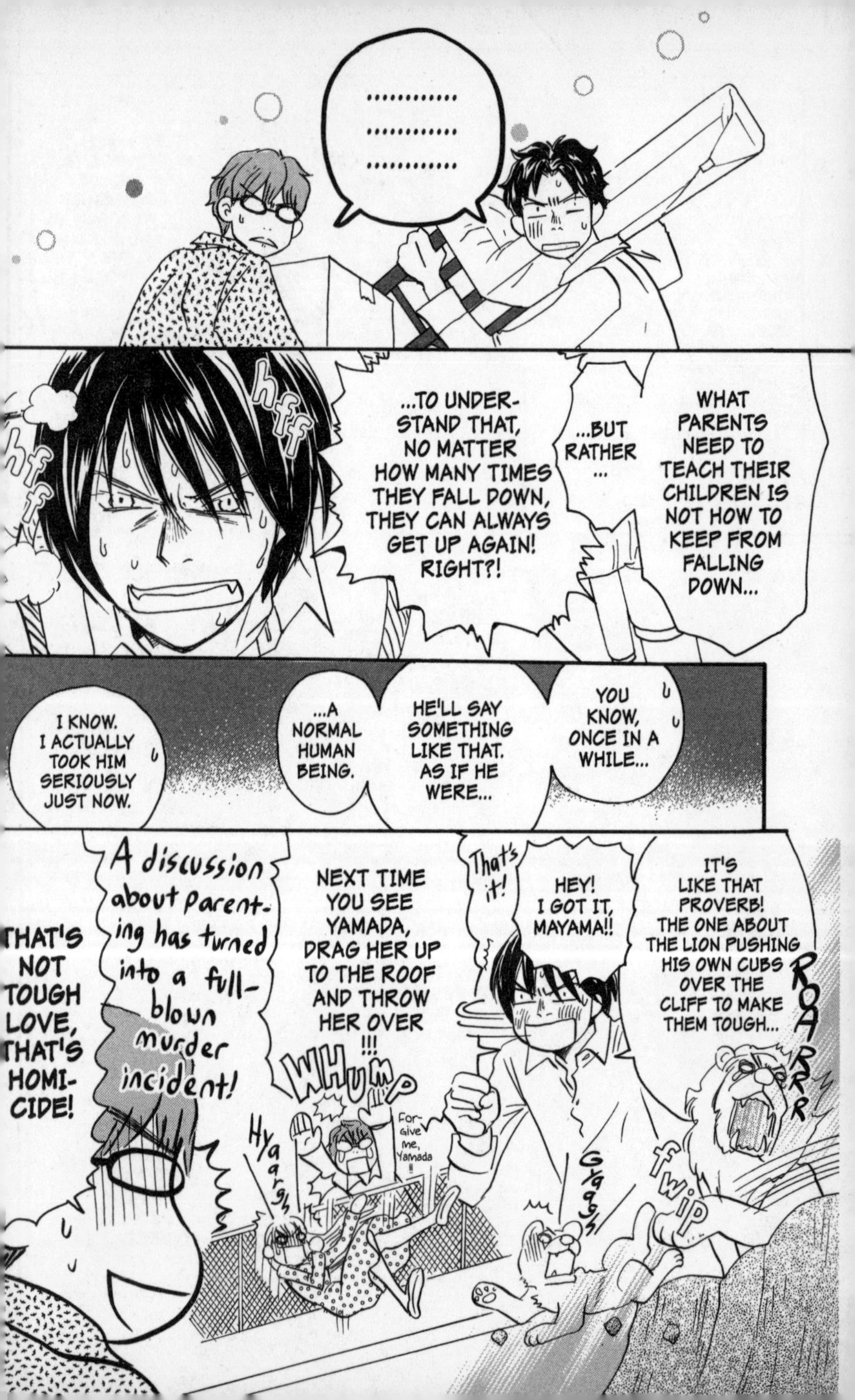
....
....
....
WHAT PARENTS NEED TO TEACH THEIR CHILDREN IS NOT HOW TO KEEP FROM FALLING DOWN...
...BUT RATHER ...
...TO UNDER-STAND THAT, NO MATTER HOW MANY TIMES THEY FALL DOWN, THEY CAN ALWAYS GET UP AGAIN! RIGHT?!
hff
hff
YOU KNOW, ONCE IN A WHILE...
HE'LL SAY SOMETHING LIKE THAT. AS IF HE WERE...
...A NORMAL HUMAN BEING.
I KNOW. I ACTUALLY TOOK HIM SERIOUSLY JUST NOW.
IT'S LIKE THAT PROVERB! THE ONE ABOUT THE LION PUSHING HIS OWN CUBS OVER THE CLIFF TO MAKE THEM TOUGH...
ROARRR
fwip
Gyaagh
HEY! I GOT IT, MAYAMA!!
That's it!
NEXT TIME YOU SEE YAMADA, DRAG HER UP TO THE ROOF AND THROW HER OVER!!!
WHUMP
Forgive me, Yamada!!
Hyaargh
A discussion about parent-ing has turned into a full-blown murder incident!
THAT'S NOT TOUGH LOVE, THAT'S HOMI-CIDE!

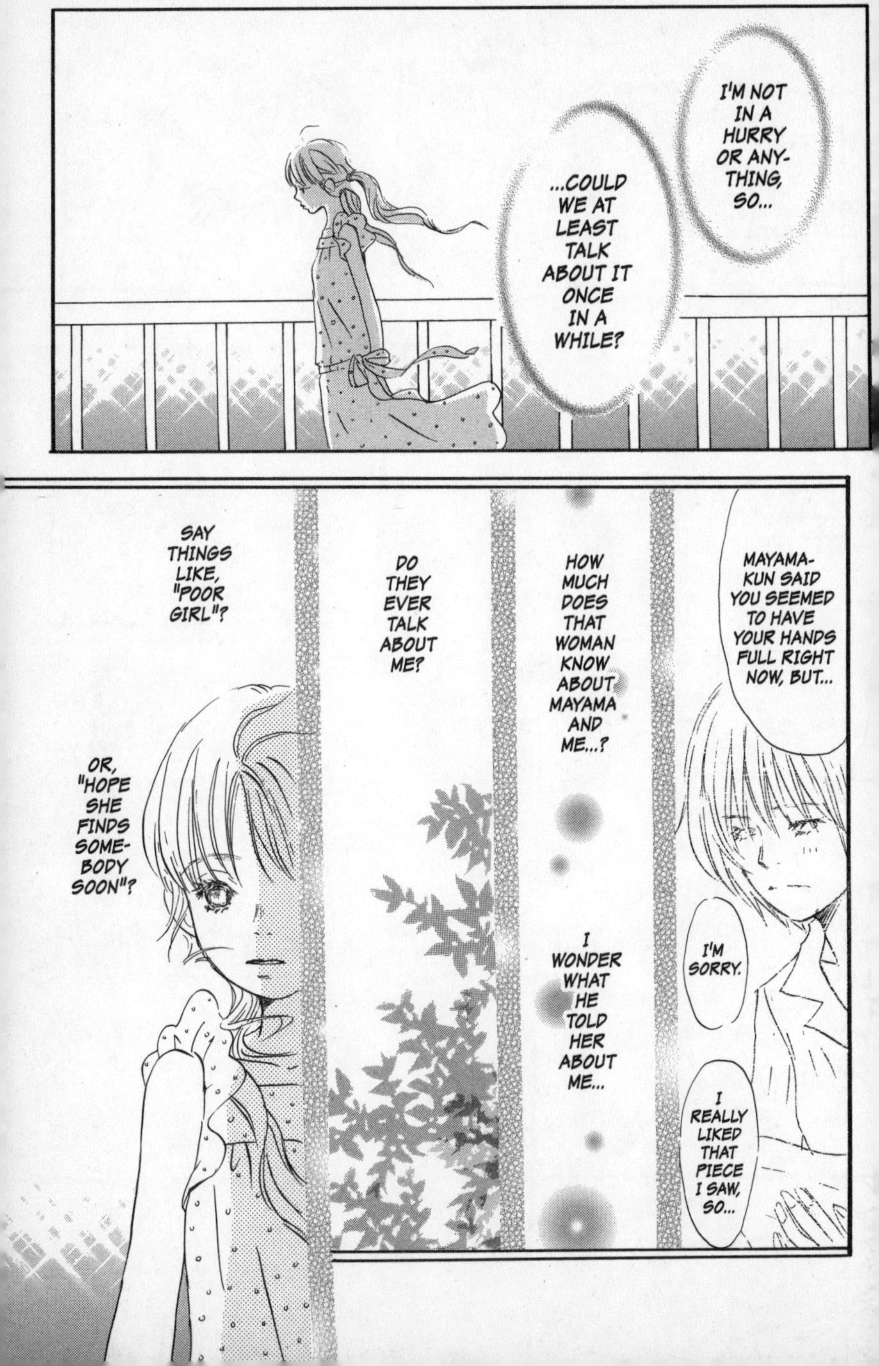
I'M NOT IN A HURRY OR ANYTHING, SO...
...COULD WE AT LEAST TALK ABOUT IT ONCE IN A WHILE?
MAYAMA-KUN SAID YOU SEEMED TO HAVE YOUR HANDS FULL RIGHT NOW, BUT...
I'M SORRY.
I REALLY LIKED THAT PIECE I SAW, SO...
HOW MUCH DOES THAT WOMAN KNOW ABOUT MAYAMA AND ME...?
I WONDER WHAT HE TOLD HER ABOUT ME...
DO THEY EVER TALK ABOUT ME?
SAY THINGS LIKE, "POOR GIRL"?
OR, "HOPE SHE FINDS SOMEBODY SOON"?

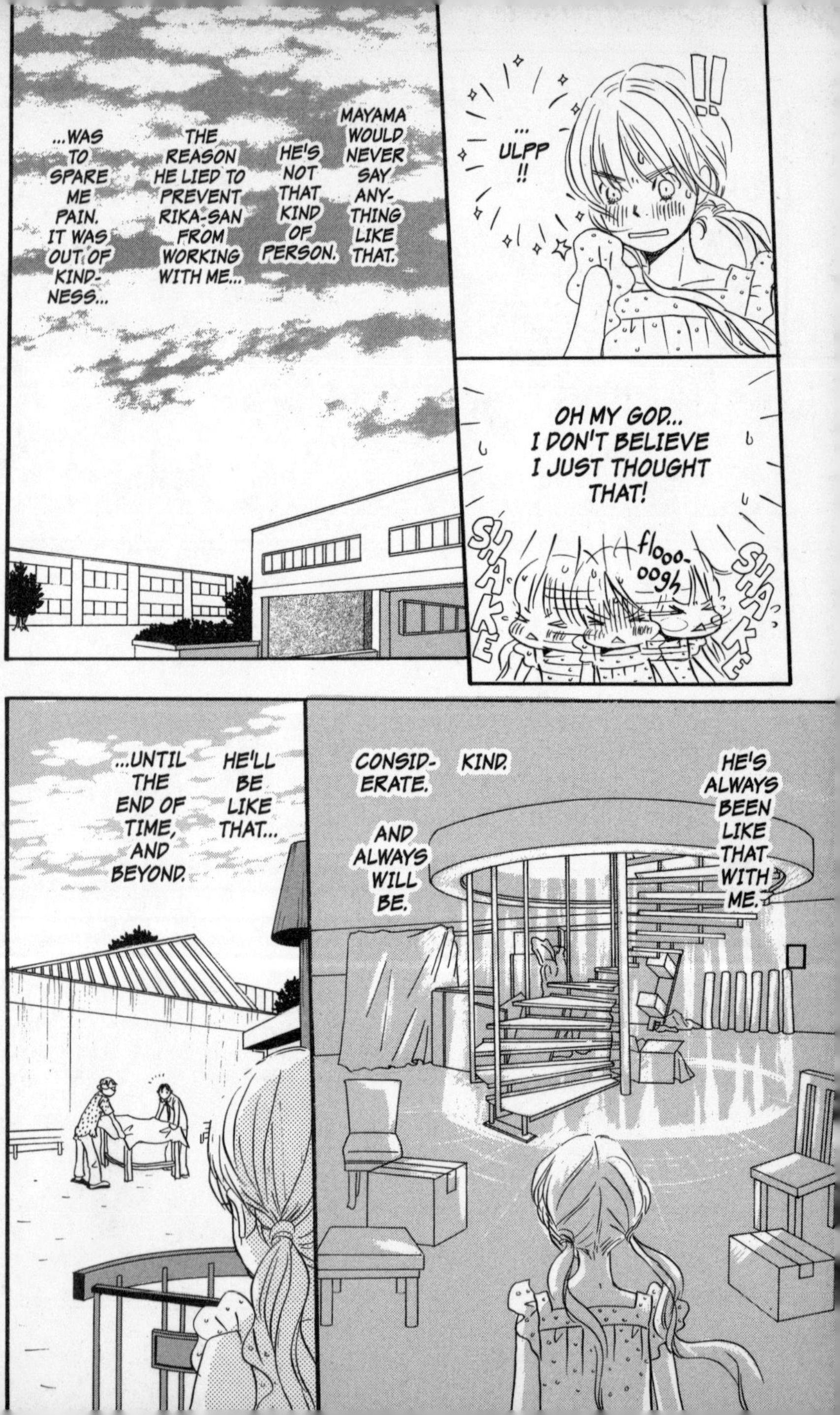
!!
...ULPP!!
OH MY GOD... I DON'T BELIEVE I JUST THOUGHT THAT!
floooogh
SHAKE
SHAKE
MAYAMA WOULD NEVER SAY ANYTHING LIKE THAT.
HE'S NOT THAT KIND OF PERSON.
THE REASON HE LIED TO PREVENT RIKA-SAN FROM WORKING WITH ME...
...WAS TO SPARE ME PAIN. IT WAS OUT OF KINDNESS...
HE'S ALWAYS BEEN LIKE THAT WITH ME.
KIND.
CONSIDERATE.
AND ALWAYS WILL BE.
HE'LL BE LIKE THAT...
...UNTIL THE END OF TIME, AND BEYOND.

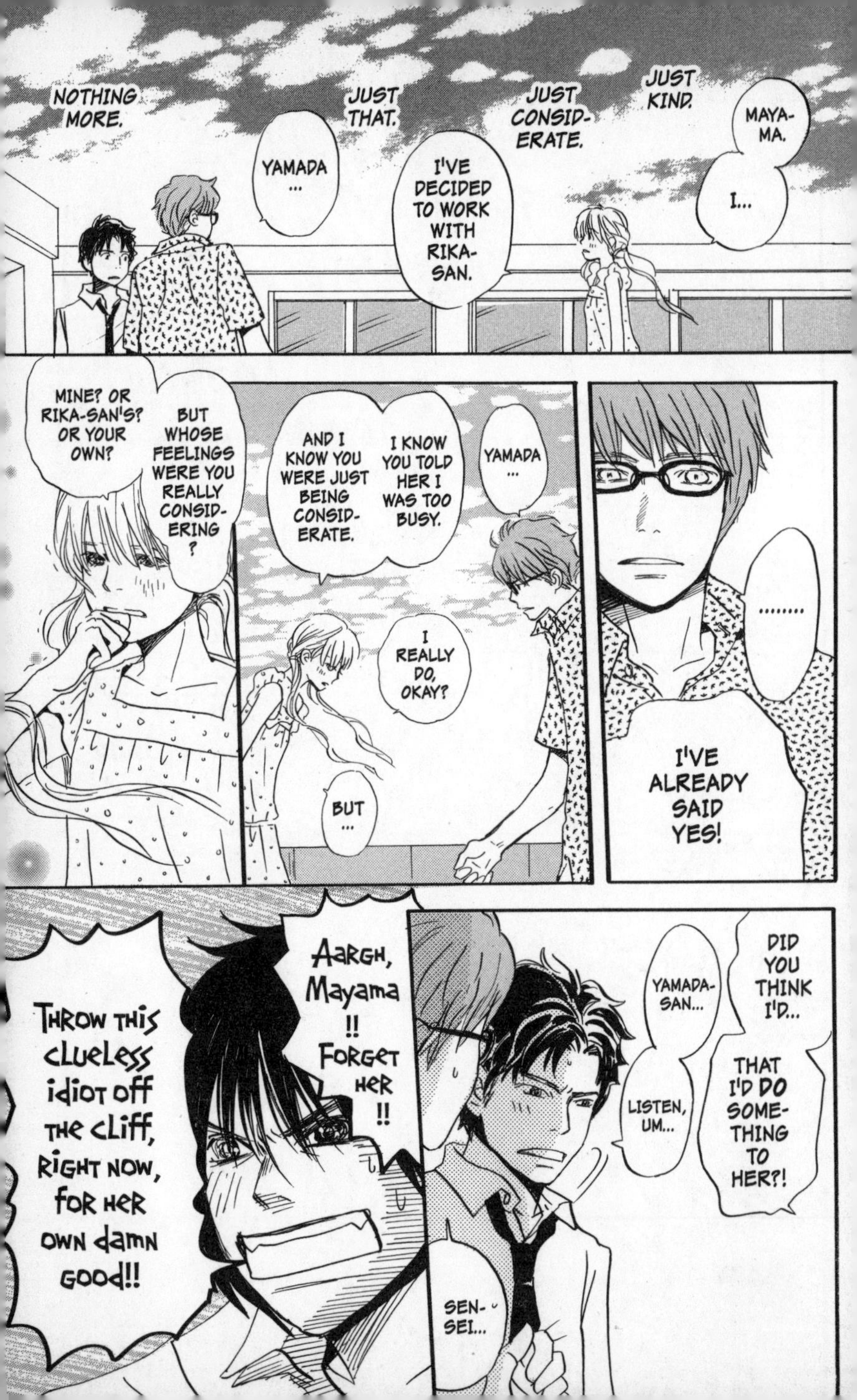
JUST KIND.
MAYAMA.
I...
JUST CONSID-ERATE.
I'VE DECIDED TO WORK WITH RIKA-SAN.
JUST THAT.
YAMADA...
NOTHING MORE.
....
I'VE ALREADY SAID YES!
YAMADA...
I KNOW YOU TOLD HER I WAS TOO BUSY.
AND I KNOW YOU WERE JUST BEING CONSID-ERATE.
I REALLY DO, OKAY?
BUT...
BUT WHOSE FEELINGS WERE YOU REALLY CONSID-ERING?
MINE? OR RIKA-SAN'S? OR YOUR OWN?
DID YOU THINK I'D...
YAMADA-SAN...
THAT I'D DO SOME-THING TO HER?!
LISTEN, UM...
SEN-SEI...
Aargh, Mayama!! Forget her!!
THROW THIS clueless idiot off the cliff, RIGHT NOW, FOR HER OWN damn GOOD!!

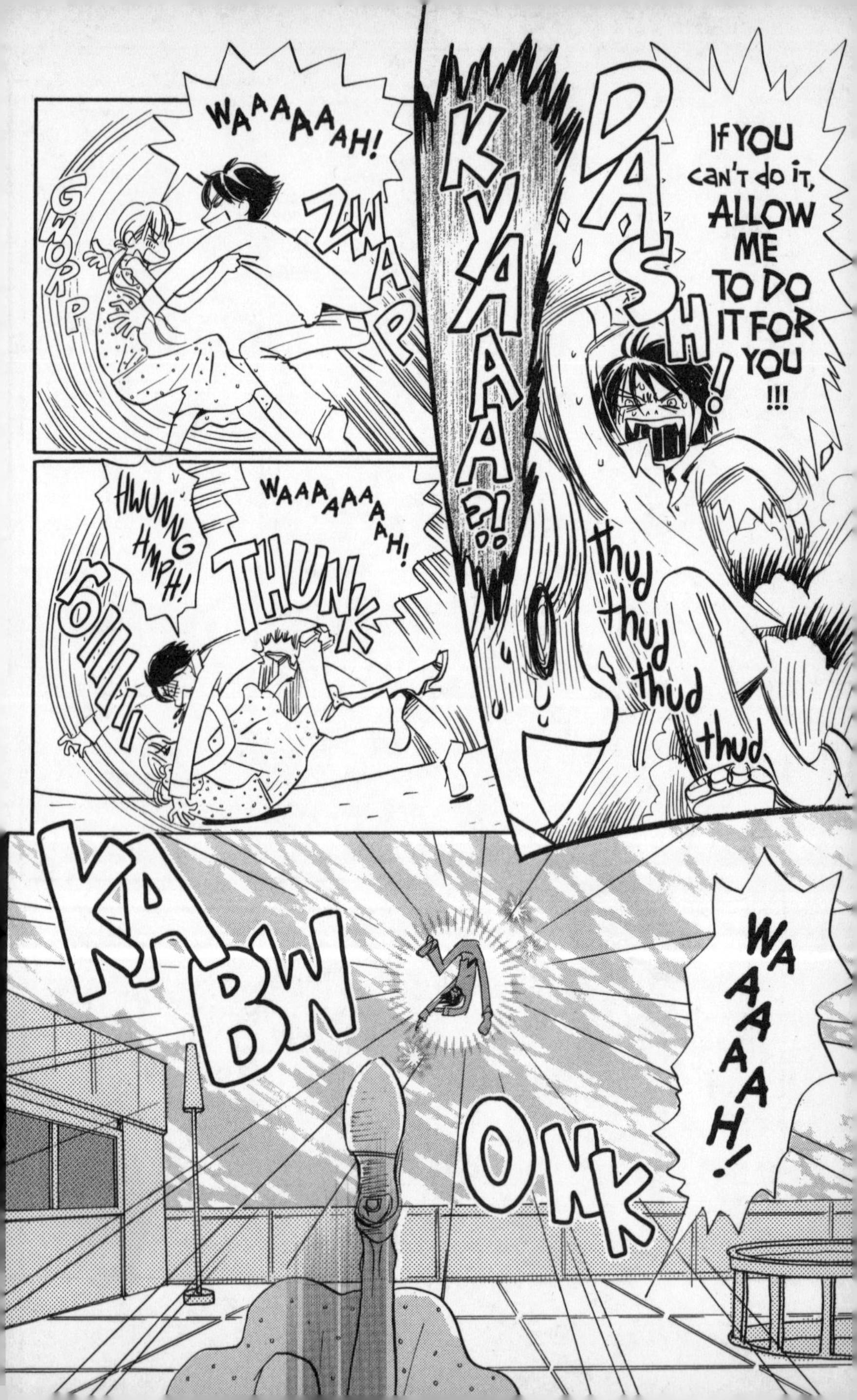
IF YOU can't do it, ALLOW ME TO DO IT FOR YOU!!!
DASH!
KYAAAA?!!
thud thud thud thud
WAAAAAAH!
ZWAP
GWORP
WAAAAAAAAH!
HWUNNG HMPH!
THUNK
WAAAAAAH!
KABWONK

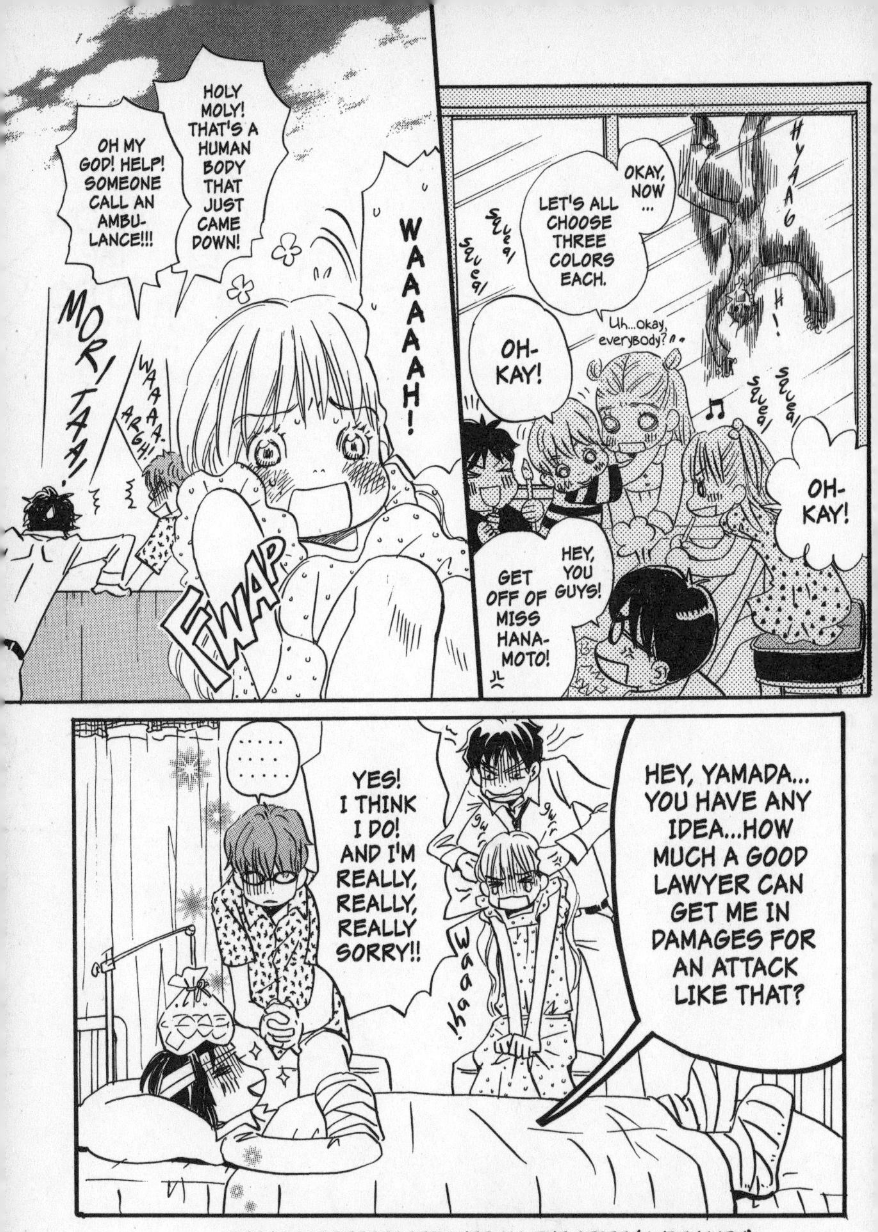
HYAAGH!
OKAY, NOW ...
LET'S ALL CHOOSE THREE COLORS EACH.
squeal squeal
OH-KAY!
Uh...okay, everybody?
squeal
OH-KAY!
HEY, YOU GUYS! GET OFF OF MISS HANA-MOTO!
WAAAAAAH!
HOLY MOLY! THAT'S A HUMAN BODY THAT JUST CAME DOWN!
OH MY GOD! HELP! SOMEONE CALL AN AMBU-LANCE!!!
WAAAAA-ARGH!
MORI TAAA!
WAP
HEY, YAMADA... YOU HAVE ANY IDEA...HOW MUCH A GOOD LAWYER CAN GET ME IN DAMAGES FOR AN ATTACK LIKE THAT?
Waaaah!
YES! I THINK I DO! AND I'M REALLY, REALLY, REALLY SORRY!!
......

WHEN I GOT DEPRESSED OVER ALL THE GRIEF (AND INJURY) I'D CAUSED EVERYBODY AND MUMBLED THAT I WISHED THERE WAS A DELETE KEY FOR CRUSHES, MORITA SAID, "OVERRULED. ON THE GROUNDS OF BEING TOTALLY UNROMANTIC," AND GRINNED AT ME THROUGH HIS BANDAGES.

chapter 43—the end—

#5:

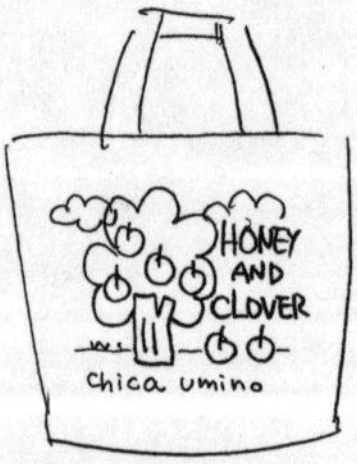
HONEY
AND
CLOVER
chica umino

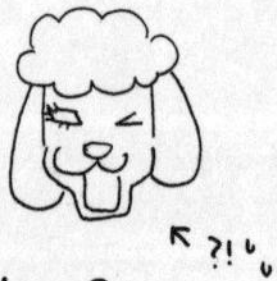
?!

Rough ideas for
Honey and Clover
goods.

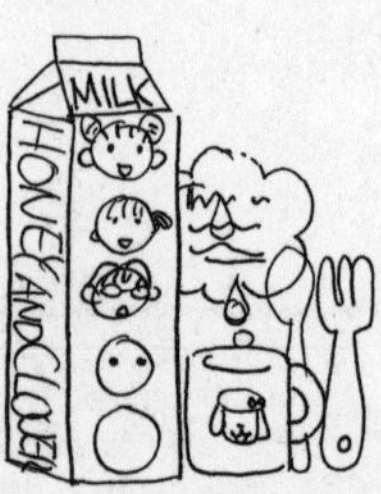
MILK
HONEY AND CLOVER

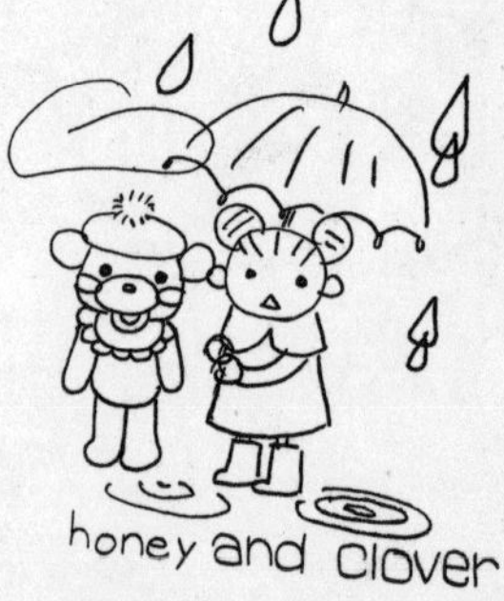
honey and clover

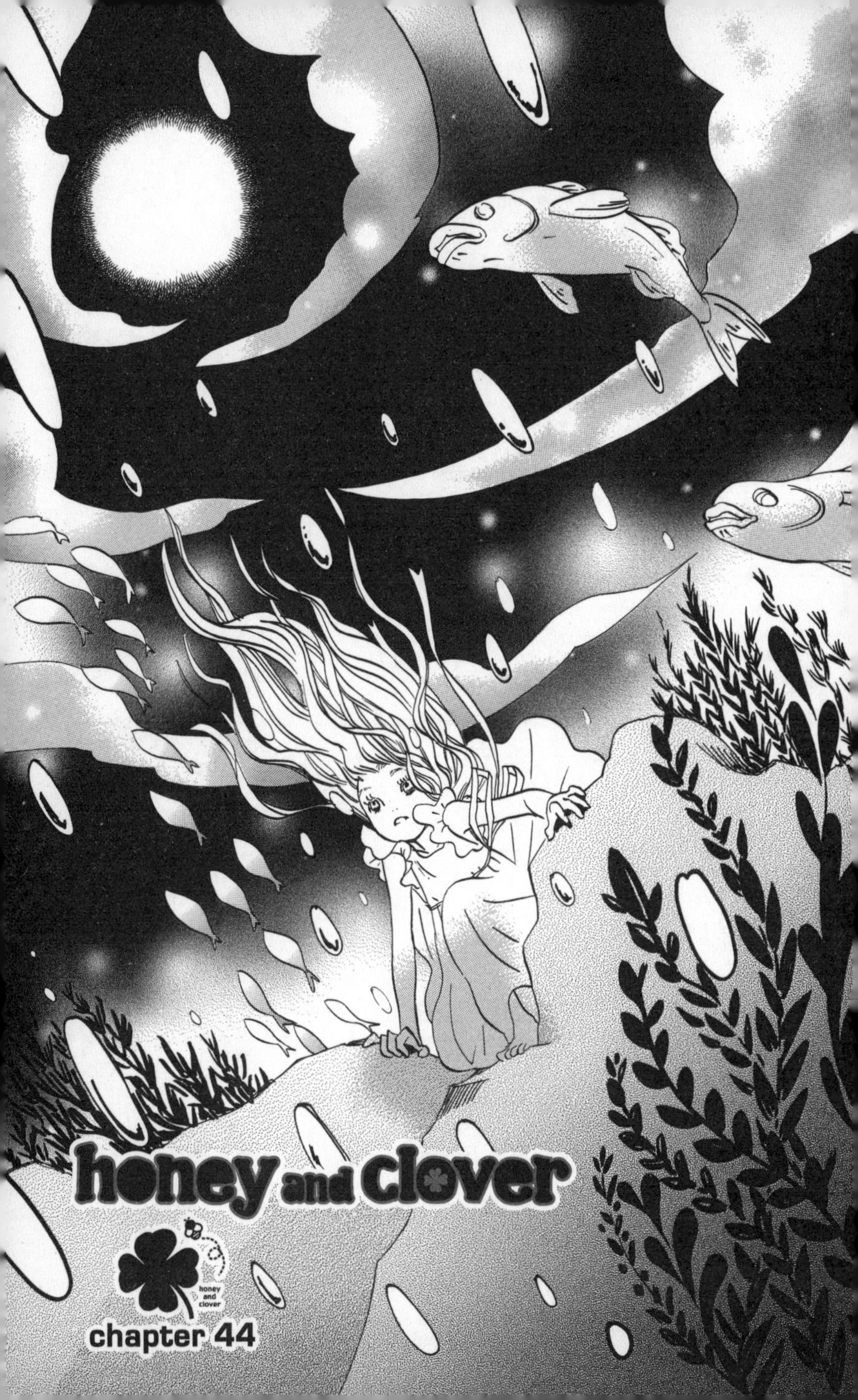
honey and clover
honey and clover
chapter 44

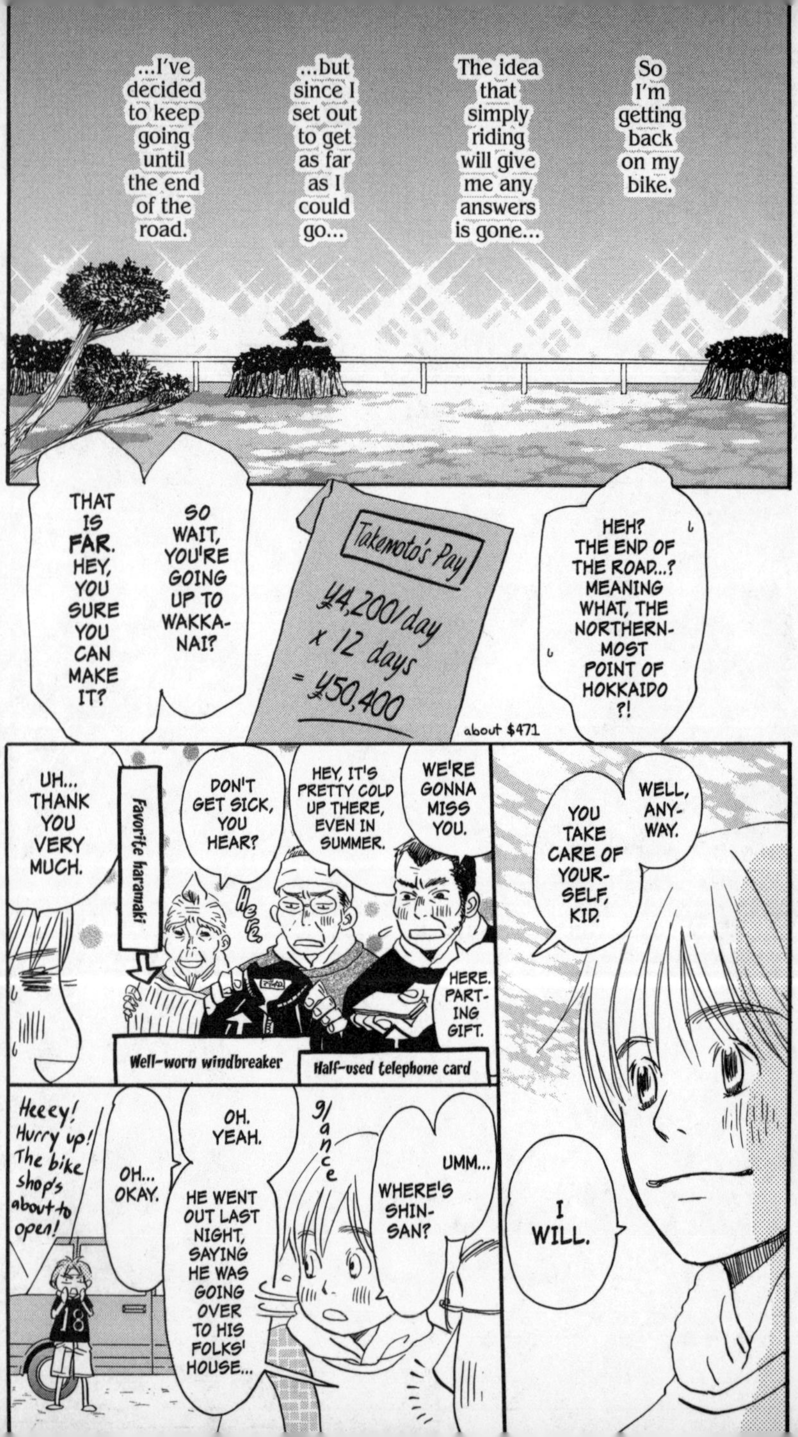
So I'm getting back on my bike.
The idea that simply riding will give me any answers is gone...
...but since I set out to get as far as I could go...
...I've decided to keep going until the end of the road.
HEH? THE END OF THE ROAD...? MEANING WHAT, THE NORTHERN-MOST POINT OF HOKKAIDO?!
Takemoto's Pay
¥4,200/day x 12 days = ¥50,400
about $471
SO WAIT, YOU'RE GOING UP TO WAKKA-NAI?
THAT IS FAR. HEY, YOU SURE YOU CAN MAKE IT?
WELL, ANY-WAY.
YOU TAKE CARE OF YOUR-SELF, KID.
I WILL.
WE'RE GONNA MISS YOU.
HEY, IT'S PRETTY COLD UP THERE, EVEN IN SUMMER.
DON'T GET SICK, YOU HEAR?
Here
HERE. PART-ING GIFT.
Half-used telephone card
Well-worn windbreaker
Favorite haramaki
UH... THANK YOU VERY MUCH.
UMM...
WHERE'S SHIN-SAN?
glance
OH. YEAH.
HE WENT OUT LAST NIGHT, SAYING HE WAS GOING OVER TO HIS FOLKS' HOUSE...
OH... OKAY.
Heeey! Hurry up! The bike shop's about to open!

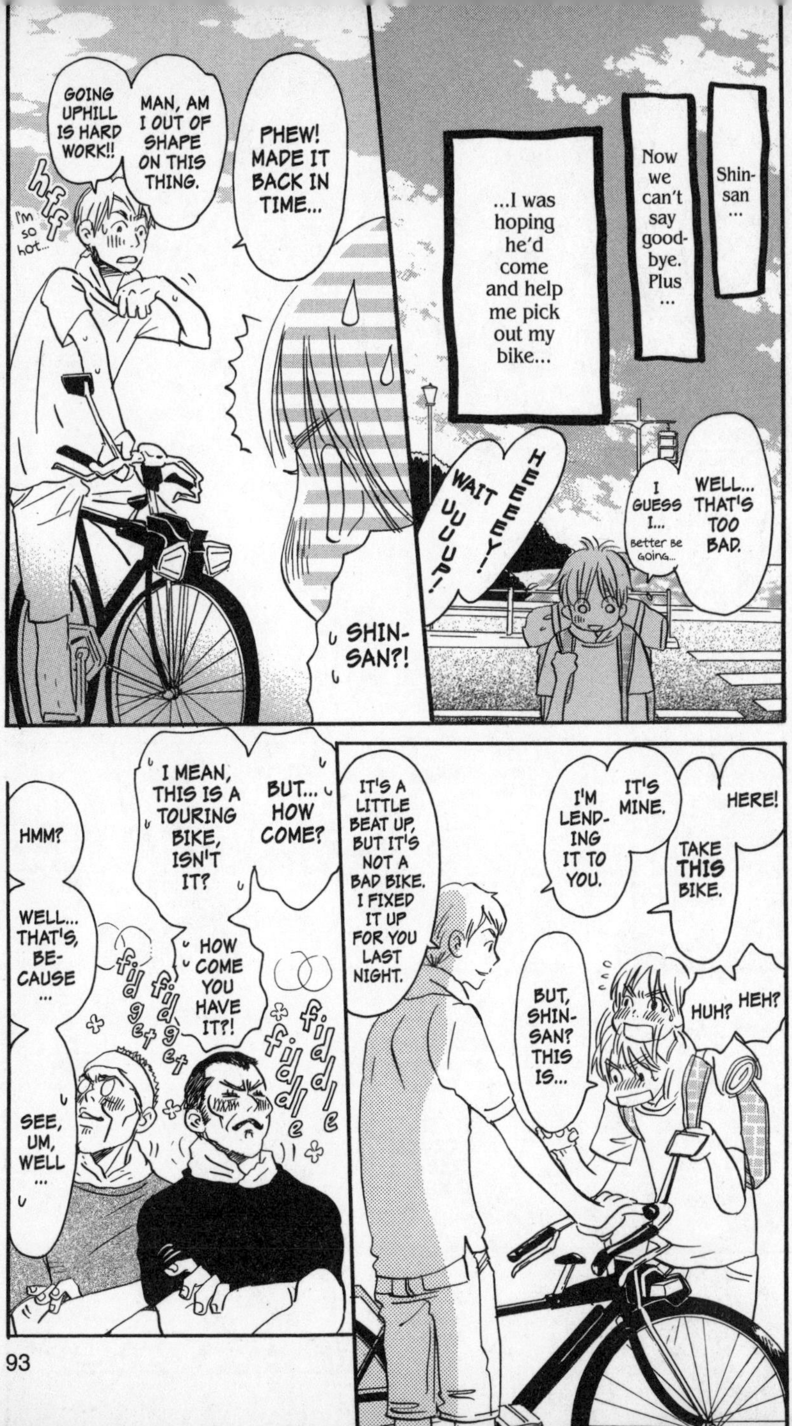
Shin-san...
Now we can't say good-bye. Plus...
...I was hoping he'd come and help me pick out my bike...
WELL... THAT'S TOO BAD.
I GUESS I... Better be going...
HEEEEY! WAIT UUUUP!
SHIN-SAN?!
PHEW! MADE IT BACK IN TIME...
MAN, AM I OUT OF SHAPE ON THIS THING.
GOING UPHILL IS HARD WORK!!
hff
I'm so hot...
HERE! TAKE THIS BIKE.
IT'S MINE. I'M LENDING IT TO YOU.
HEH?
HUH?
IT'S A LITTLE BEAT UP, BUT IT'S NOT A BAD BIKE. I FIXED IT UP FOR YOU LAST NIGHT.
BUT, SHIN-SAN? THIS IS...
BUT... HOW COME?
I MEAN, THIS IS A TOURING BIKE, ISN'T IT?
HOW COME YOU HAVE IT?!
fiddle fiddle
fidget fidget
HMM?
WELL... THAT'S, BE-CAUSE...
SEE, UM, WELL...

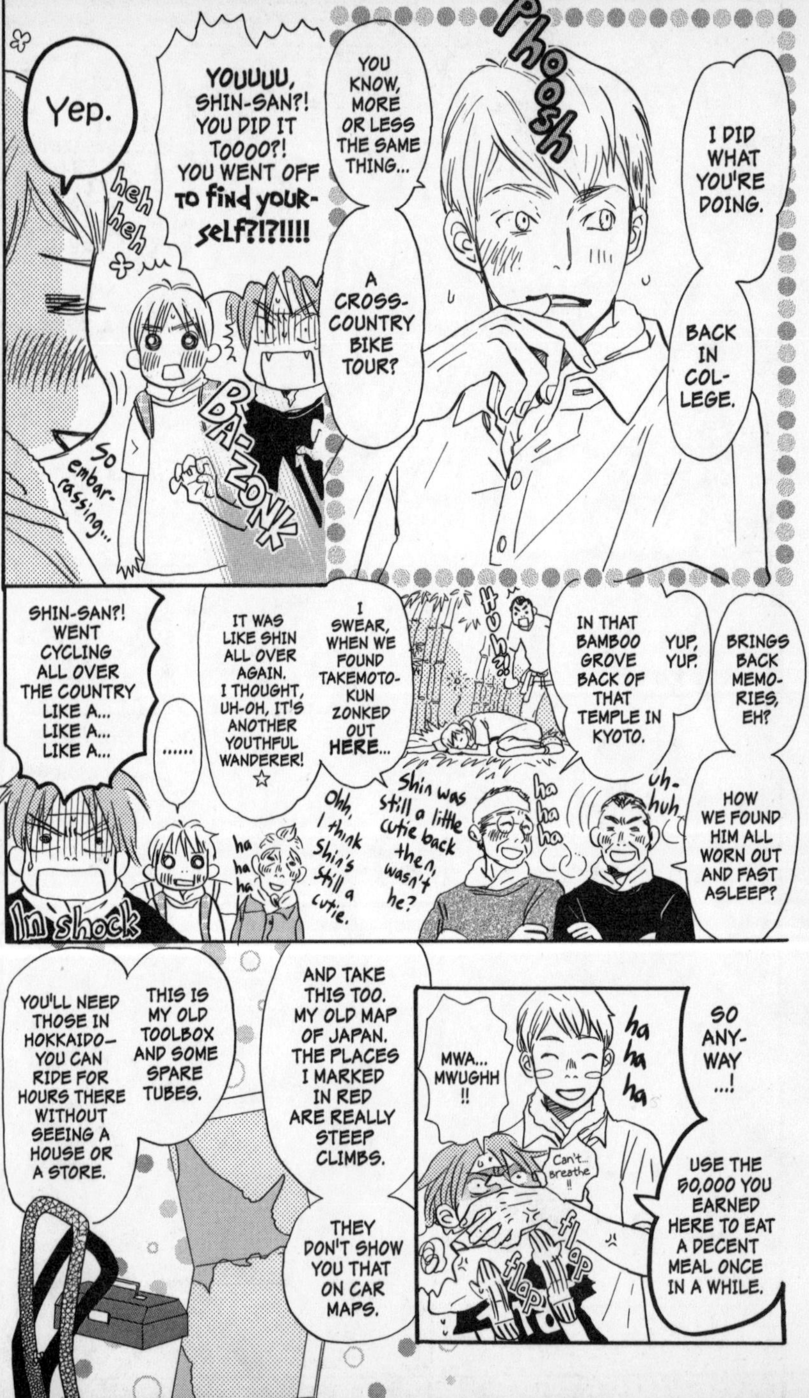
Phoosh
I DID WHAT YOU'RE DOING.
BACK IN COLLEGE.
YOU KNOW, MORE OR LESS THE SAME THING...
A CROSS-COUNTRY BIKE TOUR?
YOUUUU, SHIN-SAN?! YOU DID IT TOOOO?! YOU WENT OFF TO find yourself?!?!!!!
Yep.
heh heh
BA-ZONK
So embarrassing...
BRINGS BACK MEMORIES, EH?
HOW WE FOUND HIM ALL WORN OUT AND FAST ASLEEP?
YUP, YUP.
IN THAT BAMBOO GROVE BACK OF THAT TEMPLE IN KYOTO.
Huh?!
uh-huh
ha ha ha
Shin was still a little cutie back then, wasn't he?
I SWEAR, WHEN WE FOUND TAKEMOTO-KUN ZONKED OUT HERE...
IT WAS LIKE SHIN ALL OVER AGAIN. I THOUGHT, UH-OH, IT'S ANOTHER YOUTHFUL WANDERER! ☆
Ohh, I think Shin's still a cutie.
ha ha ha
......
SHIN-SAN?! WENT CYCLING ALL OVER THE COUNTRY LIKE A... LIKE A... LIKE A...
In shock
SO ANYWAY...!
ha ha ha
USE THE 50,000 YOU EARNED HERE TO EAT A DECENT MEAL ONCE IN A WHILE.
MWA... MWUGHH !!
Can't... Breathe !!
flap flap
AND TAKE THIS TOO. MY OLD MAP OF JAPAN. THE PLACES I MARKED IN RED ARE REALLY STEEP CLIMBS.
THEY DON'T SHOW YOU THAT ON CAR MAPS.
THIS IS MY OLD TOOLBOX AND SOME SPARE TUBES.
YOU'LL NEED THOSE IN HOKKAIDO—YOU CAN RIDE FOR HOURS THERE WITHOUT SEEING A HOUSE OR A STORE.

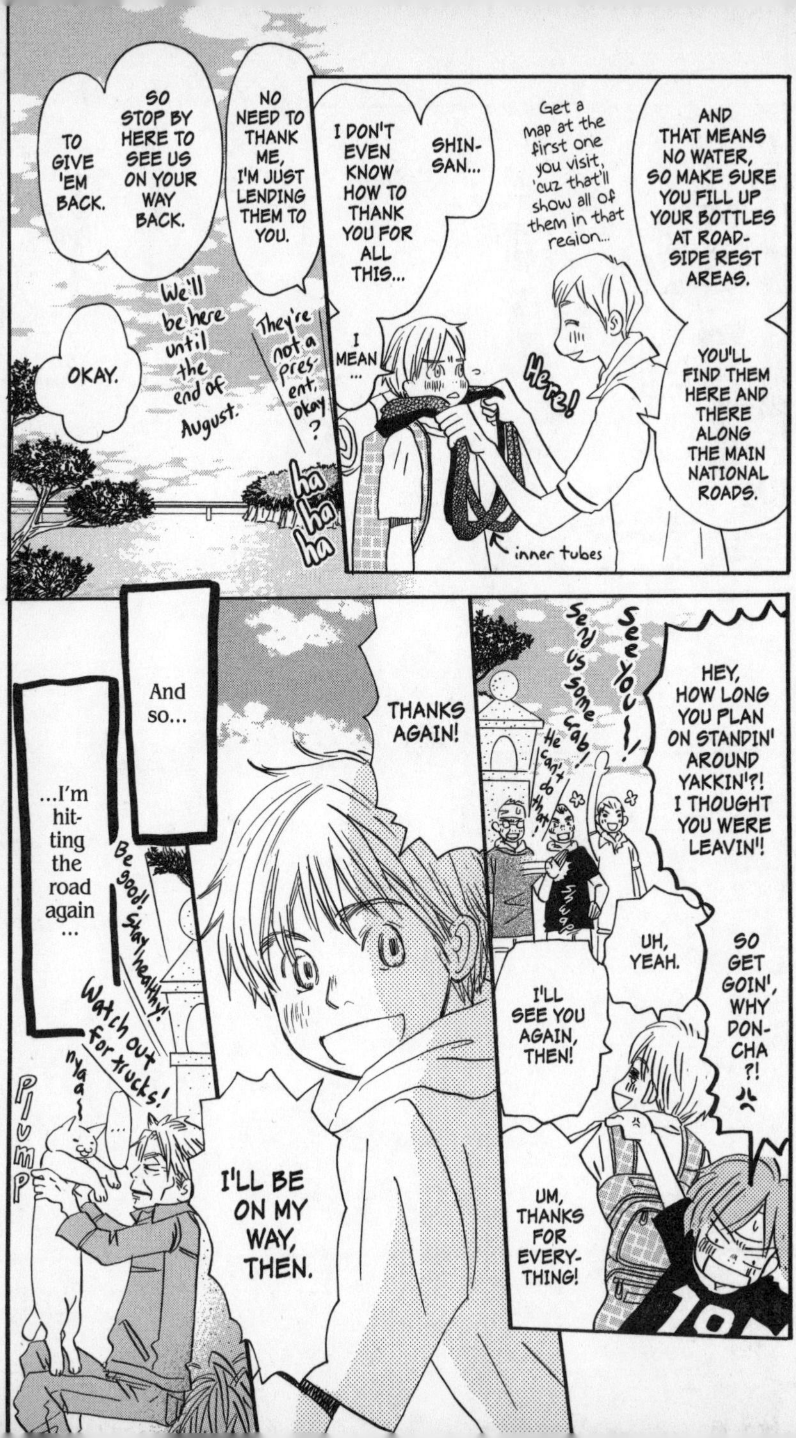
AND THAT MEANS NO WATER, SO MAKE SURE YOU FILL UP YOUR BOTTLES AT ROAD-SIDE REST AREAS.
YOU'LL FIND THEM HERE AND THERE ALONG THE MAIN NATIONAL ROADS.
Get a map at the first one you visit, 'cuz that'll show all of them in that region...
Here!
inner tubes
SHIN-SAN...
I DON'T EVEN KNOW HOW TO THANK YOU FOR ALL THIS...
I MEAN...
NO NEED TO THANK ME, I'M JUST LENDING THEM TO YOU.
They're not a present, okay?
ha ha ha
SO STOP BY HERE TO SEE US ON YOUR WAY BACK.
TO GIVE 'EM BACK.
We'll be here until the end of August.
OKAY.
See you~!
Send us some crab!
He can't do that!
HEY, HOW LONG YOU PLAN ON STANDIN' AROUND YAKKIN'?! I THOUGHT YOU WERE LEAVIN'!
UH, YEAH.
SO GET GOIN', WHY DONCHA?!
I'LL SEE YOU AGAIN, THEN!
UM, THANKS FOR EVERYTHING!
THANKS AGAIN!
And so...
I'LL BE ON MY WAY, THEN.
...I'm hitting the road again...
Be good! Stay healthy!
Watch out for trucks!
nyaa~
...
Plump

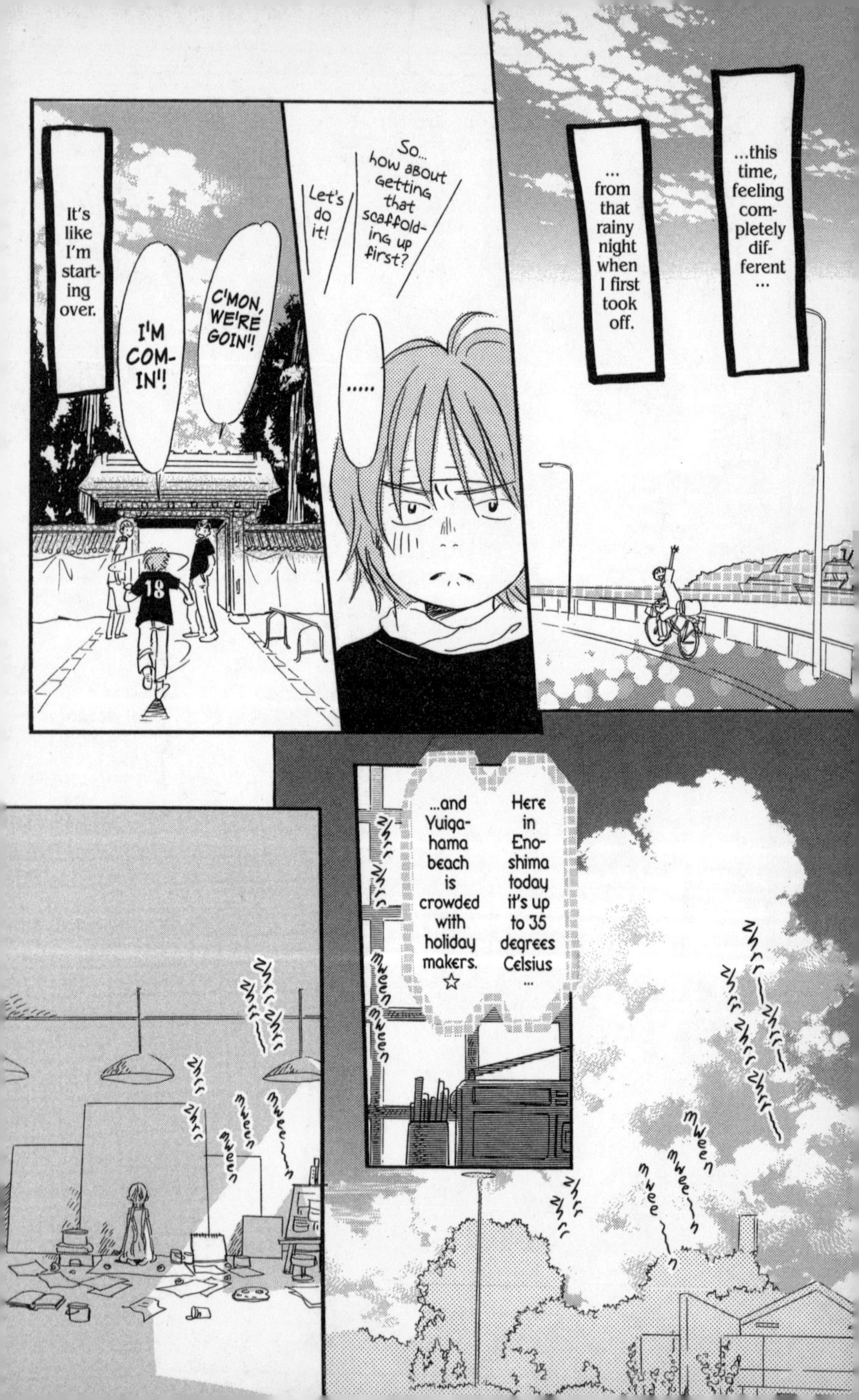
...this time, feeling com-pletely dif-ferent...
...from that rainy night when I first took off.
So... how about getting that scaffold-ing up first?
Let's do it!
.....
It's like I'm start-ing over.
C'MON, WE'RE GOIN'!
I'M COM-IN'!
Here in Eno-shima today it's up to 35 degrees Celsius...
...and Yuiga-hama beach is crowded with holiday makers. ☆
zhrr zhrr
mween mween
zhrr—zhrr—
zhrr zhrr zhrr—
mween
mwee—n
mwee—n
zhrr zhrr
zhrr zhrr zhrr—
zhrr zhrr
mwee—n
mween mween

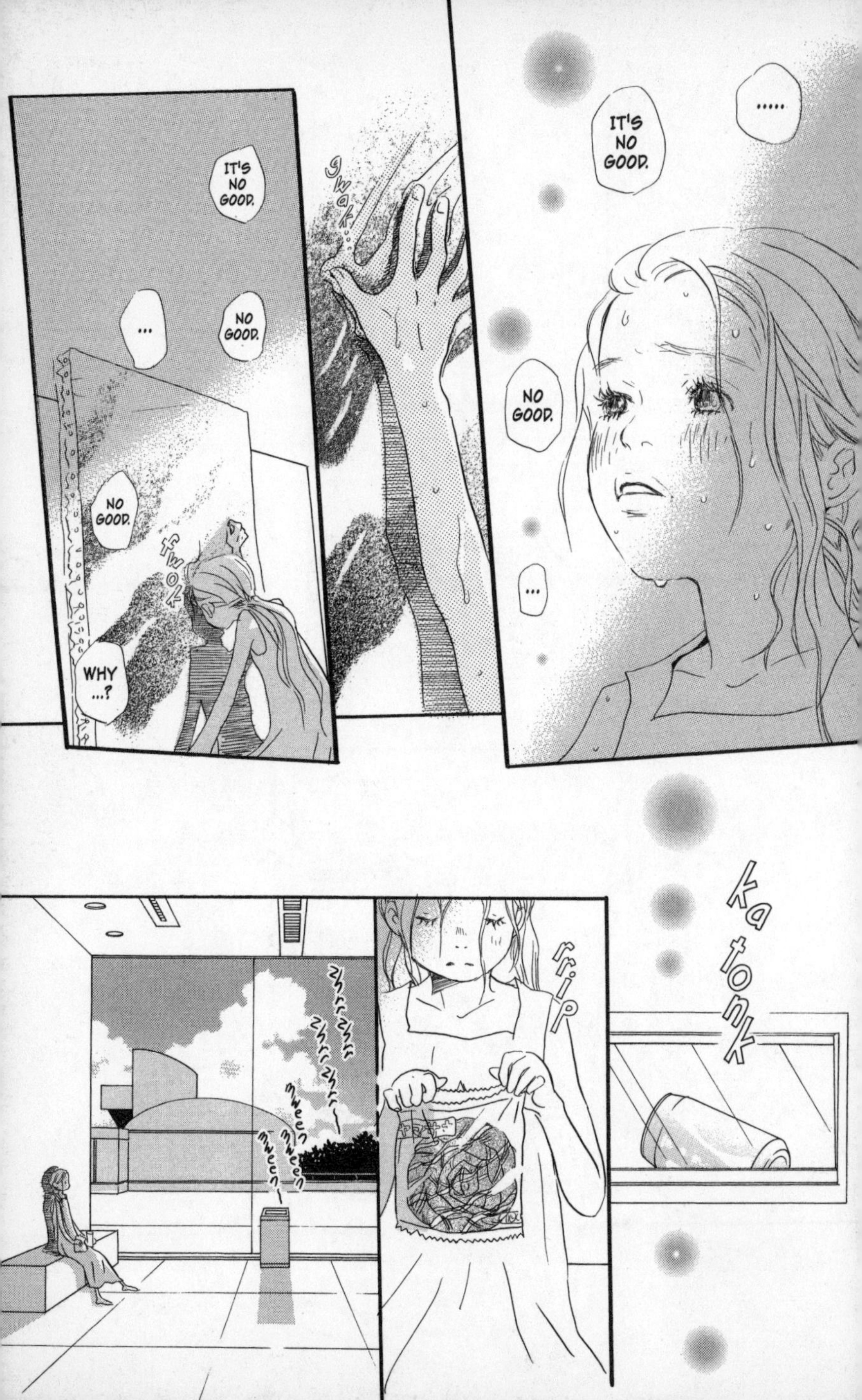

.....
IT'S NO GOOD.
NO GOOD.
...
gwak
IT'S NO GOOD.
NO GOOD.
...
NO GOOD.
fwok
WHY ...?
ka tonk
rrip
zhrrzhrr
zhrrzhrr~
mween
mween
mween~

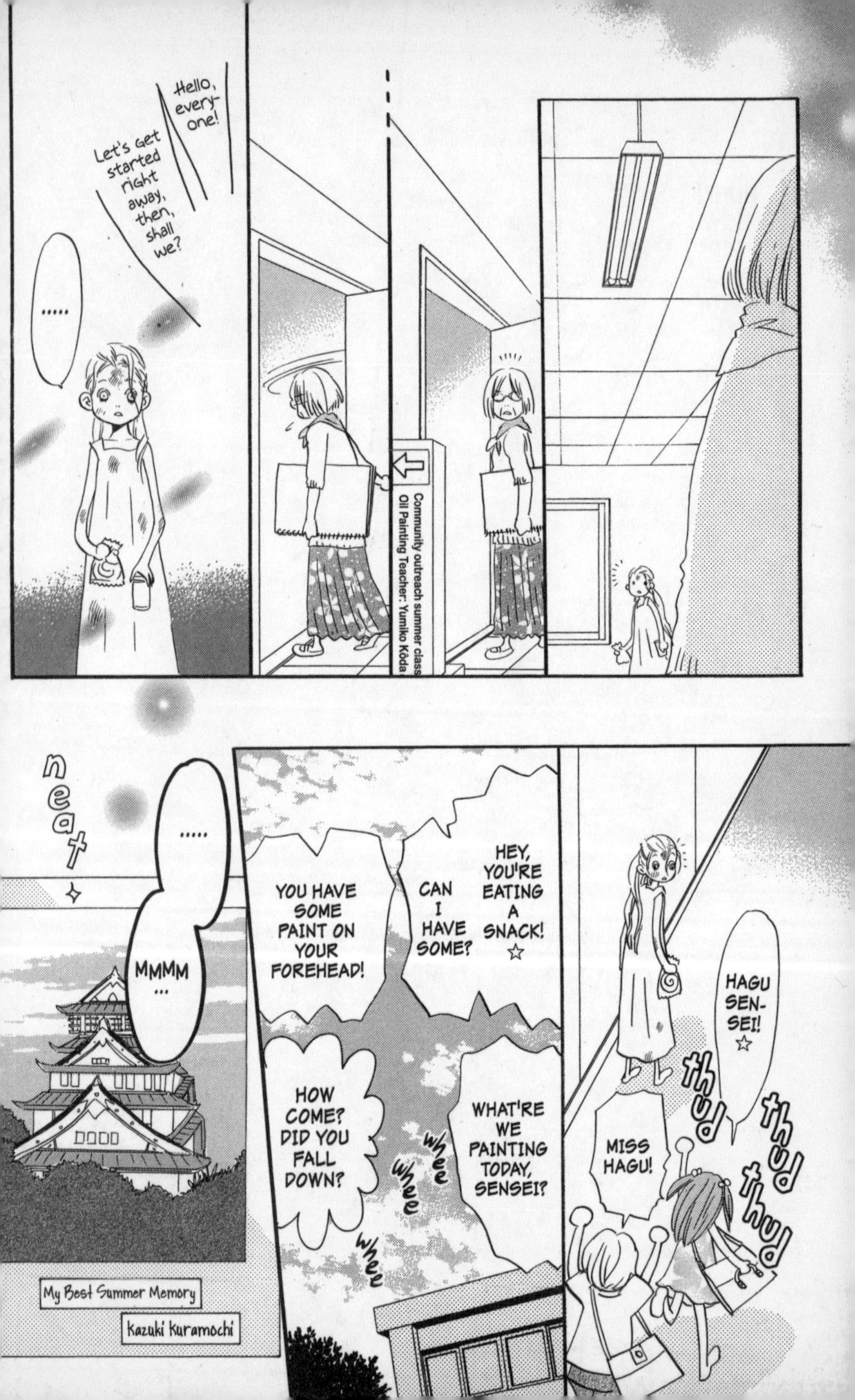
Community outreach summer class
Oil Painting Teacher: Yumiko Kōda
Hello, every-one!
Let's get started right away, then, shall we?
.....
HAGU SEN-SEI! ☆
thud thud thud
MISS HAGU!
HEY, YOU'RE EATING A SNACK! ☆
CAN I HAVE SOME?
YOU HAVE SOME PAINT ON YOUR FOREHEAD!
WHAT'RE WE PAINTING TODAY, SENSEI?
HOW COME? DID YOU FALL DOWN?
whee whee whee
.....
MMMM ...
neat
My Best Summer Memory
Kazuki Kuramochi

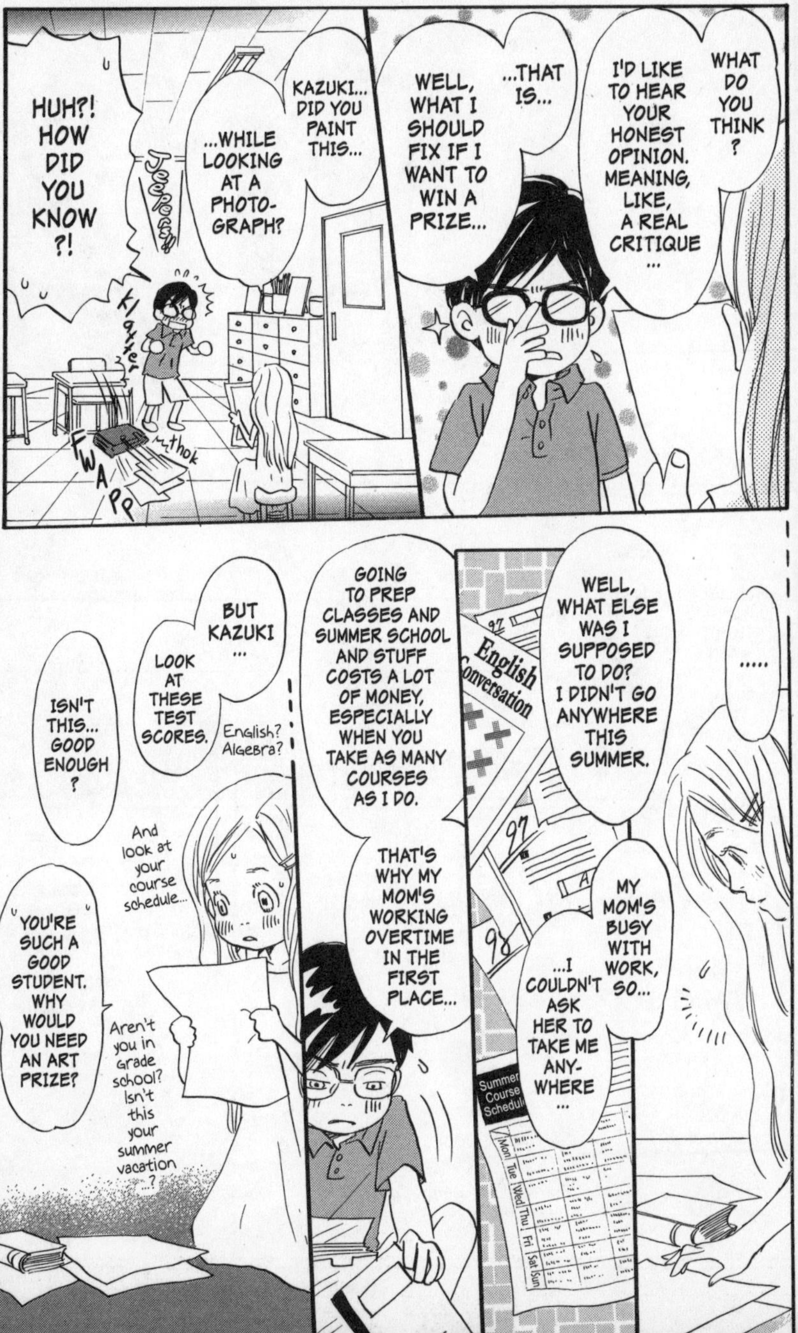
WHAT DO YOU THINK?
I'D LIKE TO HEAR YOUR HONEST OPINION. MEANING, LIKE, A REAL CRITIQUE...
...THAT IS...
WELL, WHAT I SHOULD FIX IF I WANT TO WIN A PRIZE...
KAZUKI... DID YOU PAINT THIS...
...WHILE LOOKING AT A PHOTOGRAPH?
HUH?! HOW DID YOU KNOW?!
Jeepers
klatter
thok
FWAPP
.....
WELL, WHAT ELSE WAS I SUPPOSED TO DO? I DIDN'T GO ANYWHERE THIS SUMMER.
English Conversation
97
98
MY MOM'S BUSY WITH WORK, SO...
...I COULDN'T ASK HER TO TAKE ME ANYWHERE...
Summer Course Schedule
Mon Tue Wed Thu Fri Sat Sun
GOING TO PREP CLASSES AND SUMMER SCHOOL AND STUFF COSTS A LOT OF MONEY, ESPECIALLY WHEN YOU TAKE AS MANY COURSES AS I DO.
THAT'S WHY MY MOM'S WORKING OVERTIME IN THE FIRST PLACE...
BUT KAZUKI...
LOOK AT THESE TEST SCORES.
English? Algebra?
ISN'T THIS... GOOD ENOUGH?
And look at your course schedule...
YOU'RE SUCH A GOOD STUDENT. WHY WOULD YOU NEED AN ART PRIZE?
Aren't you in Grade school? Isn't this your summer vacation...?

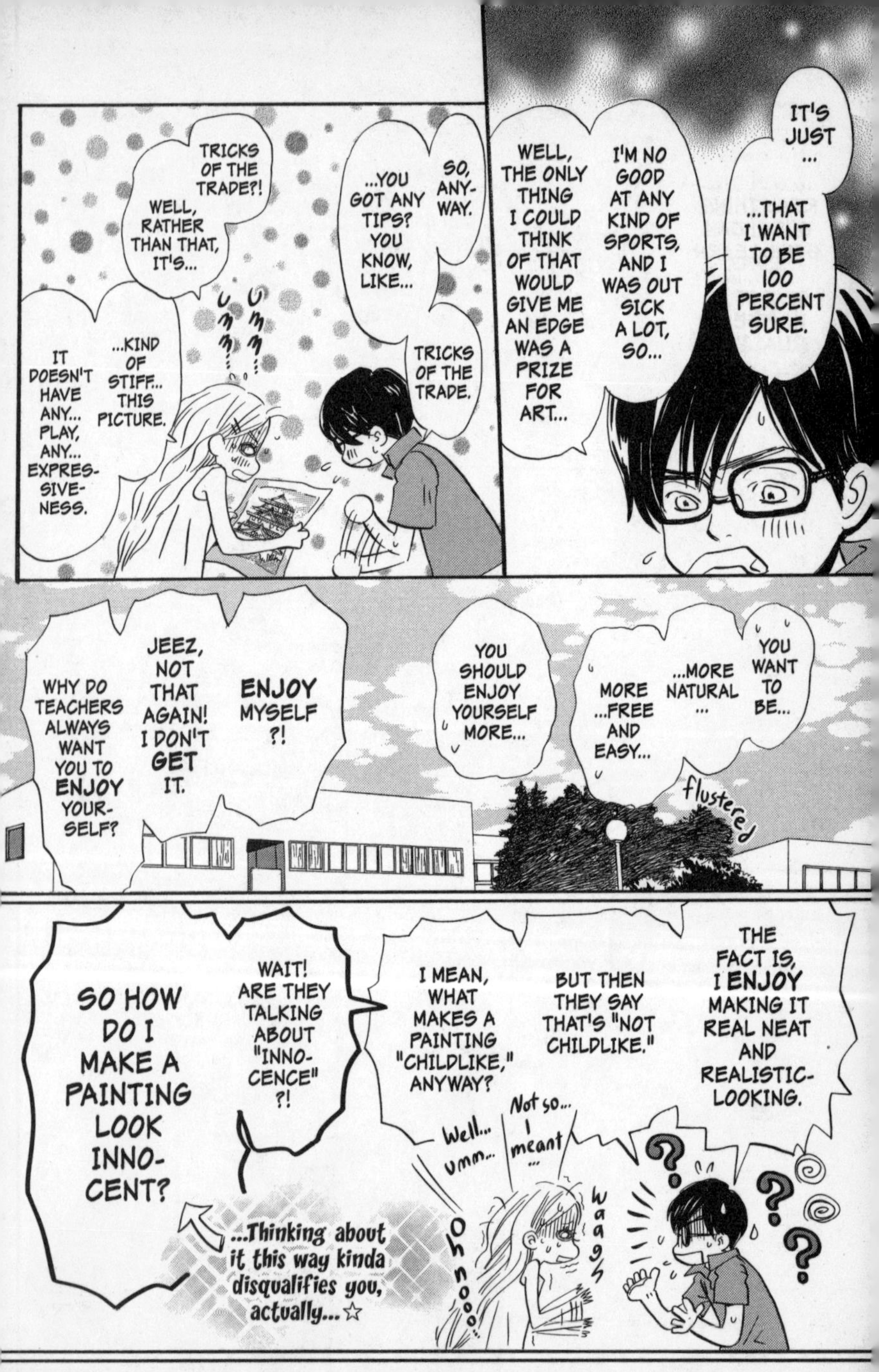
IT'S JUST ...
...THAT I WANT TO BE 100 PERCENT SURE.
I'M NO GOOD AT ANY KIND OF SPORTS, AND I WAS OUT SICK A LOT, SO...
WELL, THE ONLY THING I COULD THINK OF THAT WOULD GIVE ME AN EDGE WAS A PRIZE FOR ART...
SO, ANYWAY.
...YOU GOT ANY TIPS? YOU KNOW, LIKE...
TRICKS OF THE TRADE.
TRICKS OF THE TRADE?!
WELL, RATHER THAN THAT, IT'S...
...KIND OF STIFF... THIS PICTURE.
IT DOESN'T HAVE ANY... PLAY, ANY... EXPRESSIVENESS.
Ummm
Ummm
YOU WANT TO BE...
...MORE NATURAL...
MORE ...FREE AND EASY...
YOU SHOULD ENJOY YOURSELF MORE...
flustered
ENJOY MYSELF?!
JEEZ, NOT THAT AGAIN! I DON'T GET IT.
WHY DO TEACHERS ALWAYS WANT YOU TO ENJOY YOURSELF?
THE FACT IS, I ENJOY MAKING IT REAL NEAT AND REALISTIC-LOOKING.
BUT THEN THEY SAY THAT'S "NOT CHILDLIKE."
I MEAN, WHAT MAKES A PAINTING "CHILDLIKE," ANYWAY?
WAIT! ARE THEY TALKING ABOUT "INNOCENCE"?!
SO HOW DO I MAKE A PAINTING LOOK INNOCENT?
Not so... I meant...
Well... umm...
Waagh
Oh nooo...
...Thinking about it this way kinda disqualifies you, actually...☆

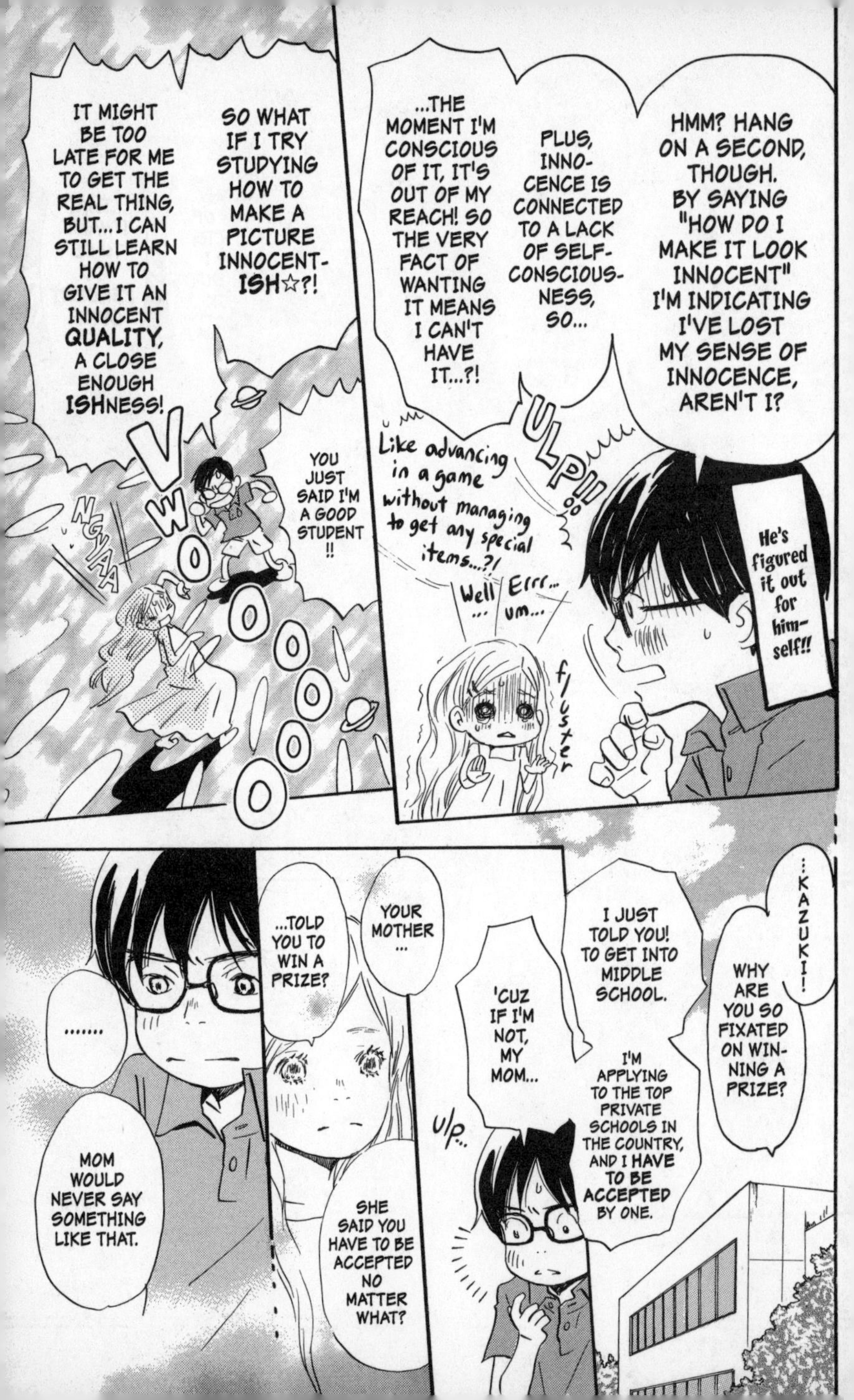
HMM? HANG ON A SECOND, THOUGH. BY SAYING "HOW DO I MAKE IT LOOK INNOCENT" I'M INDICATING I'VE LOST MY SENSE OF INNOCENCE, AREN'T I?
PLUS, INNOCENCE IS CONNECTED TO A LACK OF SELF-CONSCIOUSNESS, SO...
...THE MOMENT I'M CONSCIOUS OF IT, IT'S OUT OF MY REACH! SO THE VERY FACT OF WANTING IT MEANS I CAN'T HAVE IT...?!
ULP!!
He's figured it out for him-self!!
Like advancing in a game without managing to get any special items...?!
Well ...
Errr... um...
fluster
SO WHAT IF I TRY STUDYING HOW TO MAKE A PICTURE INNOCENT-ISH☆?!
IT MIGHT BE TOO LATE FOR ME TO GET THE REAL THING, BUT...I CAN STILL LEARN HOW TO GIVE IT AN INNOCENT QUALITY, A CLOSE ENOUGH ISHNESS!
VWOOOOOOOO
YOU JUST SAID I'M A GOOD STUDENT!!
NGYAA
...KAZUKI!
WHY ARE YOU SO FIXATED ON WINNING A PRIZE?
I JUST TOLD YOU! TO GET INTO MIDDLE SCHOOL.
I'M APPLYING TO THE TOP PRIVATE SCHOOLS IN THE COUNTRY, AND I HAVE TO BE ACCEPTED BY ONE.
'CUZ IF I'M NOT, MY MOM...
ULP...
YOUR MOTHER ...
...TOLD YOU TO WIN A PRIZE?
SHE SAID YOU HAVE TO BE ACCEPTED NO MATTER WHAT?
....
MOM WOULD NEVER SAY SOMETHING LIKE THAT.

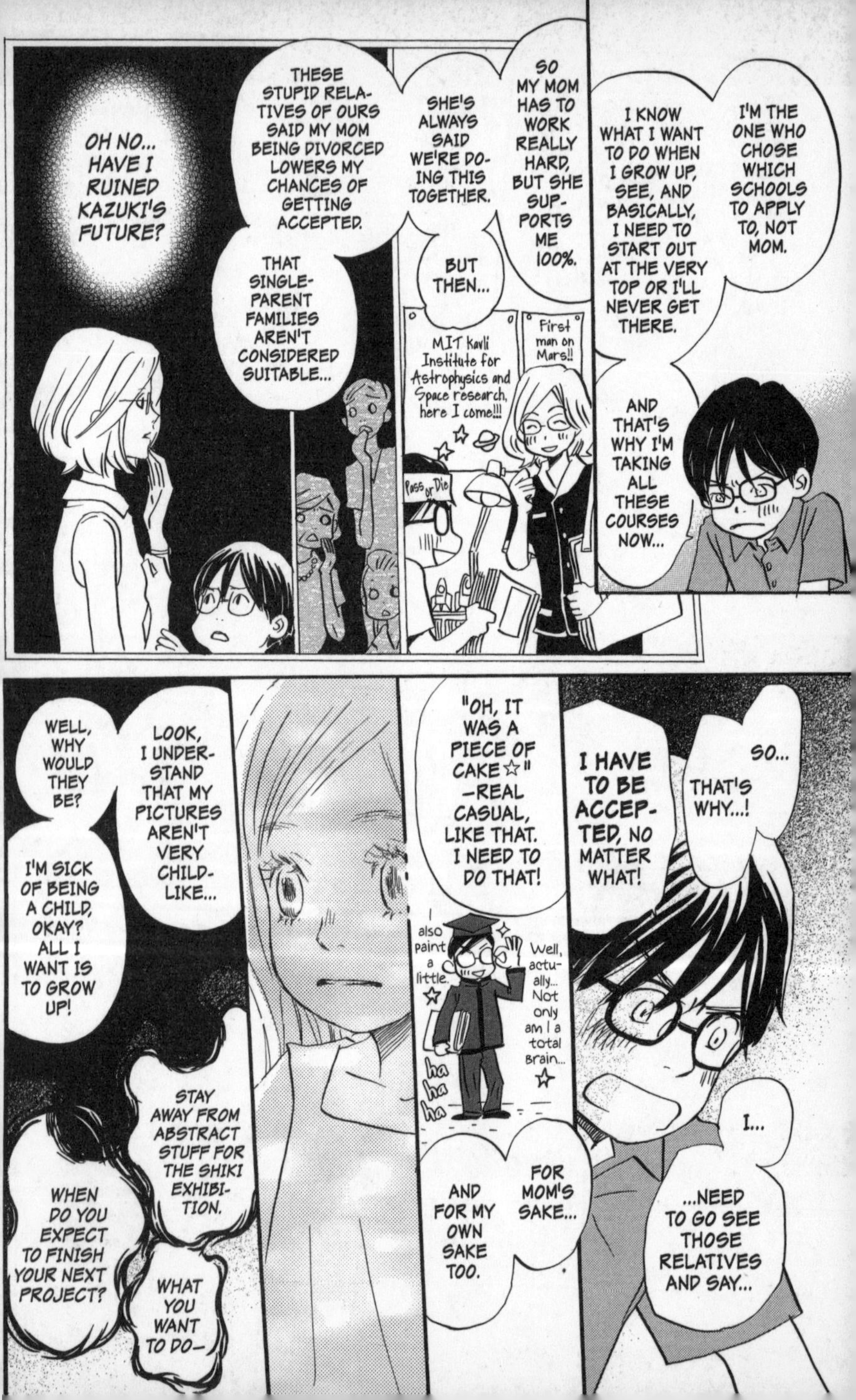
I'M THE ONE WHO CHOSE WHICH SCHOOLS TO APPLY TO, NOT MOM.
I KNOW WHAT I WANT TO DO WHEN I GROW UP, SEE, AND BASICALLY, I NEED TO START OUT AT THE VERY TOP OR I'LL NEVER GET THERE.
AND THAT'S WHY I'M TAKING ALL THESE COURSES NOW...
SO MY MOM HAS TO WORK REALLY HARD, BUT SHE SUPPORTS ME 100%.
SHE'S ALWAYS SAID WE'RE DOING THIS TOGETHER.
BUT THEN...
First man on Mars!!
MIT Kavli Institute for Astrophysics and Space research, here I come!!!
Pass or Die
THESE STUPID RELATIVES OF OURS SAID MY MOM BEING DIVORCED LOWERS MY CHANCES OF GETTING ACCEPTED.
THAT SINGLE-PARENT FAMILIES AREN'T CONSIDERED SUITABLE...
OH NO... HAVE I RUINED KAZUKI'S FUTURE?
SO... THAT'S WHY...!
I HAVE TO BE ACCEPTED, NO MATTER WHAT!
I...
...NEED TO GO SEE THOSE RELATIVES AND SAY...
"OH, IT WAS A PIECE OF CAKE☆" —REAL CASUAL, LIKE THAT. I NEED TO DO THAT!
Well, actually... Not only am I a total brain... ☆
I also paint a little. ☆
ha ha ha
FOR MOM'S SAKE...
AND FOR MY OWN SAKE TOO.
LOOK, I UNDERSTAND THAT MY PICTURES AREN'T VERY CHILDLIKE...
WELL, WHY WOULD THEY BE?
I'M SICK OF BEING A CHILD, OKAY? ALL I WANT IS TO GROW UP!
STAY AWAY FROM ABSTRACT STUFF FOR THE SHIKI EXHIBITION.
WHEN DO YOU EXPECT TO FINISH YOUR NEXT PROJECT?
WHAT YOU WANT TO DO—

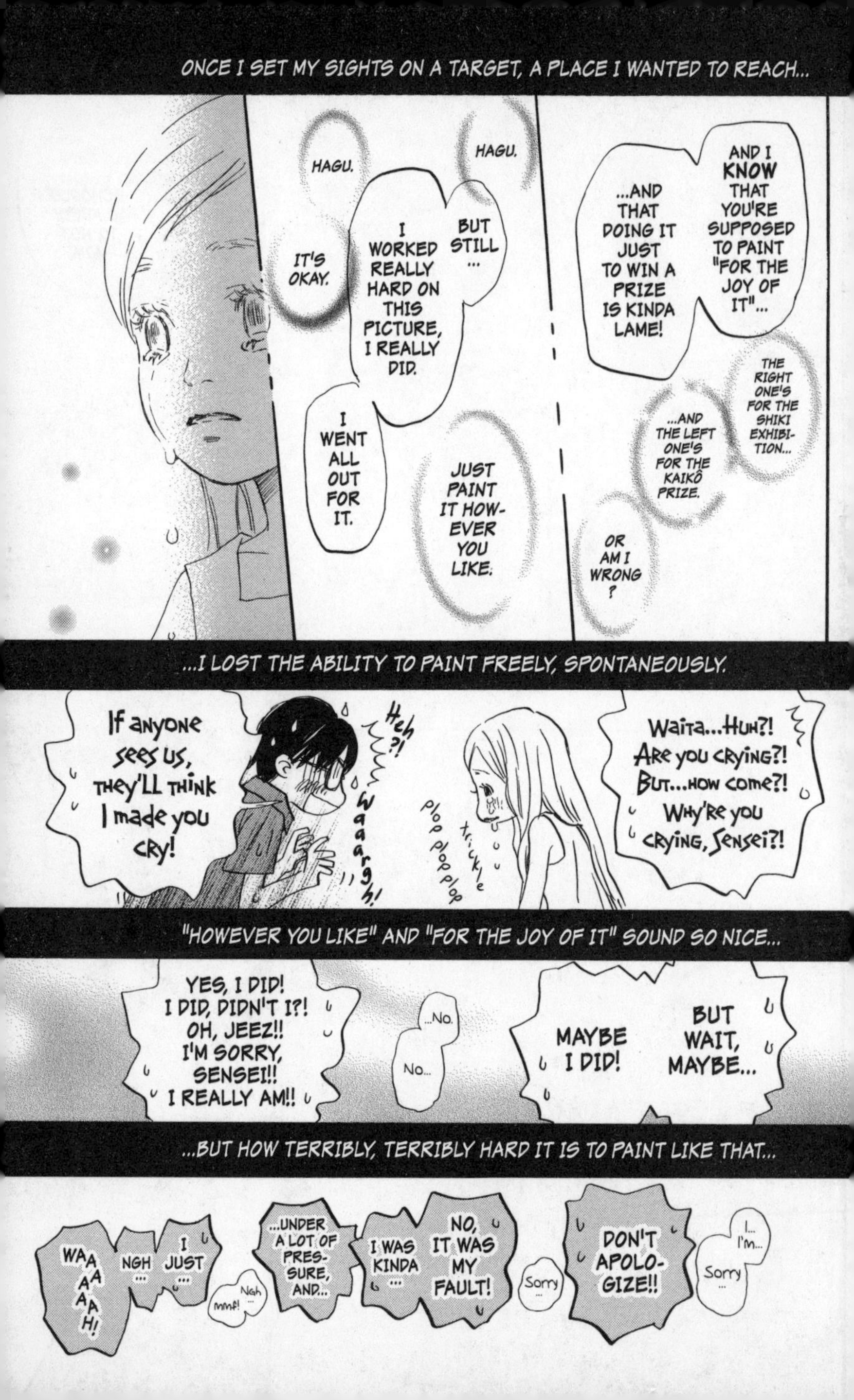
ONCE I SET MY SIGHTS ON A TARGET, A PLACE I WANTED TO REACH...
AND I KNOW THAT YOU'RE SUPPOSED TO PAINT "FOR THE JOY OF IT"...
...AND THAT DOING IT JUST TO WIN A PRIZE IS KINDA LAME!
THE RIGHT ONE'S FOR THE SHIKI EXHIBITION...
...AND THE LEFT ONE'S FOR THE KAIKÔ PRIZE.
OR AM I WRONG?
HAGU.
BUT STILL...
HAGU.
I WORKED REALLY HARD ON THIS PICTURE, I REALLY DID.
IT'S OKAY.
JUST PAINT IT HOWEVER YOU LIKE.
I WENT ALL OUT FOR IT.
...I LOST THE ABILITY TO PAINT FREELY, SPONTANEOUSLY.
Waita...Huh?! Are you crying?! But...how come?! Why're you crying, Sensei?!
trickle
plop plop plop
Heh?!
Waaargh!
If anyone sees us, they'll think I made you cry!
"HOWEVER YOU LIKE" AND "FOR THE JOY OF IT" SOUND SO NICE...
BUT WAIT, MAYBE...
MAYBE I DID!
...No.
No...
YES, I DID! I DID, DIDN'T I?! OH, JEEZ!! I'M SORRY, SENSEI!! I REALLY AM!!
...BUT HOW TERRIBLY, TERRIBLY HARD IT IS TO PAINT LIKE THAT...
I... I'm...
Sorry...
DON'T APOLOGIZE!!
Sorry...
NO, IT WAS MY FAULT!
I WAS KINDA...
...UNDER A LOT OF PRES-SURE, AND...
Ngh...
mmf!
I JUST...
NGH...
WAAAAAH!

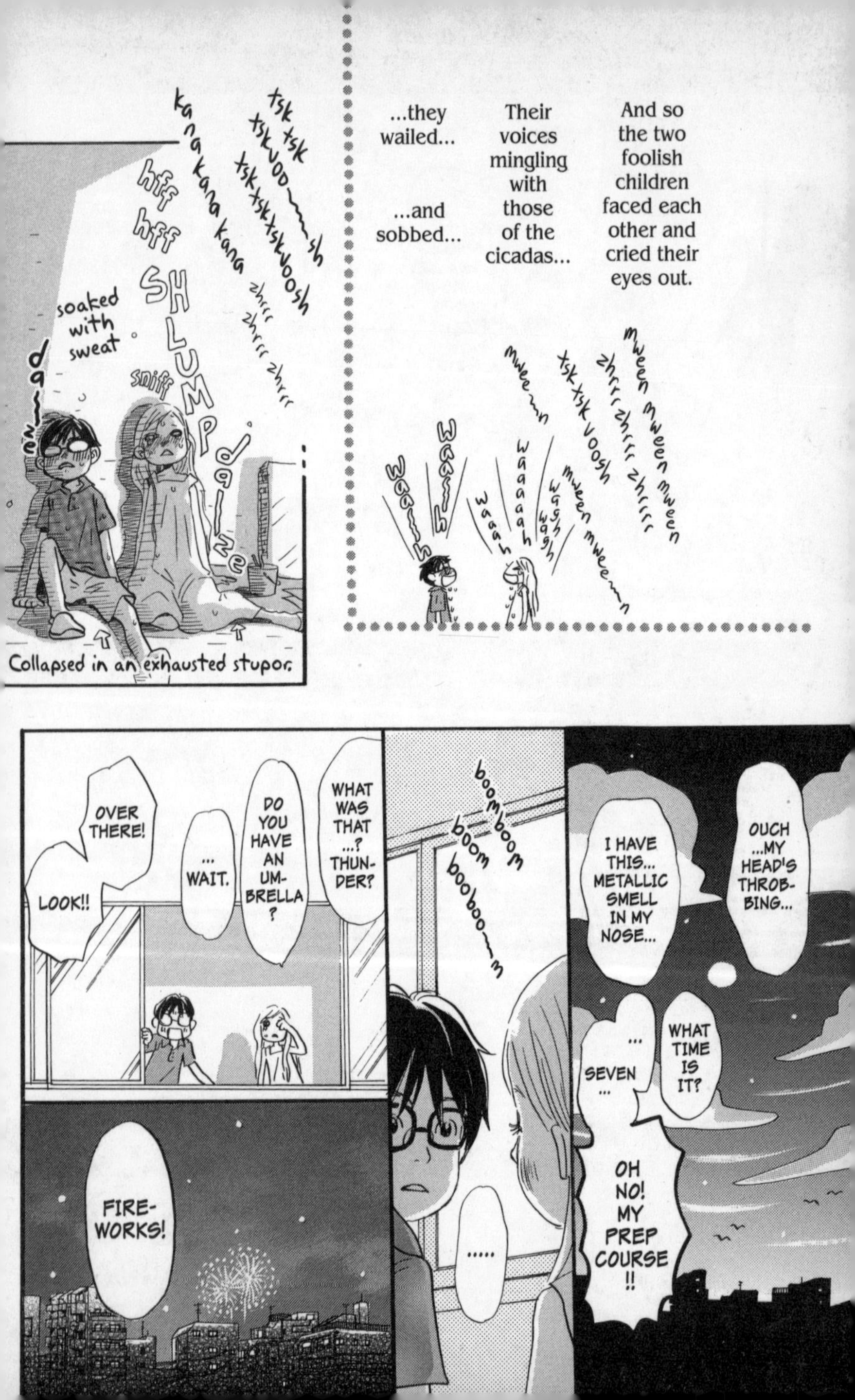
And so the two foolish children faced each other and cried their eyes out.
Their voices mingling with those of the cicadas...
...they wailed...
...and sobbed...
mween mween mween
zhrrr zhrrr zhrrr
tsk tsk voosh
mwee~n
mween mwee~n
waaaaaah
wagh wagh
waaah
waa~h
waa~h
tsk tsk
tskvoo~sh
tsk tsk tsk tskvoosh
kana kana kana kana
zhrrr zhrrr zhrrr
hff hff
SHLUMP
sniff
da~ngle
da~ze
soaked with sweat
Collapsed in an exhausted stupor.
OUCH ...MY HEAD'S THROBBING...
I HAVE THIS... METALLIC SMELL IN MY NOSE...
WHAT TIME IS IT?
... SEVEN ...
OH NO! MY PREP COURSE!!
boom boom boom boo boo~m
.....
WHAT WAS THAT ...? THUNDER?
DO YOU HAVE AN UMBRELLA?
... WAIT.
OVER THERE! LOOK!!
FIRE-WORKS!

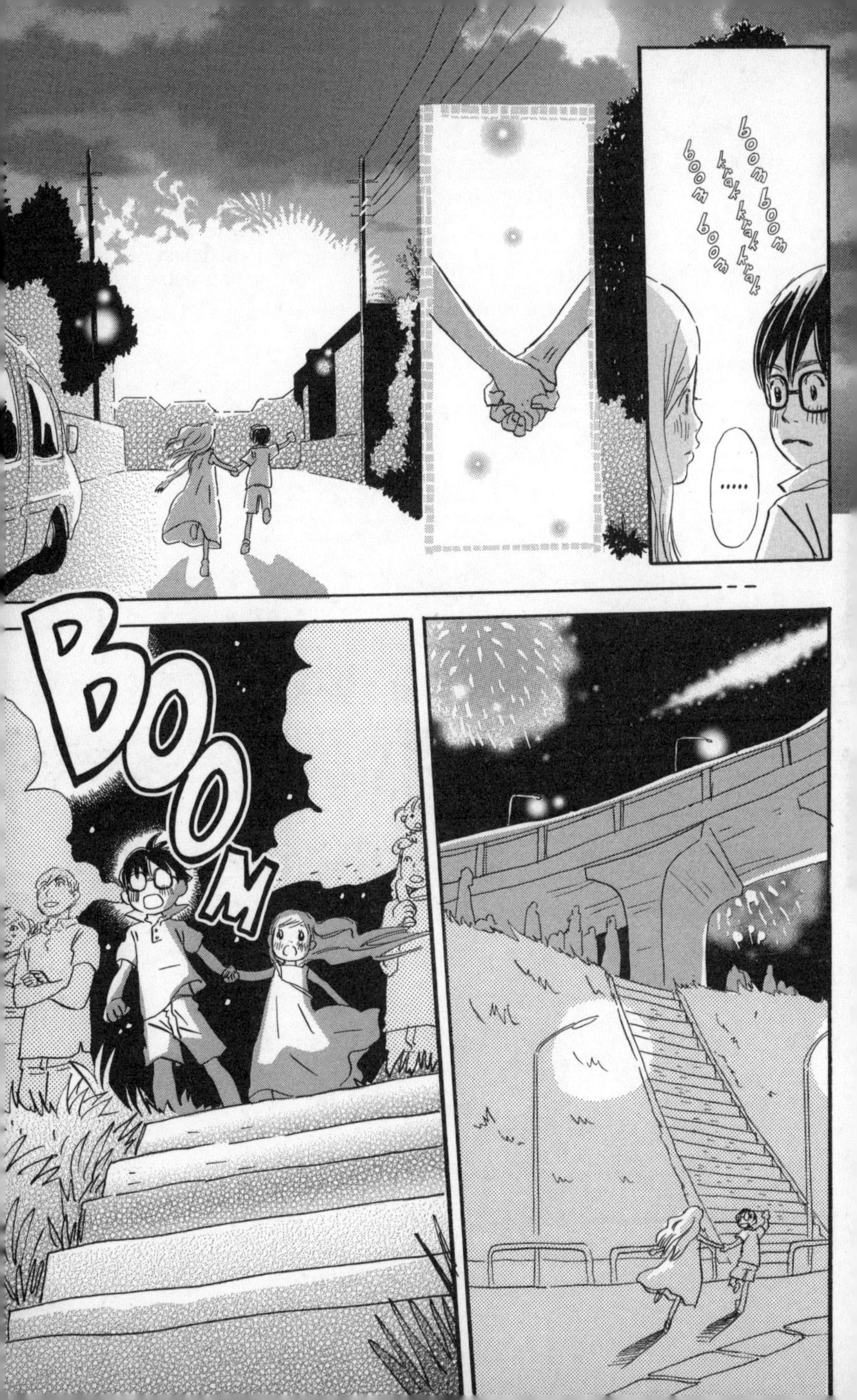
boom boom
krak krak krak
boom boom boom
......
BOOOM

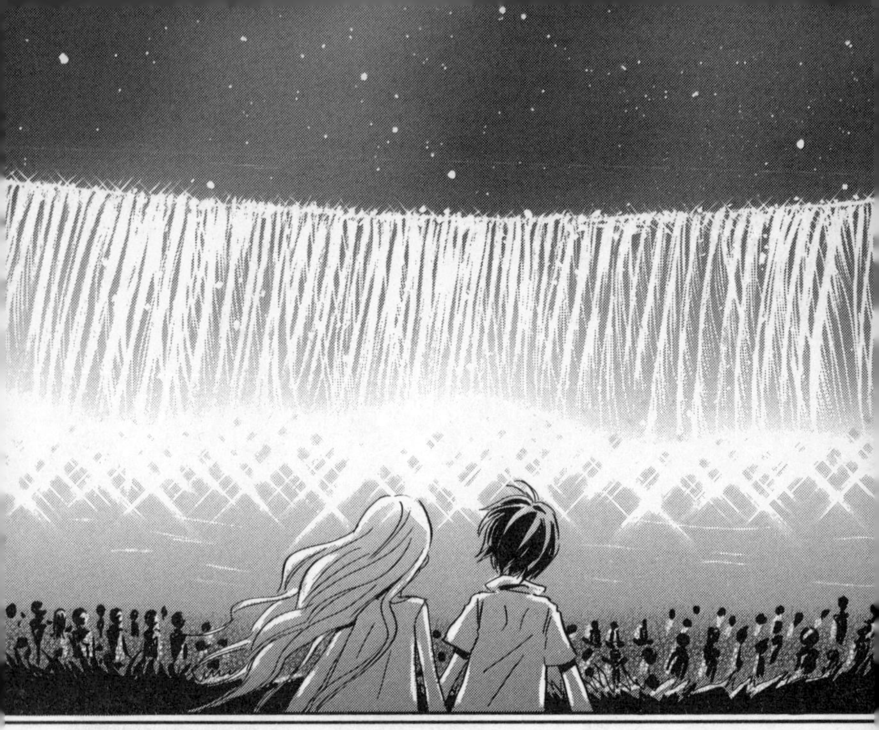

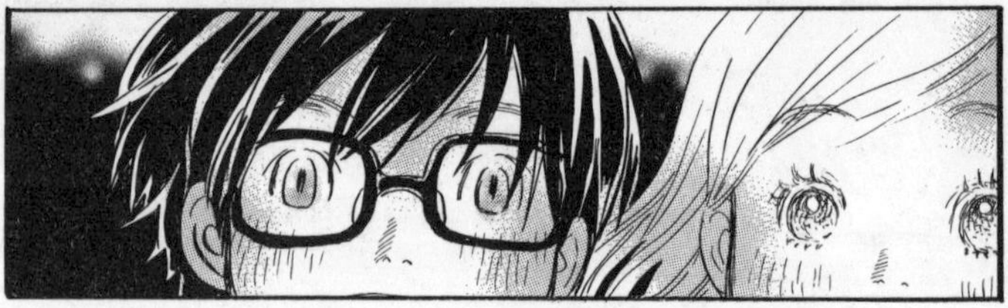

MISS HANAMOTO'S GRINNING AND SHOUTING, "WOW! HOW BEAUTIFUL!"

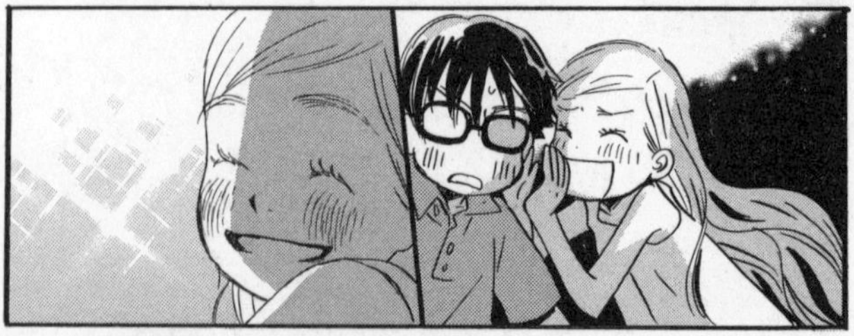

LIKE SHE HADN'T BEEN BAWLING HER EYES OUT
JUST A LITTLE WHILE AGO. (...WELL, OKAY, I WAS TOO...)

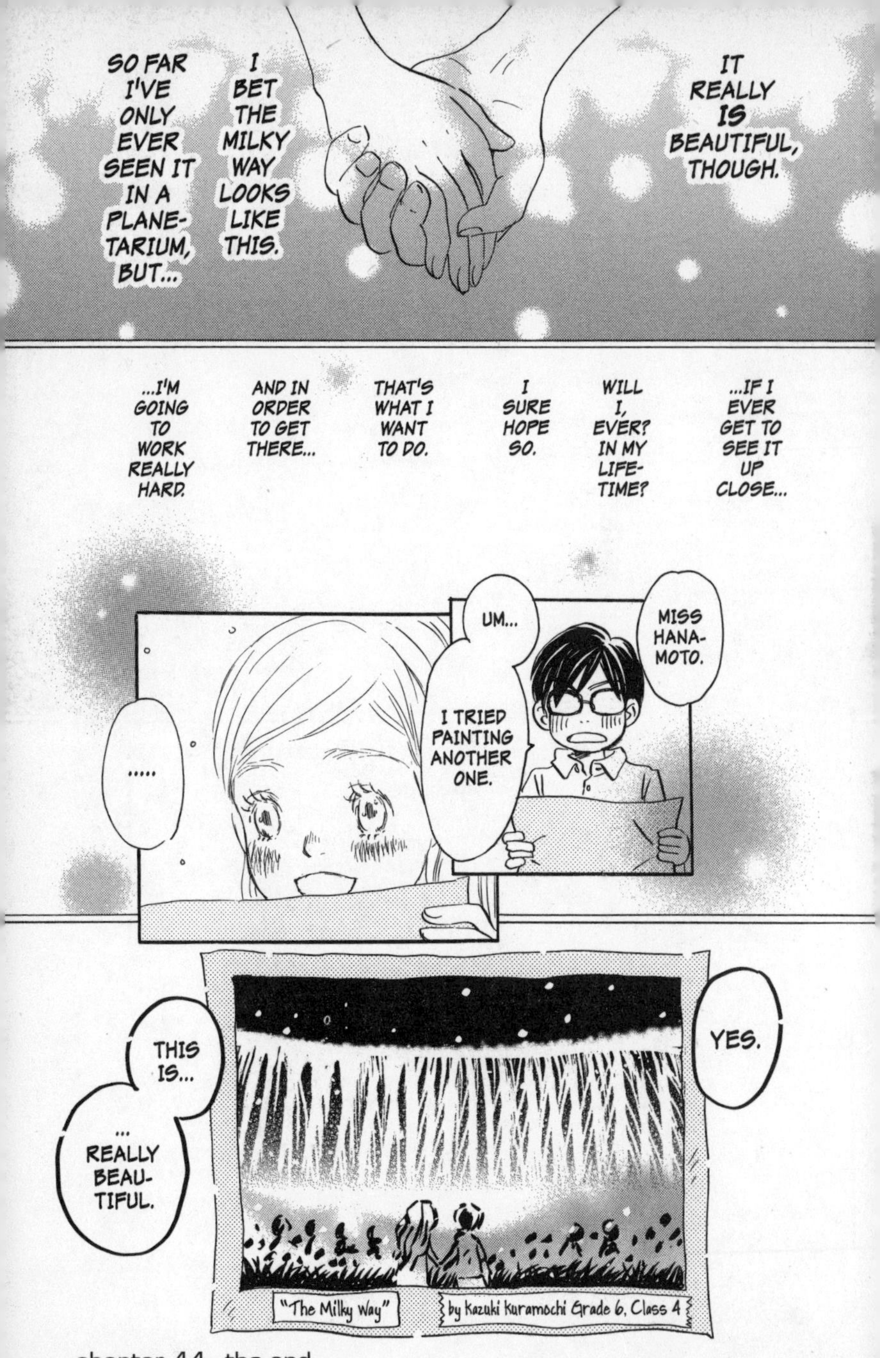
IT REALLY IS BEAUTIFUL, THOUGH.
I BET THE MILKY WAY LOOKS LIKE THIS.
SO FAR I'VE ONLY EVER SEEN IT IN A PLANETARIUM, BUT...
...IF I EVER GET TO SEE IT UP CLOSE...
WILL I, EVER? IN MY LIFETIME?
I SURE HOPE SO.
THAT'S WHAT I WANT TO DO.
AND IN ORDER TO GET THERE...
...I'M GOING TO WORK REALLY HARD.
MISS HANAMOTO.
UM...
I TRIED PAINTING ANOTHER ONE.
.....
YES.
THIS IS...
...REALLY BEAUTIFUL.
"The Milky Way"
by Kazuki Kuramochi Grade 6, Class 4

chapter 44—the end—

#6:

Someone gave me
a really pretty
bouquet, so...

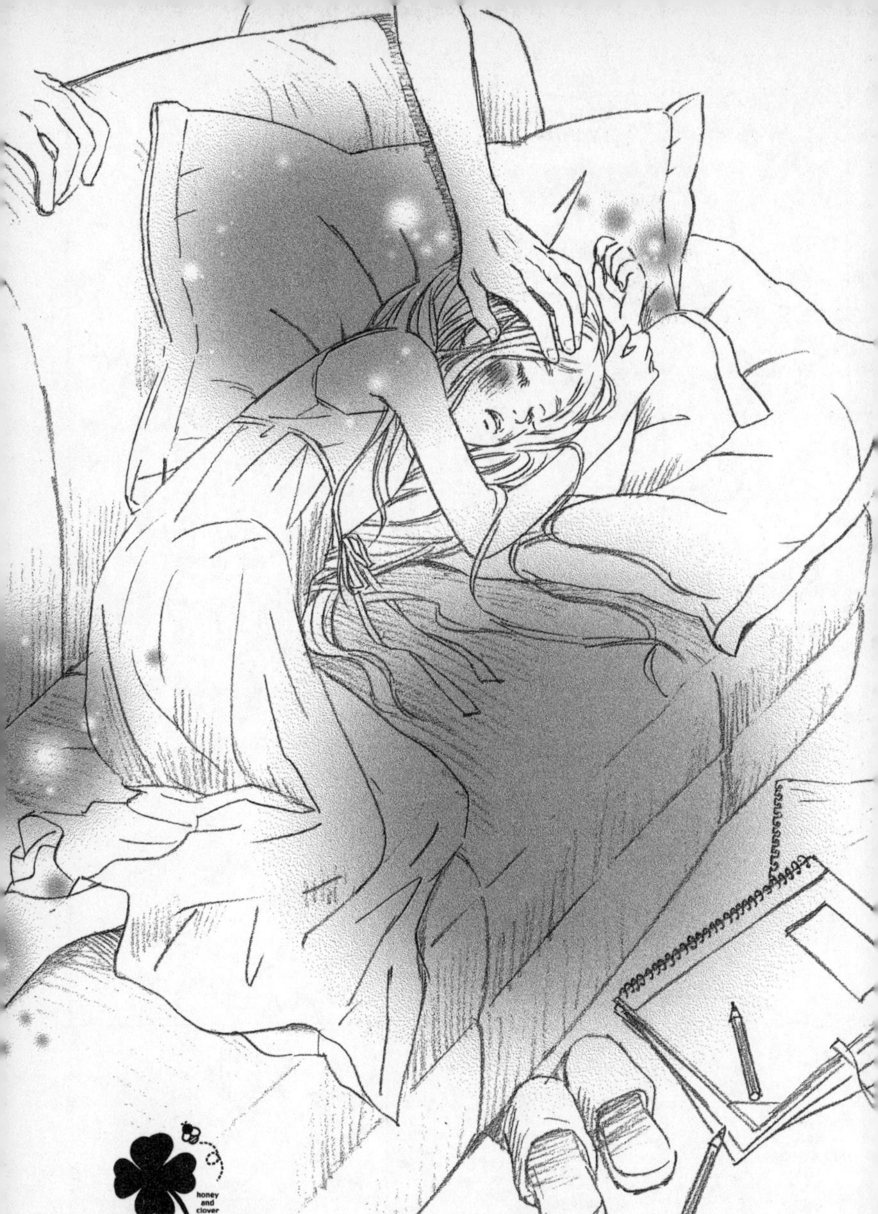

chapter 45

honey and clover

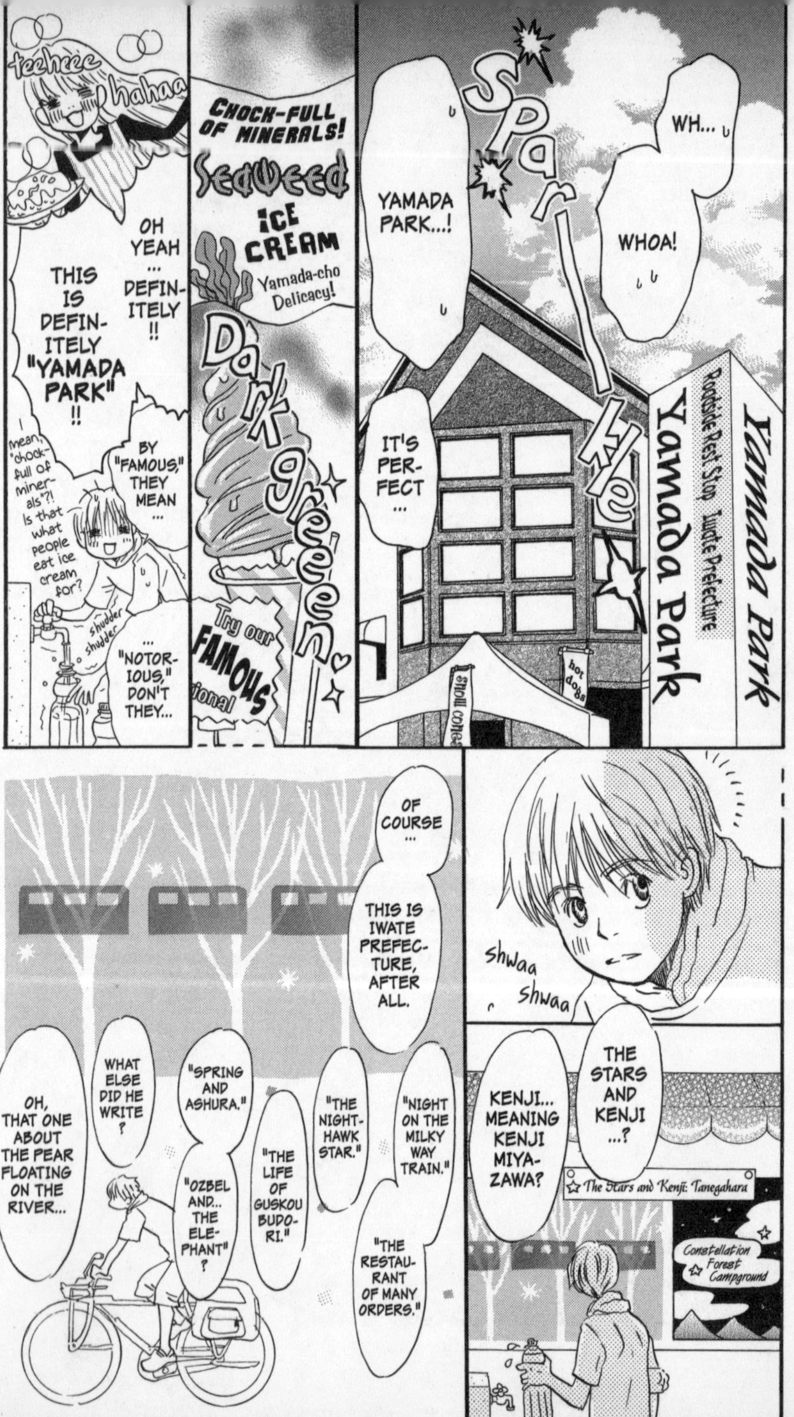
Sparkle
WH... WHOA!
YAMADA PARK...!
IT'S PERFECT...
Yamada Park
Roadside Rest Stop Iwate Prefecture
Yamada Park
hot dogs
CHOCK-FULL OF MINERALS!
Seaweed ICE CREAM
Yamada-cho Delicacy!
Dark green
Try our FAMOUS
teeheee hahaa
OH YEAH... DEFINITELY!!
THIS IS DEFINITELY "YAMADA PARK"!!
BY "FAMOUS," THEY MEAN...
... "NOTORIOUS," DON'T THEY...
shudder shudder
I mean, "chock-full of minerals"?! Is that what people eat ice cream for?
shwaa shwaa
THE STARS AND KENJI...?
KENJI... MEANING KENJI MIYAZAWA?
The Stars and Kenji: Tanegahara
Constellation Forest Campground
OF COURSE...
THIS IS IWATE PREFECTURE, AFTER ALL.
"NIGHT ON THE MILKY WAY TRAIN."
"THE NIGHTHAWK STAR."
"THE RESTAURANT OF MANY ORDERS."
"THE LIFE OF GUSKOU BUDORI."
"SPRING AND ASHURA."
"OZBEL AND... THE ELEPHANT"?
WHAT ELSE DID HE WRITE?
OH, THAT ONE ABOUT THE PEAR FLOATING ON THE RIVER...

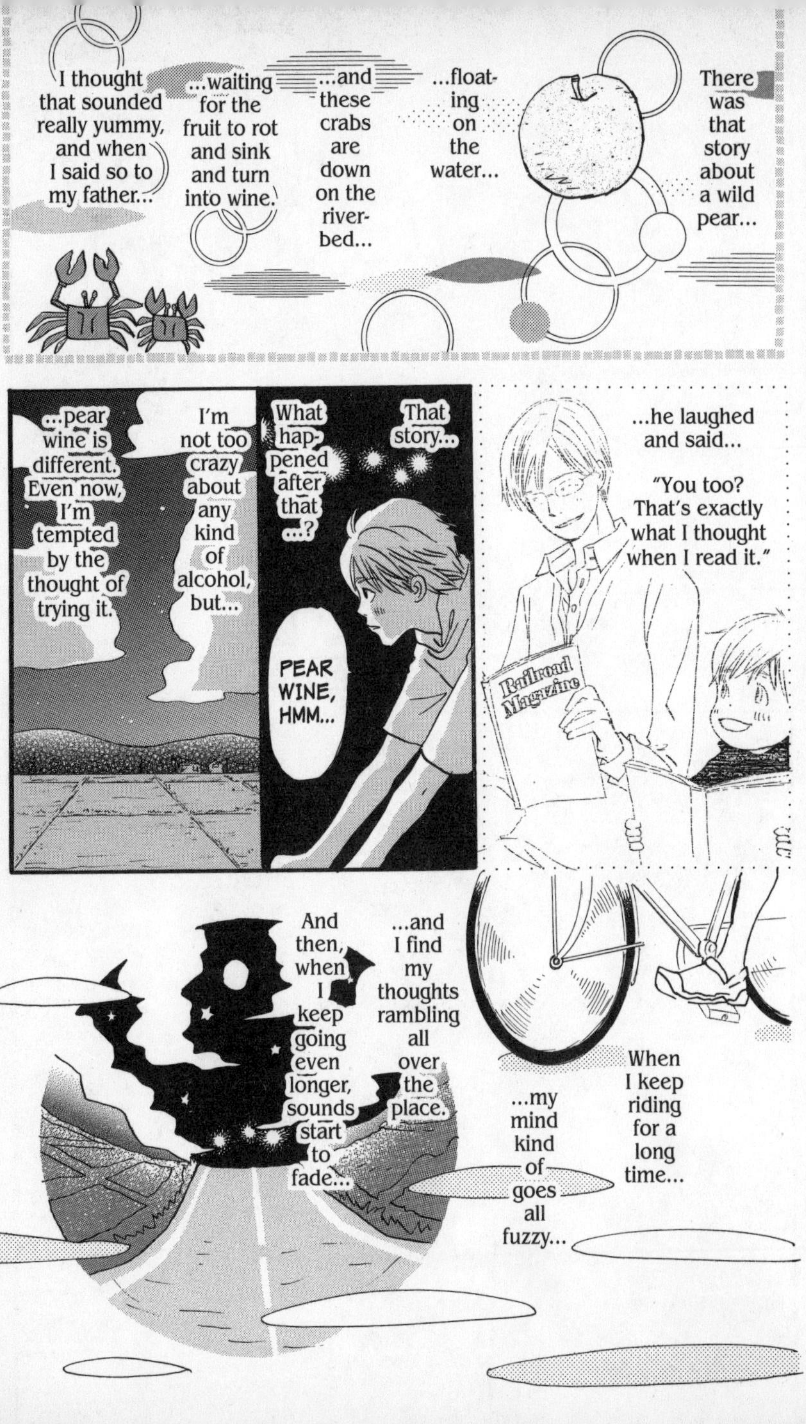
There was that story about a wild pear...
...floating on the water...
...and these crabs are down on the riverbed...
...waiting for the fruit to rot and sink and turn into wine.
I thought that sounded really yummy, and when I said so to my father...
...he laughed and said...
"You too? That's exactly what I thought when I read it."
Railroad Magazine
That story...
What happened after that...?
PEAR WINE, HMM...
I'm not too crazy about any kind of alcohol, but...
...pear wine is different. Even now, I'm tempted by the thought of trying it.
When I keep riding for a long time...
...my mind kind of goes all fuzzy...
...and I find my thoughts rambling all over the place.
And then, when I keep going even longer, sounds start to fade...

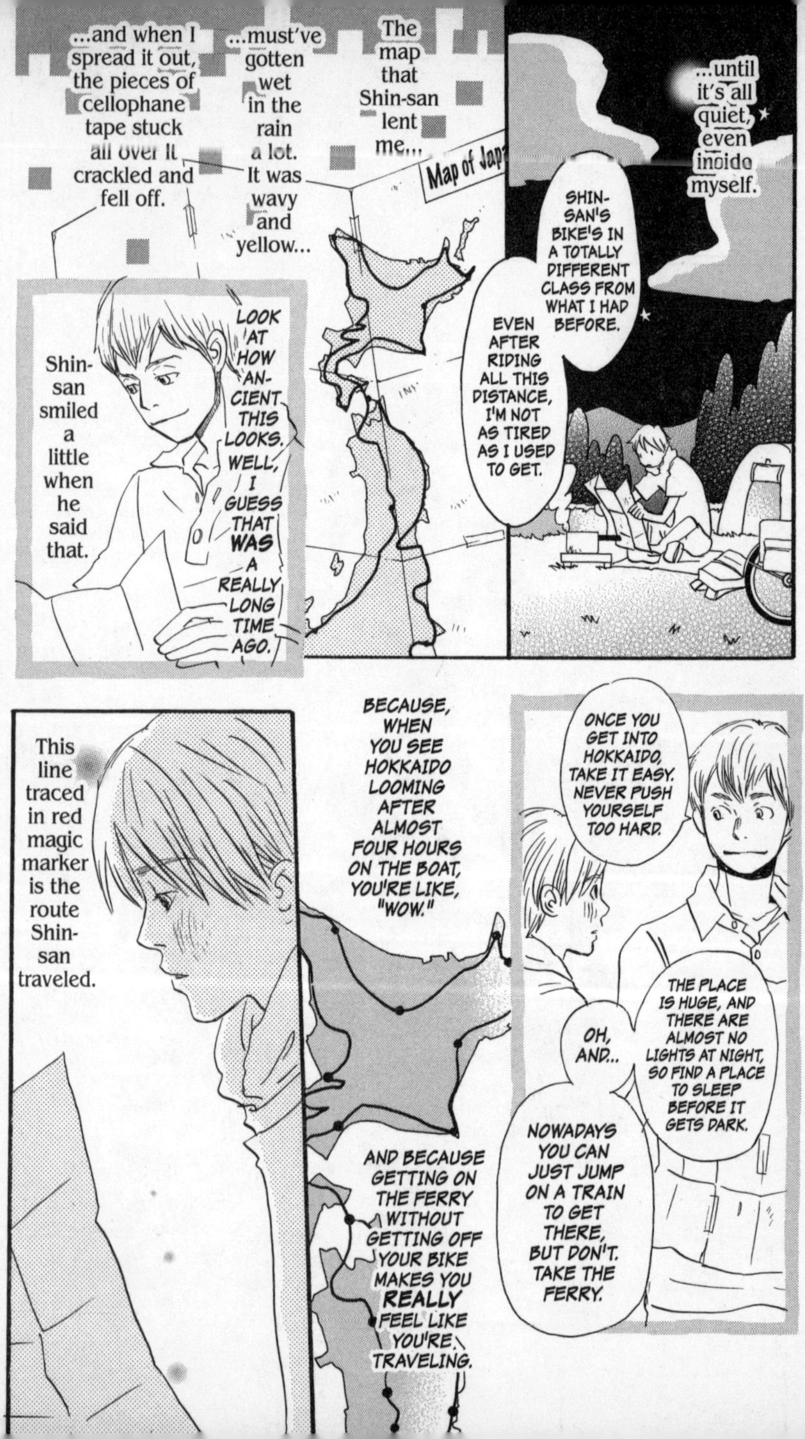
...until it's all quiet, even inside myself.
SHIN-SAN'S BIKE'S IN A TOTALLY DIFFERENT CLASS FROM WHAT I HAD BEFORE.
EVEN AFTER RIDING ALL THIS DISTANCE, I'M NOT AS TIRED AS I USED TO GET.
The map that Shin-san lent me...
...must've gotten wet in the rain a lot. It was wavy and yellow...
...and when I spread it out, the pieces of cellophane tape stuck all over it crackled and fell off.
Map of Jap
LOOK AT HOW ANCIENT THIS LOOKS. WELL, I GUESS THAT WAS A REALLY LONG TIME AGO.
Shin-san smiled a little when he said that.
ONCE YOU GET INTO HOKKAIDO, TAKE IT EASY. NEVER PUSH YOURSELF TOO HARD.
THE PLACE IS HUGE, AND THERE ARE ALMOST NO LIGHTS AT NIGHT, SO FIND A PLACE TO SLEEP BEFORE IT GETS DARK.
OH, AND...
NOWADAYS YOU CAN JUST JUMP ON A TRAIN TO GET THERE, BUT DON'T. TAKE THE FERRY.
BECAUSE, WHEN YOU SEE HOKKAIDO LOOMING AFTER ALMOST FOUR HOURS ON THE BOAT, YOU'RE LIKE, "WOW."
AND BECAUSE GETTING ON THE FERRY WITHOUT GETTING OFF YOUR BIKE MAKES YOU REALLY FEEL LIKE YOU'RE TRAVELING.
This line traced in red magic marker is the route Shin-san traveled.

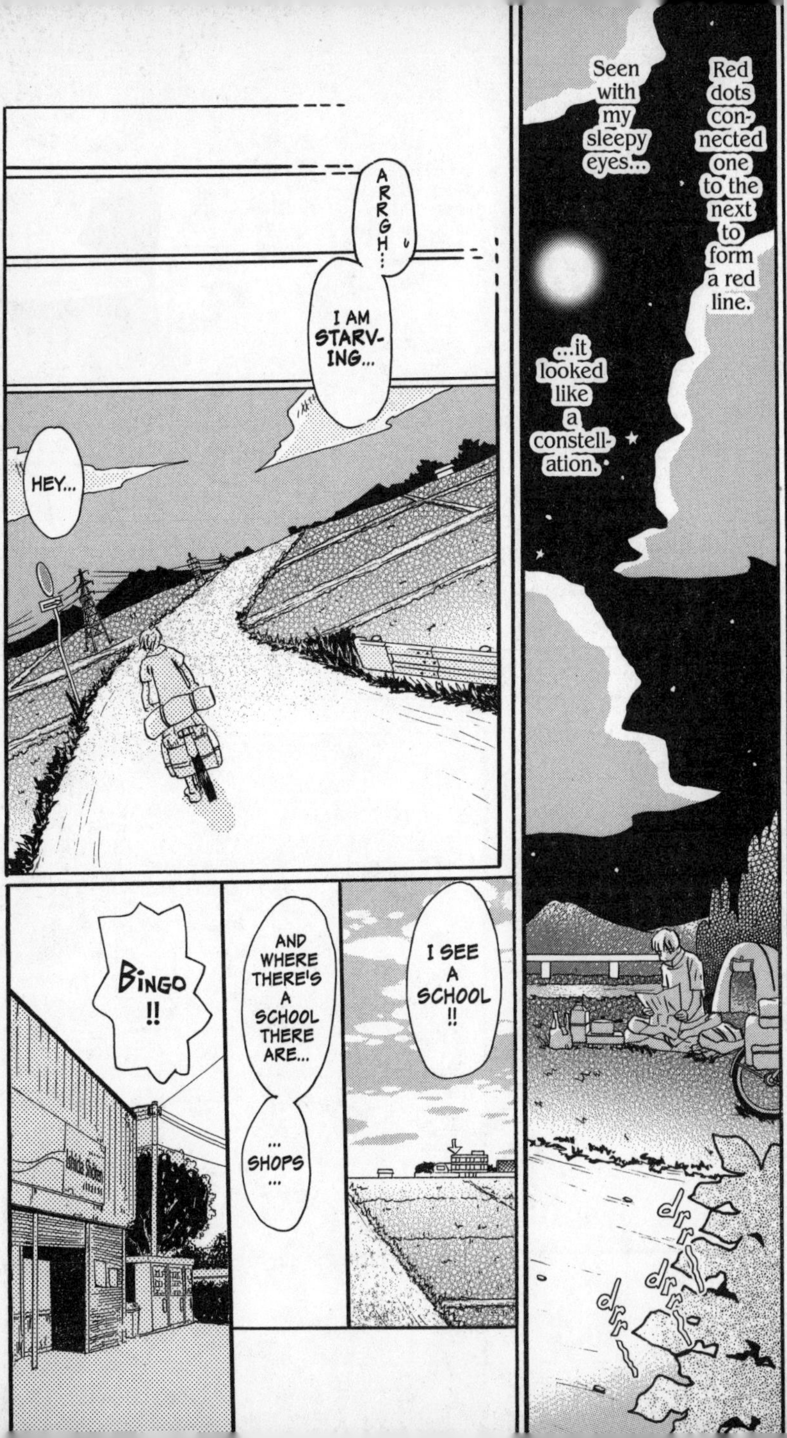
Red dots connected one to the next to form a red line.
Seen with my sleepy eyes...
...it looked like a constellation.
drr~ drr~ drr~
ARRGH...
I AM STARVING...
HEY...
I SEE A SCHOOL!!
AND WHERE THERE'S A SCHOOL THERE ARE...
...SHOPS...
BINGO!!

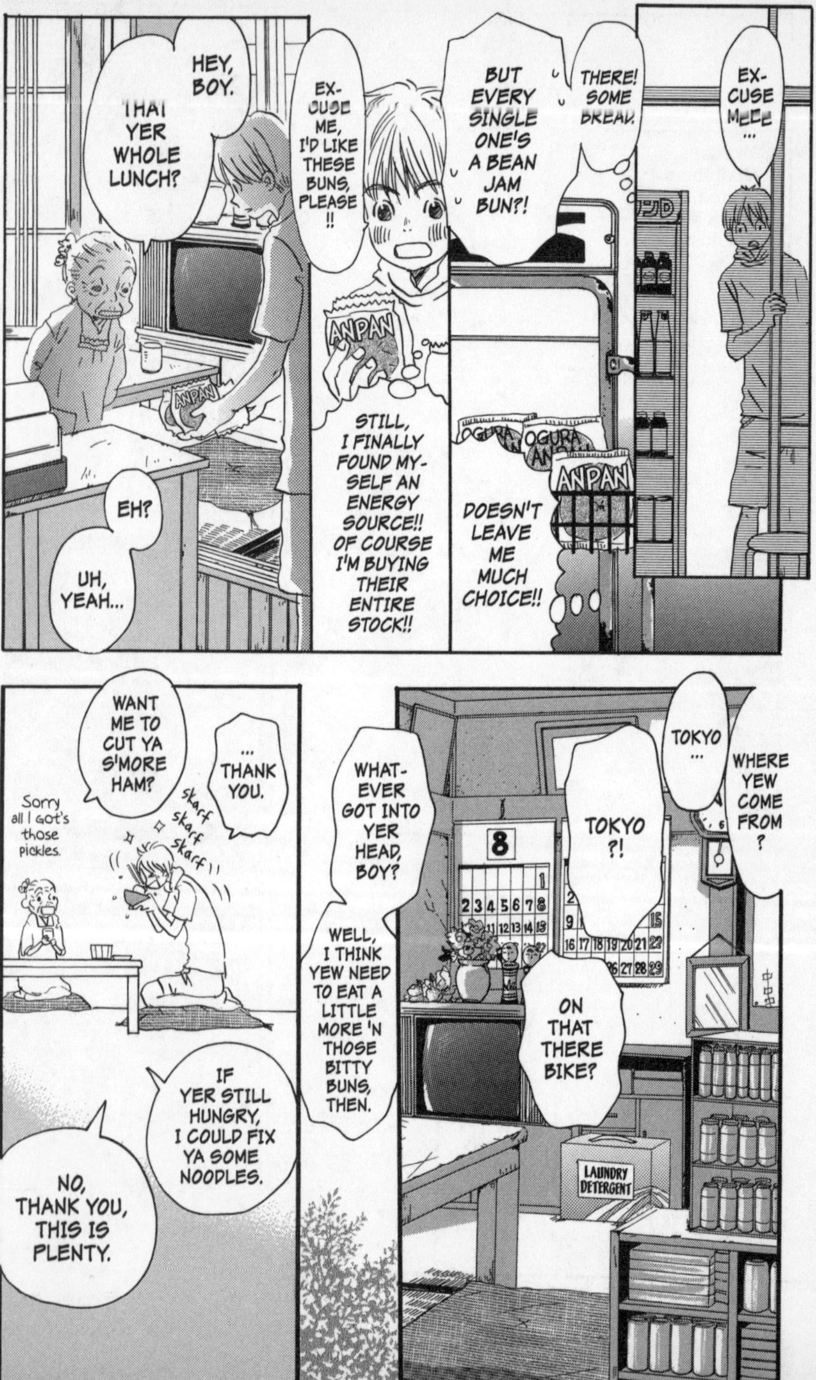
EX-CUSE MEEE...
THERE! SOME BREAD.
BUT EVERY SINGLE ONE'S A BEAN JAM BUN?!
DOESN'T LEAVE ME MUCH CHOICE!!
EX-CUSE ME, I'D LIKE THESE BUNS, PLEASE!!
ANPAN
STILL, I FINALLY FOUND MY-SELF AN ENERGY SOURCE!! OF COURSE I'M BUYING THEIR ENTIRE STOCK!!
HEY, BOY.
THAT YER WHOLE LUNCH?
EH?
UH, YEAH...
WHERE YEW COME FROM?
TOKYO...
TOKYO?!
ON THAT THERE BIKE?
LAUNDRY DETERGENT
WHAT-EVER GOT INTO YER HEAD, BOY?
WELL, I THINK YEW NEED TO EAT A LITTLE MORE 'N THOSE BITTY BUNS, THEN.
WANT ME TO CUT YA S'MORE HAM?
... THANK YOU.
Sorry all I got's those pickles.
skarf skarf skarf
IF YER STILL HUNGRY, I COULD FIX YA SOME NOODLES.
NO, THANK YOU, THIS IS PLENTY.

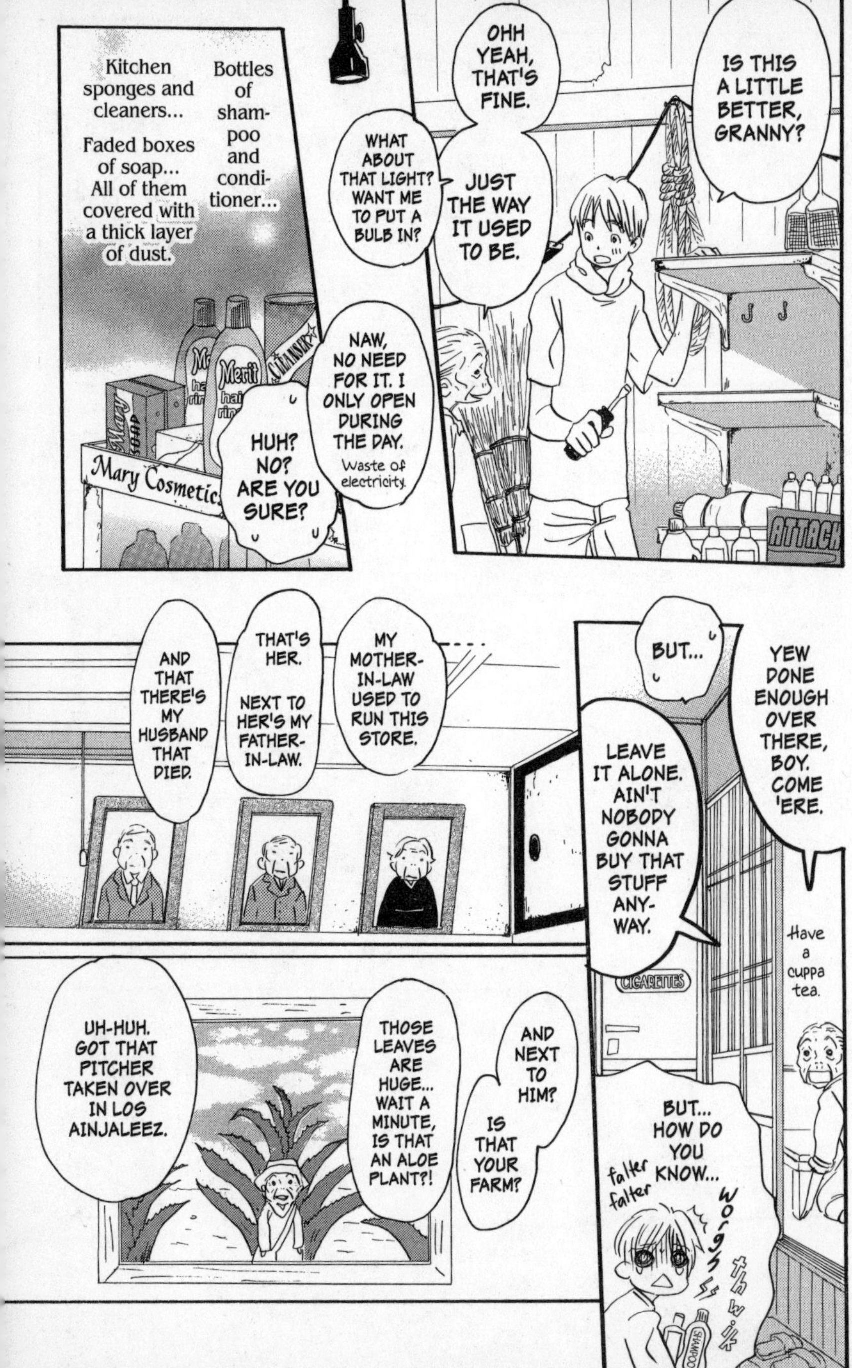
IS THIS A LITTLE BETTER, GRANNY?
OHH YEAH, THAT'S FINE.
JUST THE WAY IT USED TO BE.
WHAT ABOUT THAT LIGHT? WANT ME TO PUT A BULB IN?
NAW, NO NEED FOR IT. I ONLY OPEN DURING THE DAY.
Waste of electricity.
ATTACH
Bottles of shampoo and conditioner...
Kitchen sponges and cleaners...
Faded boxes of soap... All of them covered with a thick layer of dust.
HUH? NO? ARE YOU SURE?
Merit
CLEANSER
Mary Cosmetics
YEW DONE ENOUGH OVER THERE, BOY. COME 'ERE.
BUT...
LEAVE IT ALONE. AIN'T NOBODY GONNA BUY THAT STUFF ANYWAY.
Have a cuppa tea.
CIGARETTES
BUT... HOW DO YOU KNOW...
falter falter
SHAMPOO
MY MOTHER-IN-LAW USED TO RUN THIS STORE.
THAT'S HER.
NEXT TO HER'S MY FATHER-IN-LAW.
AND THAT THERE'S MY HUSBAND THAT DIED.
AND NEXT TO HIM?
IS THAT YOUR FARM?
THOSE LEAVES ARE HUGE... WAIT A MINUTE, IS THAT AN ALOE PLANT?!
UH-HUH. GOT THAT PITCHER TAKEN OVER IN LOS AINJALEEZ.

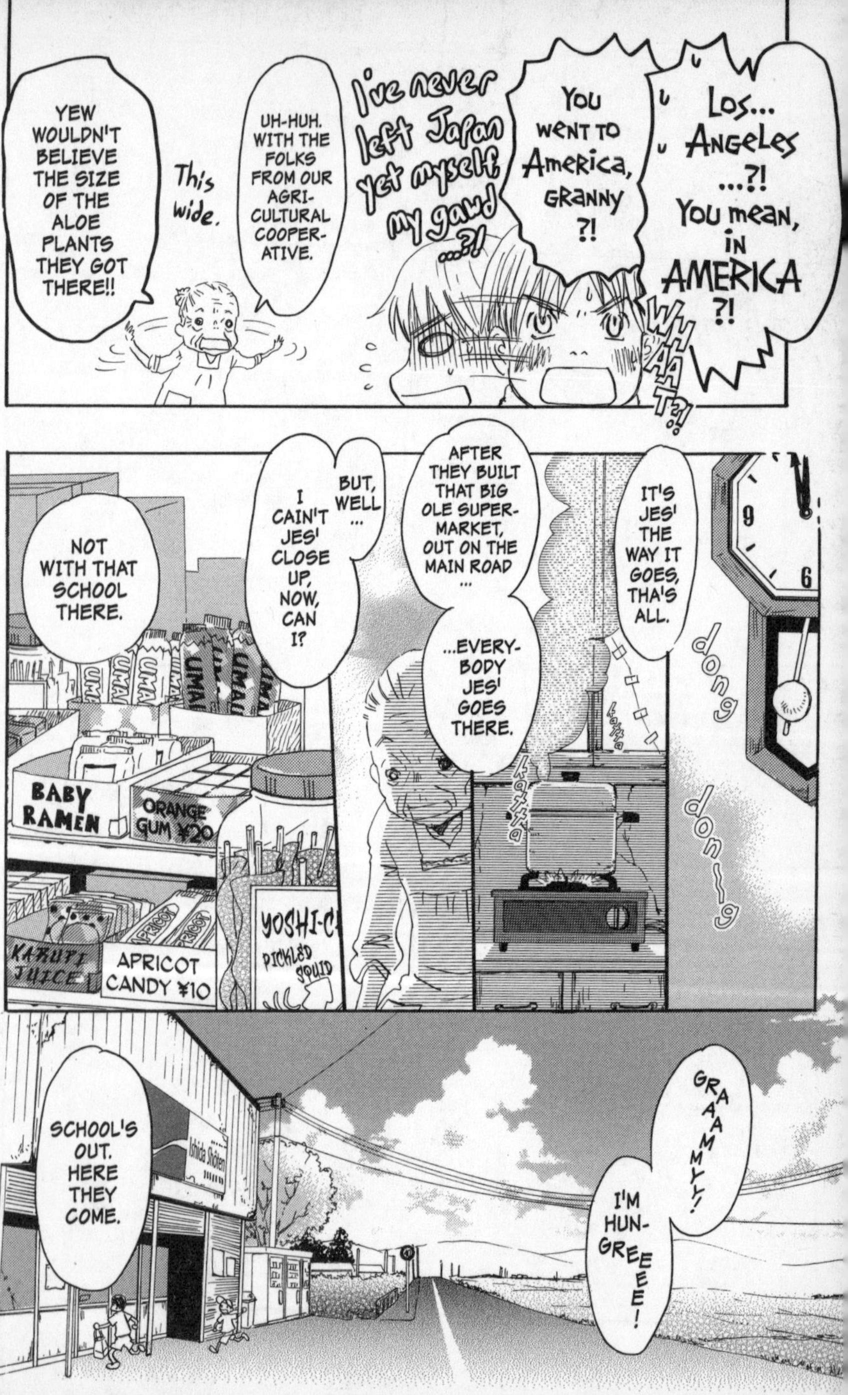
Los... Angeles ...?! You mean, in AMERICA?!
WHAAAT?!
You went to America, granny?!
I've never left Japan yet myself, my gawd ...?!
UH-HUH. WITH THE FOLKS FROM OUR AGRI-CULTURAL COOPER-ATIVE.
This wide.
YEW WOULDN'T BELIEVE THE SIZE OF THE ALOE PLANTS THEY GOT THERE!!
dong dong~g
IT'S JES' THE WAY IT GOES, THA'S ALL.
katta katta
AFTER THEY BUILT THAT BIG OLE SUPER-MARKET, OUT ON THE MAIN ROAD ...
...EVERY-BODY JES' GOES THERE.
BUT, WELL ...
I CAIN'T JES' CLOSE UP, NOW, CAN I?
NOT WITH THAT SCHOOL THERE.
UMAI
BABY RAMEN
ORANGE GUM ¥20
YOSHI-C
PICKLED SQUID
APRICOT
KARUTI JUICE
APRICOT CANDY ¥10
GRAAAMMYY!
I'M HUN-GREEEE!
SCHOOL'S OUT. HERE THEY COME.
Ishida Shoten

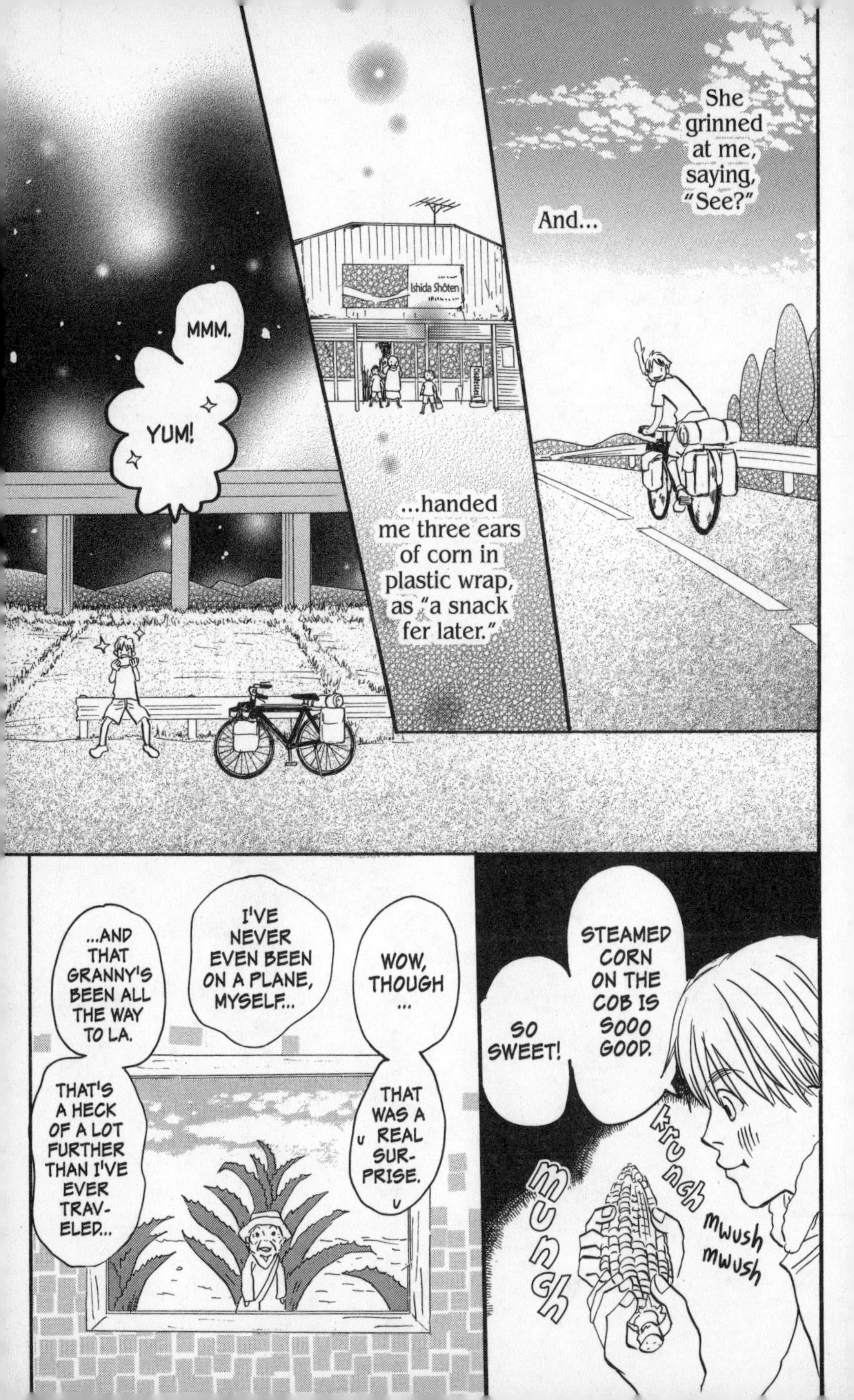
She grinned at me, saying, "See?"
And...
Ishida Shôten
...handed me three ears of corn in plastic wrap, as "a snack fer later."
MMM.
YUM!
STEAMED CORN ON THE COB IS SOOO GOOD.
SO SWEET!
krunch
munch
mwush mwush
WOW, THOUGH...
THAT WAS A REAL SURPRISE.
I'VE NEVER EVEN BEEN ON A PLANE, MYSELF...
...AND THAT GRANNY'S BEEN ALL THE WAY TO LA.
THAT'S A HECK OF A LOT FURTHER THAN I'VE EVER TRAVELED...

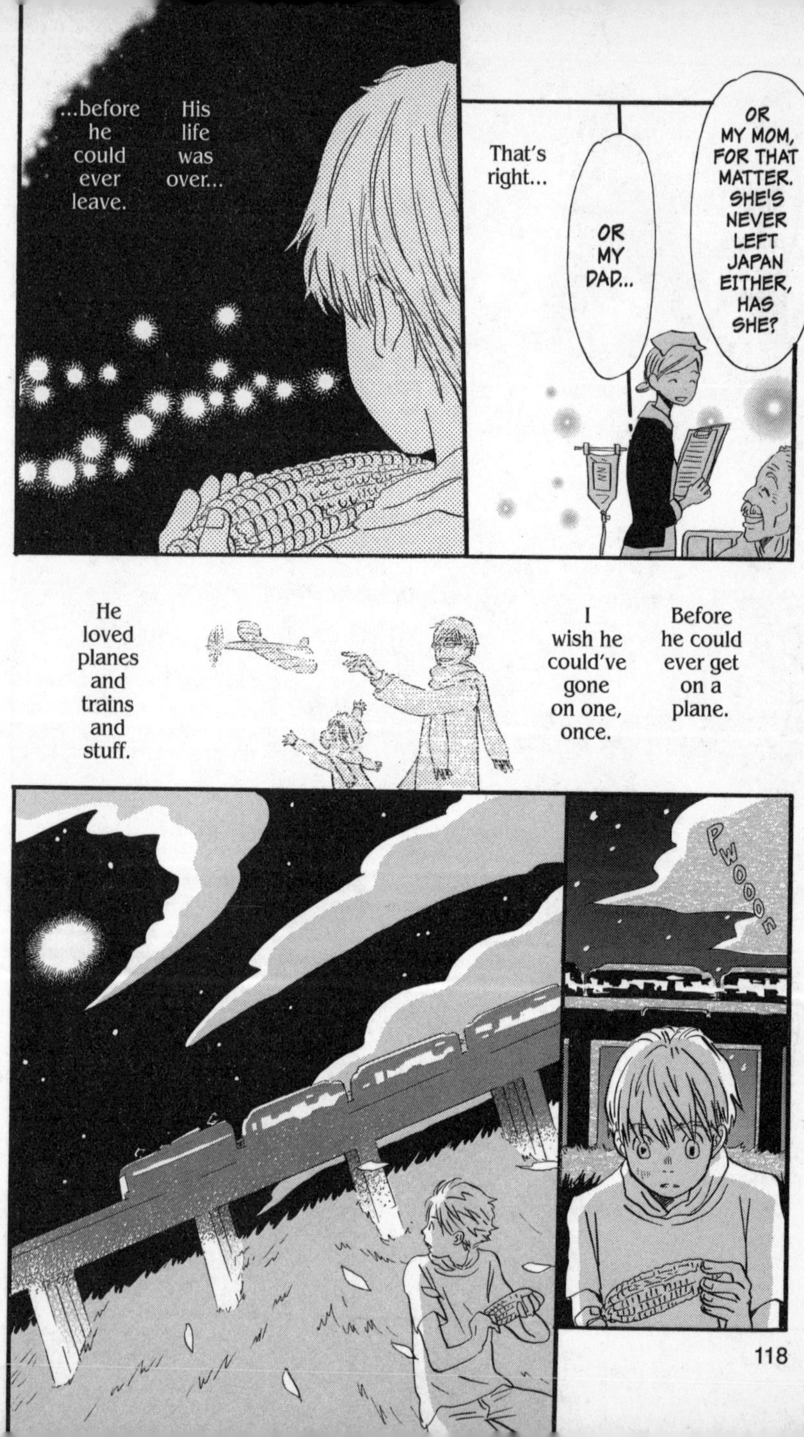
OR MY MOM, FOR THAT MATTER. SHE'S NEVER LEFT JAPAN EITHER, HAS SHE?
OR MY DAD...
That's right...
His life was over...
...before he could ever leave.
Before he could ever get on a plane.
I wish he could've gone on one, once.
He loved planes and trains and stuff.
PWOOOO

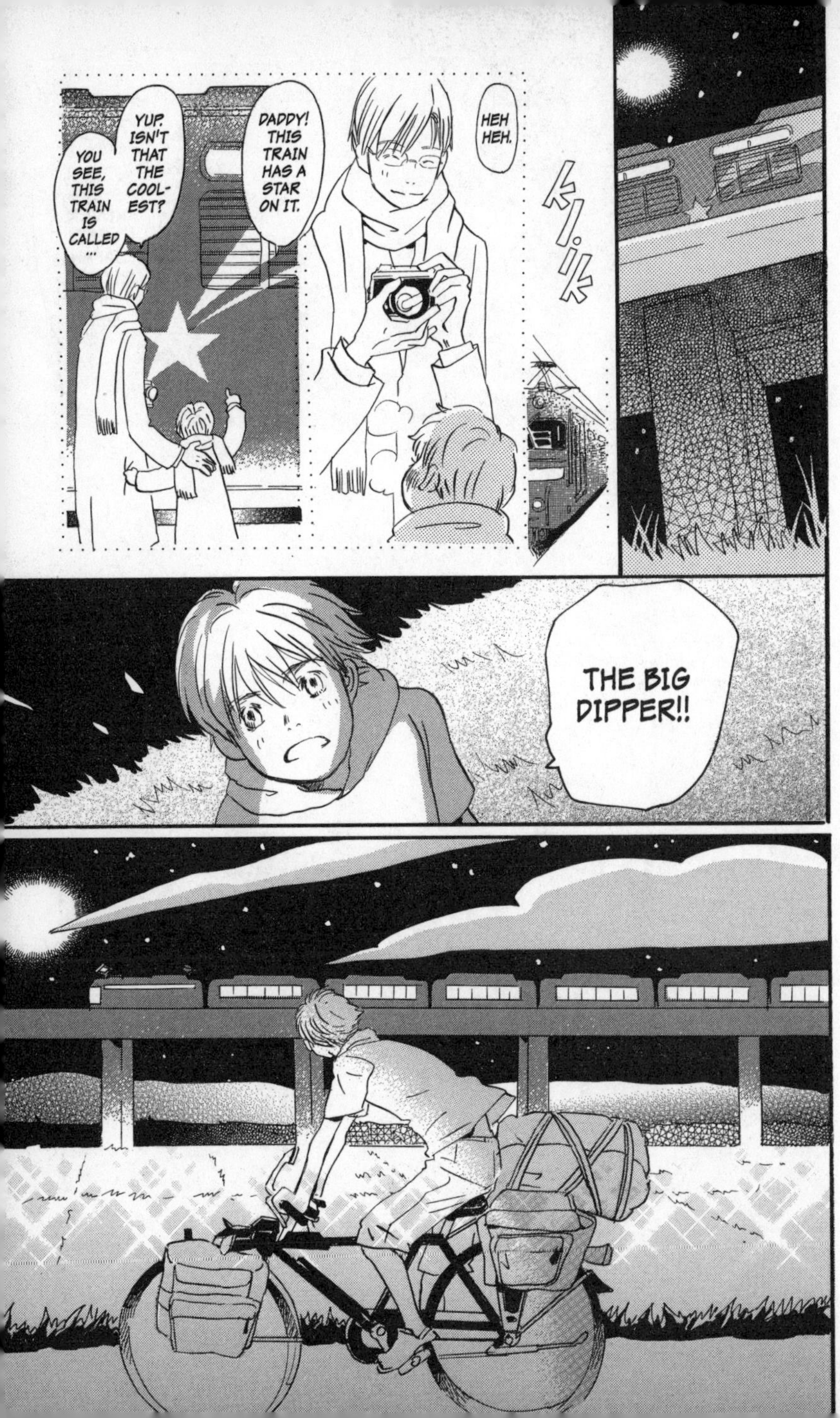
KLIK
HEH HEH.
DADDY! THIS TRAIN HAS A STAR ON IT.
YUP. ISN'T THAT THE COOL-EST?
YOU SEE, THIS TRAIN IS CALLED ...
THE BIG DIPPER!!

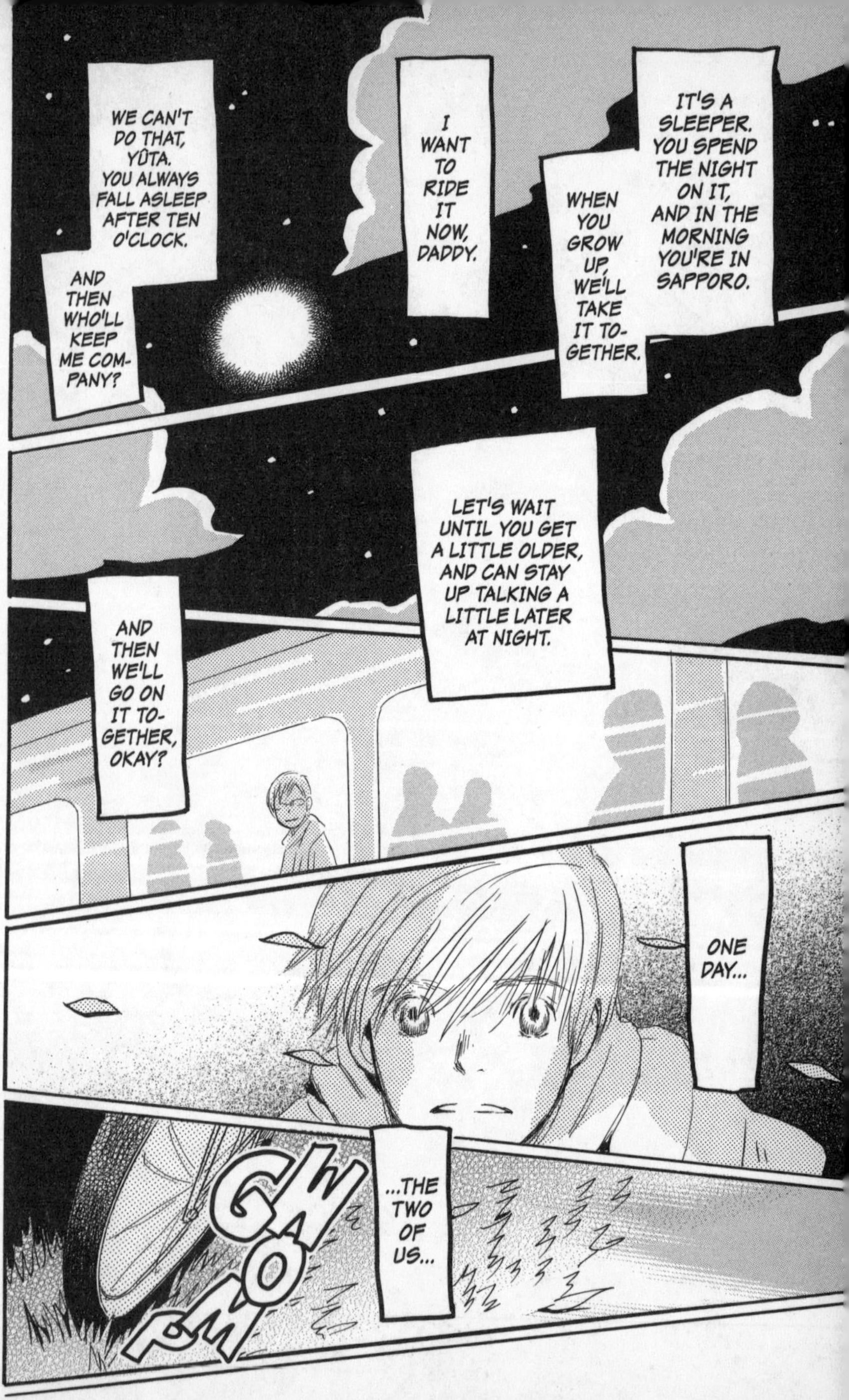
IT'S A SLEEPER. YOU SPEND THE NIGHT ON IT, AND IN THE MORNING YOU'RE IN SAPPORO.
WHEN YOU GROW UP, WE'LL TAKE IT TO-GETHER.
I WANT TO RIDE IT NOW, DADDY.
WE CAN'T DO THAT, YÛTA. YOU ALWAYS FALL ASLEEP AFTER TEN O'CLOCK.
AND THEN WHO'LL KEEP ME COM-PANY?
LET'S WAIT UNTIL YOU GET A LITTLE OLDER, AND CAN STAY UP TALKING A LITTLE LATER AT NIGHT.
AND THEN WE'LL GO ON IT TO-GETHER, OKAY?
ONE DAY...
...THE TWO OF US...
GWOMP

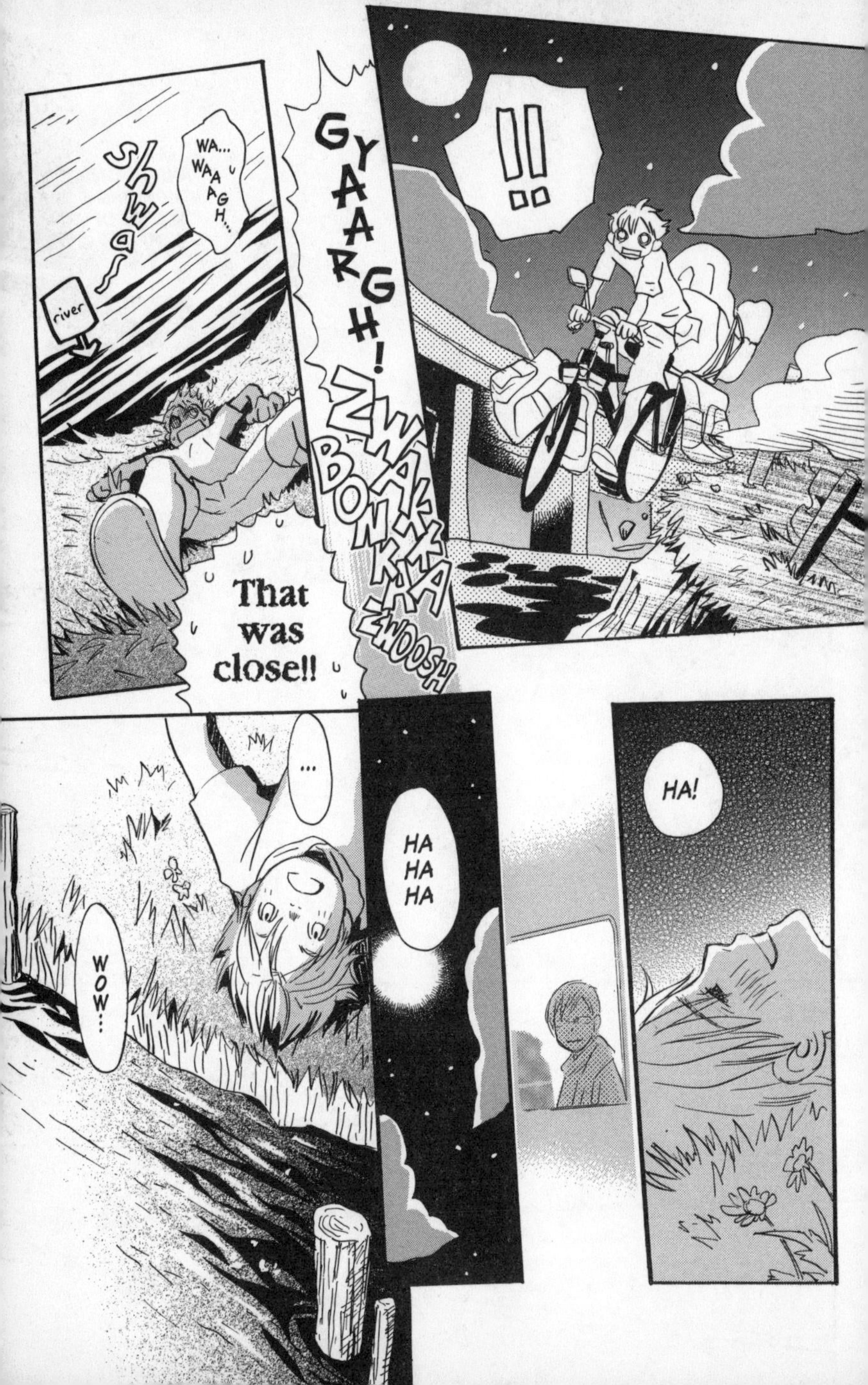
!!
GYAARGH!
ZWAKKA
BONKA
ZWOOSH
WA... WAAAGH...
shwa~
river
That was close!!
HA!
HA HA HA
...
WOW...

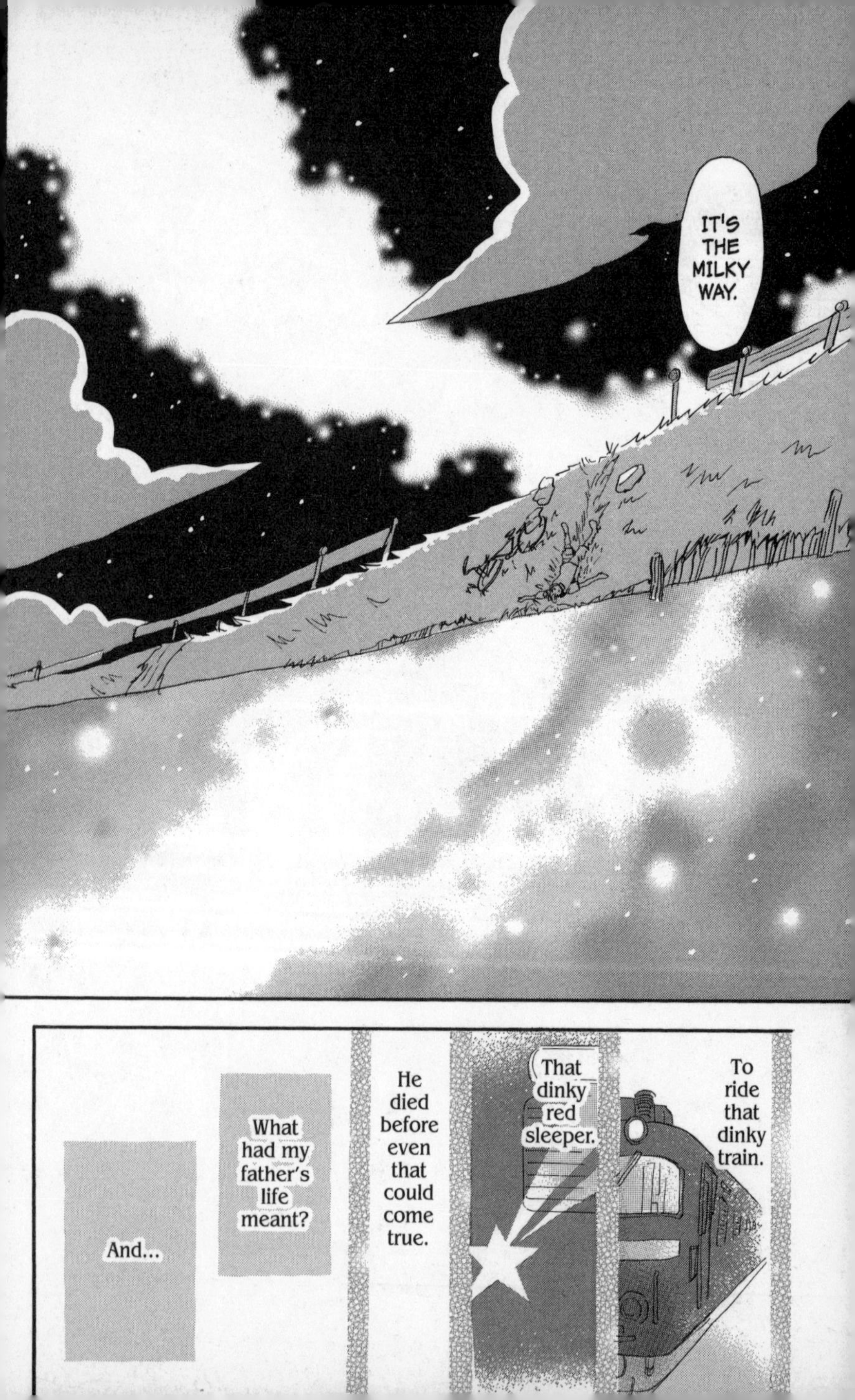
IT'S THE MILKY WAY.
To ride that dinky train.
That dinky red sleeper.
He died before even that could come true.
What had my father's life meant?
And...

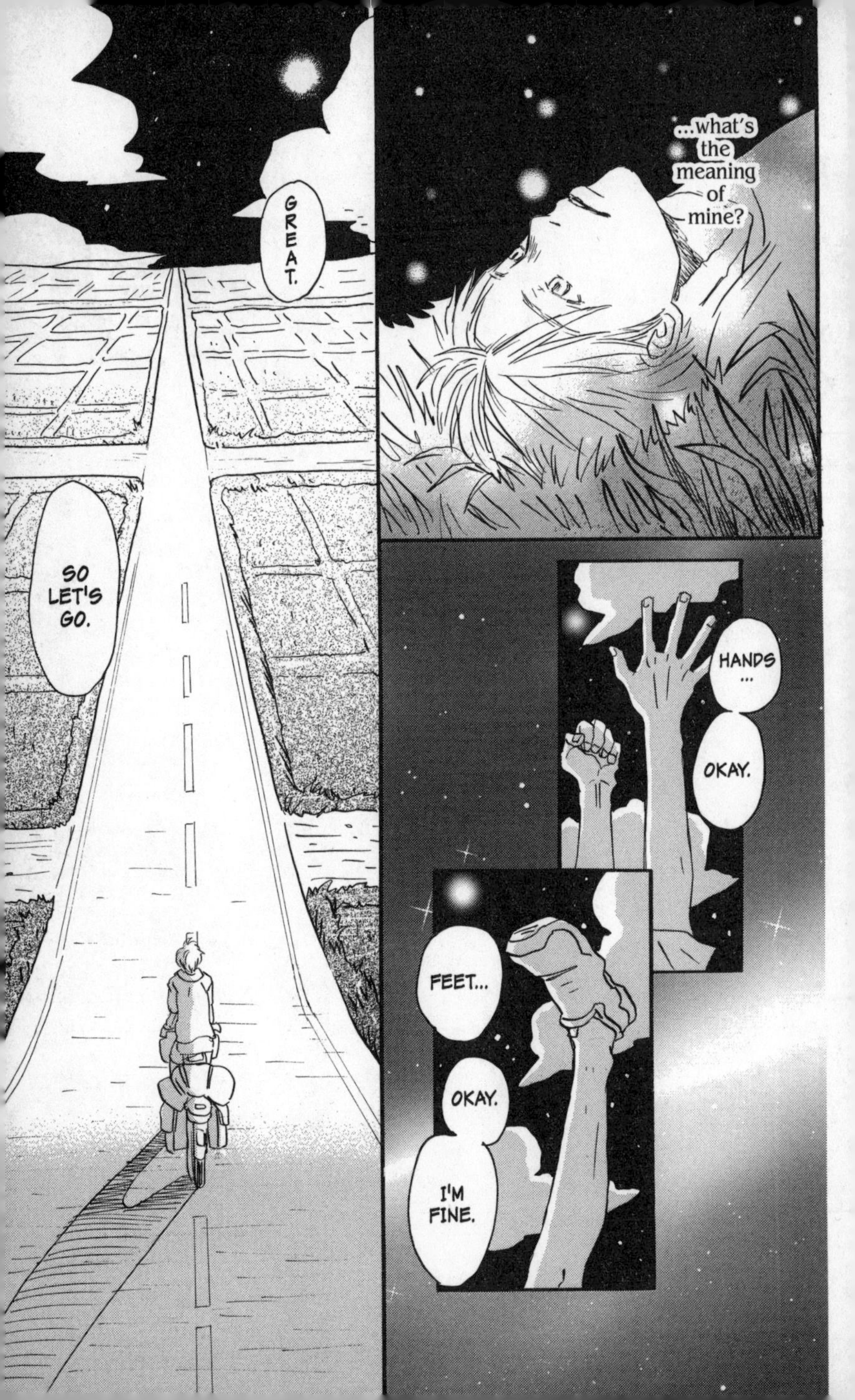
...what's the meaning of mine?
HANDS ...
OKAY.
FEET...
OKAY.
I'M FINE.
GREAT.
SO LET'S GO.

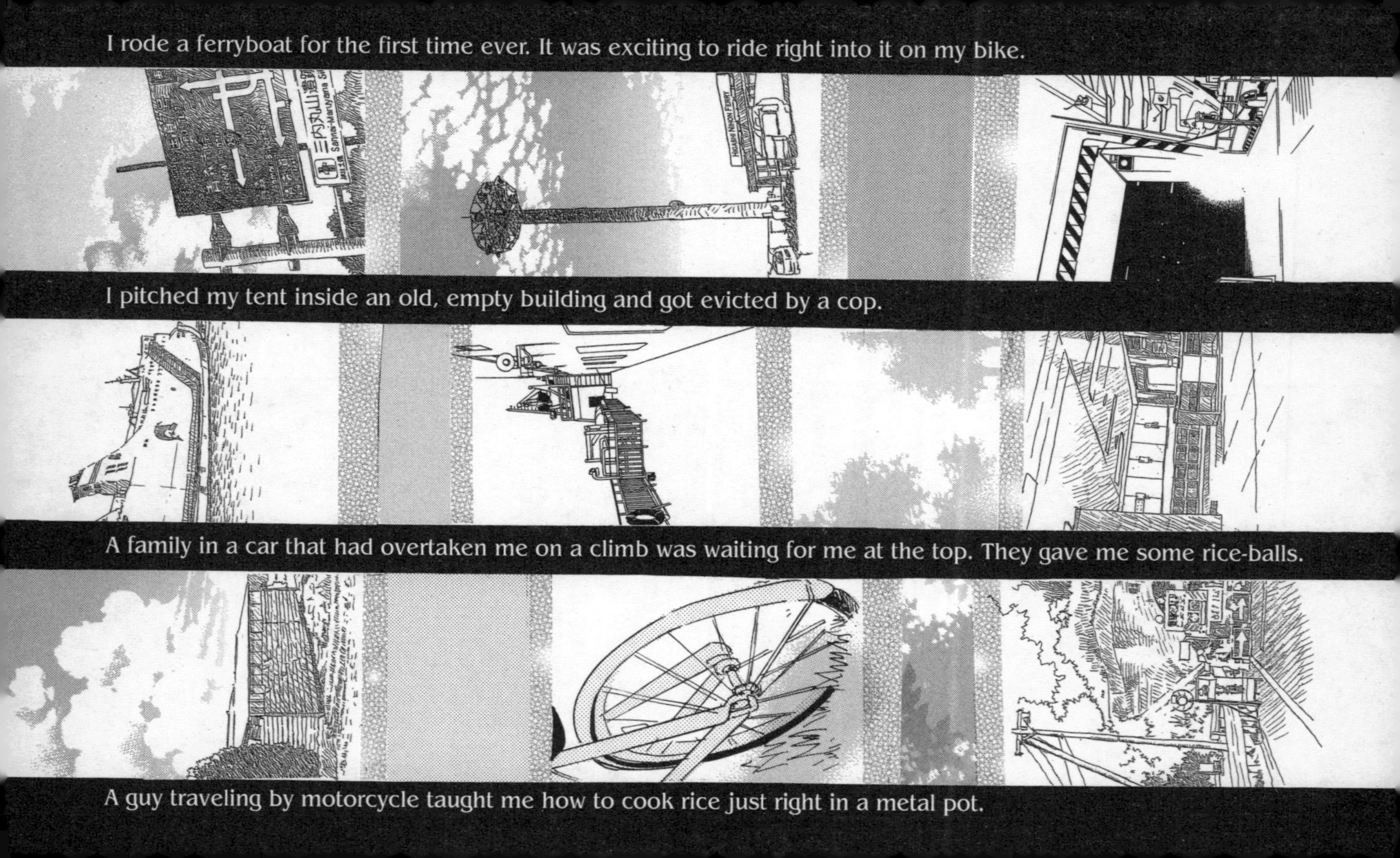
I rode a ferryboat for the first time ever. It was exciting to ride right into it on my bike.
HIGASHI NIHON FERRY
I pitched my tent inside an old, empty building and got evicted by a cop.
A family in a car that had overtaken me on a climb was waiting for me at the top. They gave me some rice-balls.
A guy traveling by motorcycle taught me how to cook rice just right in a metal pot.

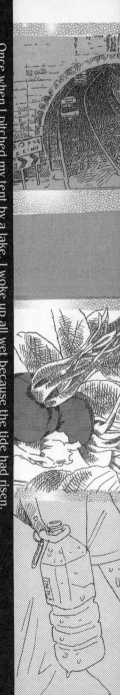

I stopped a few times for a couple days of work filling silos with hay.

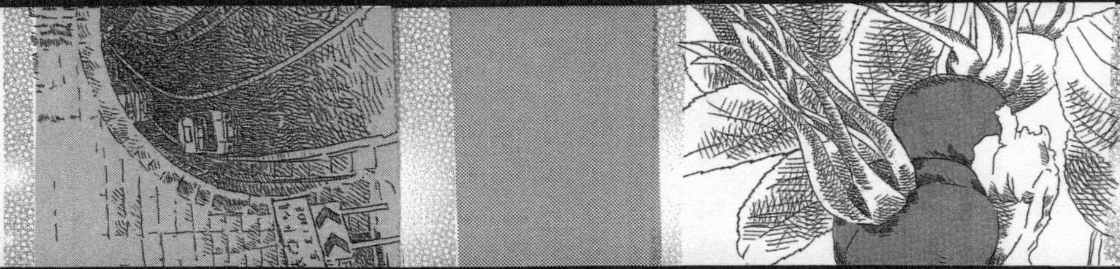

Once when I pitched my tent by a lake, I woke up all wet because the tide had risen.

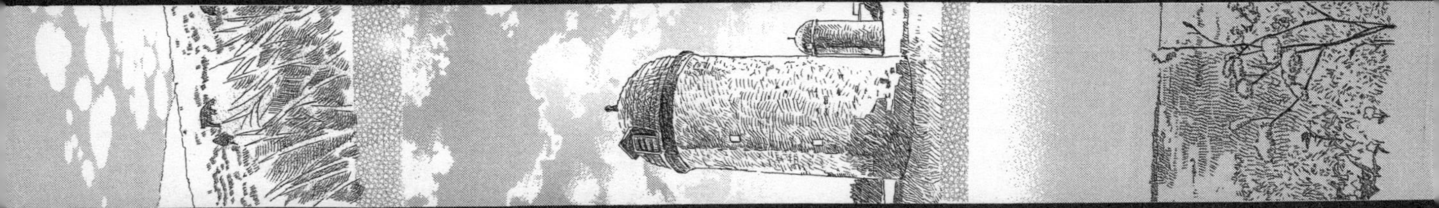

I saw the sea shining lead-grey. I saw the shadows of clouds crossing the road.

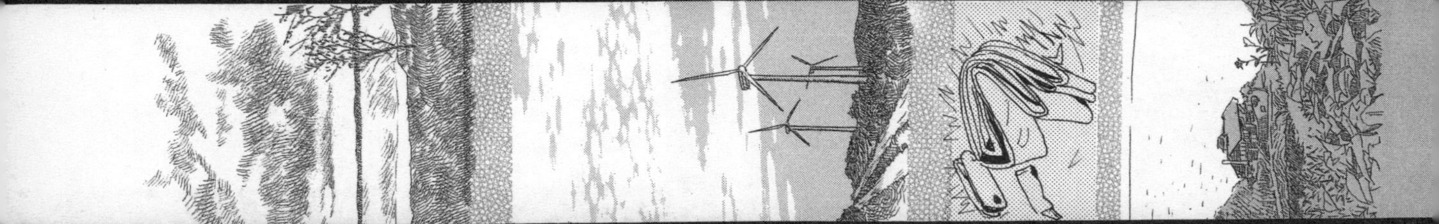

I rode and ate and slept and got up and rode some more.

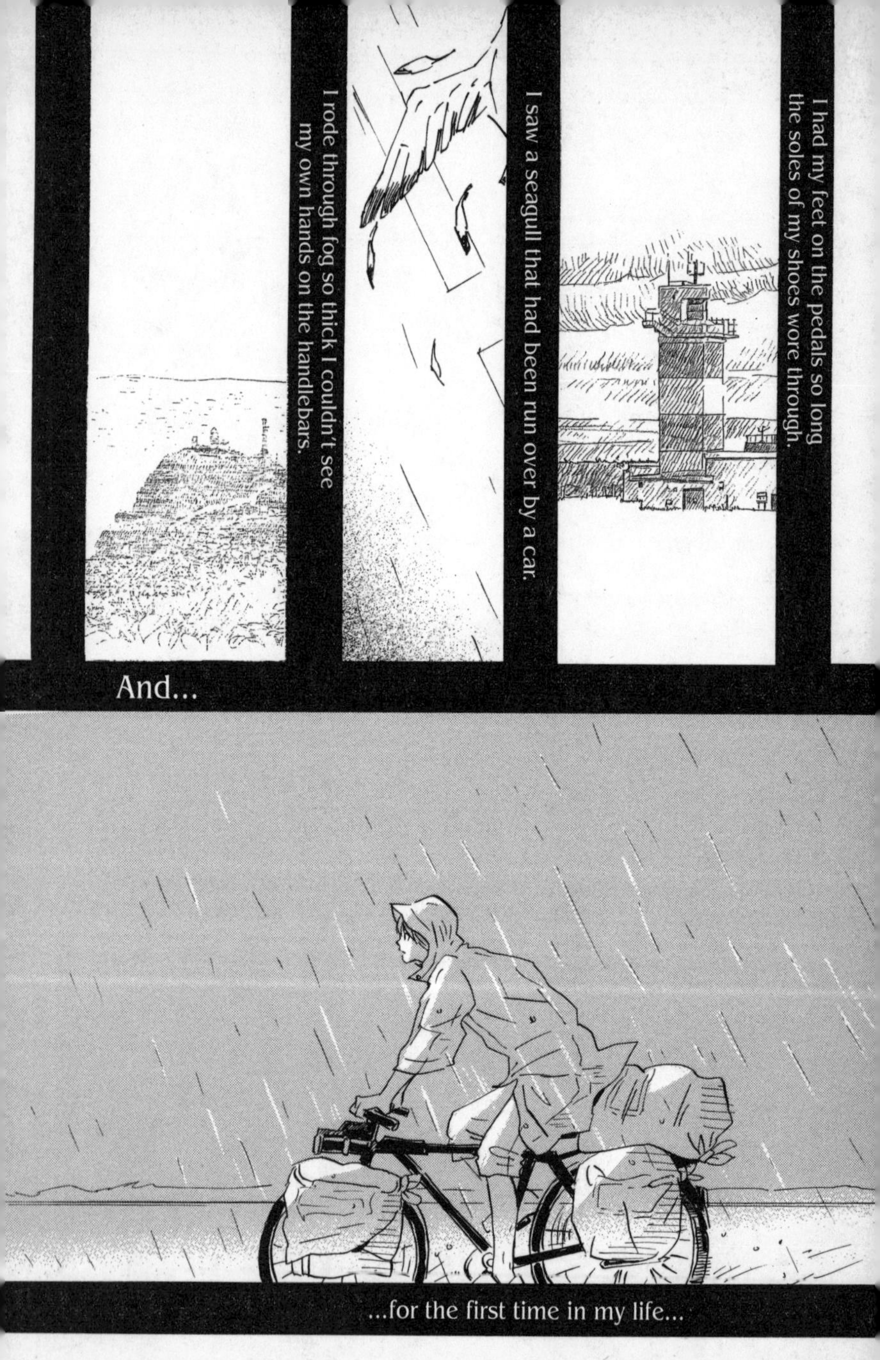
I had my feet on the pedals so long the soles of my shoes wore through.
I saw a seagull that had been run over by a car.
I rode through fog so thick I couldn't see my own hands on the handlebars.
And...
...for the first time in my life...

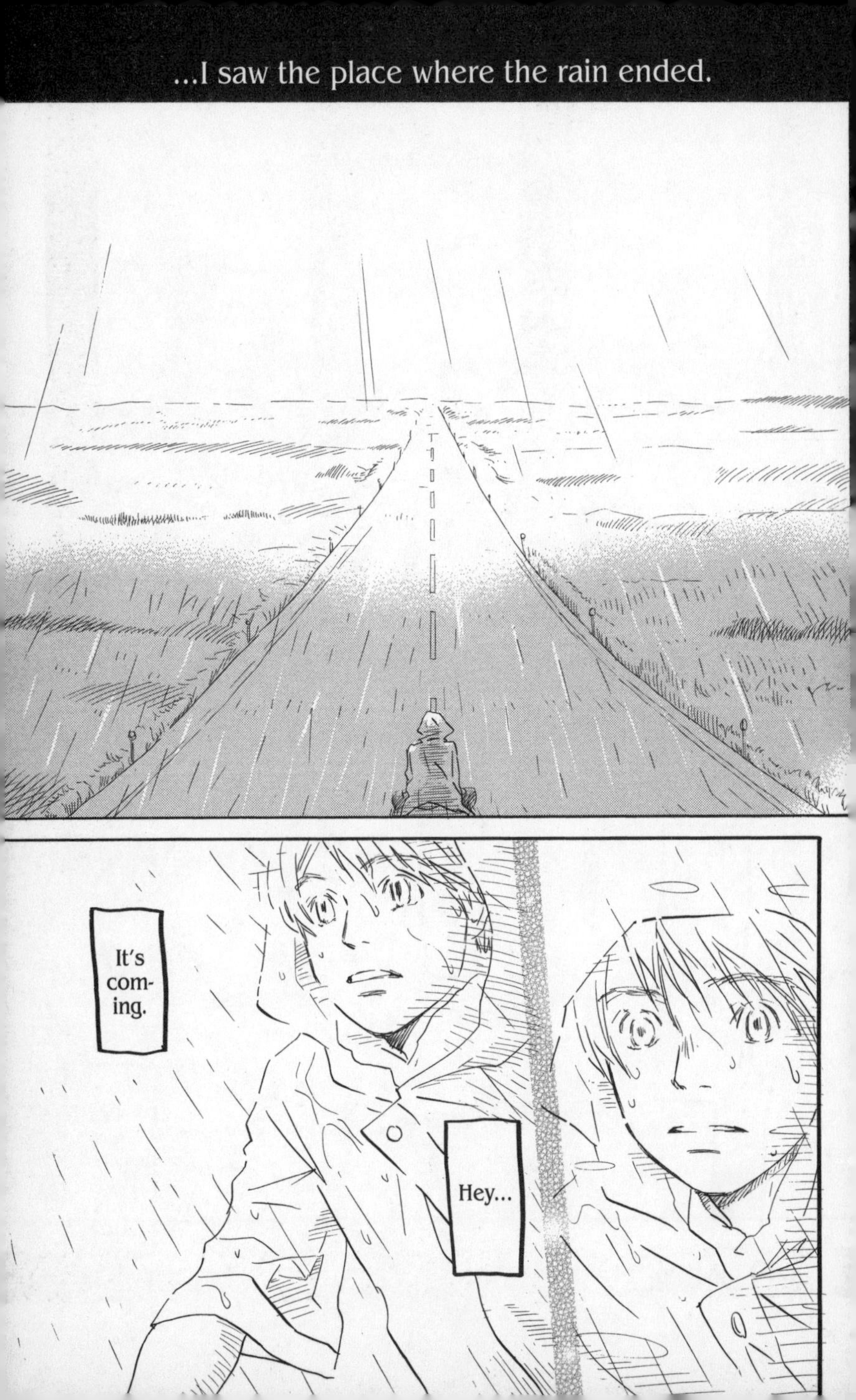
...I saw the place where the rain ended.
Hey...
It's coming.

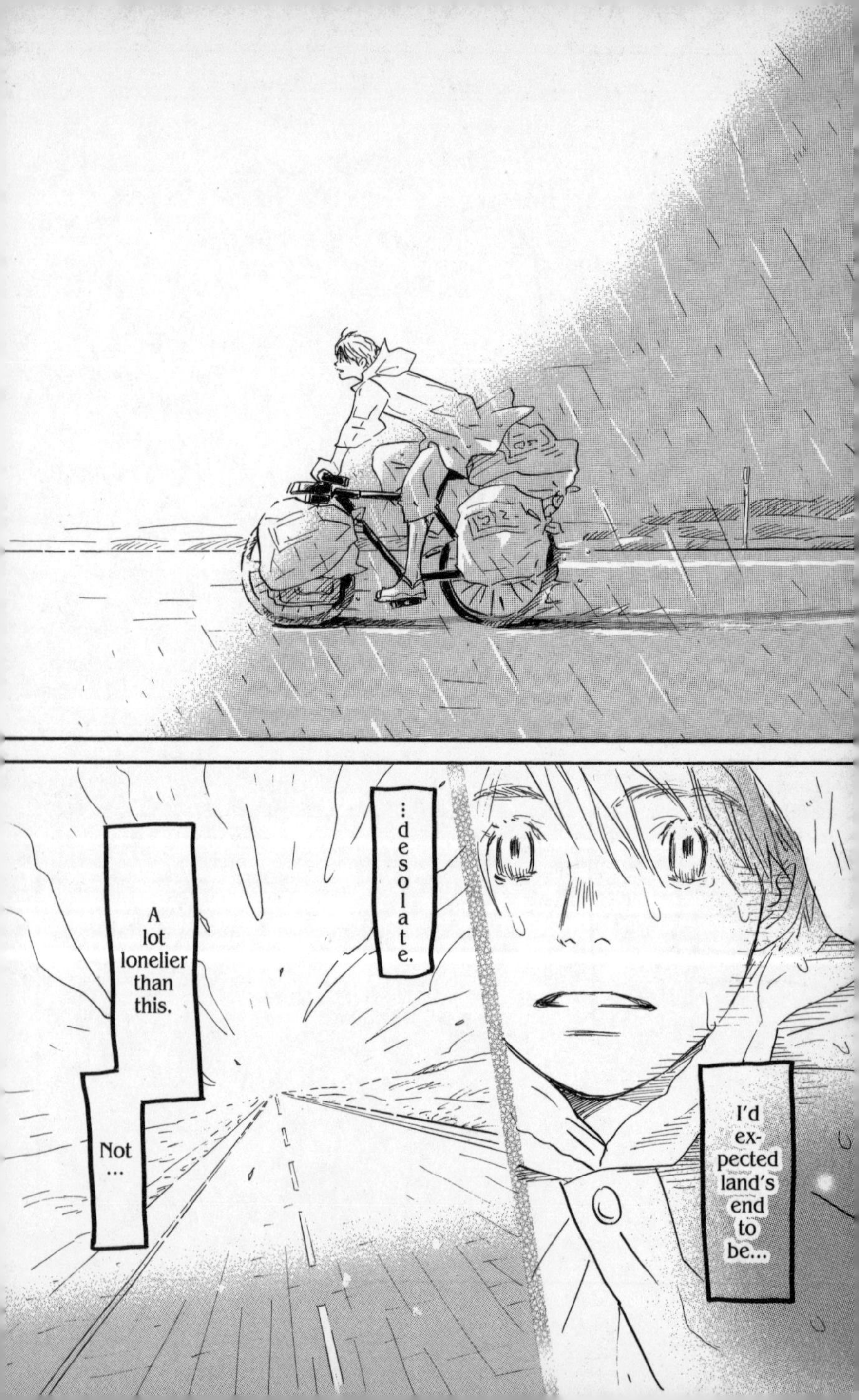
I'd expected land's end to be...
...desolate.
A lot lonelier than this.
Not...

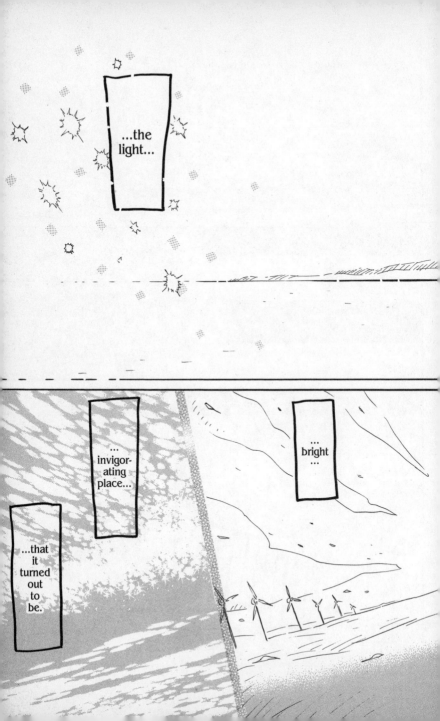

...the light...

...
invigor-
ating
place...

...
bright
...

...that
it
turned
out
to
be.

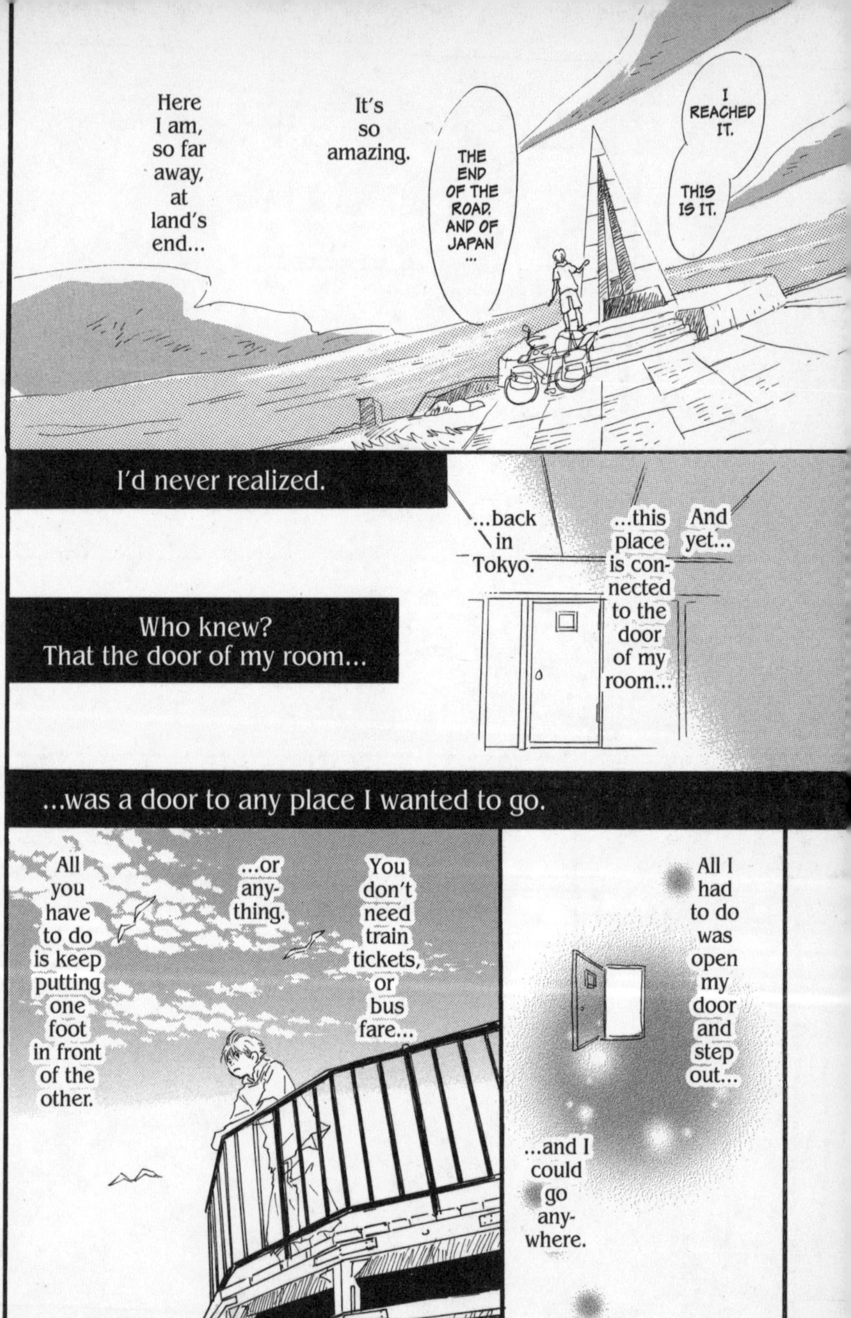
I REACHED IT.
THIS IS IT.
THE END OF THE ROAD. AND OF JAPAN...
It's so amazing.
Here I am, so far away, at land's end...
And yet...
...this place is connected to the door of my room...
...back in Tokyo.
I'd never realized.
Who knew? That the door of my room...
...was a door to any place I wanted to go.
All I had to do was open my door and step out...
...and I could go anywhere.
You don't need train tickets, or bus fare...
...or anything.
All you have to do is keep putting one foot in front of the other.

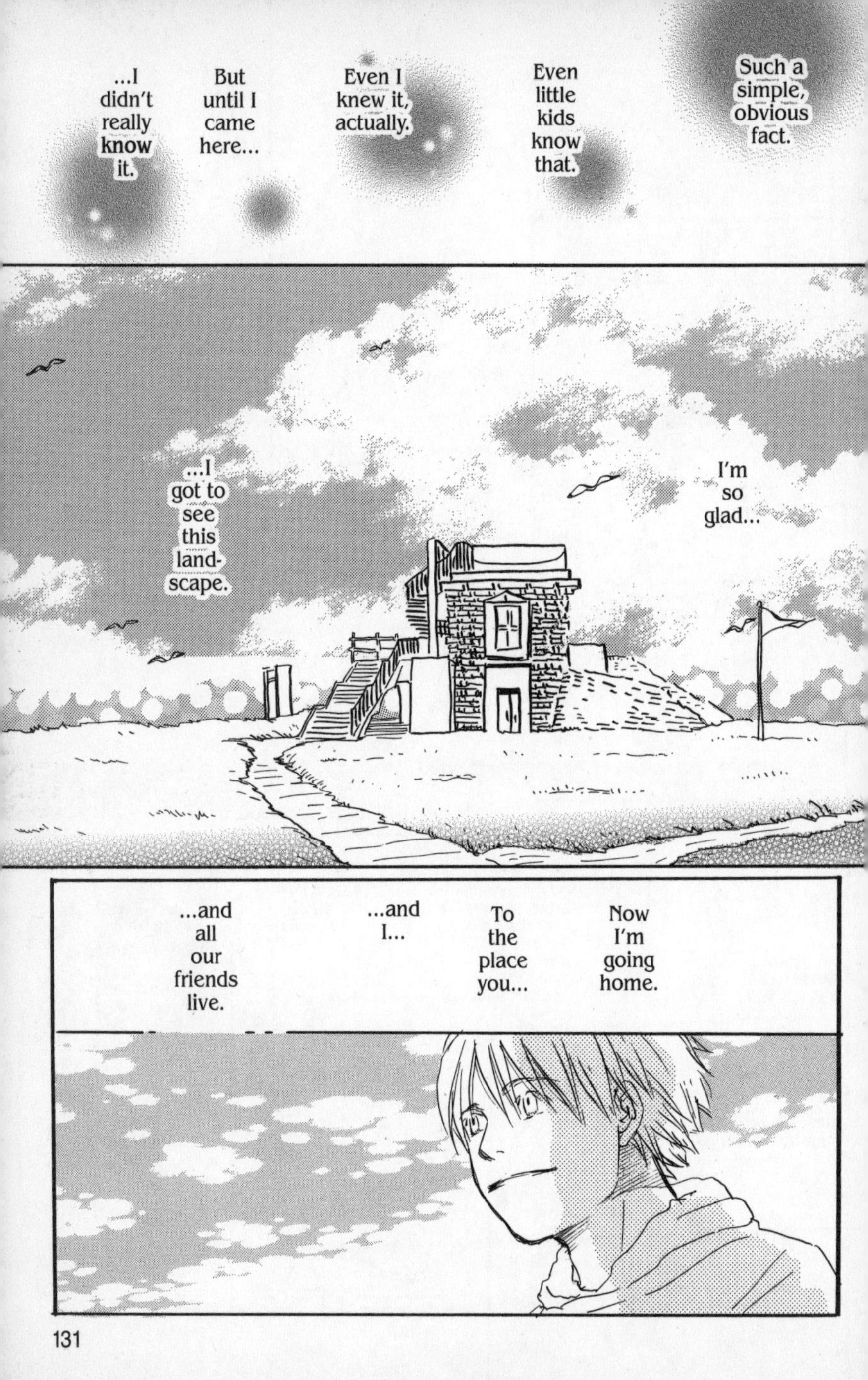
Such a simple, obvious fact.
Even little kids know that.
Even I knew it, actually.
But until I came here...
...I didn't really **know** it.
I'm so glad...
...I got to see this land-scape.
Now I'm going home.
To the place you...
...and I...
...and all our friends live.

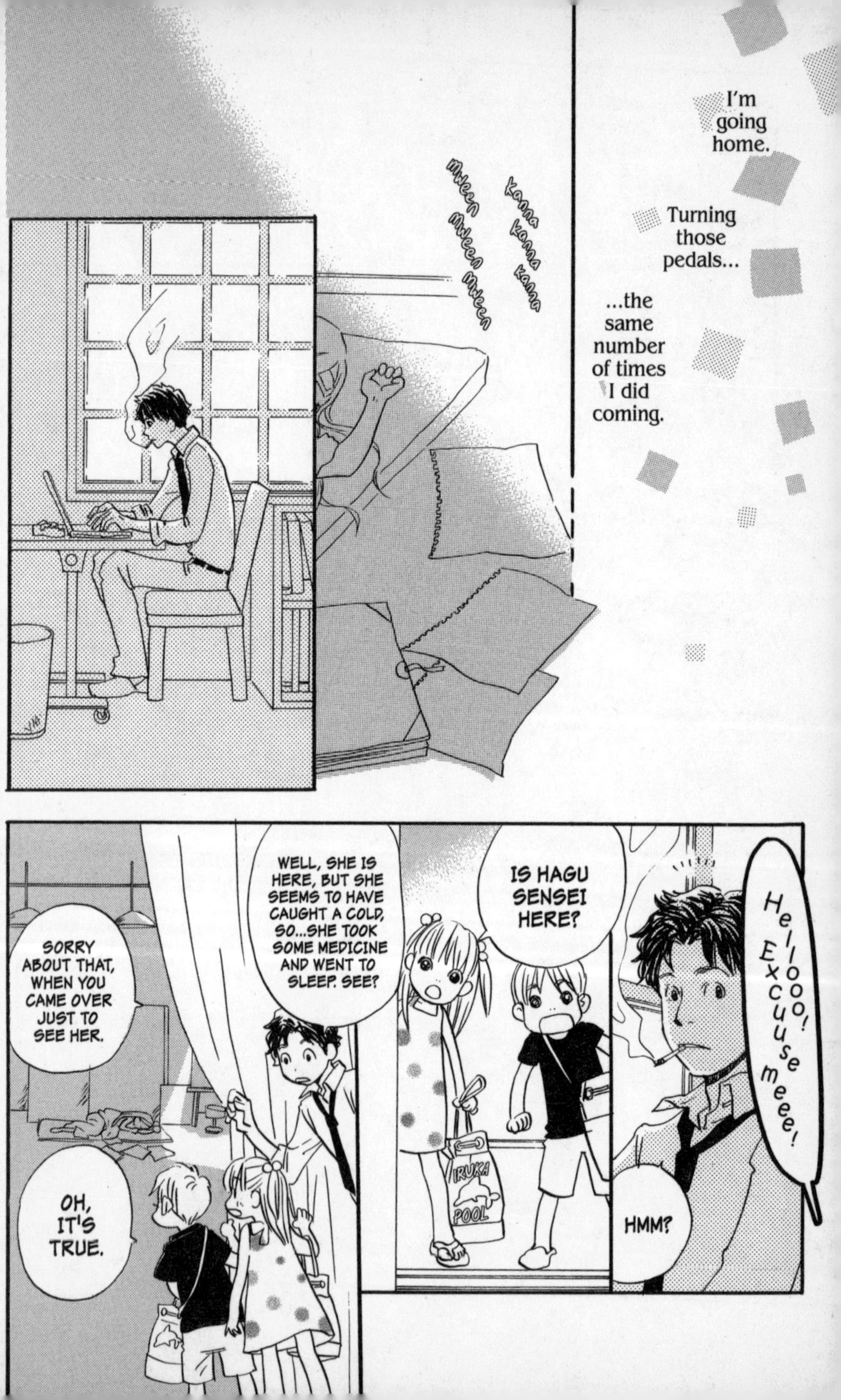
I'm going home.
Turning those pedals...
...the same number of times I did coming.
Kanna kanna kanna
Mween mween mween
Hellooo! Excuuse meee!
HMM?
IS HAGU SENSEI HERE?
WELL, SHE IS HERE, BUT SHE SEEMS TO HAVE CAUGHT A COLD, SO...SHE TOOK SOME MEDICINE AND WENT TO SLEEP. SEE?
SORRY ABOUT THAT, WHEN YOU CAME OVER JUST TO SEE HER.
OH, IT'S TRUE.
IRUKA POOL

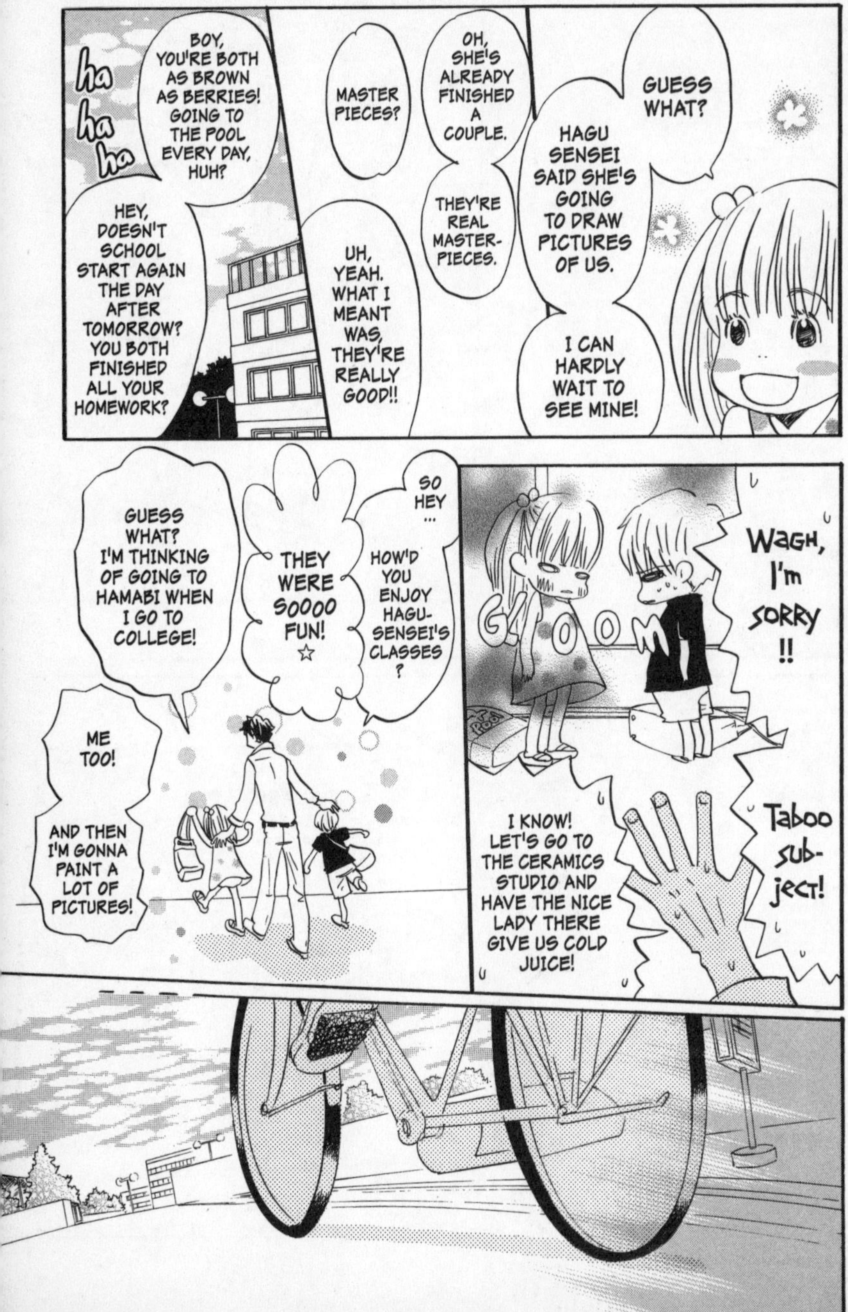
GUESS WHAT?
HAGU SENSEI SAID SHE'S GOING TO DRAW PICTURES OF US.
I CAN HARDLY WAIT TO SEE MINE!
OH, SHE'S ALREADY FINISHED A COUPLE.
MASTER PIECES?
THEY'RE REAL MASTER-PIECES.
UH, YEAH. WHAT I MEANT WAS, THEY'RE REALLY GOOD!!
BOY, YOU'RE BOTH AS BROWN AS BERRIES! GOING TO THE POOL EVERY DAY, HUH?
ha ha ha
HEY, DOESN'T SCHOOL START AGAIN THE DAY AFTER TOMORROW? YOU BOTH FINISHED ALL YOUR HOMEWORK?
GLOOM
Wagh, I'm sorry!!
Taboo subject!
I KNOW! LET'S GO TO THE CERAMICS STUDIO AND HAVE THE NICE LADY THERE GIVE US COLD JUICE!
SO HEY... HOW'D YOU ENJOY HAGU-SENSEI'S CLASSES?
THEY WERE SOOOO FUN! ☆
GUESS WHAT? I'M THINKING OF GOING TO HAMABI WHEN I GO TO COLLEGE!
ME TOO!
AND THEN I'M GONNA PAINT A LOT OF PICTURES!

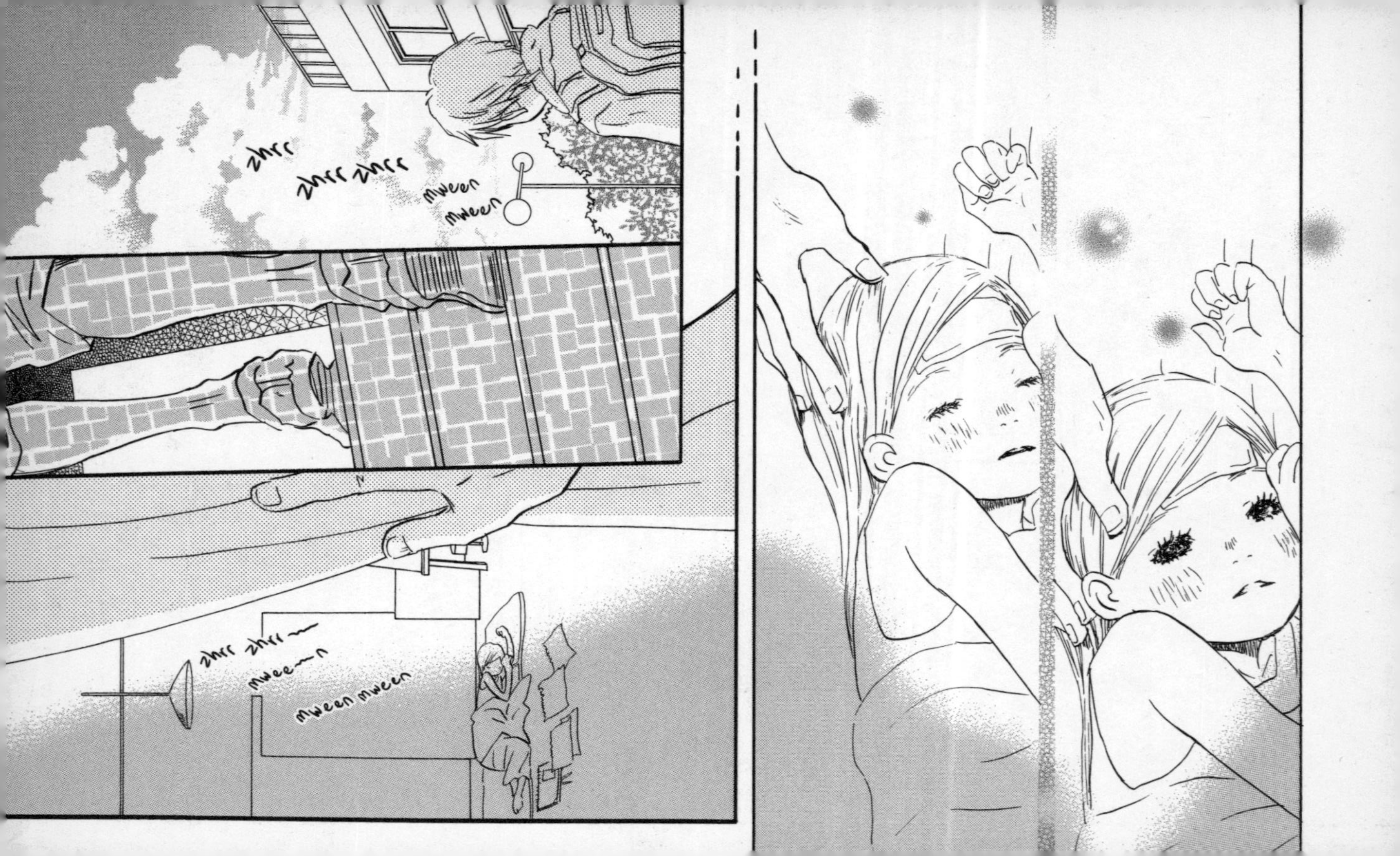
zhrr
zhrr zhrr
mween
mween
zhrr zhrr~~
mwee~n
mween mween

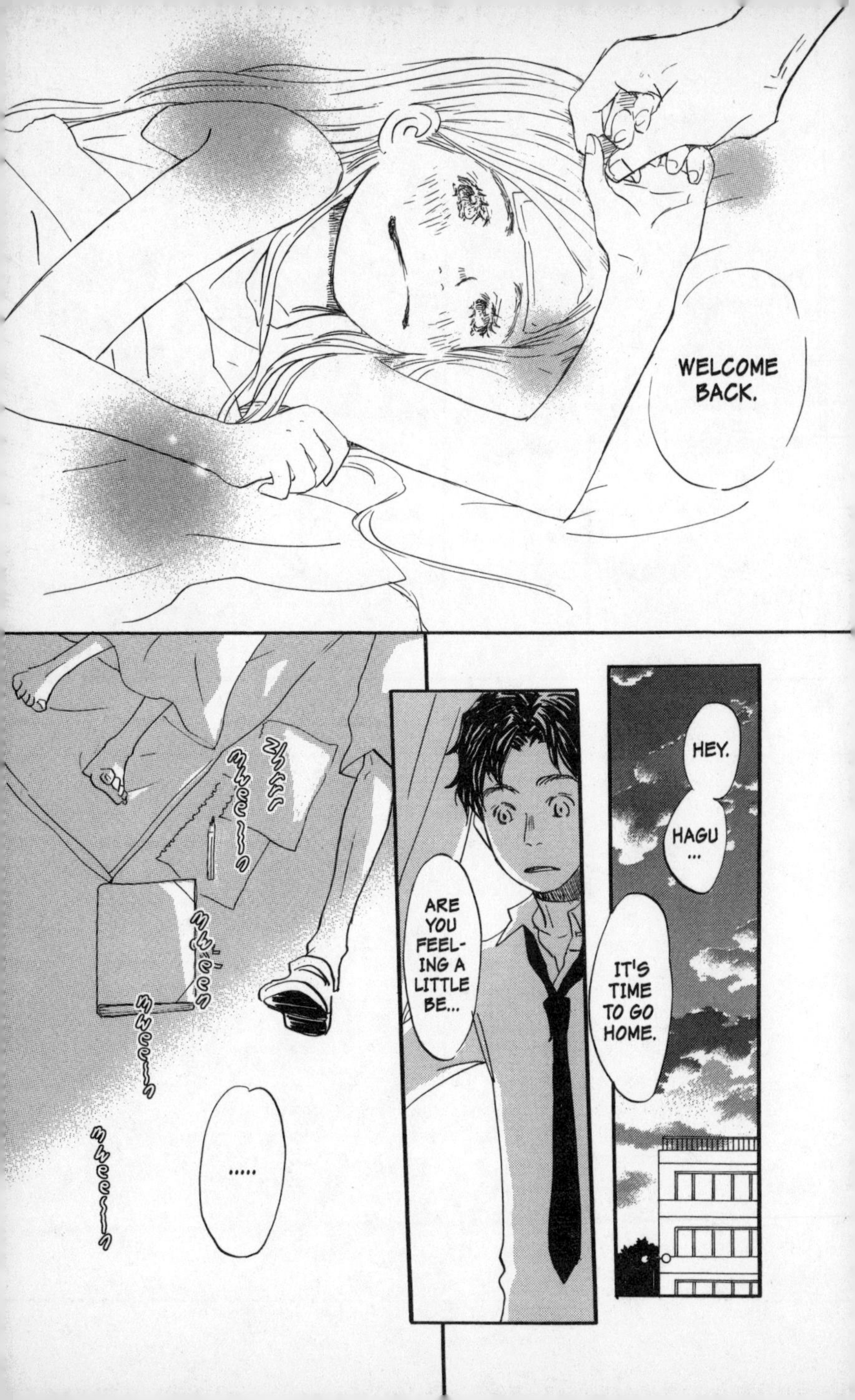
WELCOME BACK.
HEY.
HAGU...
IT'S TIME TO GO HOME.
ARE YOU FEELING A LITTLE BE...
zhrrr
mwee~~n
mweeen
mwee~~n
.....
mwee~~n

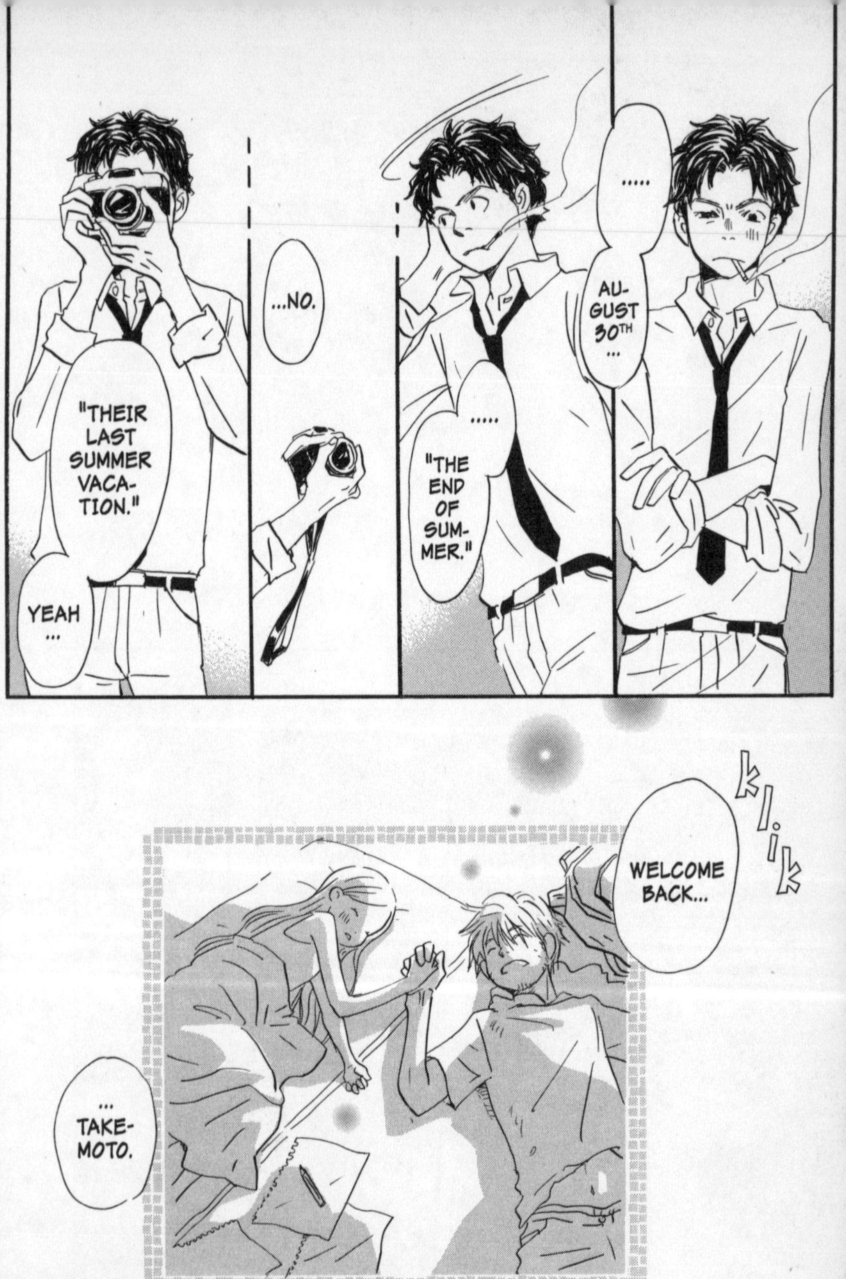
.....
AU-GUST 30TH ...
.....
"THE END OF SUM-MER."
...NO.
"THEIR LAST SUMMER VACA-TION."
YEAH ...
KLIK
WELCOME BACK...
... TAKE-MOTO.

chapter 45—the end—

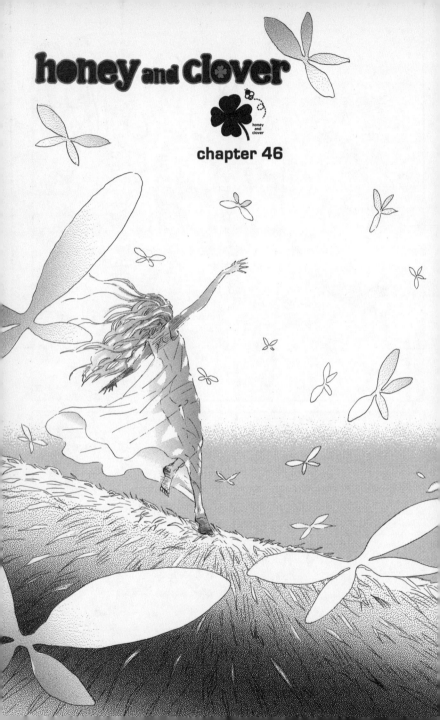

honey and clover

honey and clover

chapter 46

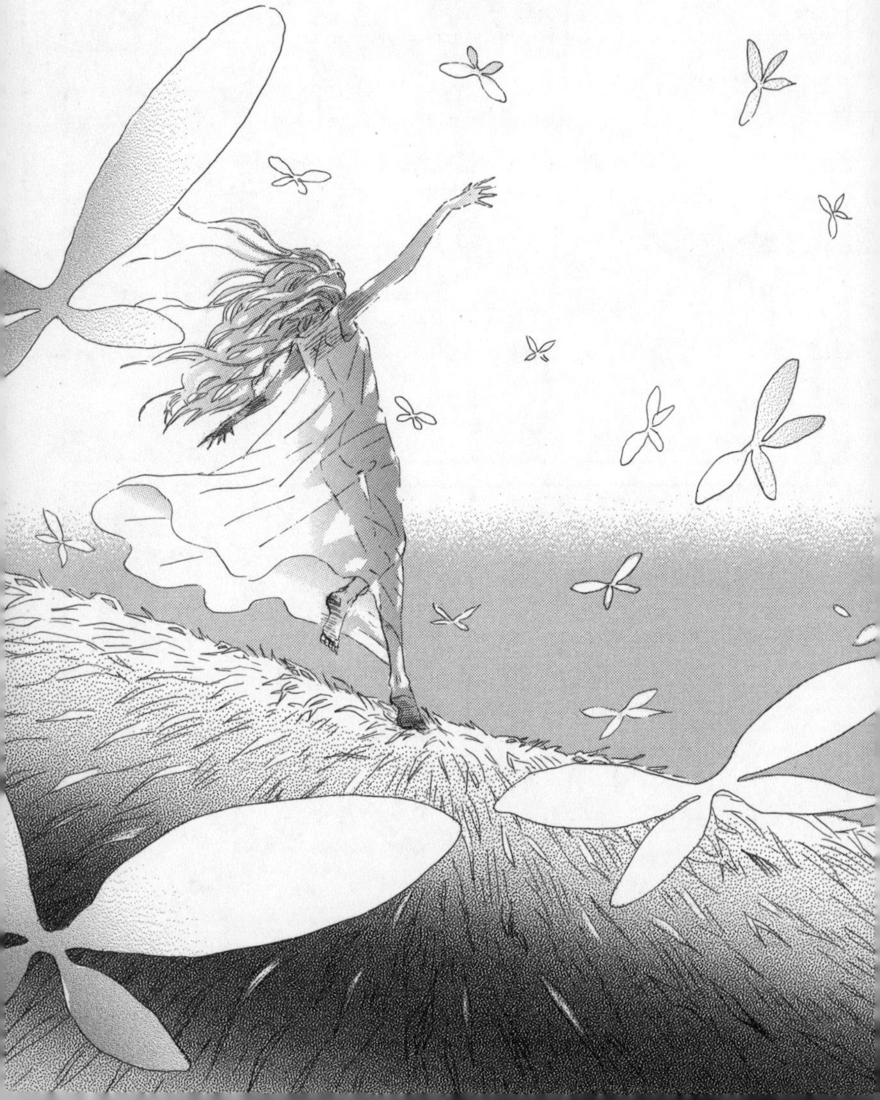

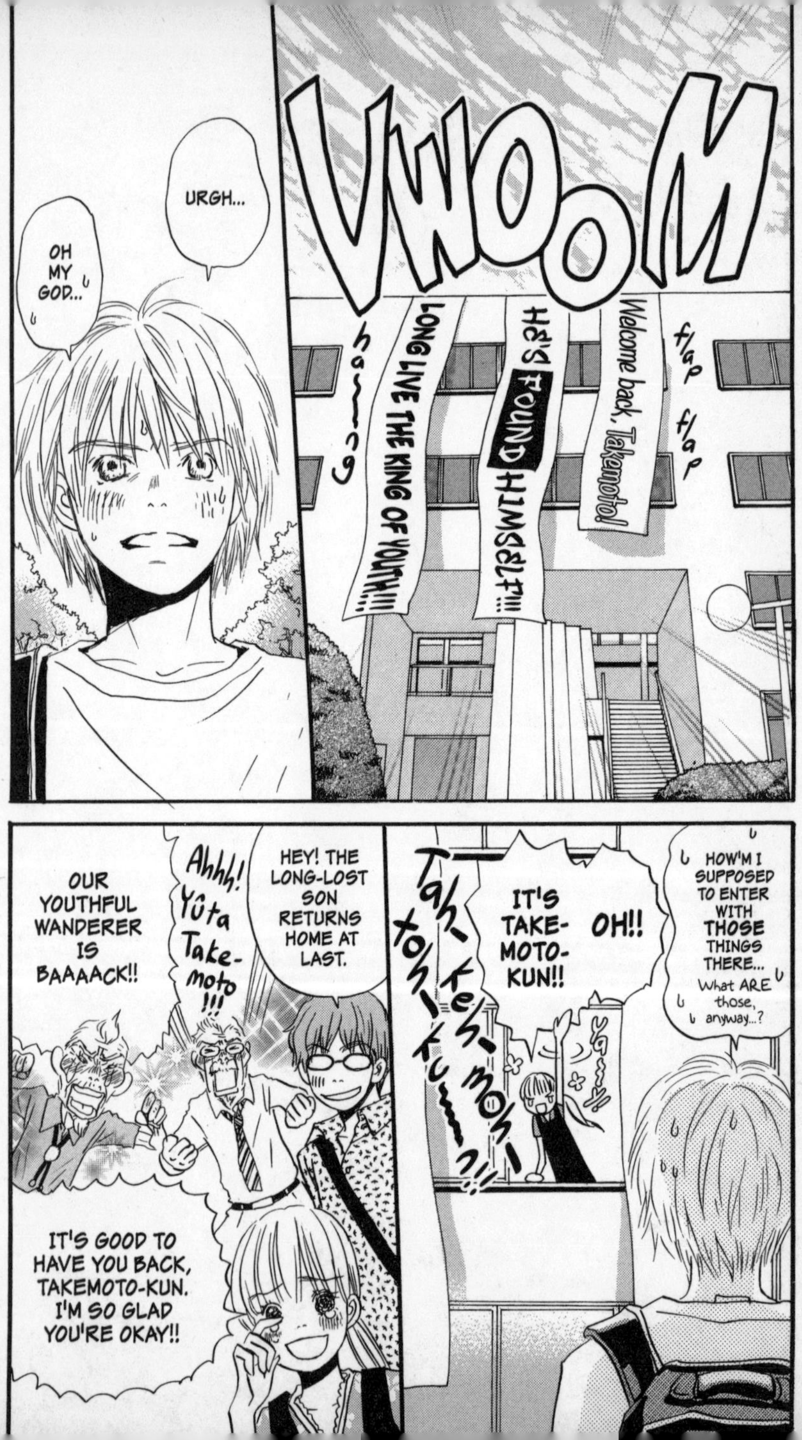
VWOOM
Welcome back, Takemoto!
He's FOUND HIMSELF!!!
LONG LIVE THE KING OF YOUTH!!!
flap flap
URGH...
OH MY GOD...
HOW'M I SUPPOSED TO ENTER WITH THOSE THINGS THERE...
What ARE those, anyway...?
OH!!
IT'S TAKE-MOTO-KUN!!
Tak-keh-moh-toh-ku~n!!
HEY! THE LONG-LOST SON RETURNS HOME AT LAST.
Ahhh! Yûta Take-moto!!!
OUR YOUTHFUL WANDERER IS BAAAACK!!
IT'S GOOD TO HAVE YOU BACK, TAKEMOTO-KUN. I'M SO GLAD YOU'RE OKAY!!

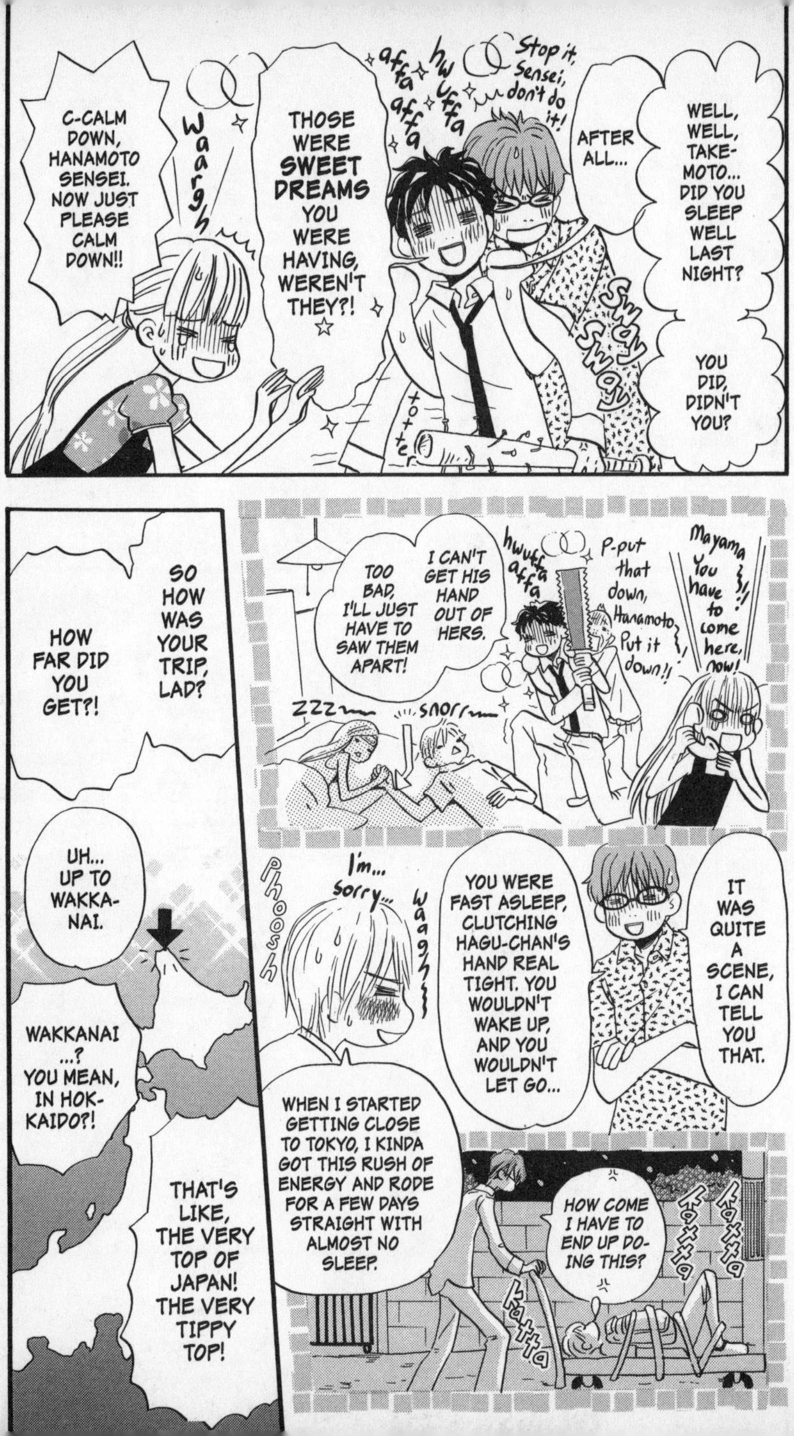
WELL, WELL, TAKE-MOTO... DID YOU SLEEP WELL LAST NIGHT?
YOU DID, DIDN'T YOU?
Sway Sway
AFTER ALL...
Stop it, Sensei, don't do it!
hwuffa affa
affa affa
THOSE WERE SWEET DREAMS YOU WERE HAVING, WEREN'T THEY?! ☆
totter
Waargh
C-CALM DOWN, HANAMOTO SENSEI. NOW JUST PLEASE CALM DOWN!!
Mayama You have to come here, now!
P-put that down, Hanamoto, Put it down!!
hwuffa affa
I CAN'T GET HIS HAND OUT OF HERS.
TOO BAD, I'LL JUST HAVE TO SAW THEM APART!
snorr
ZZZ
IT WAS QUITE A SCENE, I CAN TELL YOU THAT.
YOU WERE FAST ASLEEP, CLUTCHING HAGU-CHAN'S HAND REAL TIGHT. YOU WOULDN'T WAKE UP, AND YOU WOULDN'T LET GO...
Waaagh
I'm... sorry...
Phoosh
WHEN I STARTED GETTING CLOSE TO TOKYO, I KINDA GOT THIS RUSH OF ENERGY AND RODE FOR A FEW DAYS STRAIGHT WITH ALMOST NO SLEEP.
kattakatta
HOW COME I HAVE TO END UP DOING THIS?
katta
SO HOW WAS YOUR TRIP, LAD?
HOW FAR DID YOU GET?!
UH... UP TO WAKKANAI.
WAKKANAI...? YOU MEAN, IN HOKKAIDO?!
THAT'S LIKE, THE VERY TOP OF JAPAN! THE VERY TIPPY TOP!

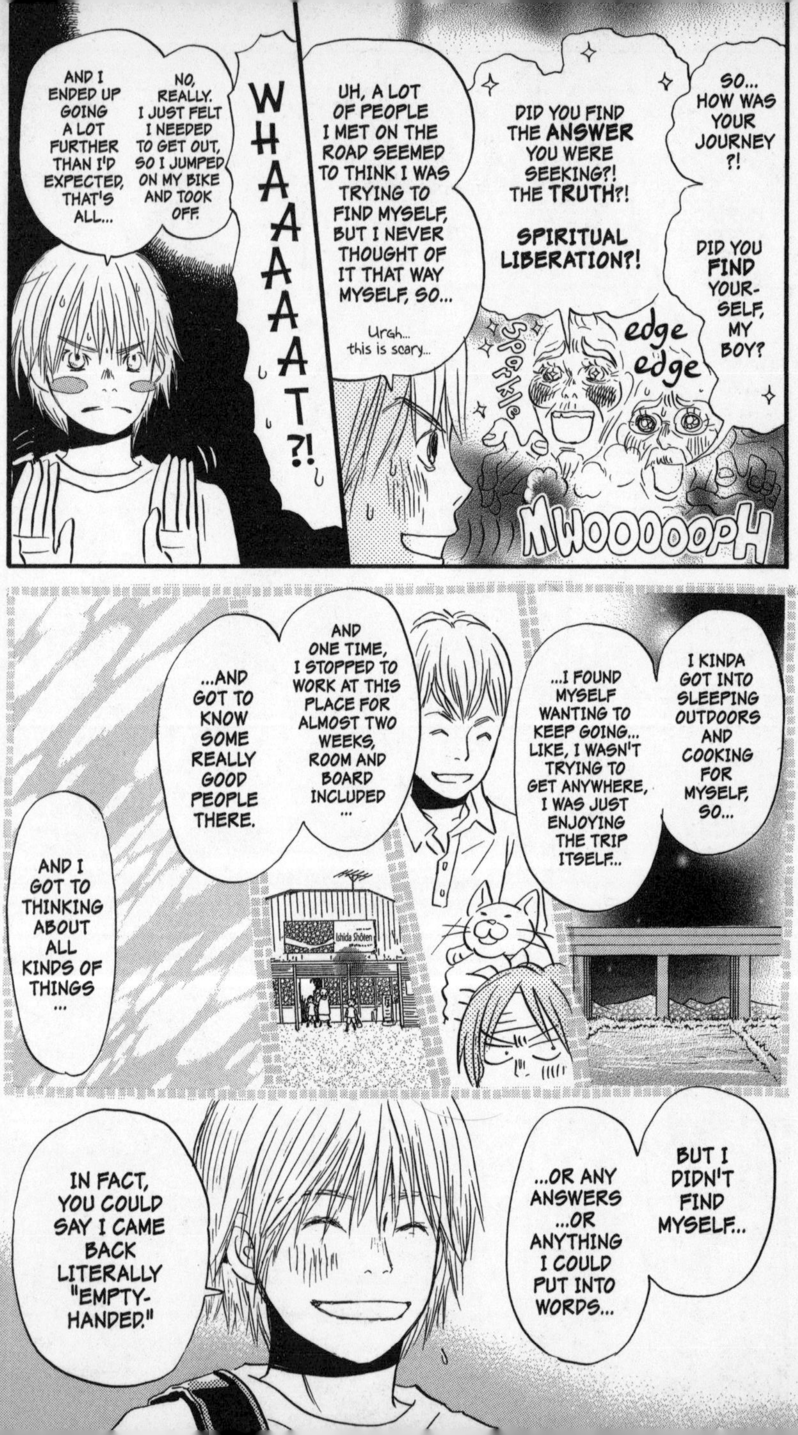
SO... HOW WAS YOUR JOURNEY ?!
DID YOU FIND YOURSELF, MY BOY?
DID YOU FIND THE ANSWER YOU WERE SEEKING?! THE TRUTH?!
SPIRITUAL LIBERATION?!
Sparkle
edge edge
MWOOOOOPH
UH, A LOT OF PEOPLE I MET ON THE ROAD SEEMED TO THINK I WAS TRYING TO FIND MYSELF, BUT I NEVER THOUGHT OF IT THAT WAY MYSELF, SO...
Urgh... this is scary...
WHAAAAAT?!
NO, REALLY. I JUST FELT I NEEDED TO GET OUT, SO I JUMPED ON MY BIKE AND TOOK OFF.
AND I ENDED UP GOING A LOT FURTHER THAN I'D EXPECTED, THAT'S ALL...
I KINDA GOT INTO SLEEPING OUTDOORS AND COOKING FOR MYSELF, SO...
...I FOUND MYSELF WANTING TO KEEP GOING... LIKE, I WASN'T TRYING TO GET ANYWHERE, I WAS JUST ENJOYING THE TRIP ITSELF...
AND ONE TIME, I STOPPED TO WORK AT THIS PLACE FOR ALMOST TWO WEEKS, ROOM AND BOARD INCLUDED ...
...AND GOT TO KNOW SOME REALLY GOOD PEOPLE THERE.
Ishida Shōten
AND I GOT TO THINKING ABOUT ALL KINDS OF THINGS ...
BUT I DIDN'T FIND MYSELF...
...OR ANY ANSWERS ...OR ANYTHING I COULD PUT INTO WORDS...
IN FACT, YOU COULD SAY I CAME BACK LITERALLY "EMPTY-HANDED."

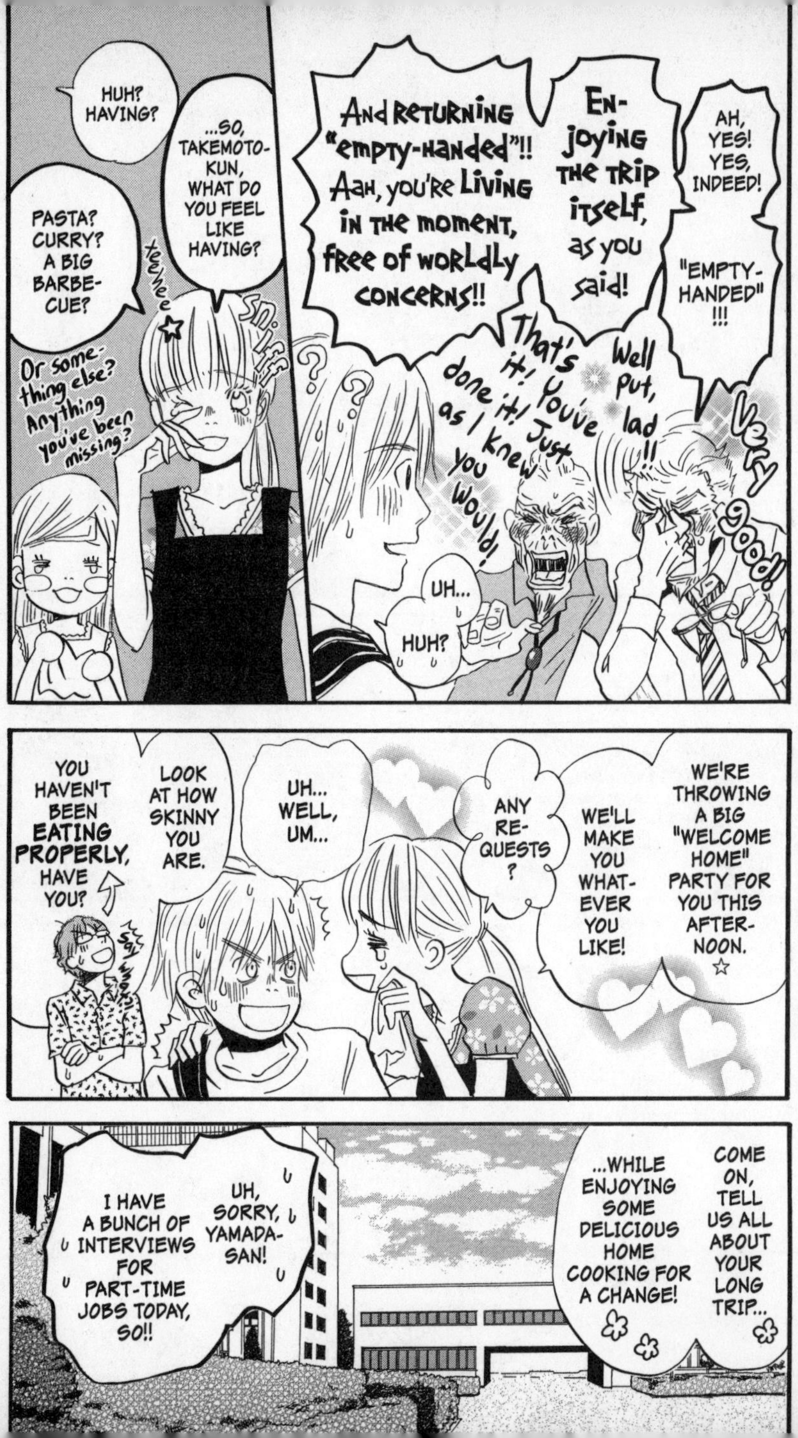
AH, YES! YES, INDEED!
"EMPTY-HANDED"!!!
Enjoying the trip itself, as you said!
And returning "empty-handed"!! Aah, you're living in the moment, free of worldly concerns!!
Very good!
Well put, lad!!
That's it! You've done it! Just as I knew you would!
UH...
HUH?
...SO, TAKEMOTO-KUN, WHAT DO YOU FEEL LIKE HAVING?
HUH? HAVING?
teehee
sniff
PASTA? CURRY? A BIG BARBECUE?
Or something else? Anything you've been missing?
WE'RE THROWING A BIG "WELCOME HOME" PARTY FOR YOU THIS AFTERNOON. ☆
WE'LL MAKE YOU WHATEVER YOU LIKE!
ANY REQUESTS?
UH... WELL, UM...
LOOK AT HOW SKINNY YOU ARE.
YOU HAVEN'T BEEN EATING PROPERLY, HAVE YOU?
COME ON, TELL US ALL ABOUT YOUR LONG TRIP...
...WHILE ENJOYING SOME DELICIOUS HOME COOKING FOR A CHANGE!
UH, SORRY, YAMADA-SAN!
I HAVE A BUNCH OF INTERVIEWS FOR PART-TIME JOBS TODAY, SO!!

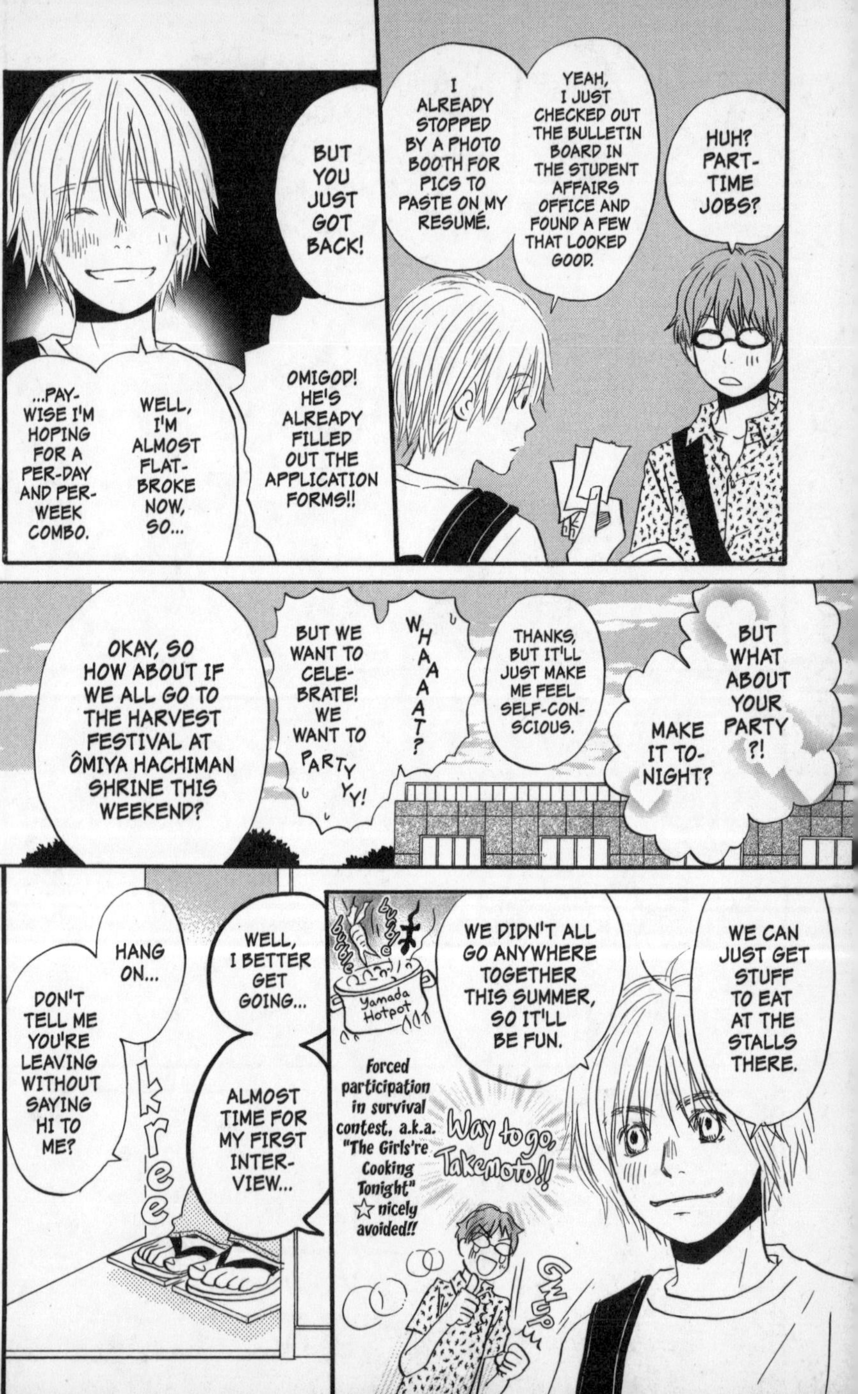
HUH? PART-TIME JOBS?
YEAH, I JUST CHECKED OUT THE BULLETIN BOARD IN THE STUDENT AFFAIRS OFFICE AND FOUND A FEW THAT LOOKED GOOD.
I ALREADY STOPPED BY A PHOTO BOOTH FOR PICS TO PASTE ON MY RESUMÉ.
BUT YOU JUST GOT BACK!
OMIGOD! HE'S ALREADY FILLED OUT THE APPLICATION FORMS!!
WELL, I'M ALMOST FLAT-BROKE NOW, SO...
...PAY-WISE I'M HOPING FOR A PER-DAY AND PER-WEEK COMBO.
BUT WHAT ABOUT YOUR PARTY?!
MAKE IT TO-NIGHT?
THANKS, BUT IT'LL JUST MAKE ME FEEL SELF-CONSCIOUS.
WHAAAAT?
BUT WE WANT TO CELE-BRATE! WE WANT TO PARTYYY!
OKAY, SO HOW ABOUT IF WE ALL GO TO THE HARVEST FESTIVAL AT ÔMIYA HACHIMAN SHRINE THIS WEEKEND?
WE CAN JUST GET STUFF TO EAT AT THE STALLS THERE.
WE DIDN'T ALL GO ANYWHERE TOGETHER THIS SUMMER, SO IT'LL BE FUN.
Yamada Hotpot
Forced participation in survival contest, a.k.a. "The Girls're Cooking Tonight" ☆ nicely avoided!!
Way to go, Takemoto!!
GWUP
WELL, I BETTER GET GOING...
ALMOST TIME FOR MY FIRST INTER-VIEW...
HANG ON...
DON'T TELL ME YOU'RE LEAVING WITHOUT SAYING HI TO ME?
kree

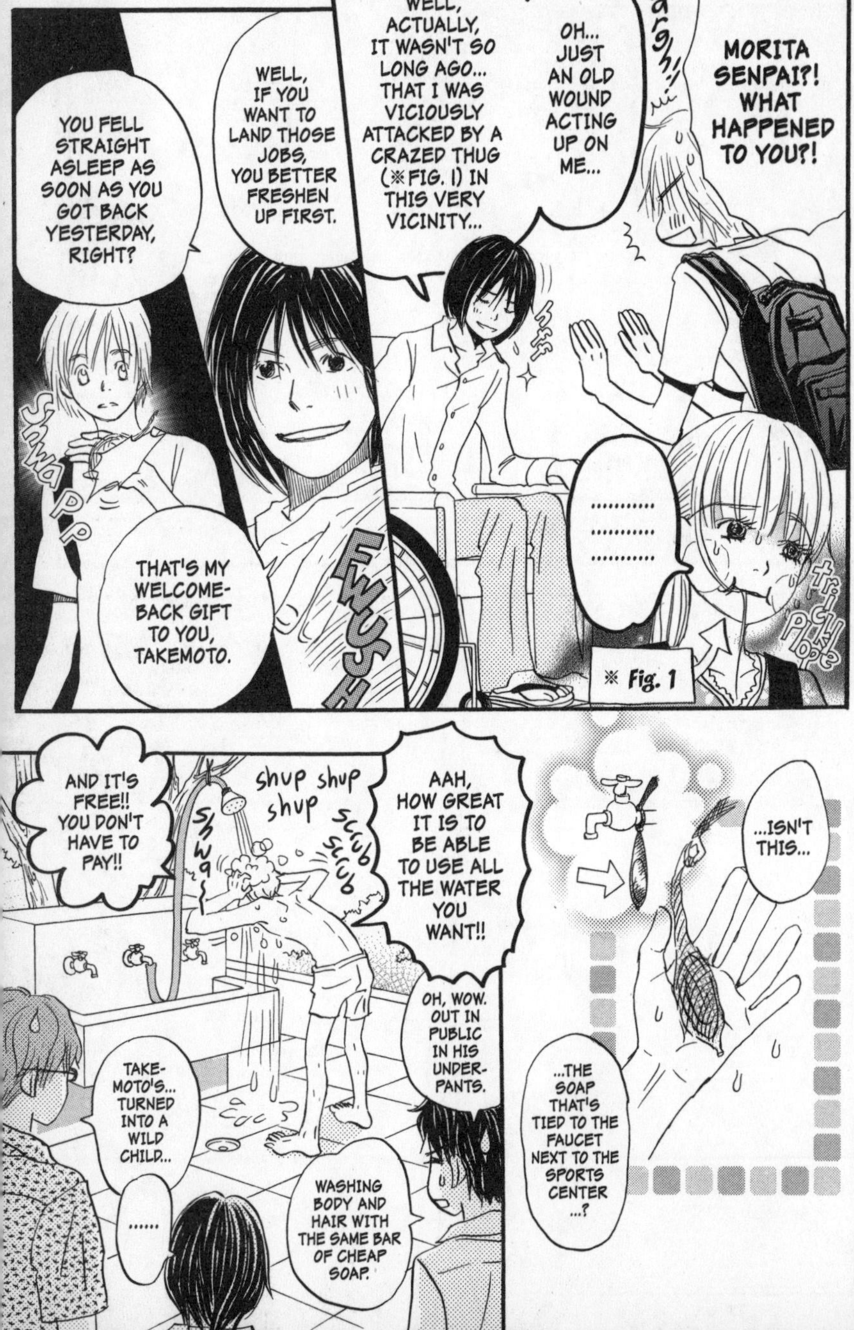
MORITA SENPAI?! WHAT HAPPENED TO YOU?!
Wargh!!
OH... JUST AN OLD WOUND ACTING UP ON ME...
WELL, ACTUALLY, IT WASN'T SO LONG AGO... THAT I WAS VICIOUSLY ATTACKED BY A CRAZED THUG (※FIG. 1) IN THIS VERY VICINITY...
hff
....
....
....
trickly plope
※ Fig. 1
WELL, IF YOU WANT TO LAND THOSE JOBS, YOU BETTER FRESHEN UP FIRST.
FWUSH
YOU FELL STRAIGHT ASLEEP AS SOON AS YOU GOT BACK YESTERDAY, RIGHT?
Shwapp
THAT'S MY WELCOME-BACK GIFT TO YOU, TAKEMOTO.
...ISN'T THIS...
...THE SOAP THAT'S TIED TO THE FAUCET NEXT TO THE SPORTS CENTER ...?
AAH, HOW GREAT IT IS TO BE ABLE TO USE ALL THE WATER YOU WANT!!
shup shup shup
scrub scrub
shwa~
AND IT'S FREE!! YOU DON'T HAVE TO PAY!!
OH, WOW. OUT IN PUBLIC IN HIS UNDER-PANTS.
TAKE-MOTO'S... TURNED INTO A WILD CHILD...
WASHING BODY AND HAIR WITH THE SAME BAR OF CHEAP SOAP.
......

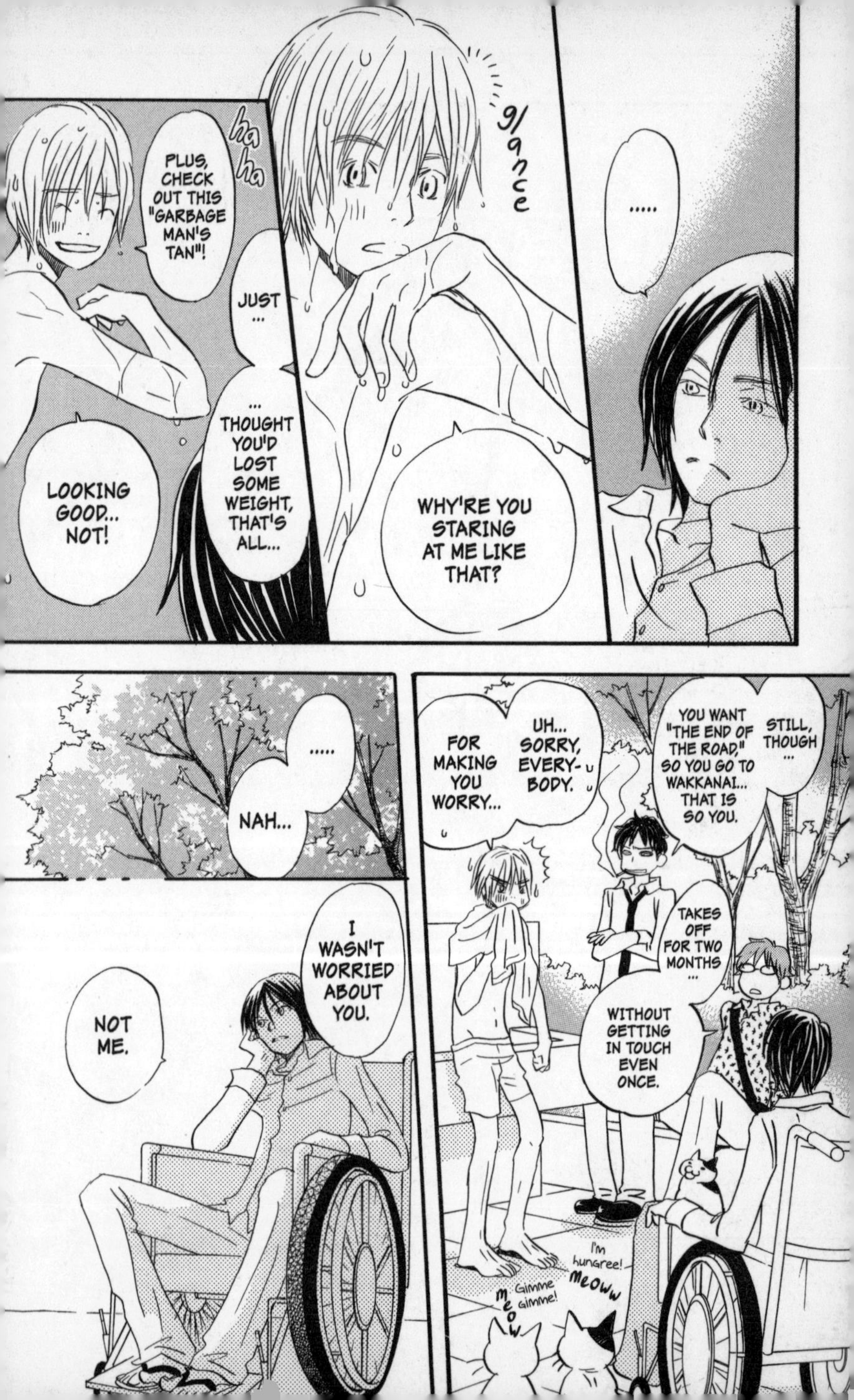
.....
glance
WHY'RE YOU STARING AT ME LIKE THAT?
JUST ...
... THOUGHT YOU'D LOST SOME WEIGHT, THAT'S ALL...
PLUS, CHECK OUT THIS "GARBAGE MAN'S TAN"!
ha ha
LOOKING GOOD... NOT!
STILL, THOUGH ...
YOU WANT "THE END OF THE ROAD," SO YOU GO TO WAKKANAI... THAT IS SO YOU.
TAKES OFF FOR TWO MONTHS ...
WITHOUT GETTING IN TOUCH EVEN ONCE.
UH... SORRY, EVERY-BODY.
FOR MAKING YOU WORRY...
I'm hungree!
MEOWW
Gimme Gimme!
meow
.....
NAH...
I WASN'T WORRIED ABOUT YOU.
NOT ME.

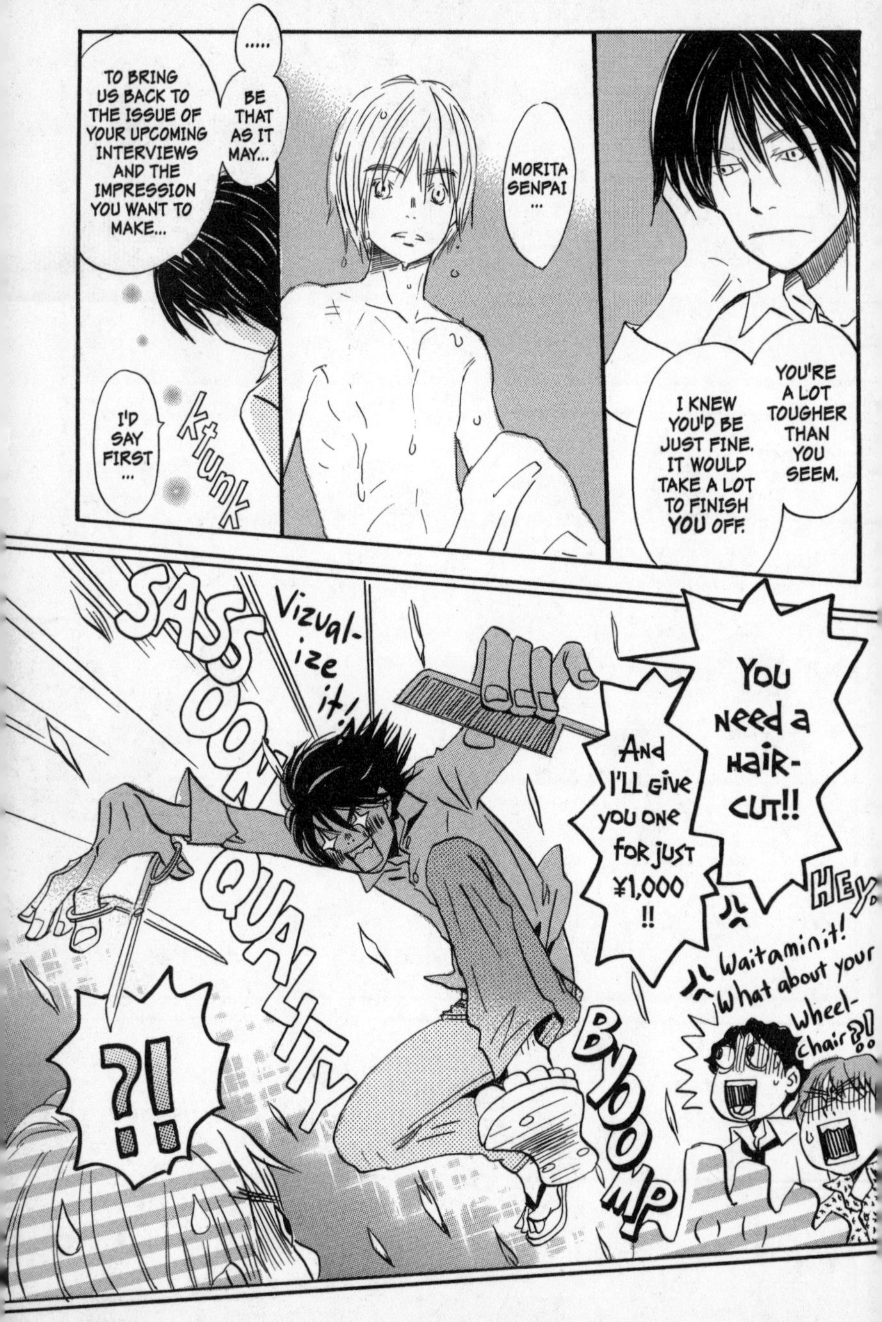
YOU'RE A LOT TOUGHER THAN YOU SEEM.
I KNEW YOU'D BE JUST FINE. IT WOULD TAKE A LOT TO FINISH YOU OFF.
MORITA SENPAI ...
......
BE THAT AS IT MAY...
TO BRING US BACK TO THE ISSUE OF YOUR UPCOMING INTERVIEWS AND THE IMPRESSION YOU WANT TO MAKE...
ktunk
I'D SAY FIRST ...
You need a HAIR-CUT!!
And I'll give you one for just ¥1,000 !!
Vizual-ize it!
SASSOON QUALITY
HEY.
Waitaminit! What about your wheel-chair?!
BYOOOM!
?!!

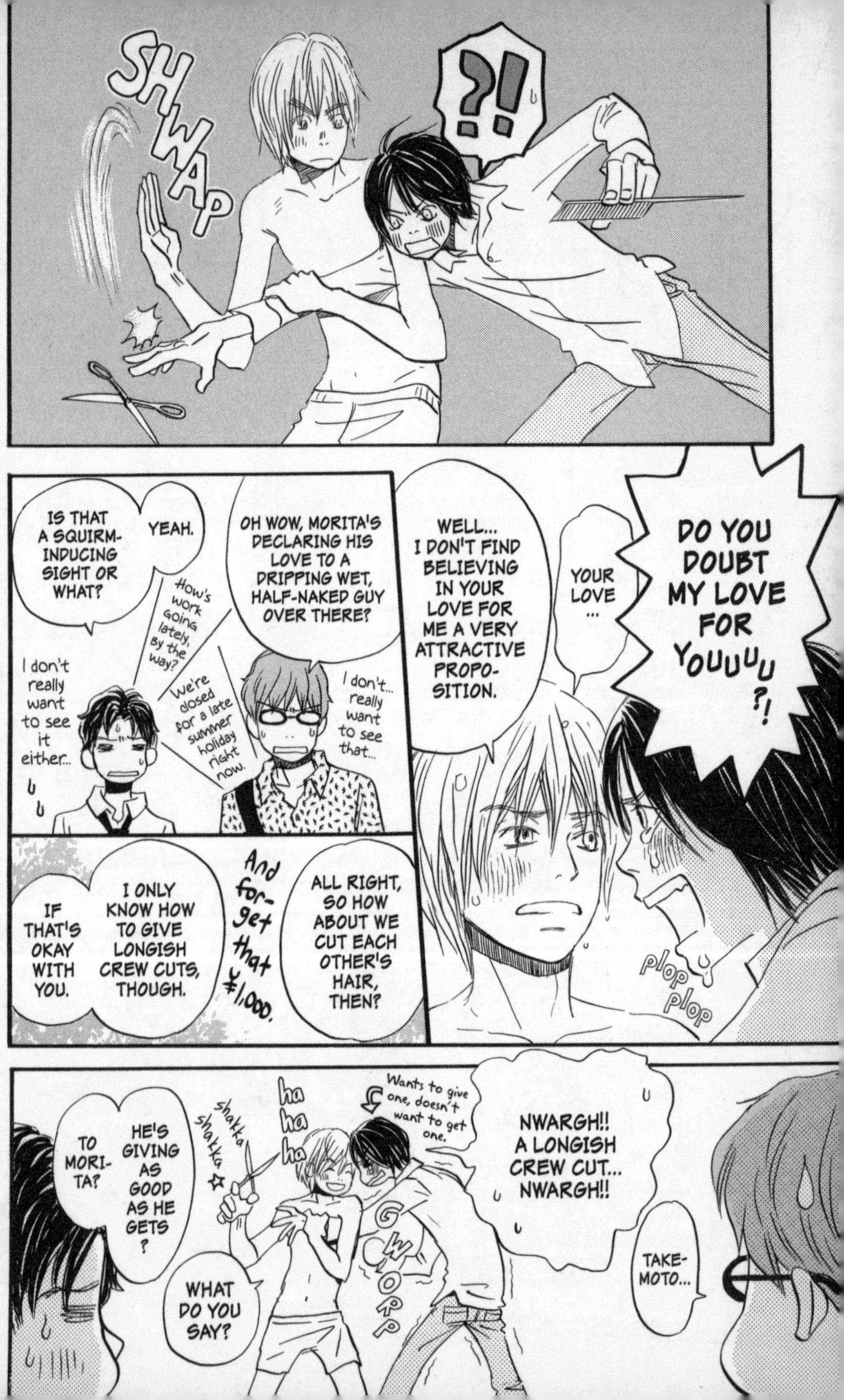
SHWAP
?!
DO YOU DOUBT MY LOVE FOR YOUUUU?!
YOUR LOVE...
WELL... I DON'T FIND BELIEVING IN YOUR LOVE FOR ME A VERY ATTRACTIVE PROPO-SITION.
plop plop
OH WOW, MORITA'S DECLARING HIS LOVE TO A DRIPPING WET, HALF-NAKED GUY OVER THERE?
YEAH.
IS THAT A SQUIRM-INDUCING SIGHT OR WHAT?
I don't... really want to see that...
How's work going lately, by the way?
We're closed for a late summer holiday right now.
I don't really want to see it either...
ALL RIGHT, SO HOW ABOUT WE CUT EACH OTHER'S HAIR, THEN?
And for-get that ¥1,000.
I ONLY KNOW HOW TO GIVE LONGISH CREW CUTS, THOUGH.
IF THAT'S OKAY WITH YOU.
TAKE-MOTO...
NWARGH!! A LONGISH CREW CUT... NWARGH!!
Wants to give one, doesn't want to get one.
GWORP
ha ha ha
shakka shakka ☆
WHAT DO YOU SAY?
HE'S GIVING AS GOOD AS HE GETS?
TO MORI-TA?

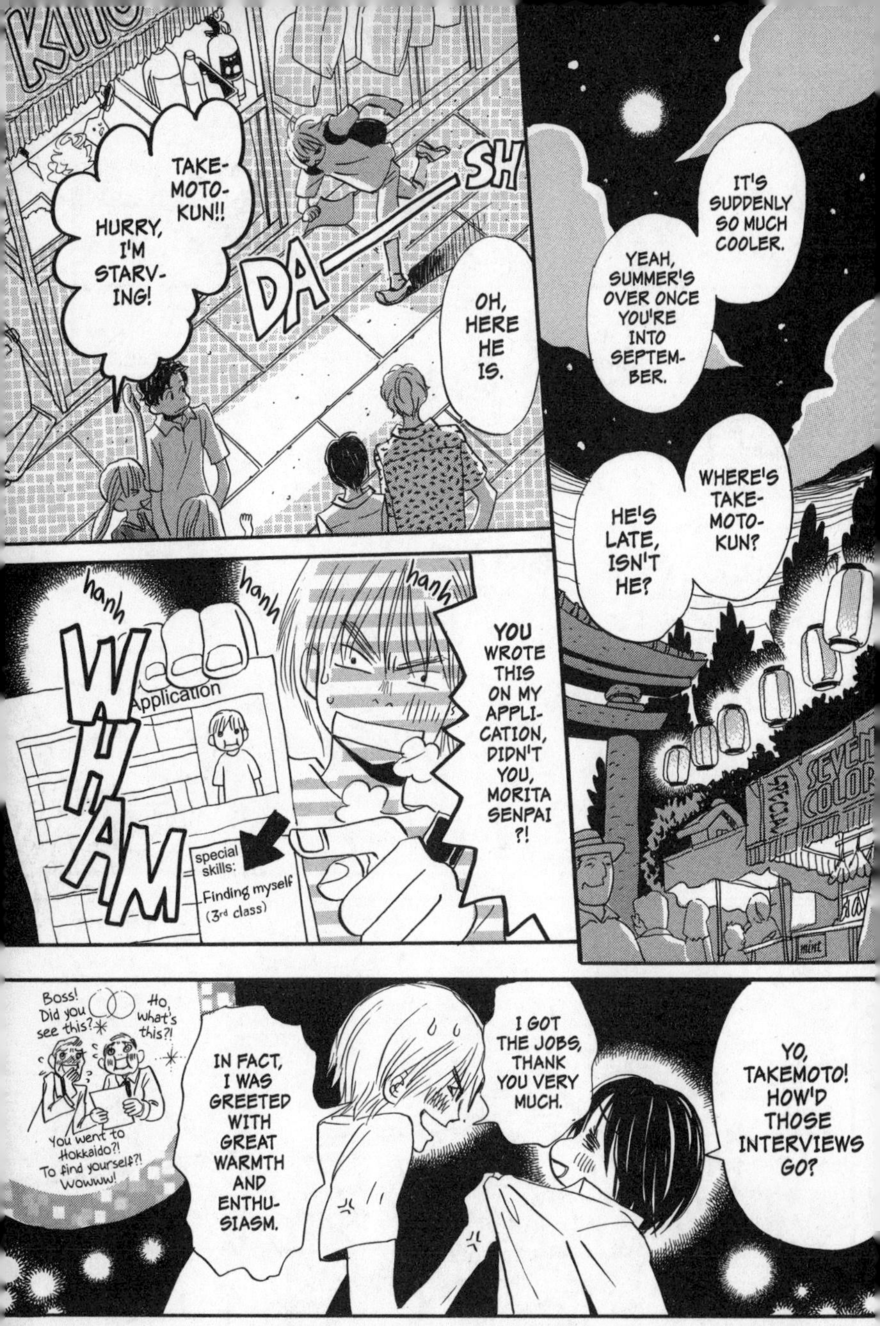
IT'S SUDDENLY SO MUCH COOLER.
YEAH, SUMMER'S OVER ONCE YOU'RE INTO SEPTEMBER.
WHERE'S TAKEMOTO-KUN?
HE'S LATE, ISN'T HE?
OH, HERE HE IS.
DA
SH
TAKEMOTO-KUN!!
HURRY, I'M STARVING!
hanh
hanh
YOU WROTE THIS ON MY APPLICATION, DIDN'T YOU, MORITA SENPAI?!
WHAM
Application
special skills:
Finding myself (3rd class)
YO, TAKEMOTO! HOW'D THOSE INTERVIEWS GO?
I GOT THE JOBS, THANK YOU VERY MUCH.
IN FACT, I WAS GREETED WITH GREAT WARMTH AND ENTHUSIASM.
Ho, what's this?!
Boss! Did you see this?
You went to Hokkaido?! To find yourself?! Wowww!

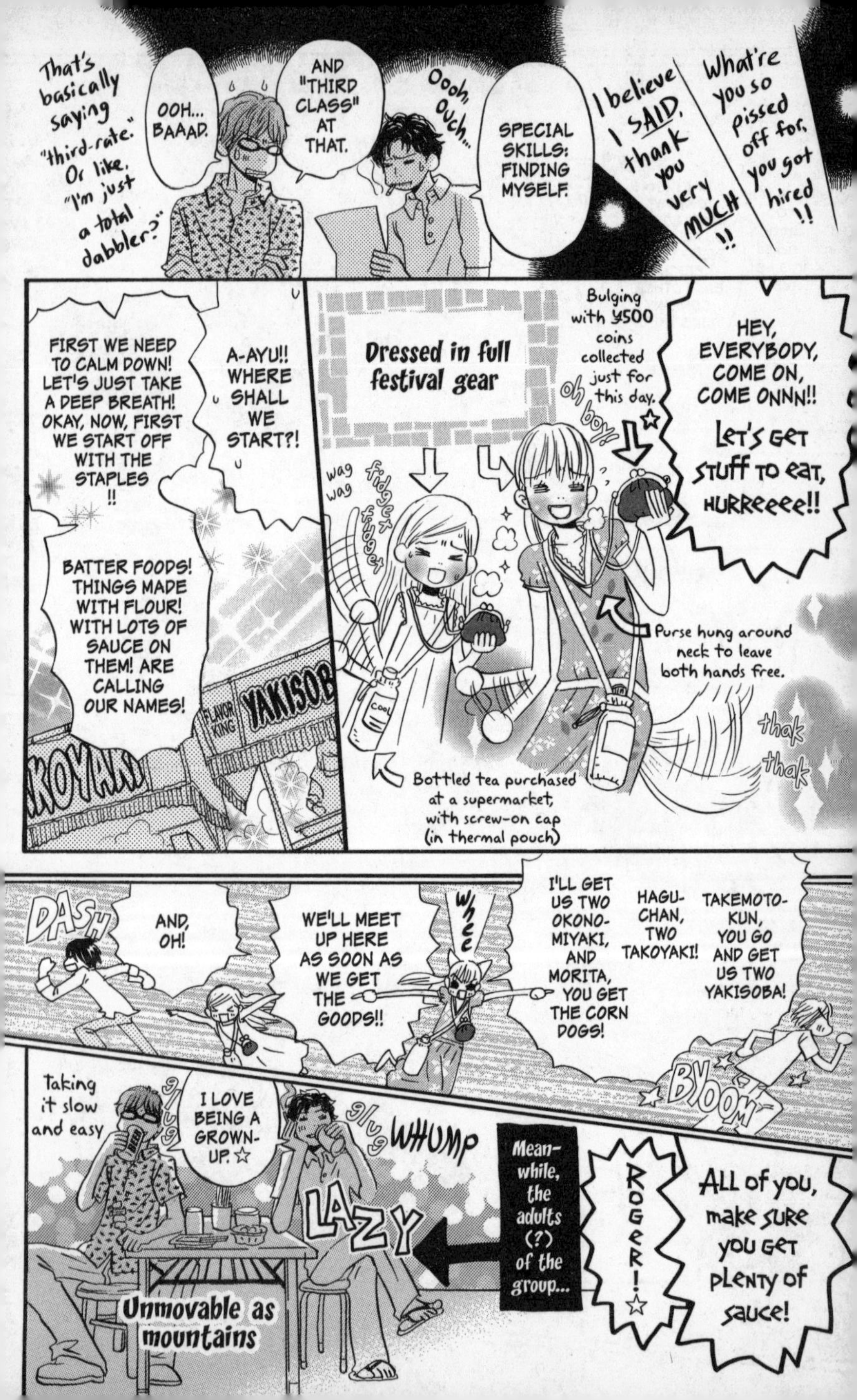
What're you so pissed off for, you got hired!!
I believe I SAID, thank you very MUCH!!
SPECIAL SKILLS: FINDING MYSELF.
Oooh, ouch...
AND "THIRD CLASS" AT THAT.
OOH... BAAAD.
That's basically saying "third-rate." Or like, "I'm just a total dabbler?"
HEY, EVERYBODY, COME ON, COME ONNN!!
LET'S GET STUFF TO EAT, HURREEEE!!
Bulging with ¥500 coins collected just for this day. ☆
oh boy!
Dressed in full festival gear
wag wag
fidget fidget
Purse hung around neck to leave both hands free.
thak thak
COOL
Bottled tea purchased at a supermarket, with screw-on cap (in thermal pouch)
A-AYU!! WHERE SHALL WE START?!
FIRST WE NEED TO CALM DOWN! LET'S JUST TAKE A DEEP BREATH! OKAY, NOW, FIRST WE START OFF WITH THE STAPLES!!
BATTER FOODS! THINGS MADE WITH FLOUR! WITH LOTS OF SAUCE ON THEM! ARE CALLING OUR NAMES!
FLAVOR KING
YAKISOB
TAKEMOTO-KUN, YOU GO AND GET US TWO YAKISOBA!
HAGU-CHAN, TWO TAKOYAKI!
I'LL GET US TWO OKONOMIYAKI, AND MORITA, YOU GET THE CORN DOGS!
whee
BYOOM
WE'LL MEET UP HERE AS SOON AS WE GET THE GOODS!!
AND, OH!
DASH
ALL of you, make sure you get plenty of sauce!
ROGER! ☆
Meanwhile, the adults (?) of the group...
LAZY
WHUMP
glug
I LOVE BEING A GROWN-UP. ☆
glug
taking it slow and easy
Unmovable as mountains

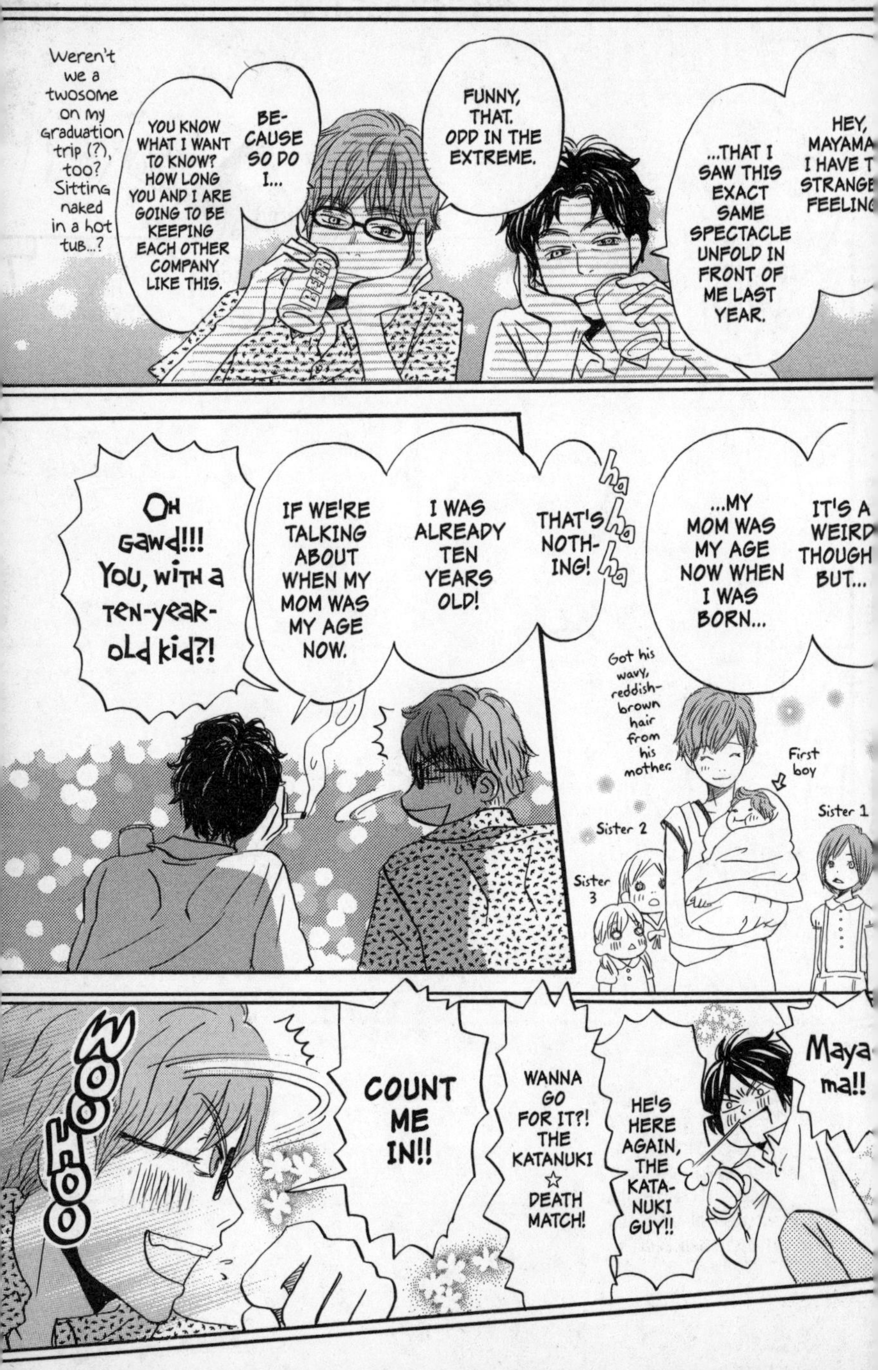
HEY, MAYAMA I HAVE T STRANGE FEELING
...THAT I SAW THIS EXACT SAME SPECTACLE UNFOLD IN FRONT OF ME LAST YEAR.
FUNNY, THAT. ODD IN THE EXTREME.
BE-CAUSE SO DO I...
YOU KNOW WHAT I WANT TO KNOW? HOW LONG YOU AND I ARE GOING TO BE KEEPING EACH OTHER COMPANY LIKE THIS.
Weren't we a twosome on my Graduation trip (?), too? Sitting naked in a hot tub...?
BEER
IT'S A WEIRD THOUGH BUT...
...MY MOM WAS MY AGE NOW WHEN I WAS BORN...
Got his wavy, reddish-brown hair from his mother.
First boy
Sister 1
Sister 2
Sister 3
ha ha ha
THAT'S NOTH-ING!
I WAS ALREADY TEN YEARS OLD!
IF WE'RE TALKING ABOUT WHEN MY MOM WAS MY AGE NOW.
Oh gawd!!! You, with a ten-year-old kid?!
Maya ma!!
HE'S HERE AGAIN, THE KATA-NUKI GUY!!
WANNA GO FOR IT?! THE KATANUKI ☆ DEATH MATCH!
COUNT ME IN!!
WOOHOOHOO

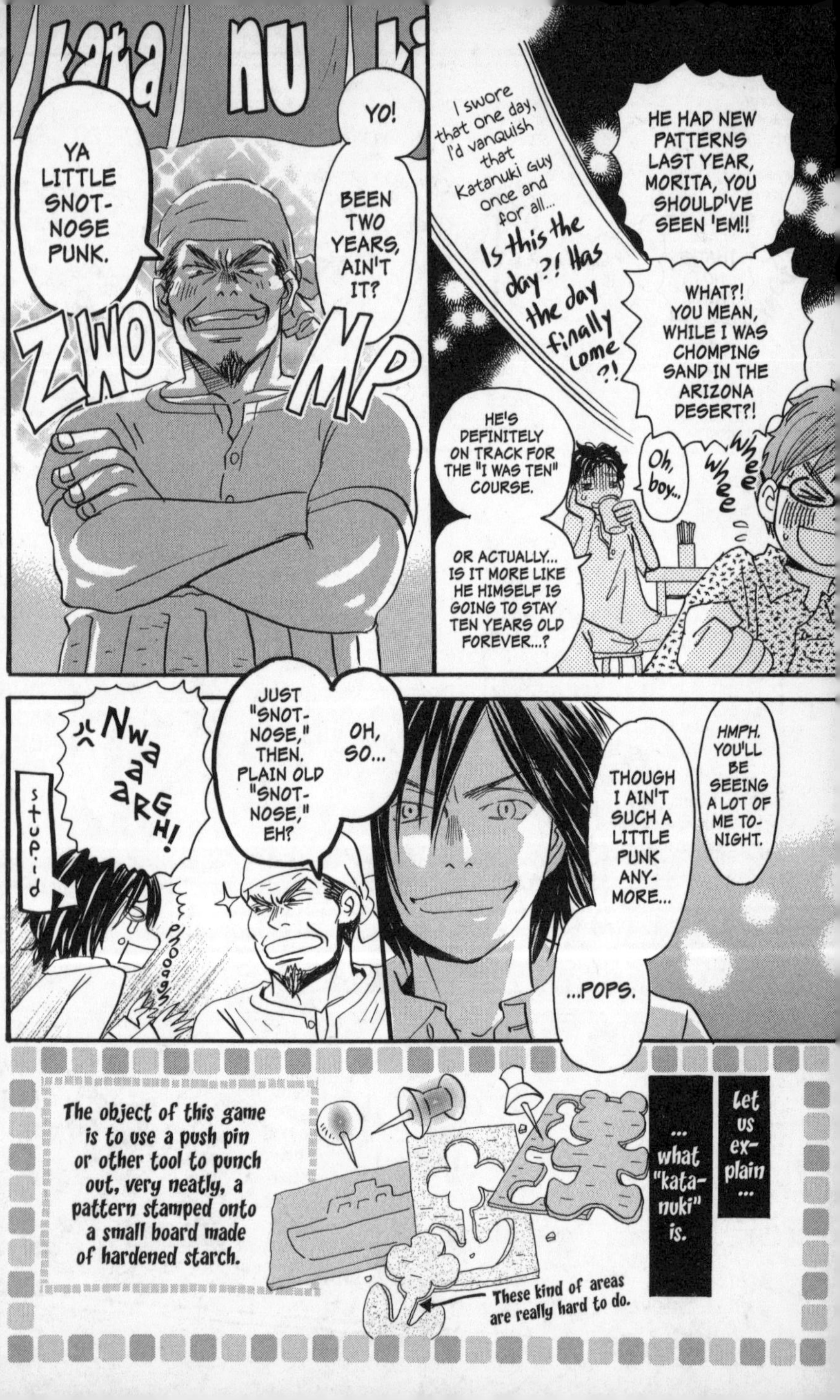
HE HAD NEW PATTERNS LAST YEAR, MORITA, YOU SHOULD'VE SEEN 'EM!!
I swore that one day, I'd vanquish that Katanuki Guy once and for all... Is this the day?! Has the day finally come?!
WHAT?! YOU MEAN, WHILE I WAS CHOMPING SAND IN THE ARIZONA DESERT?!
whee whee
Oh, boy...
HE'S DEFINITELY ON TRACK FOR THE "I WAS TEN" COURSE.
OR ACTUALLY... IS IT MORE LIKE HE HIMSELF IS GOING TO STAY TEN YEARS OLD FOREVER...?
kata nu ki
YO!
BEEN TWO YEARS, AIN'T IT?
YA LITTLE SNOT-NOSE PUNK.
ZWOMP
HMPH. YOU'LL BE SEEING A LOT OF ME TO-NIGHT.
THOUGH I AIN'T SUCH A LITTLE PUNK ANY-MORE...
...POPS.
OH, SO...
JUST "SNOT-NOSE," THEN. PLAIN OLD "SNOT-NOSE," EH?
Nwaaargh!
stupid
Let us ex-plain...
...what "kata-nuki" is.
The object of this game is to use a push pin or other tool to punch out, very neatly, a pattern stamped onto a small board made of hardened starch.
These kind of areas are really hard to do.

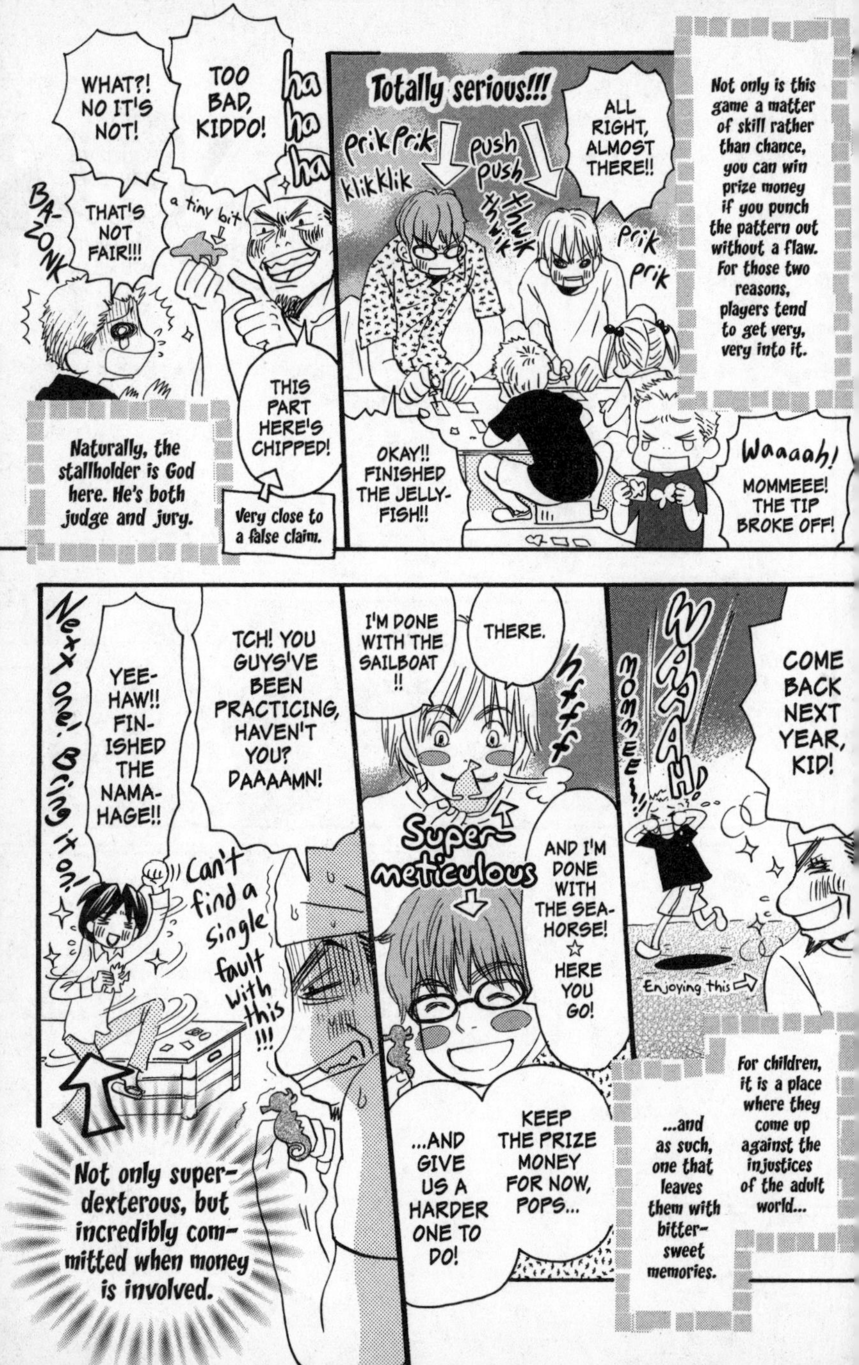
Not only is this game a matter of skill rather than chance, you can win prize money if you punch the pattern out without a flaw. For those two reasons, players tend to get very, very into it.
Totally serious!!!
ALL RIGHT, ALMOST THERE!!
prik prik klikklik
push push thwik thwik
prik prik
OKAY!! FINISHED THE JELLY-FISH!!
Waaaah!
MOMMEEE! THE TIP BROKE OFF!
THIS PART HERE'S CHIPPED!
Very close to a false claim.
WHAT?! NO IT'S NOT!
TOO BAD, KIDDO!
ha ha ha
a tiny bit
THAT'S NOT FAIR!!!
BA-ZONK
Naturally, the stallholder is God here. He's both judge and jury.
COME BACK NEXT YEAR, KID!
WAAAH!
MOMMEEE~!!
Enjoying this
THERE.
I'M DONE WITH THE SAILBOAT!!
hffff
Super-meticulous
AND I'M DONE WITH THE SEA-HORSE! ☆ HERE YOU GO!
KEEP THE PRIZE MONEY FOR NOW, POPS...
...AND GIVE US A HARDER ONE TO DO!
For children, it is a place where they come up against the injustices of the adult world...
...and as such, one that leaves them with bitter-sweet memories.
TCH! YOU GUYS'VE BEEN PRACTICING, HAVEN'T YOU? DAAAAMN!
YEE-HAW!! FIN-ISHED THE NAMA-HAGE!!
Next one! Bring it on!
Can't find a single fault with this!!!
Not only super-dexterous, but incredibly com-mitted when money is involved.

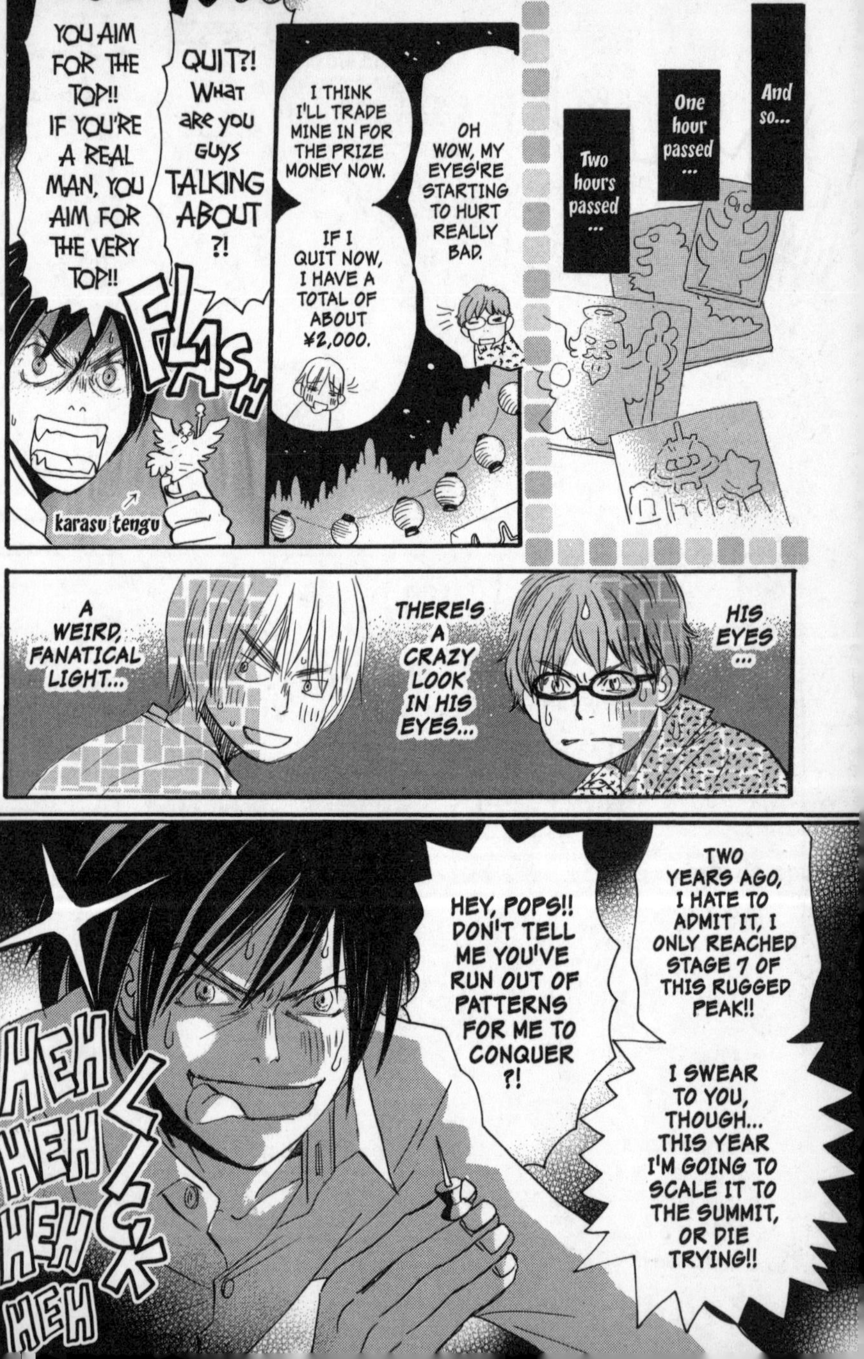
And so...
One hour passed...
Two hours passed...
OH WOW, MY EYES'RE STARTING TO HURT REALLY BAD.
I THINK I'LL TRADE MINE IN FOR THE PRIZE MONEY NOW.
IF I QUIT NOW, I HAVE A TOTAL OF ABOUT ¥2,000.
QUIT?! What are you guys TALKING ABOUT?!
YOU AIM FOR THE TOP!! IF YOU'RE A REAL MAN, YOU AIM FOR THE VERY TOP!!
FLASH
karasu tengu
HIS EYES...
THERE'S A CRAZY LOOK IN HIS EYES...
A WEIRD, FANATICAL LIGHT...
TWO YEARS AGO, I HATE TO ADMIT IT, I ONLY REACHED STAGE 7 OF THIS RUGGED PEAK!!
I SWEAR TO YOU, THOUGH... THIS YEAR I'M GOING TO SCALE IT TO THE SUMMIT, OR DIE TRYING!!
HEY, POPS!! DON'T TELL ME YOU'VE RUN OUT OF PATTERNS FOR ME TO CONQUER?!
LICK
HEH HEH HEH HEH

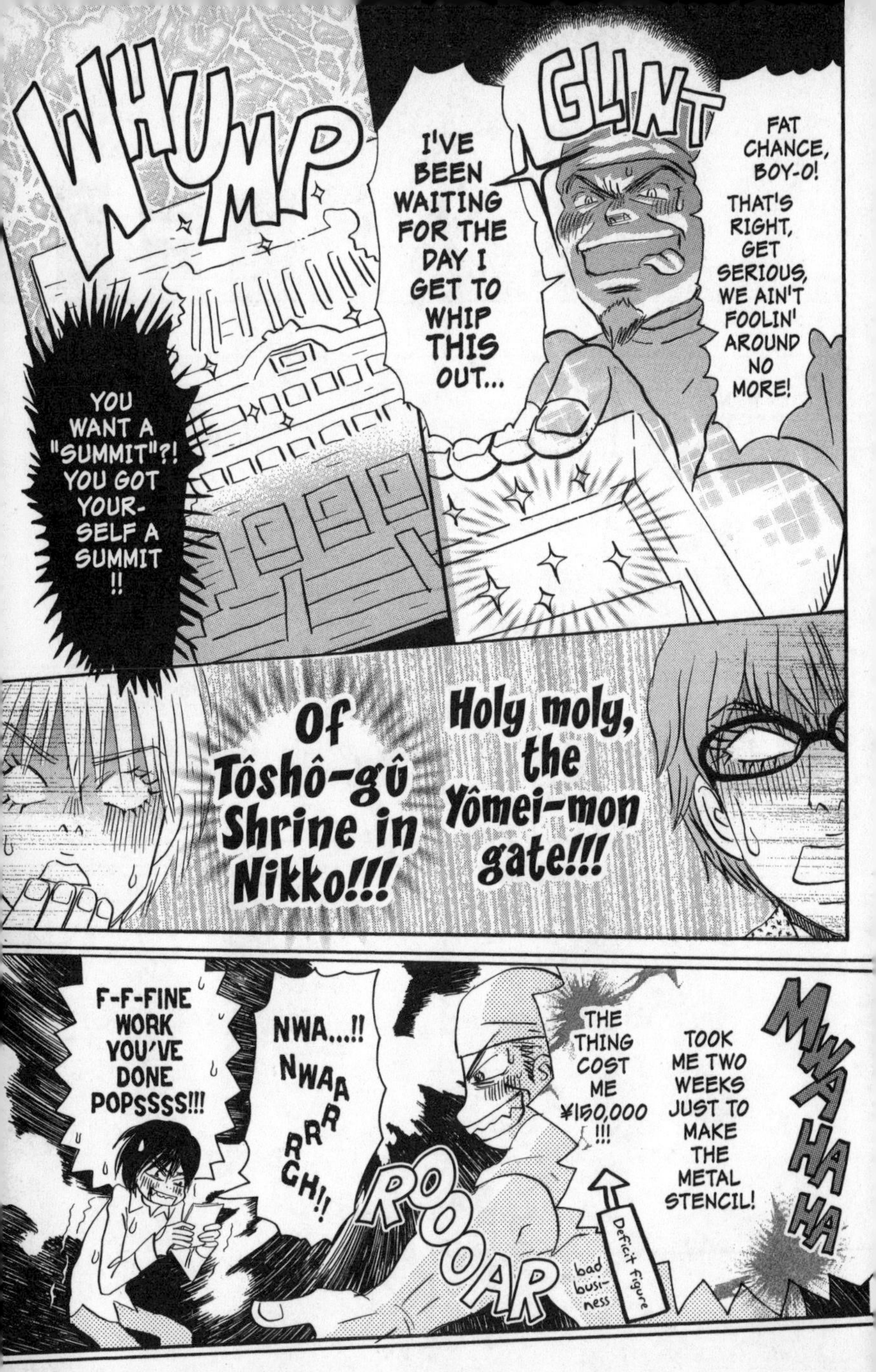
GLINT
FAT CHANCE, BOY-O!
THAT'S RIGHT, GET SERIOUS, WE AIN'T FOOLIN' AROUND NO MORE!
I'VE BEEN WAITING FOR THE DAY I GET TO WHIP THIS OUT...
WHUMP
YOU WANT A "SUMMIT"?! YOU GOT YOURSELF A SUMMIT !!
Holy moly, the Yômei-mon gate!!!
Of Tôshô-gû Shrine in Nikko!!!
MWAHAHAHA
TOOK ME TWO WEEKS JUST TO MAKE THE METAL STENCIL!
THE THING COST ME ¥150,000 !!!
Deficit figure
bad busi-ness
NWA...!! NWAARRRRGH!!
ROOOOAR
F-F-FINE WORK YOU'VE DONE POPSSSS!!!

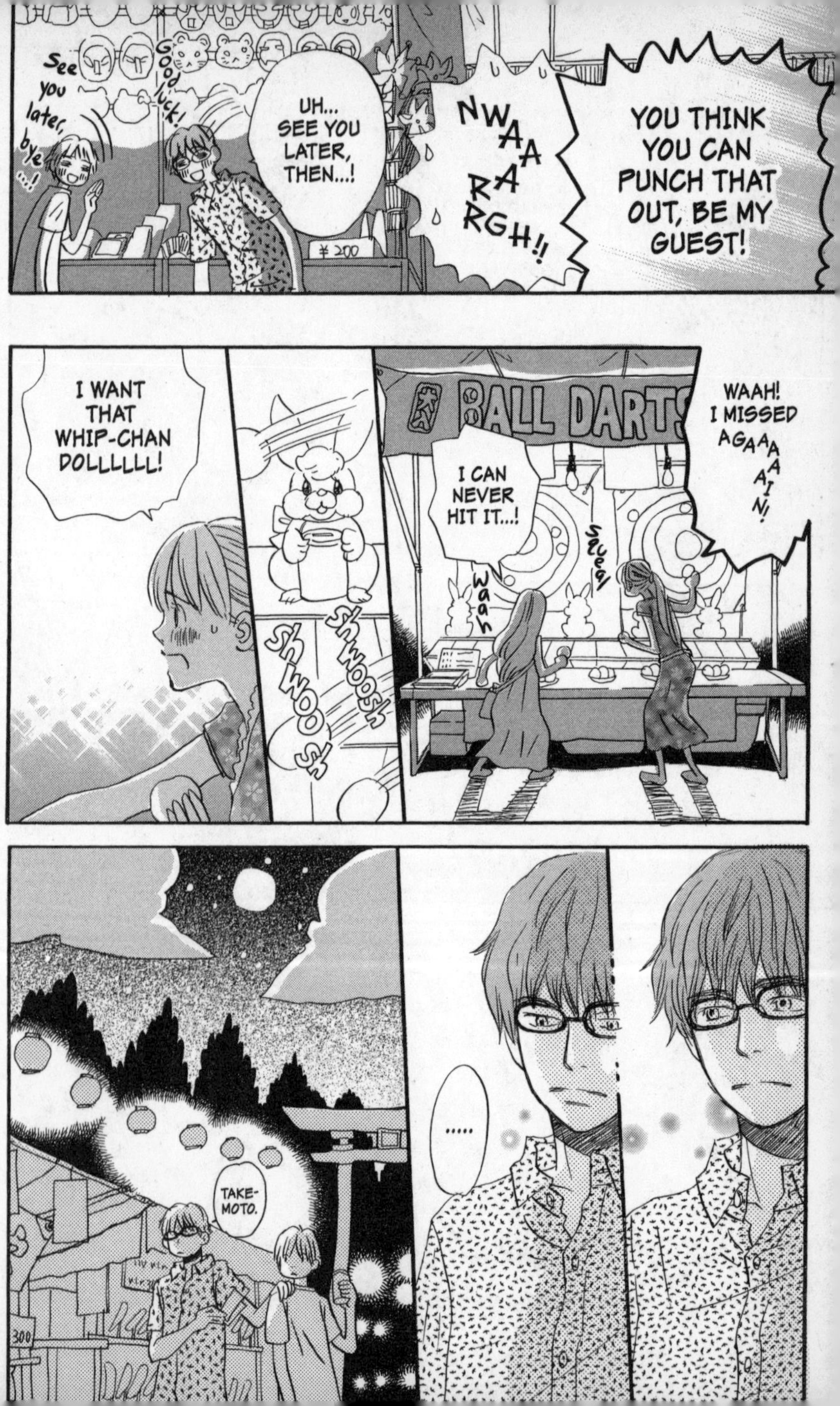
YOU THINK YOU CAN PUNCH THAT OUT, BE MY GUEST!
NWAAAARRGH!!
UH... SEE YOU LATER, THEN...!
Good luck!
See you later, bye...!
¥200
WAAH! I MISSED AGAAAAAIN!
BALL DARTS
I CAN NEVER HIT IT...!
Squeal
Waah
Shwoosh
Shwoosh
I WANT THAT WHIP-CHAN DOLLLLLL!
.....
TAKE-MOTO.
300

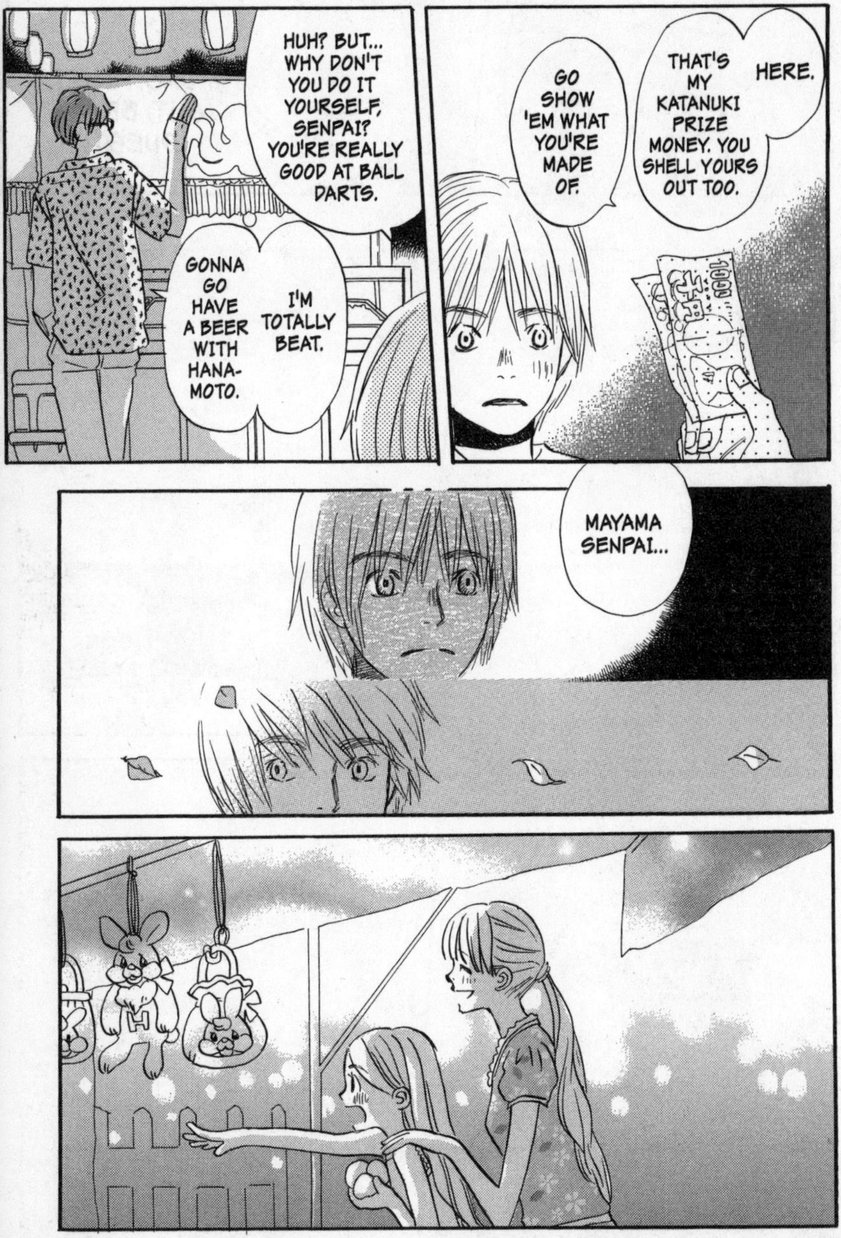
HERE.
THAT'S MY KATANUKI PRIZE MONEY. YOU SHELL YOURS OUT TOO.
GO SHOW 'EM WHAT YOU'RE MADE OF.
HUH? BUT... WHY DON'T YOU DO IT YOURSELF, SENPAI? YOU'RE REALLY GOOD AT BALL DARTS.
I'M TOTALLY BEAT.
GONNA GO HAVE A BEER WITH HANA-MOTO.
MAYAMA SENPAI...

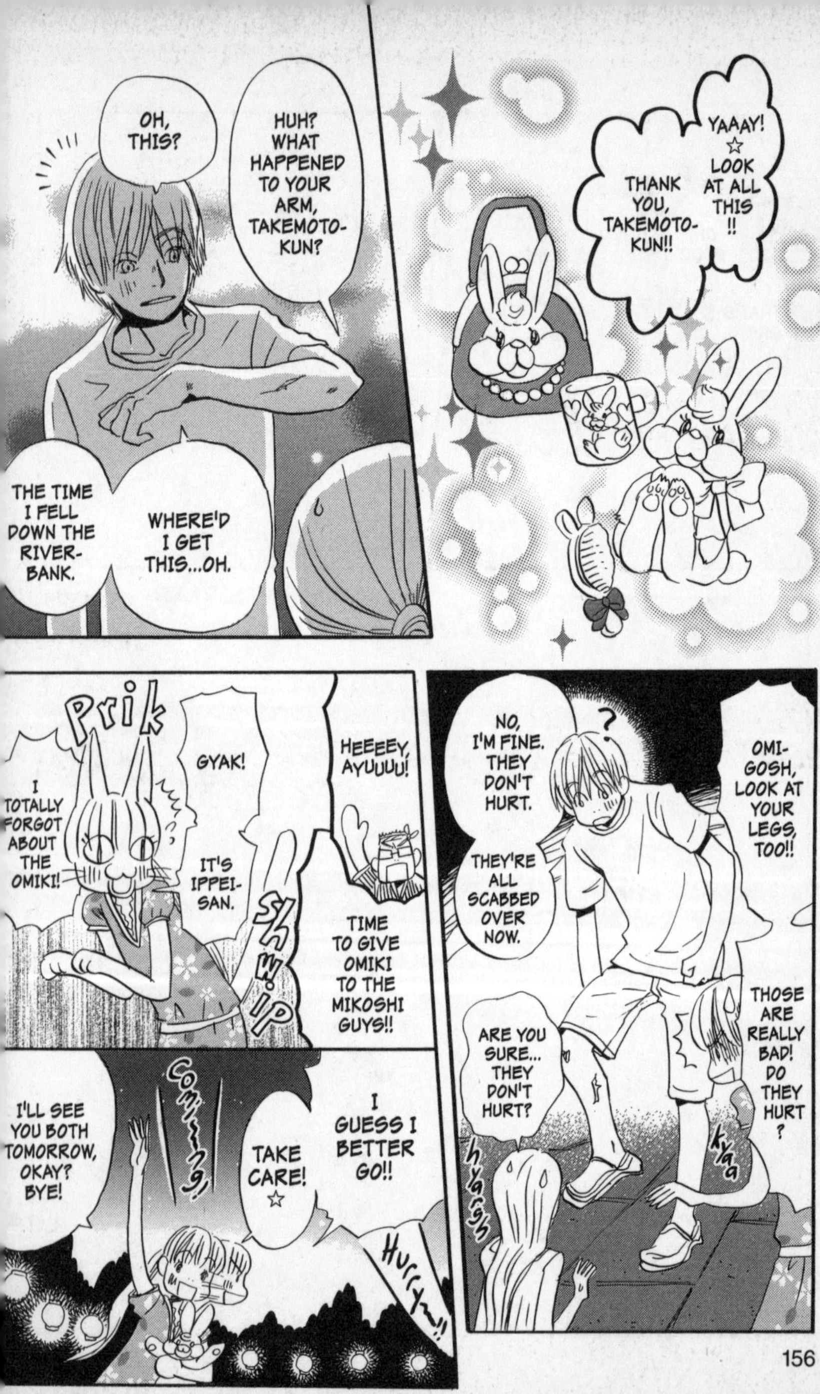
YAAAY! ☆ LOOK AT ALL THIS!!
THANK YOU, TAKEMOTO-KUN!!
HUH? WHAT HAPPENED TO YOUR ARM, TAKEMOTO-KUN?
OH, THIS?
WHERE'D I GET THIS...OH.
THE TIME I FELL DOWN THE RIVER-BANK.
OMI-GOSH, LOOK AT YOUR LEGS, TOO!!
NO, I'M FINE. THEY DON'T HURT.
THEY'RE ALL SCABBED OVER NOW.
THOSE ARE REALLY BAD! DO THEY HURT?
ARE YOU SURE... THEY DON'T HURT?
HEEEEY, AYUUUU!
TIME TO GIVE OMIKI TO THE MIKOSHI GUYS!!
GYAK!
Prik
IT'S IPPEI-SAN.
Shwip
I TOTALLY FORGOT ABOUT THE OMIKI!
I GUESS I BETTER GO!!
TAKE CARE! ☆
Comi~ng!
Hurry~!!
I'LL SEE YOU BOTH TOMORROW, OKAY? BYE!

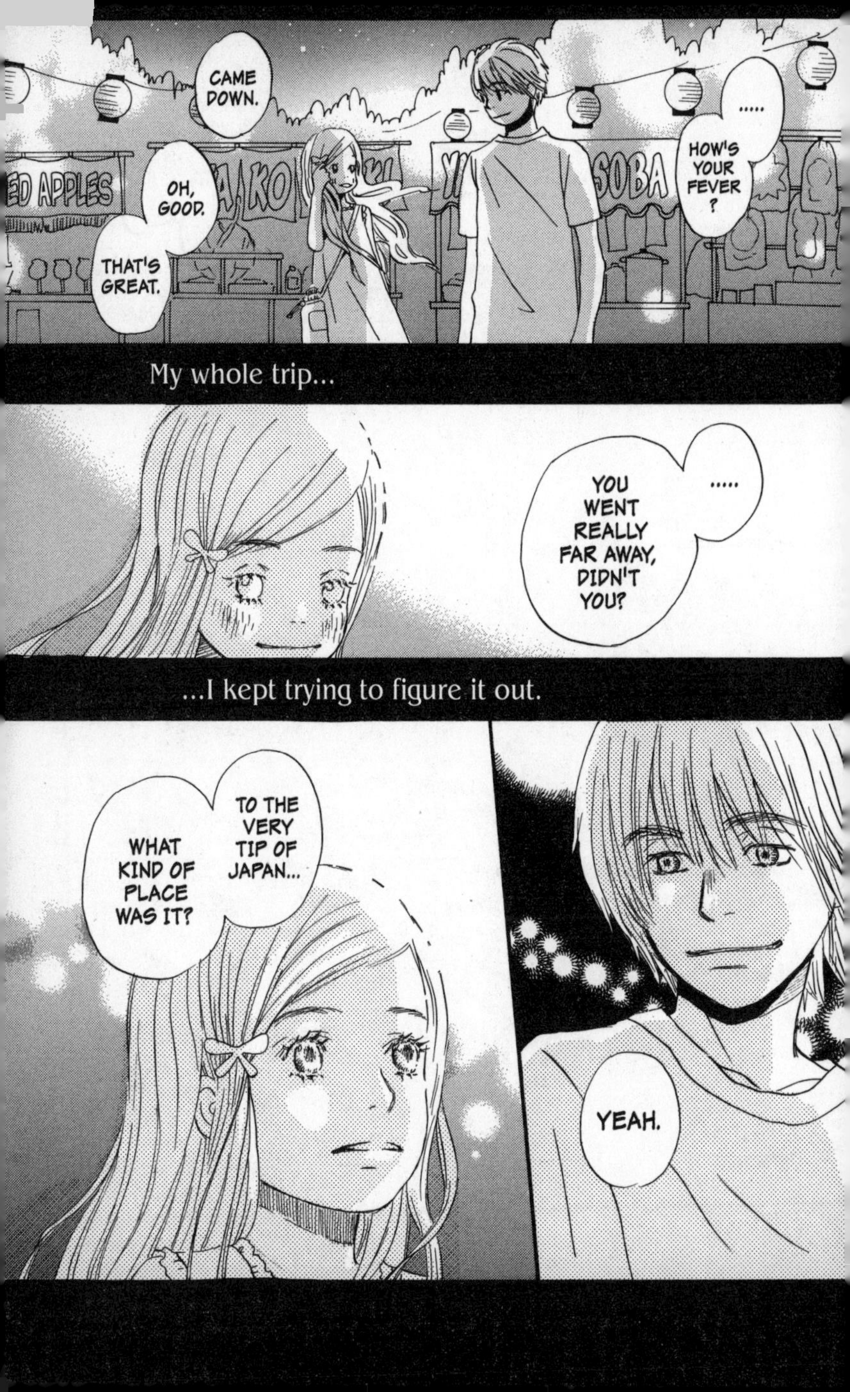
.....
HOW'S YOUR FEVER ?
SOBA
CAME DOWN.
OH, GOOD.
THAT'S GREAT.
ED APPLES
My whole trip...
.....
YOU WENT REALLY FAR AWAY, DIDN'T YOU?
...I kept trying to figure it out.
YEAH.
TO THE VERY TIP OF JAPAN...
WHAT KIND OF PLACE WAS IT?

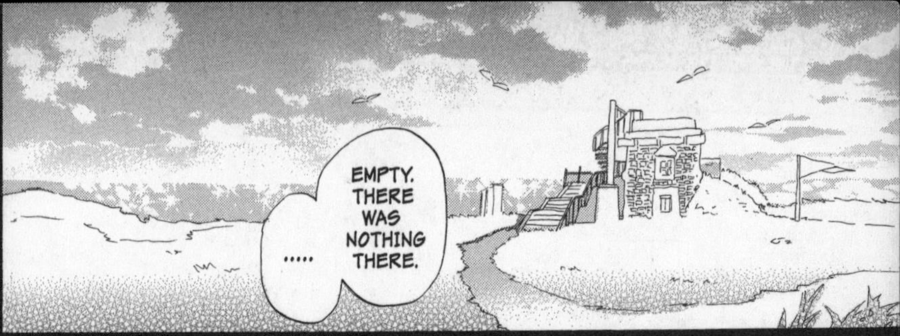
EMPTY. THERE WAS NOTHING THERE.
.....

I wanted to see how far I could go if I kept riding without ever looking back.

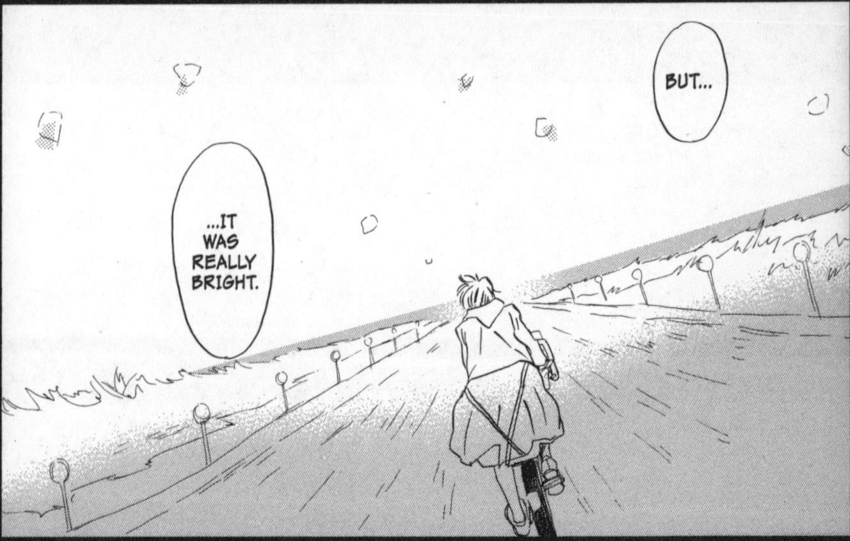
BUT...
...IT WAS REALLY BRIGHT.

I kept wondering why I wanted to do that...

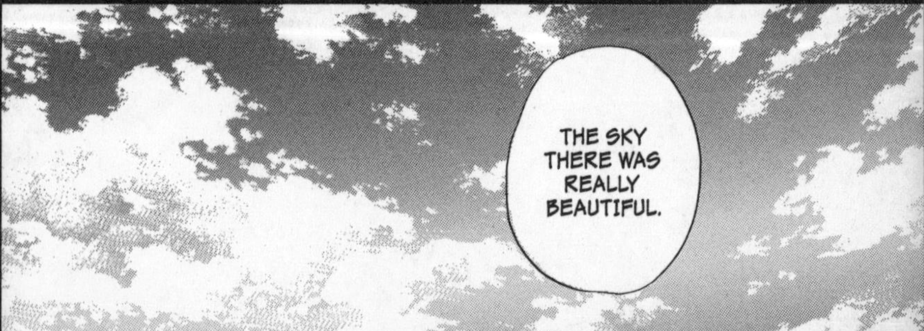
THE SKY THERE WAS REALLY BEAUTIFUL.

...and now, I finally knew.

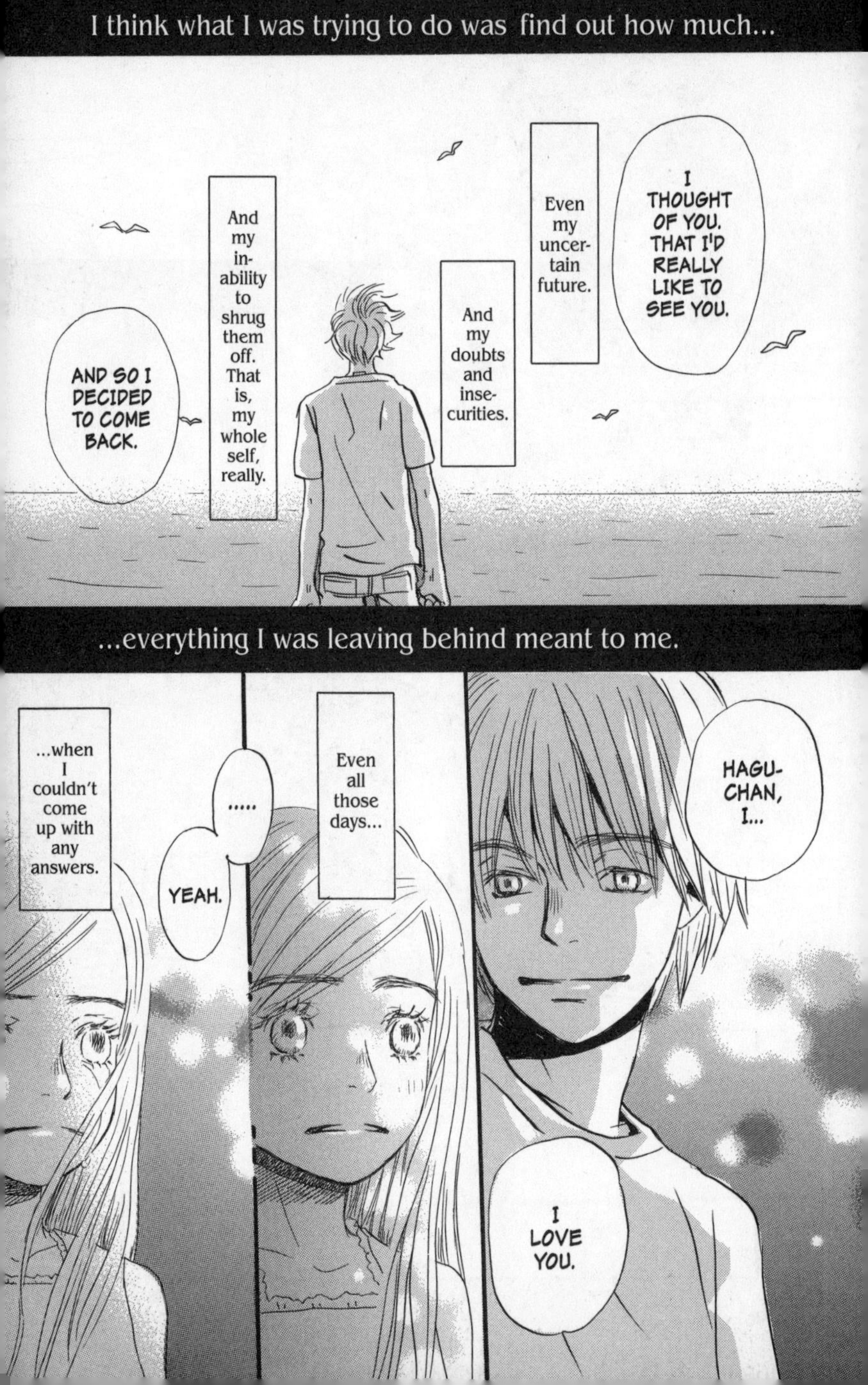
I think what I was trying to do was find out how much...
I THOUGHT OF YOU. THAT I'D REALLY LIKE TO SEE YOU.
Even my uncer-tain future.
And my doubts and inse-curities.
And my in-ability to shrug them off. That is, my whole self, really.
AND SO I DECIDED TO COME BACK.
...everything I was leaving behind meant to me.
HAGU-CHAN, I...
I LOVE YOU.
Even all those days...
......
YEAH.
...when I couldn't come up with any answers.

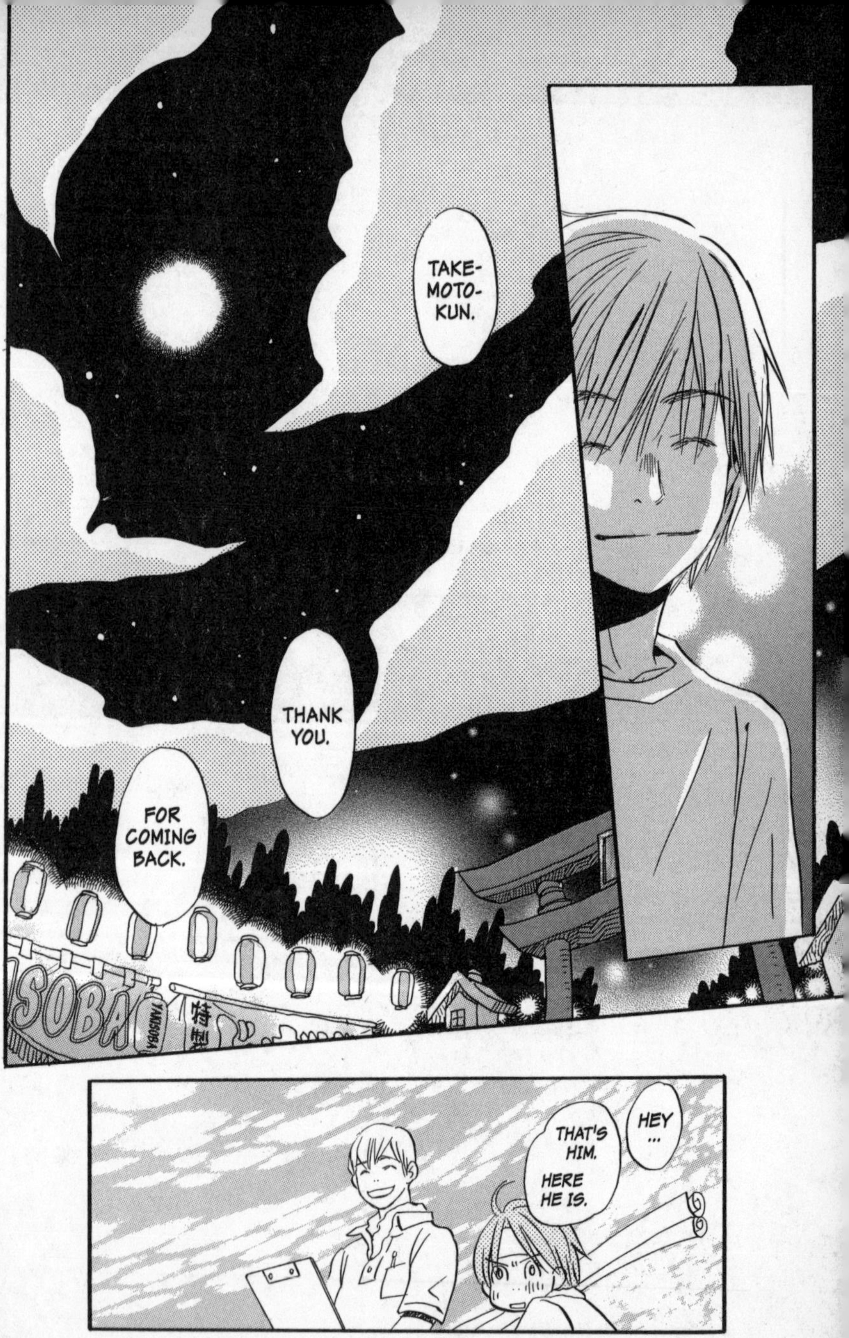
TAKE-MOTO-KUN.
THANK YOU.
FOR COMING BACK.
YAKISOBA
HEY ...
THAT'S HIM.
HERE HE IS.

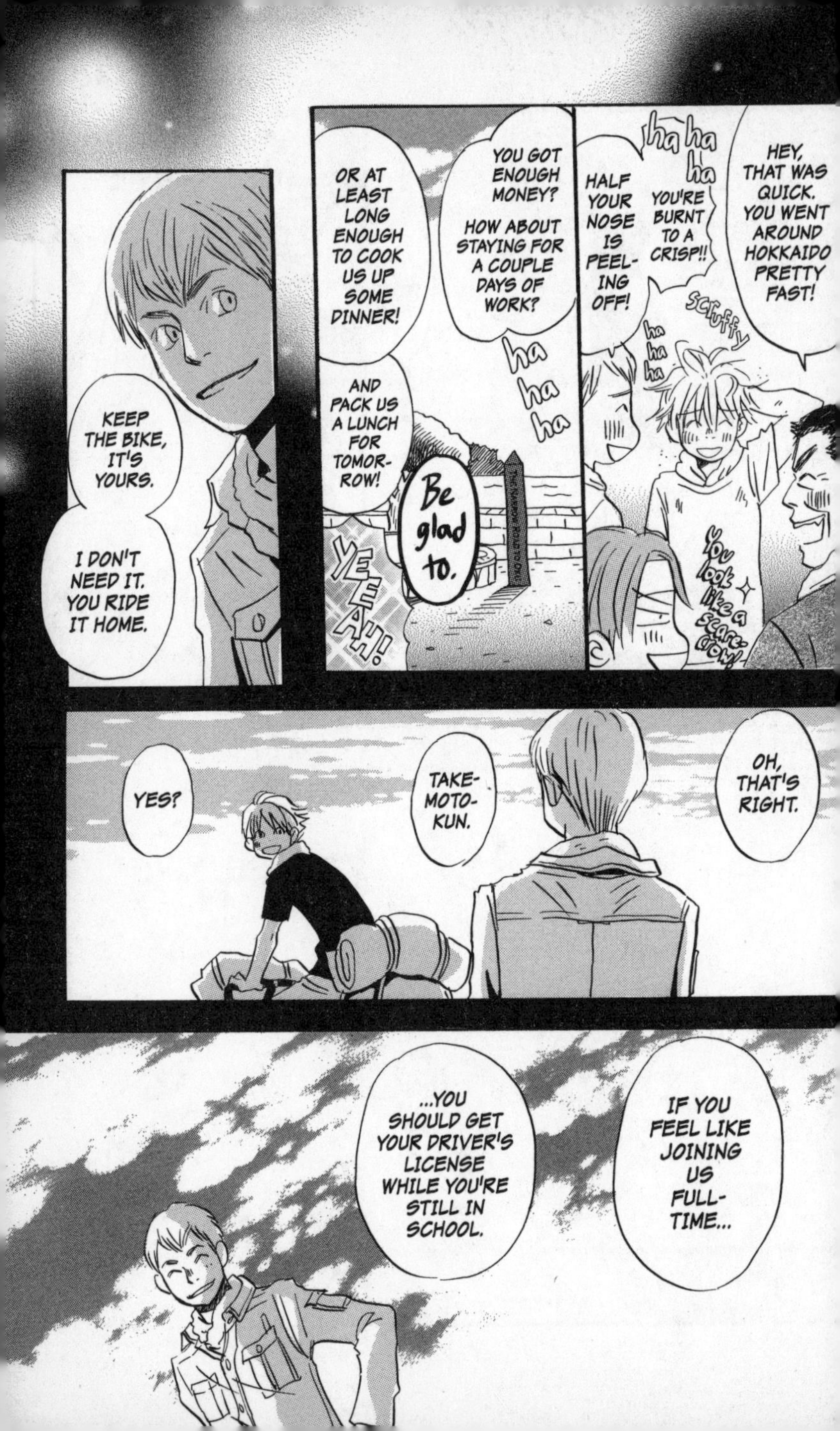
HEY, THAT WAS QUICK. YOU WENT AROUND HOKKAIDO PRETTY FAST!
ha ha ha
YOU'RE BURNT TO A CRISP!!
HALF YOUR NOSE IS PEEL-ING OFF!
scruffy
ha ha ha
You look like a scare-crow!
YOU GOT ENOUGH MONEY? HOW ABOUT STAYING FOR A COUPLE DAYS OF WORK?
OR AT LEAST LONG ENOUGH TO COOK US UP SOME DINNER!
ha ha ha
AND PACK US A LUNCH FOR TOMOR-ROW!
Be glad to.
YEEAH!
KEEP THE BIKE, IT'S YOURS.
I DON'T NEED IT. YOU RIDE IT HOME.
OH, THAT'S RIGHT.
TAKE-MOTO-KUN.
YES?
IF YOU FEEL LIKE JOINING US FULL-TIME...
...YOU SHOULD GET YOUR DRIVER'S LICENSE WHILE YOU'RE STILL IN SCHOOL.

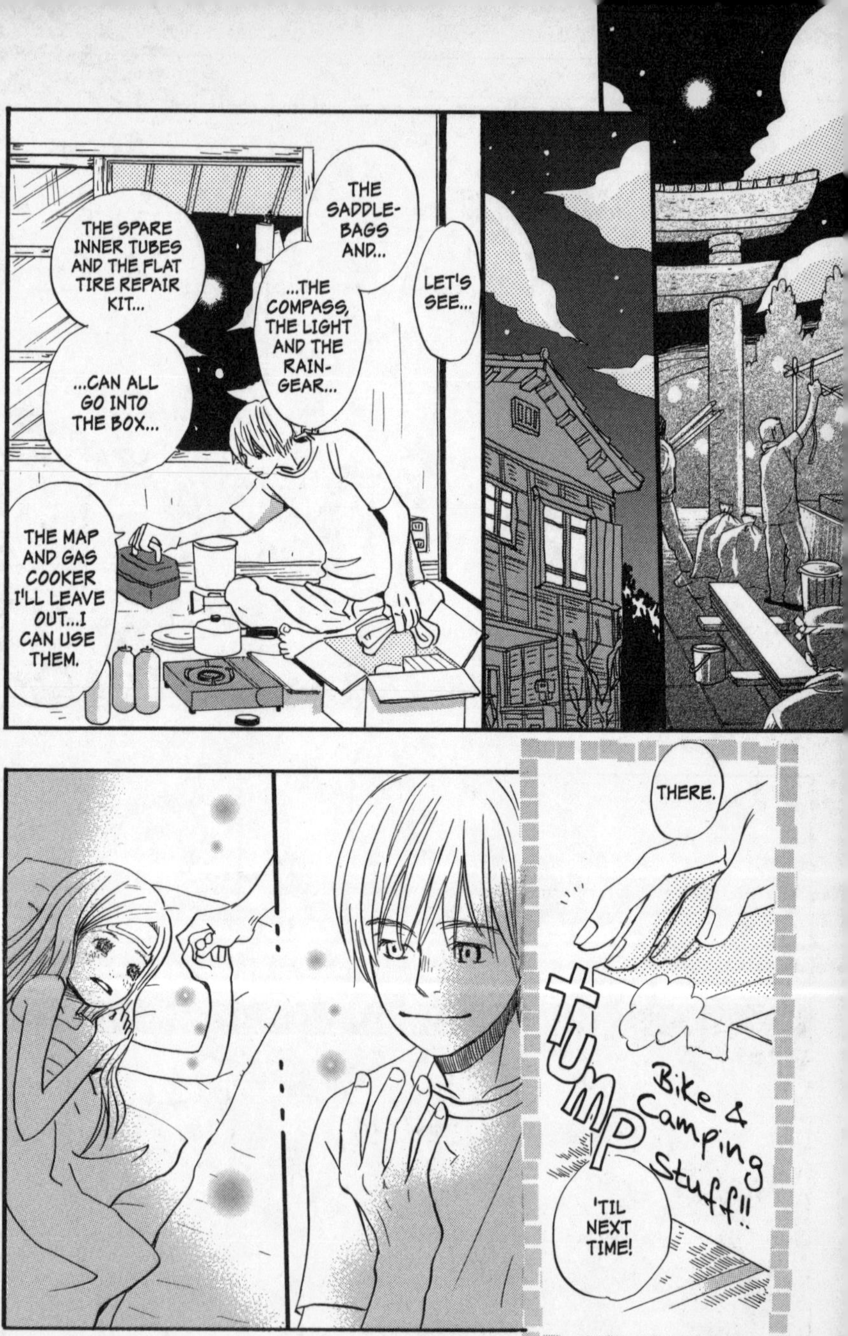
LET'S SEE...
THE SADDLE-BAGS AND...
...THE COMPASS, THE LIGHT AND THE RAIN-GEAR...
THE SPARE INNER TUBES AND THE FLAT TIRE REPAIR KIT...
...CAN ALL GO INTO THE BOX...
THE MAP AND GAS COOKER I'LL LEAVE OUT...I CAN USE THEM.
THERE.
TUMP
Bike & Camping Stuff!!
'TIL NEXT TIME!

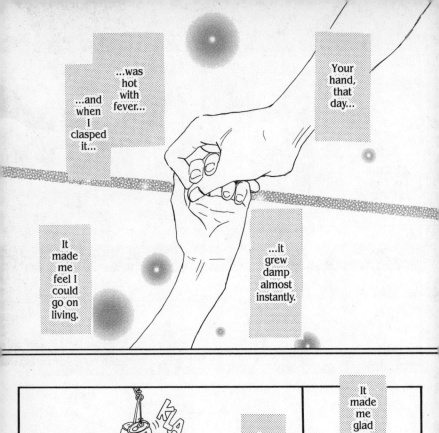

Your hand, that day...
...was hot with fever...
...and when I clasped it...
...it grew damp almost instantly.
It made me feel I could go on living.
It made me glad I'd come back...
...from the bottom...
...of my heart.
KLANK
KLONK
Mikan
—And that's why...
KLANK
YEAH? MAYAMA SENPAI? WHAT IS IT?

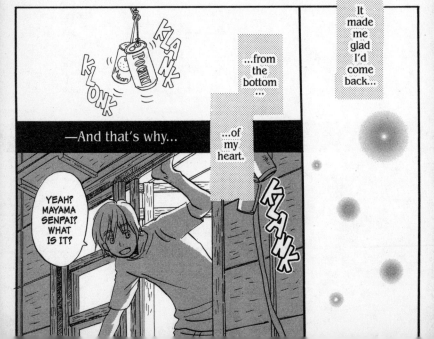

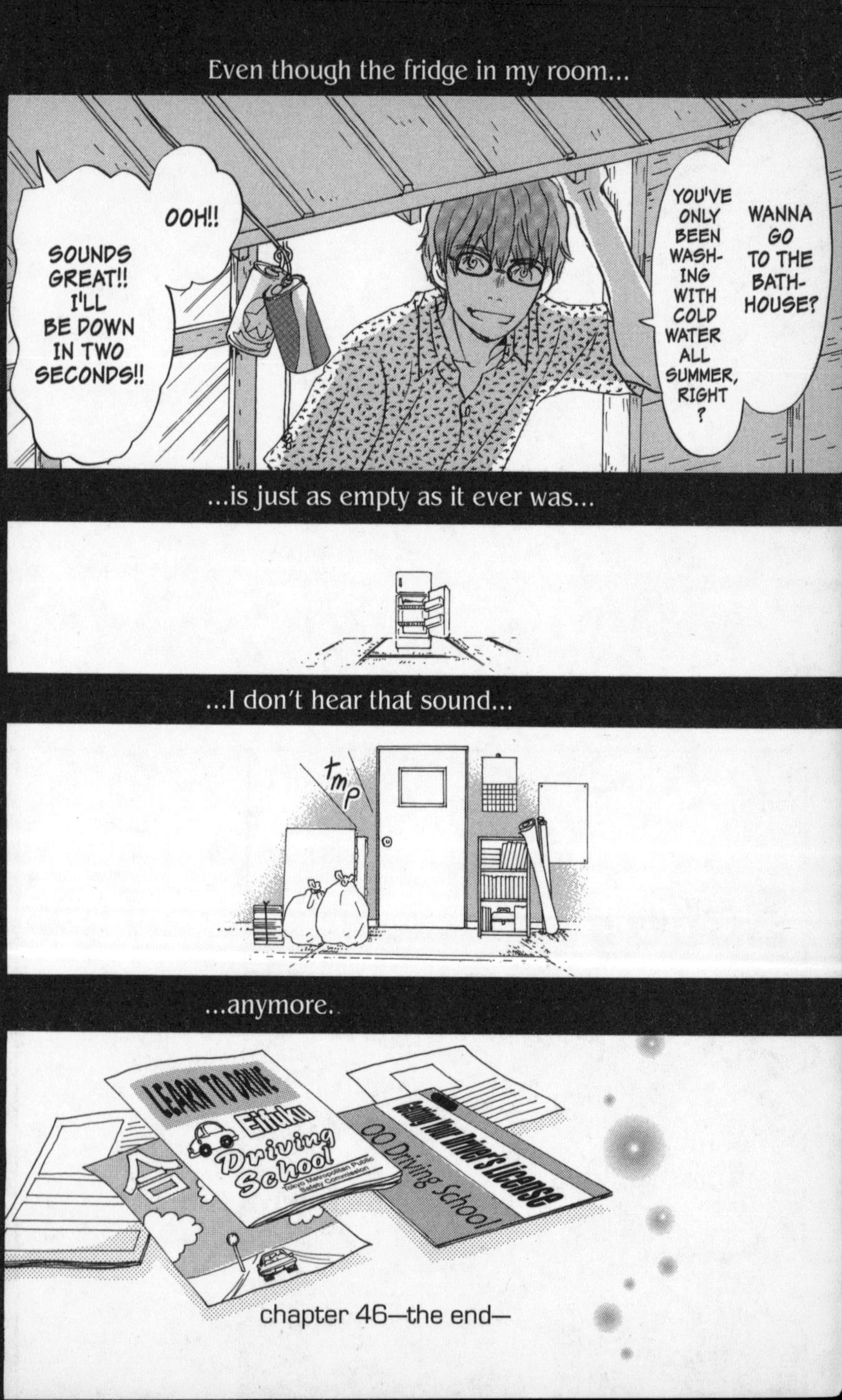
Even though the fridge in my room...
WANNA GO TO THE BATH-HOUSE?
YOU'VE ONLY BEEN WASH-ING WITH COLD WATER ALL SUMMER, RIGHT?
OOH!!
SOUNDS GREAT!! I'LL BE DOWN IN TWO SECONDS!!
...is just as empty as it ever was...
...I don't hear that sound...
tmp
...anymore.
LEARN TO DRIVE
Eifuku Driving School
Tokyo Metropolitan Public Safety Commission
Getting Your Driver's License
○○ Driving School
chapter 46—the end—

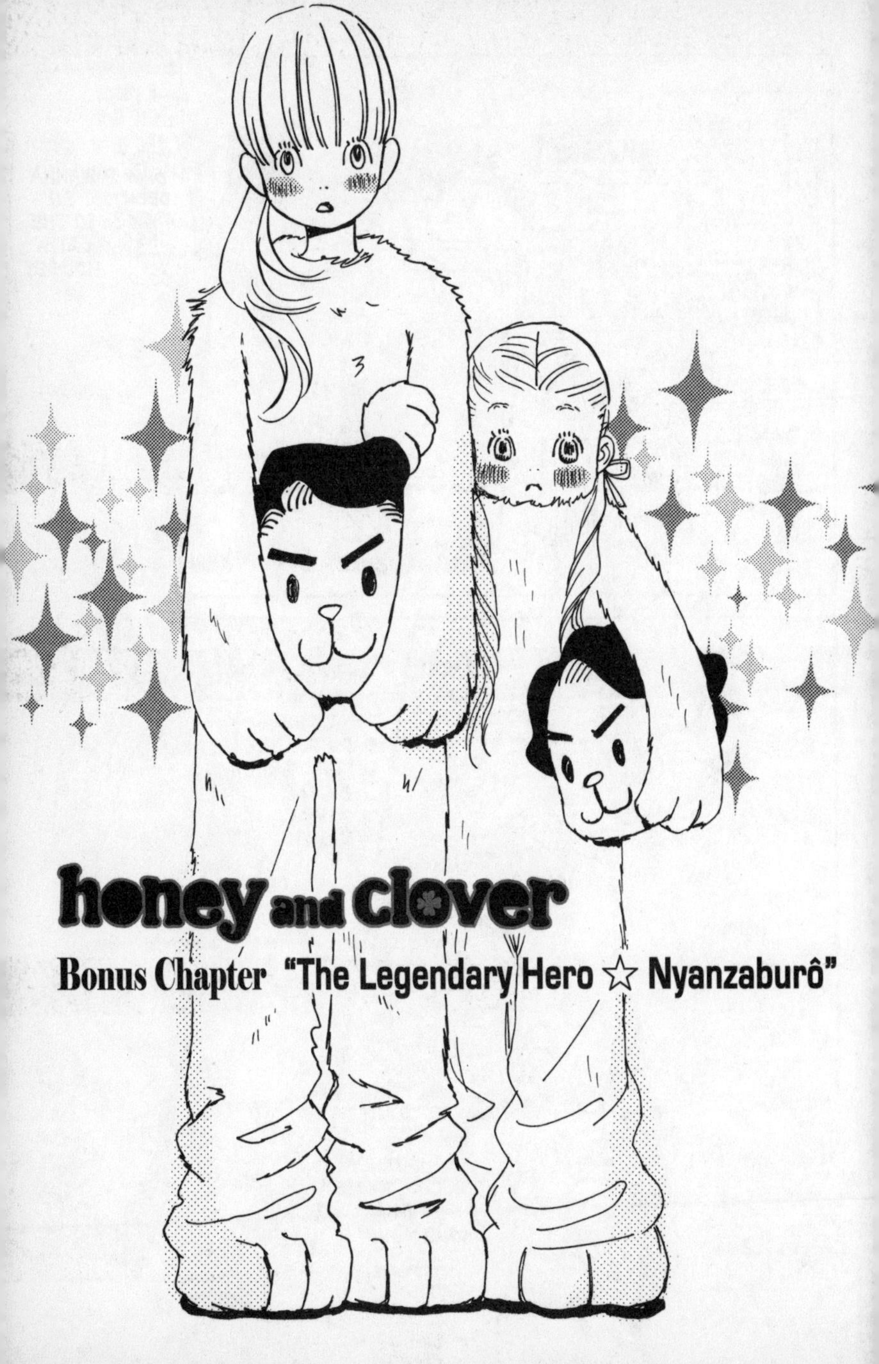

honey and clover

Bonus Chapter "The Legendary Hero ☆ Nyanzaburô"

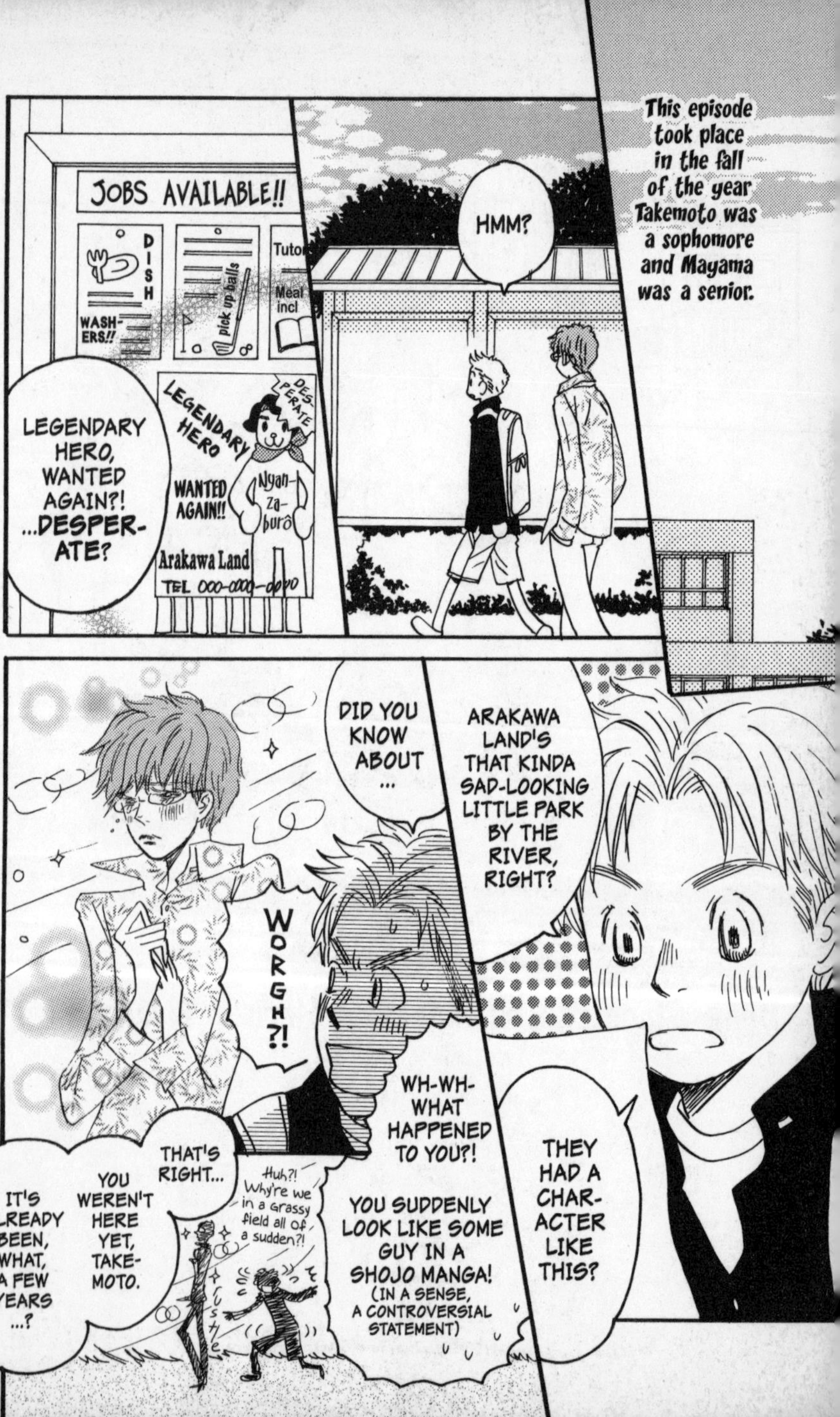
This episode took place in the fall of the year Takemoto was a sophomore and Mayama was a senior.
HMM?
JOBS AVAILABLE!!
DISH WASHERS!!
pick up balls
Tutor
Meal incl
LEGENDARY HERO
DES-PERATE
WANTED AGAIN!!
Nyan-za-burô
Arakawa Land
TEL 000-0000-0000
LEGENDARY HERO, WANTED AGAIN?! ...DESPERATE?
ARAKAWA LAND'S THAT KINDA SAD-LOOKING LITTLE PARK BY THE RIVER, RIGHT?
THEY HAD A CHARACTER LIKE THIS?
DID YOU KNOW ABOUT ...
WORGH?!
WH-WH-WHAT HAPPENED TO YOU?!
YOU SUDDENLY LOOK LIKE SOME GUY IN A SHOJO MANGA! (IN A SENSE, A CONTROVERSIAL STATEMENT)
Huh?! Why're we in a grassy field all of a sudden?!
rustle
THAT'S RIGHT...
YOU WEREN'T HERE YET, TAKEMOTO.
IT'S ALREADY BEEN, WHAT, A FEW YEARS ...?

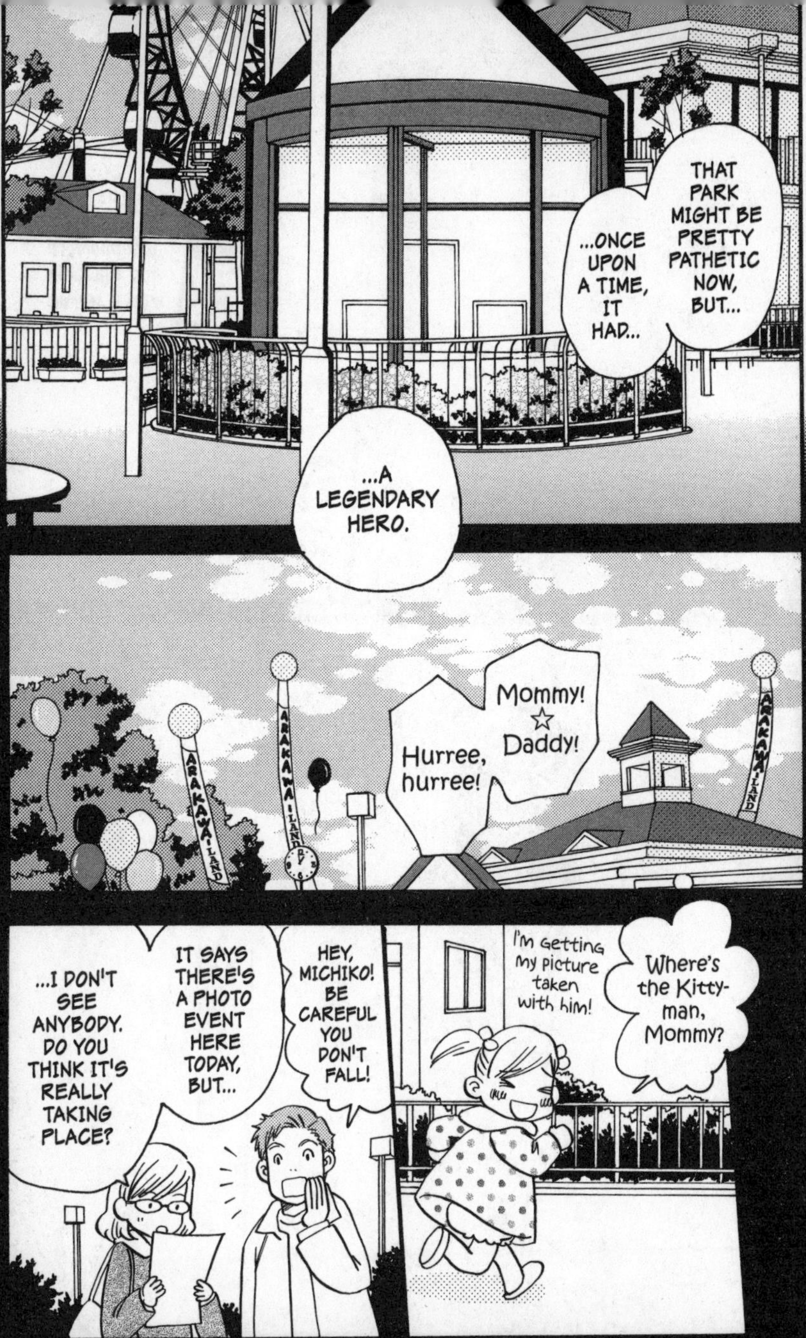
THAT PARK MIGHT BE PRETTY PATHETIC NOW, BUT...
...ONCE UPON A TIME, IT HAD...
...A LEGENDARY HERO.
Mommy! ☆ Daddy!
Hurree, hurree!
ARAKAWA LAND
Where's the Kitty-man, Mommy?
I'm getting my picture taken with him!
HEY, MICHIKO! BE CAREFUL YOU DON'T FALL!
IT SAYS THERE'S A PHOTO EVENT HERE TODAY, BUT...
...I DON'T SEE ANYBODY. DO YOU THINK IT'S REALLY TAKING PLACE?

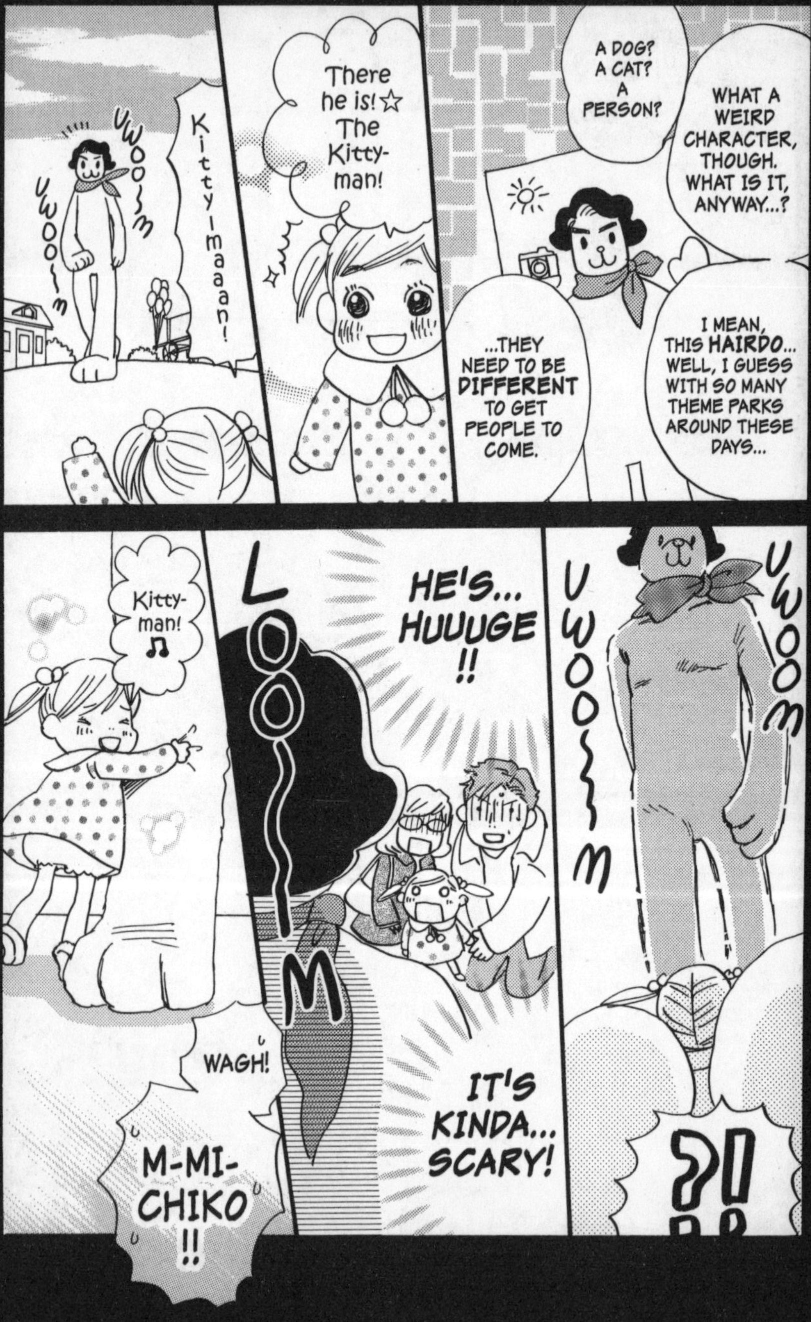
WHAT A WEIRD CHARACTER, THOUGH. WHAT IS IT, ANYWAY...?
A DOG? A CAT? A PERSON?
I MEAN, THIS **HAIRDO**... WELL, I GUESS WITH SO MANY THEME PARKS AROUND THESE DAYS...
...THEY NEED TO BE **DIFFERENT** TO GET PEOPLE TO COME.
There he is! ☆ The Kitty-man!
UWOO~M
UWOO~M
Kitty-maaaan!
UWOOOM
UWOO~M
?!!
HE'S... HUUUGE!!
LOOO~M
IT'S KINDA... SCARY!
WAGH!
M-MI-CHIKO!!
Kitty-man! ♫

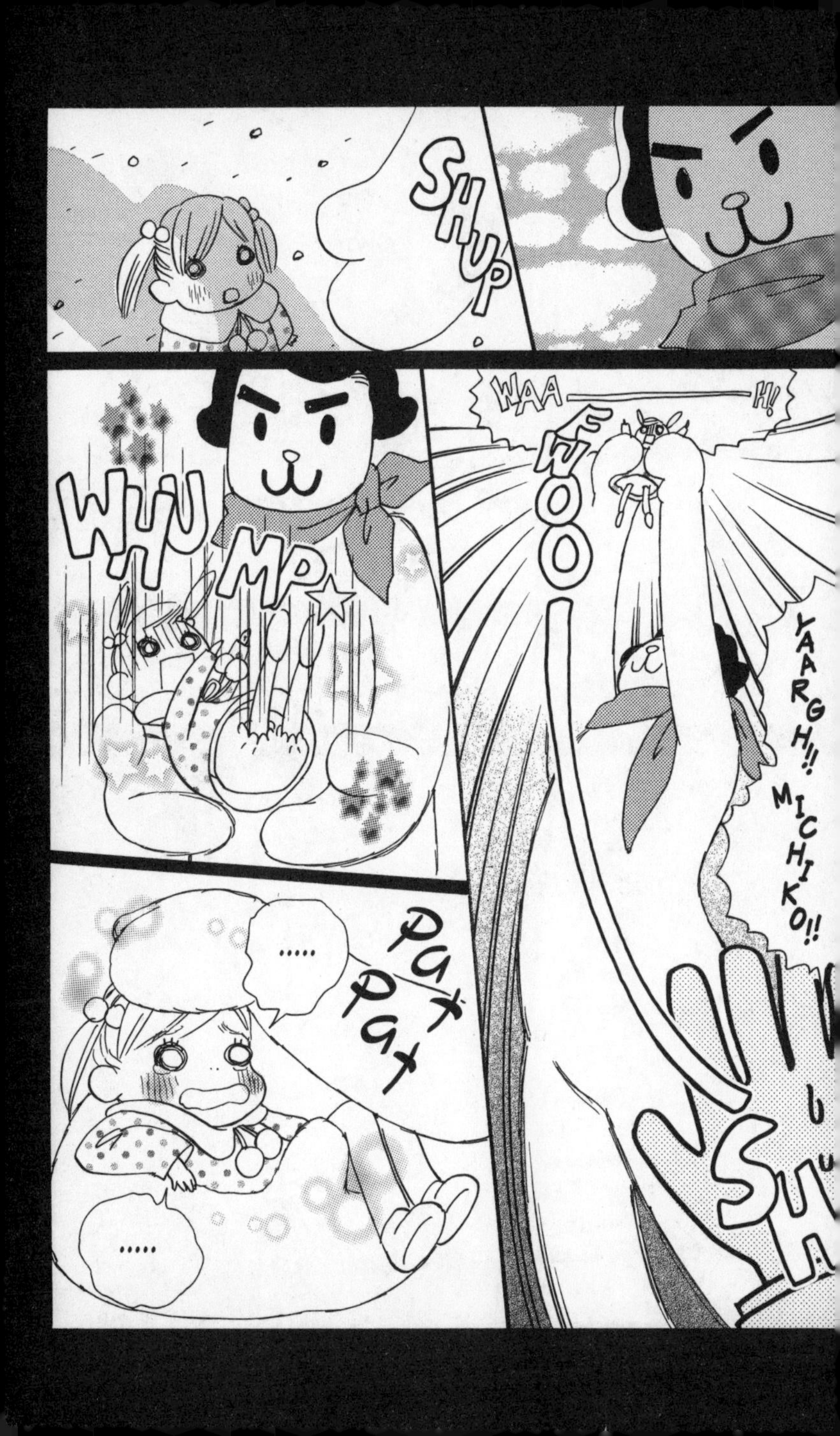
SHUP
WAA——H!
FWOOO!
YAARGH!! MICHIKO!!
WHUMP
......
Pat Pat
......

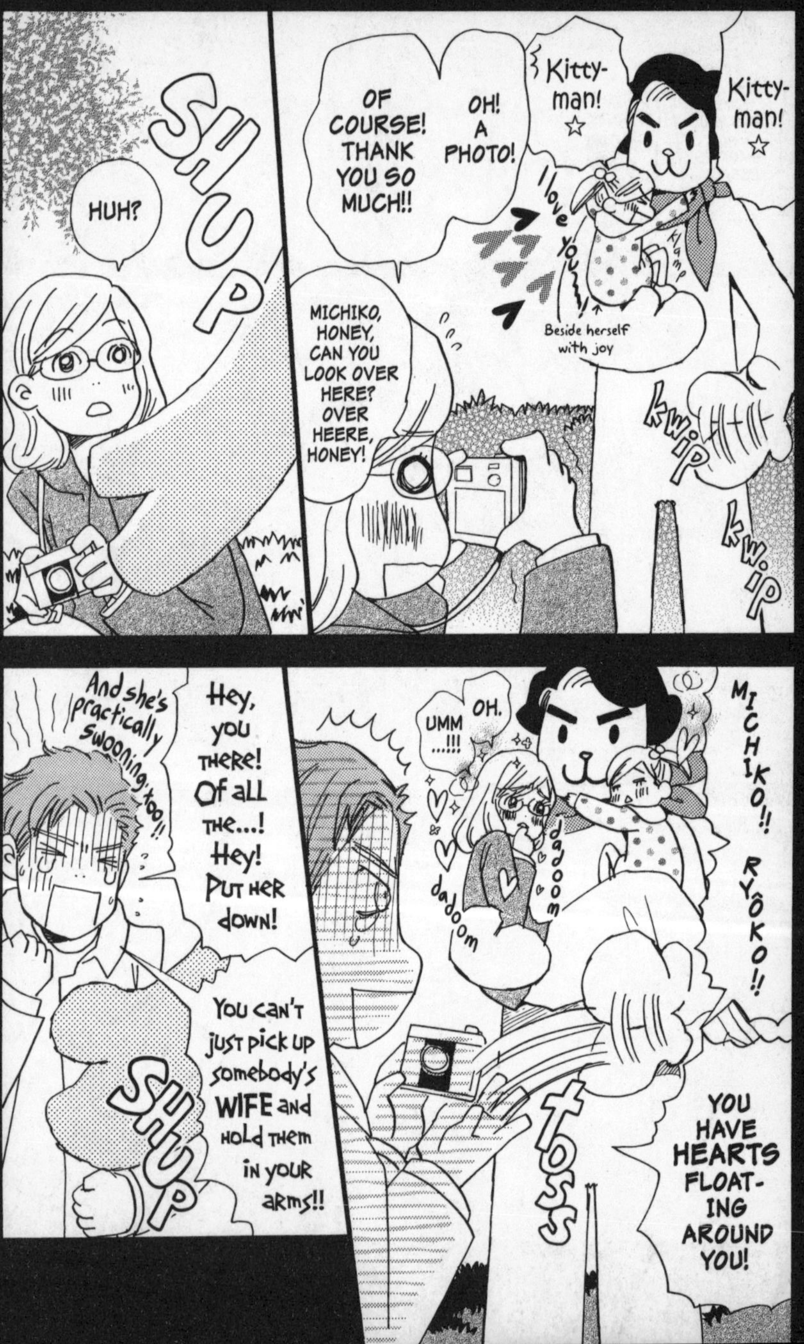
Kitty-man! ☆
Kitty-man! ☆
OH! A PHOTO!
OF COURSE! THANK YOU SO MUCH!!
I love you
klamp
Beside herself with joy
kwip
kwip
MICHIKO, HONEY, CAN YOU LOOK OVER HERE? OVER HEERE, HONEY!
SHUP
HUH?
MICHIKO!! RYÔKO!!
OH.
UMM ...!!!
dadoom
dadoom
YOU HAVE HEARTS FLOATING AROUND YOU!
toss
Hey, you there! Of all the...! Hey! Put her down!
And she's practically swooning, too!!
You can't just pick up somebody's WIFE and hold them in your arms!!
SHUP

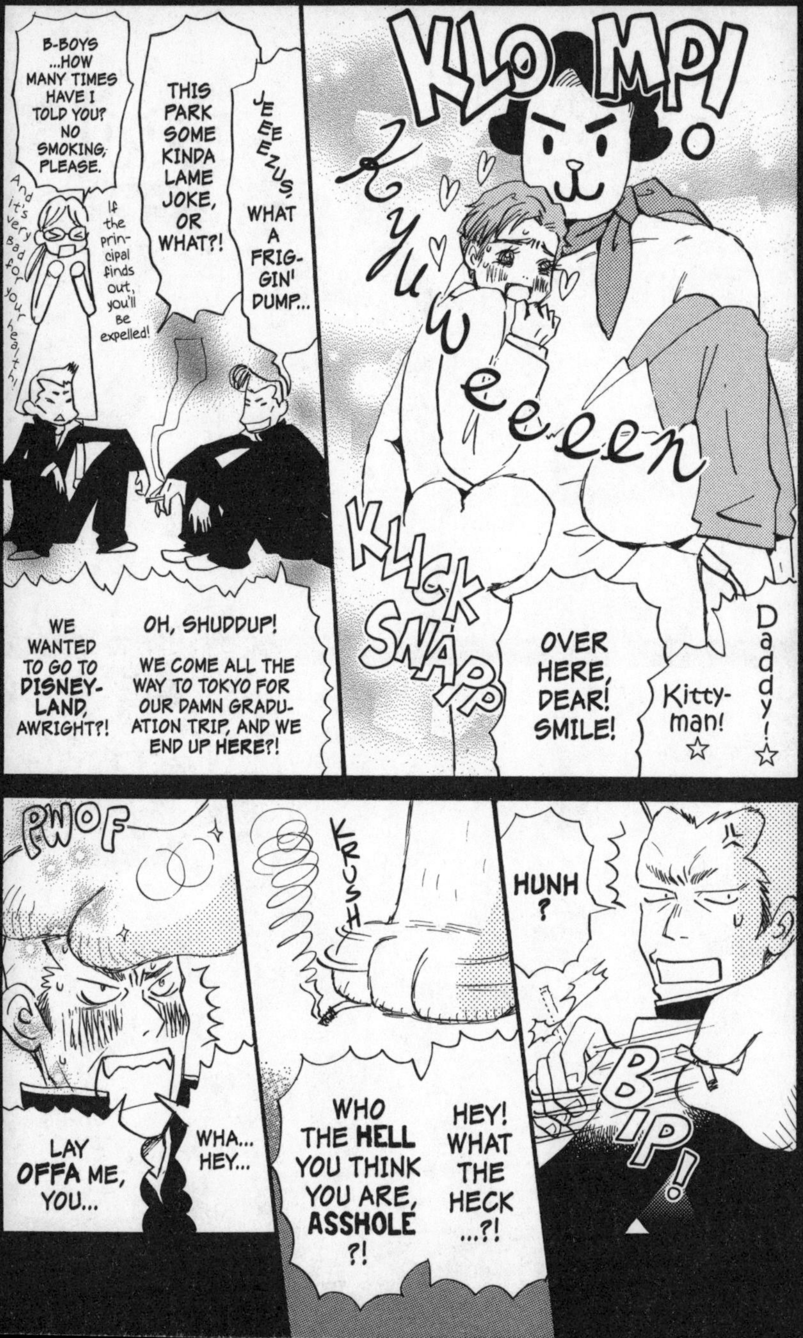
KLOMP!
kyuweeeen
KLICK SNAPP
Daddy! ☆
Kitty-man! ☆
OVER HERE, DEAR! SMILE!
JEEEEZUS, WHAT A FRIGGIN' DUMP...
THIS PARK SOME KINDA LAME JOKE, OR WHAT?!
B-BOYS ...HOW MANY TIMES HAVE I TOLD YOU? NO SMOKING, PLEASE.
And it's very bad for your health!
If the principal finds out, you'll be expelled!
OH, SHUDDUP!
WE COME ALL THE WAY TO TOKYO FOR OUR DAMN GRADUATION TRIP, AND WE END UP HERE?!
WE WANTED TO GO TO DISNEYLAND, AWRIGHT?!
HUNH?
BIP!
HEY! WHAT THE HECK ...?!
KRUSH
WHO THE HELL YOU THINK YOU ARE, ASSHOLE?!
PWOF
WHA... HEY...
LAY OFFA ME, YOU...

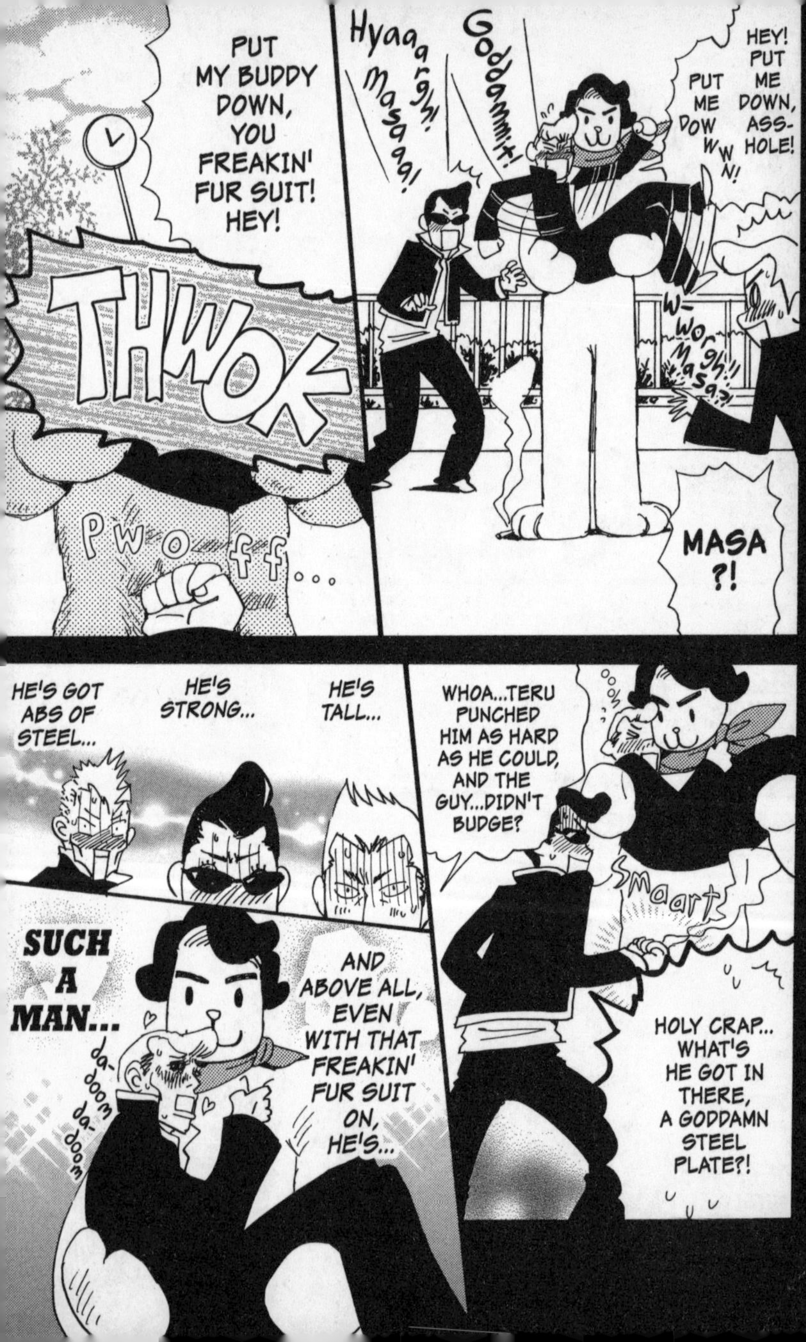
HEY! PUT ME DOWN, ASS-HOLE!
PUT ME DOWWWN!
Goddammit!
Hyaaargh! Masaaa!
W-worgh! Masa?!
MASA?!
PUT MY BUDDY DOWN, YOU FREAKIN' FUR SUIT! HEY!
THWOK
pwofff...
ooh
WHOA...TERU PUNCHED HIM AS HARD AS HE COULD, AND THE GUY...DIDN'T BUDGE?
Smaart
HOLY CRAP... WHAT'S HE GOT IN THERE, A GODDAMN STEEL PLATE?!
HE'S TALL...
HE'S STRONG...
HE'S GOT ABS OF STEEL...
AND ABOVE ALL, EVEN WITH THAT FREAKIN' FUR SUIT ON, HE'S...
SUCH A MAN...
da-doom da-doom

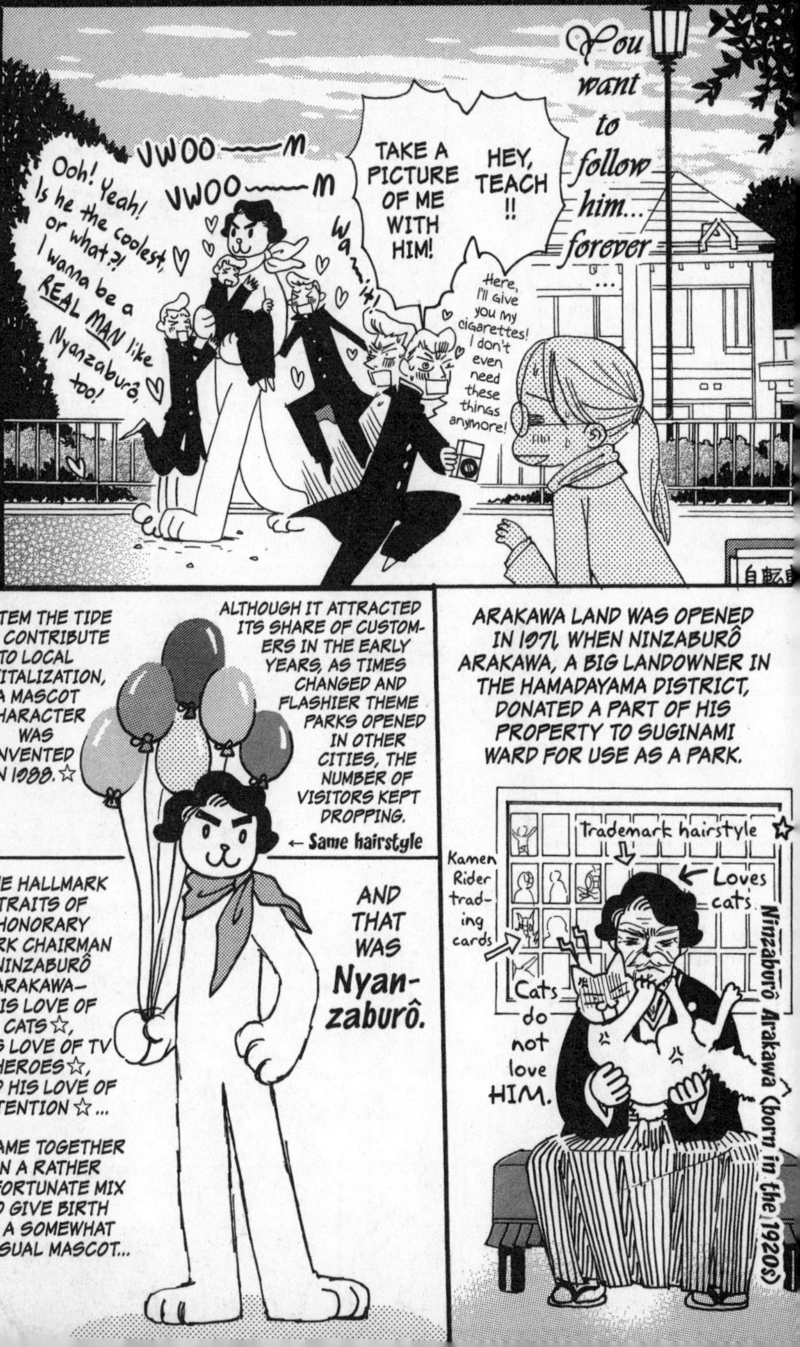
You want to follow him... forever...
HEY, TEACH!!
TAKE A PICTURE OF ME WITH HIM!
Here, I'll give you my cigarettes! I don't even need these things anymore!
Wa~it!
VWOO——M
VWOO——M
Ooh! Yeah! Is he the coolest, or what?! I wanna be a REAL MAN like Nyanzaburô, too!
ARAKAWA LAND WAS OPENED IN 1971, WHEN NINZABURÔ ARAKAWA, A BIG LANDOWNER IN THE HAMADAYAMA DISTRICT, DONATED A PART OF HIS PROPERTY TO SUGINAMI WARD FOR USE AS A PARK.
Trademark hairstyle ☆
Loves cats
Kamen Rider trading cards
Cats do not love HIM.
Ninzaburô Arakawa (born in the 1920s)
ALTHOUGH IT ATTRACTED ITS SHARE OF CUSTOMERS IN THE EARLY YEARS, AS TIMES CHANGED AND FLASHIER THEME PARKS OPENED IN OTHER CITIES, THE NUMBER OF VISITORS KEPT DROPPING.
← Same hairstyle
TO STEM THE TIDE AND CONTRIBUTE TO LOCAL REVITALIZATION, A MASCOT CHARACTER WAS INVENTED IN 1988.☆
AND THAT WAS Nyanzaburô.
THE HALLMARK TRAITS OF HONORARY PARK CHAIRMAN NINZABURÔ ARAKAWA—HIS LOVE OF CATS☆, HIS LOVE OF TV HEROES☆, AND HIS LOVE OF ATTENTION☆...
...CAME TOGETHER IN A RATHER UNFORTUNATE MIX TO GIVE BIRTH TO A SOMEWHAT UNUSUAL MASCOT...

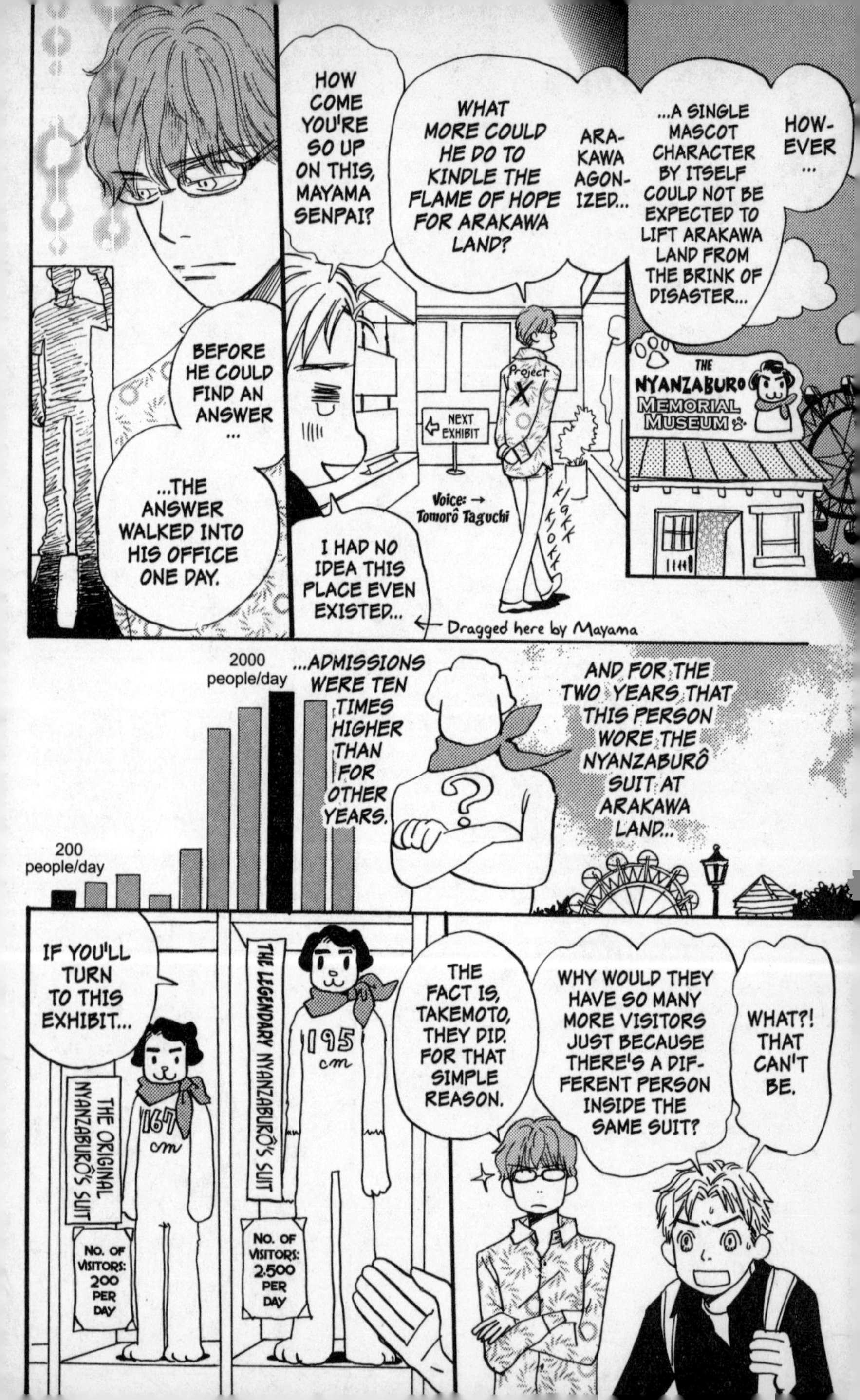
HOW-EVER...
...A SINGLE MASCOT CHARACTER BY ITSELF COULD NOT BE EXPECTED TO LIFT ARAKAWA LAND FROM THE BRINK OF DISASTER...
THE NYANZABURO MEMORIAL MUSEUM
ARA-KAWA AGON-IZED...
WHAT MORE COULD HE DO TO KINDLE THE FLAME OF HOPE FOR ARAKAWA LAND?
HOW COME YOU'RE SO UP ON THIS, MAYAMA SENPAI?
Project X
NEXT EXHIBIT
klokk klokk
Voice: → Tomorô Taguchi
I HAD NO IDEA THIS PLACE EVEN EXISTED...
Dragged here by Mayama
BEFORE HE COULD FIND AN ANSWER...
...THE ANSWER WALKED INTO HIS OFFICE ONE DAY.
AND FOR THE TWO YEARS THAT THIS PERSON WORE THE NYANZABURÔ SUIT AT ARAKAWA LAND...
...ADMISSIONS WERE TEN TIMES HIGHER THAN FOR OTHER YEARS.
2000 people/day
200 people/day
WHAT?! THAT CAN'T BE.
WHY WOULD THEY HAVE SO MANY MORE VISITORS JUST BECAUSE THERE'S A DIF-FERENT PERSON INSIDE THE SAME SUIT?
THE FACT IS, TAKEMOTO, THEY DID. FOR THAT SIMPLE REASON.
THE LEGENDARY NYANZABURÔ'S SUIT
195 cm
NO. OF VISITORS: 2,500 PER DAY
IF YOU'LL TURN TO THIS EXHIBIT...
THE ORIGINAL NYANZABURÔ'S SUIT
167 cm
NO. OF VISITORS: 200 PER DAY

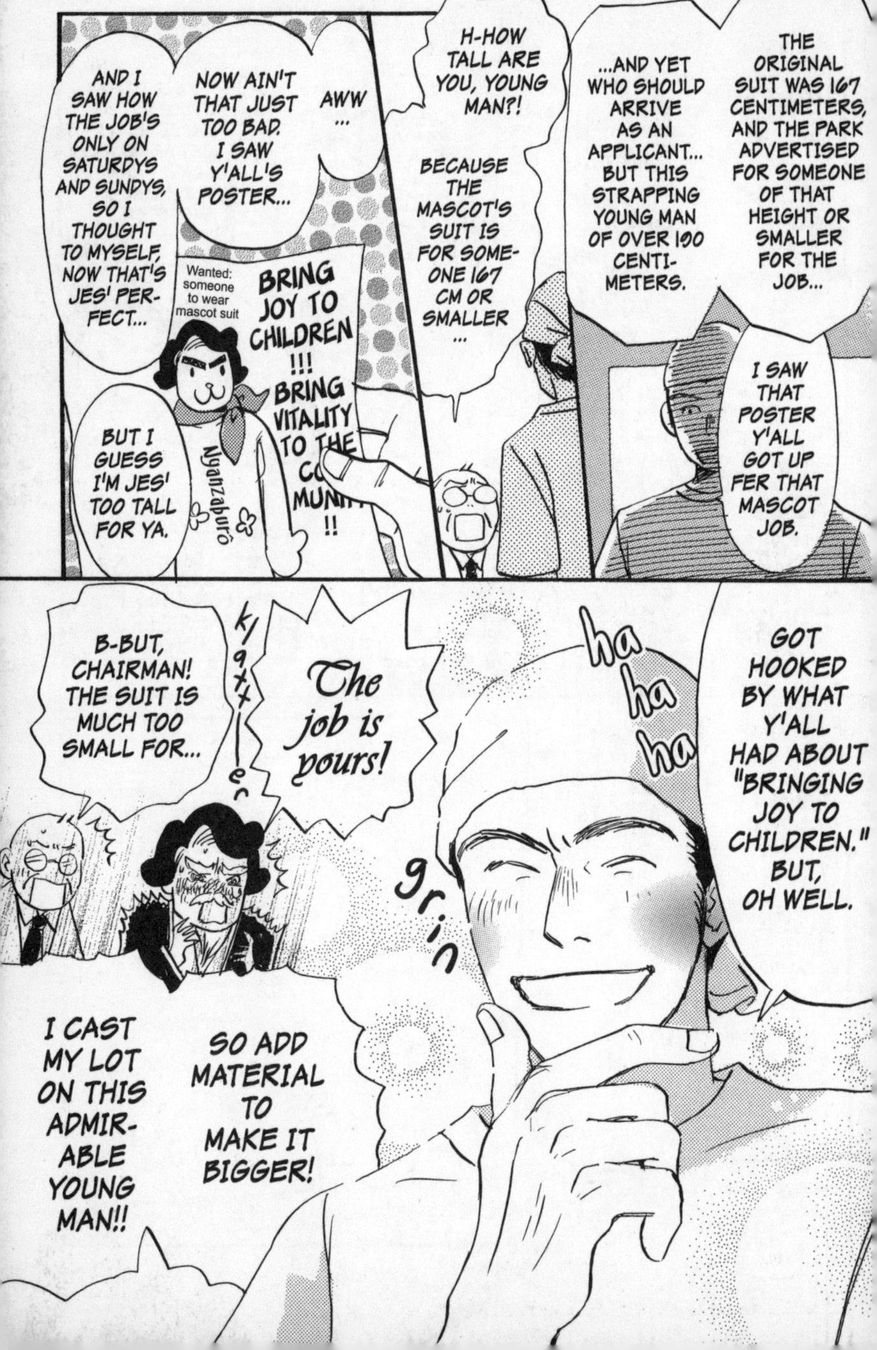
THE ORIGINAL SUIT WAS 167 CENTIMETERS, AND THE PARK ADVERTISED FOR SOMEONE OF THAT HEIGHT OR SMALLER FOR THE JOB...
...AND YET WHO SHOULD ARRIVE AS AN APPLICANT... BUT THIS STRAPPING YOUNG MAN OF OVER 190 CENTI-METERS.
I SAW THAT POSTER Y'ALL GOT UP FER THAT MASCOT JOB.
H-HOW TALL ARE YOU, YOUNG MAN?!
BECAUSE THE MASCOT'S SUIT IS FOR SOME-ONE 167 CM OR SMALLER ...
AWW ...
NOW AIN'T THAT JUST TOO BAD. I SAW Y'ALL'S POSTER...
AND I SAW HOW THE JOB'S ONLY ON SATURDYS AND SUNDYS, SO I THOUGHT TO MYSELF, NOW THAT'S JES' PER-FECT...
Wanted: someone to wear mascot suit
BRING JOY TO CHILDREN !!! BRING VITALITY TO THE
Nyanzaburō
BUT I GUESS I'M JES' TOO TALL FOR YA.
GOT HOOKED BY WHAT Y'ALL HAD ABOUT "BRINGING JOY TO CHILDREN." BUT, OH WELL.
ha ha ha
grin
The job is yours!
B-BUT, CHAIRMAN! THE SUIT IS MUCH TOO SMALL FOR...
SO ADD MATERIAL TO MAKE IT BIGGER!
I CAST MY LOT ON THIS ADMIR-ABLE YOUNG MAN!!

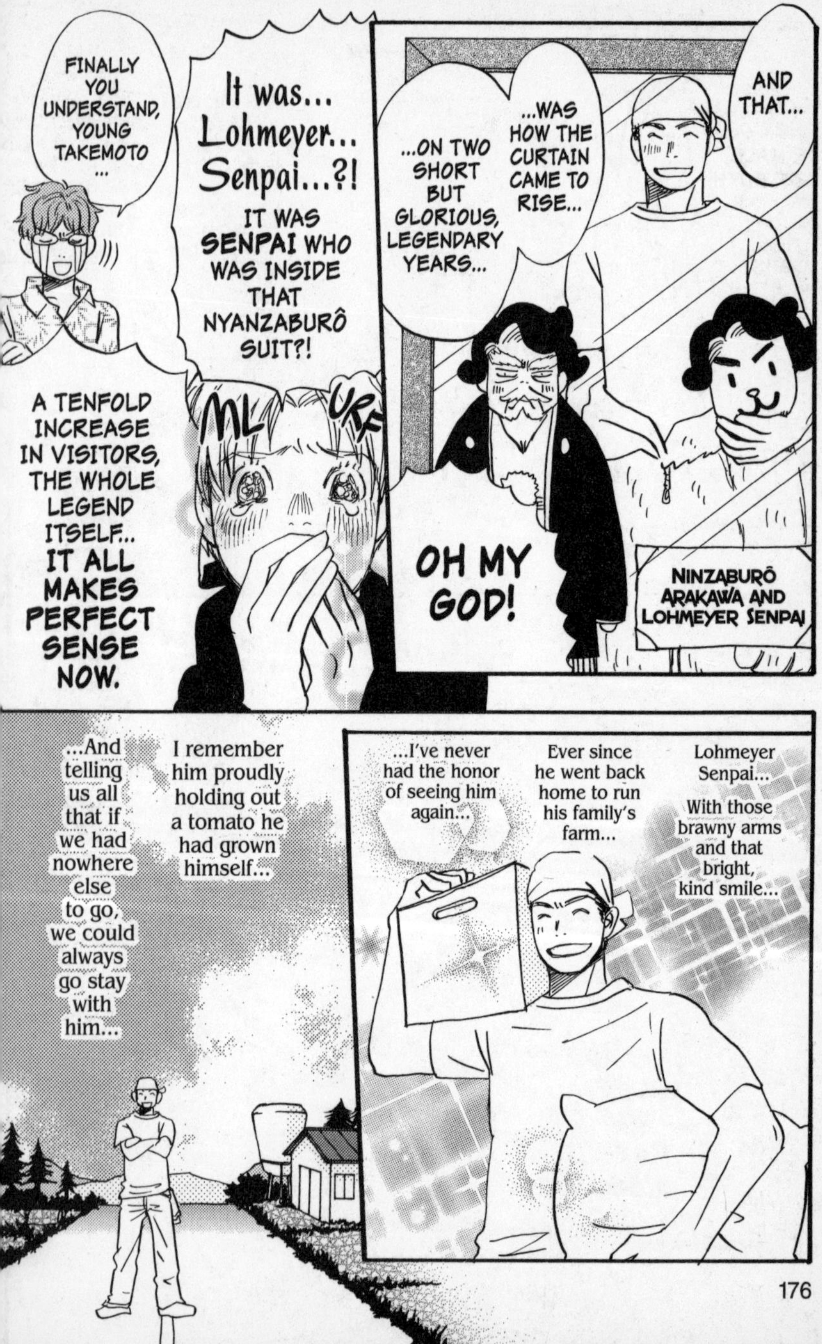
AND THAT...
...WAS HOW THE CURTAIN CAME TO RISE...
...ON TWO SHORT BUT GLORIOUS, LEGENDARY YEARS...
NINZABURÔ ARAKAWA AND LOHMEYER SENPAI
OH MY GOD!
It was... Lohmeyer... Senpai...?!
IT WAS SENPAI WHO WAS INSIDE THAT NYANZABURÔ SUIT?!
FINALLY YOU UNDERSTAND, YOUNG TAKEMOTO ...
MLURF
A TENFOLD INCREASE IN VISITORS, THE WHOLE LEGEND ITSELF... IT ALL MAKES PERFECT SENSE NOW.
Lohmeyer Senpai...
With those brawny arms and that bright, kind smile...
Ever since he went back home to run his family's farm...
...I've never had the honor of seeing him again...
I remember him proudly holding out a tomato he had grown himself...
...And telling us all that if we had nowhere else to go, we could always go stay with him...

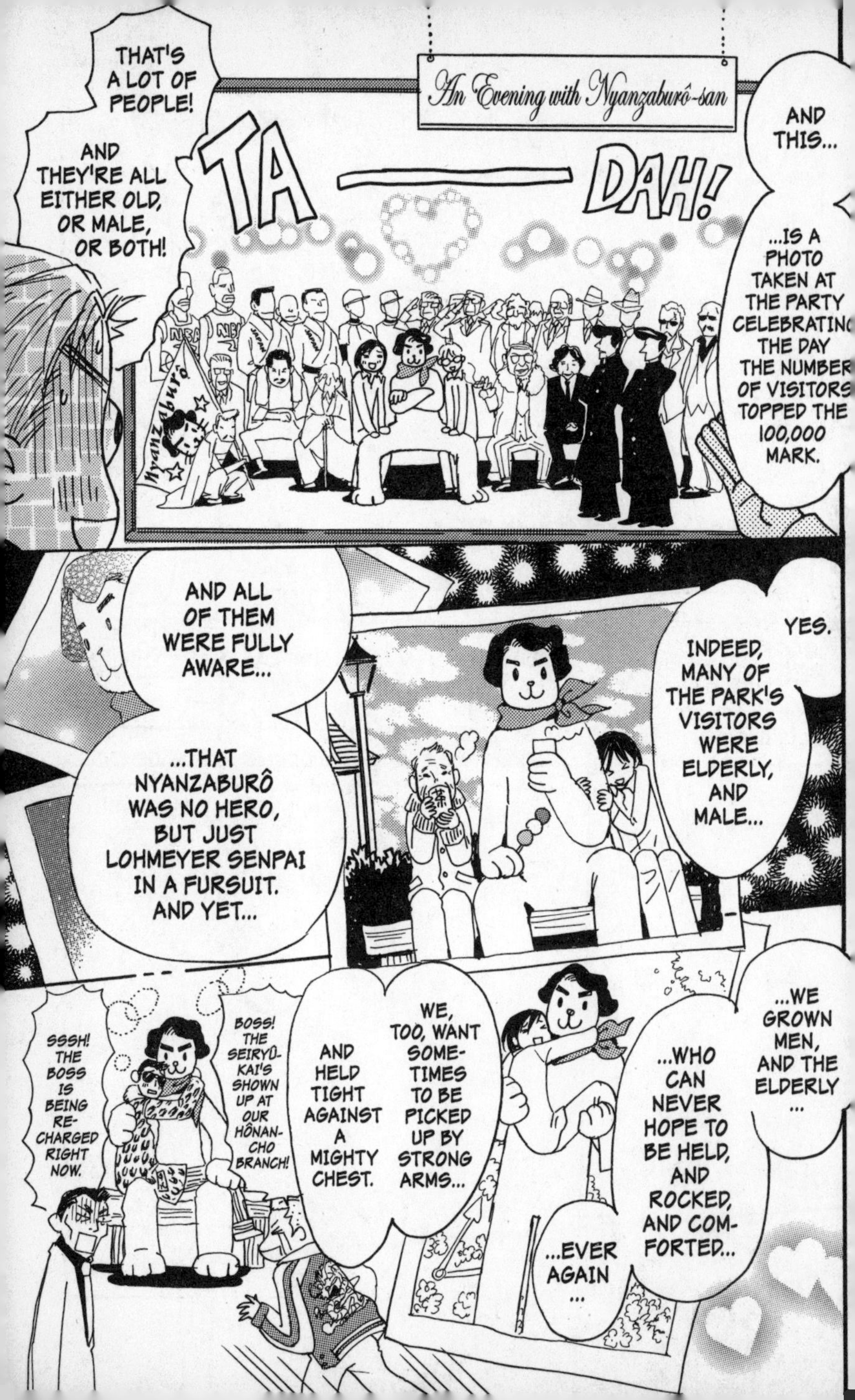
AND THIS...
...IS A PHOTO TAKEN AT THE PARTY CELEBRATING THE DAY THE NUMBER OF VISITORS TOPPED THE 100,000 MARK.
An Evening with Nyanzaburô-san
TA—DAH!
THAT'S A LOT OF PEOPLE!
AND THEY'RE ALL EITHER OLD, OR MALE, OR BOTH!
Nyanzaburô
YES.
INDEED, MANY OF THE PARK'S VISITORS WERE ELDERLY, AND MALE...
AND ALL OF THEM WERE FULLY AWARE...
...THAT NYANZABURÔ WAS NO HERO, BUT JUST LOHMEYER SENPAI IN A FURSUIT. AND YET...
...WE GROWN MEN, AND THE ELDERLY ...
...WHO CAN NEVER HOPE TO BE HELD, AND ROCKED, AND COMFORTED...
...EVER AGAIN ...
WE, TOO, WANT SOMETIMES TO BE PICKED UP BY STRONG ARMS...
AND HELD TIGHT AGAINST A MIGHTY CHEST.
BOSS! THE SEIRYÛ-KAI'S SHOWN UP AT OUR HÔNAN-CHO BRANCH!
SSSH! THE BOSS IS BEING RECHARGED RIGHT NOW.

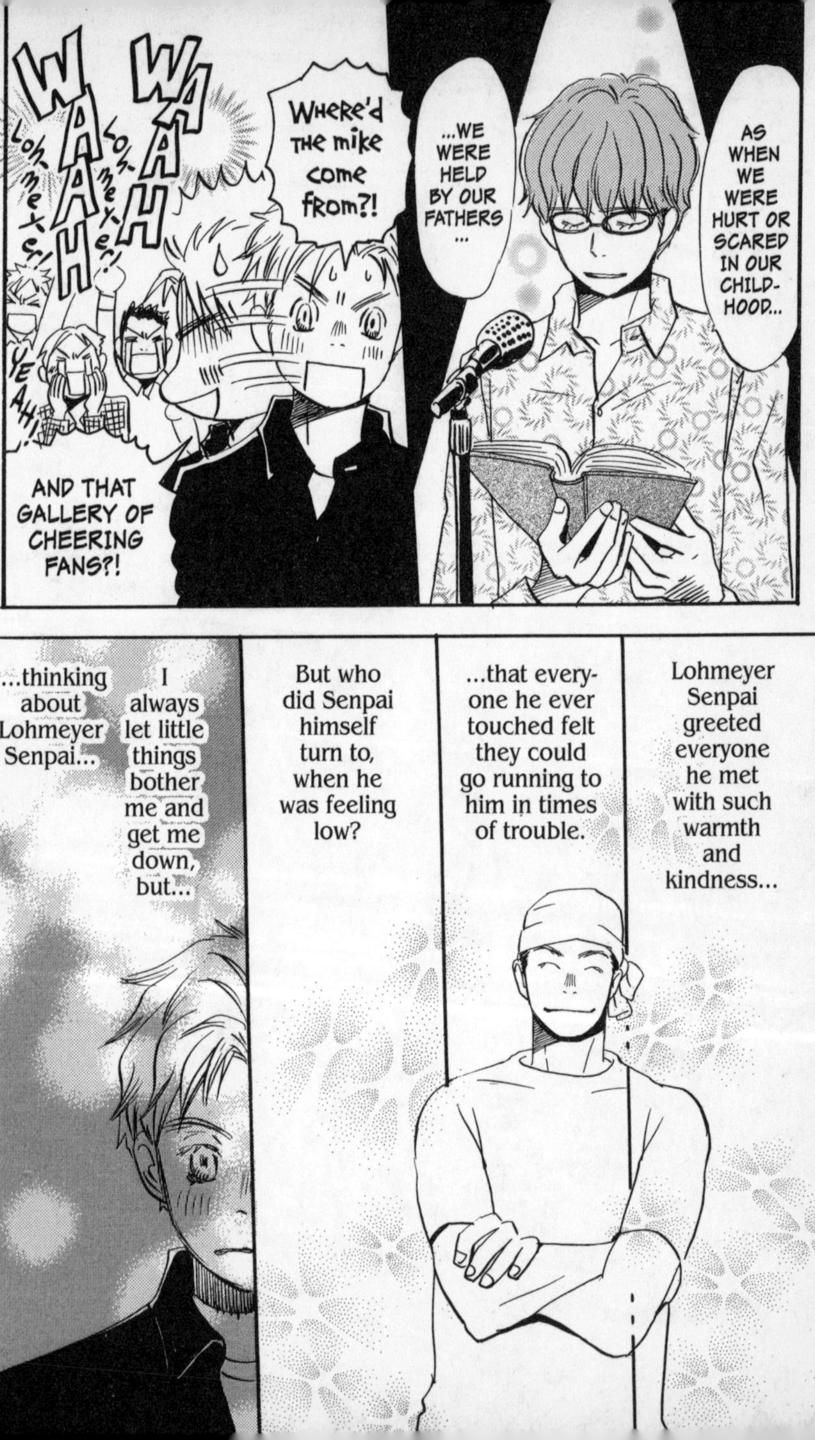
AS WHEN WE WERE HURT OR SCARED IN OUR CHILDHOOD...
...WE WERE HELD BY OUR FATHERS...
Where'd the mike come from?!
WAAAH
Lohmeyer!
WAAAAH
Lohmeyer!
YEAH!
AND THAT GALLERY OF CHEERING FANS?!
Lohmeyer Senpai greeted everyone he met with such warmth and kindness...
...that everyone he ever touched felt they could go running to him in times of trouble.
But who did Senpai himself turn to, when he was feeling low?
I always let little things bother me and get me down, but...
...thinking about Lohmeyer Senpai...

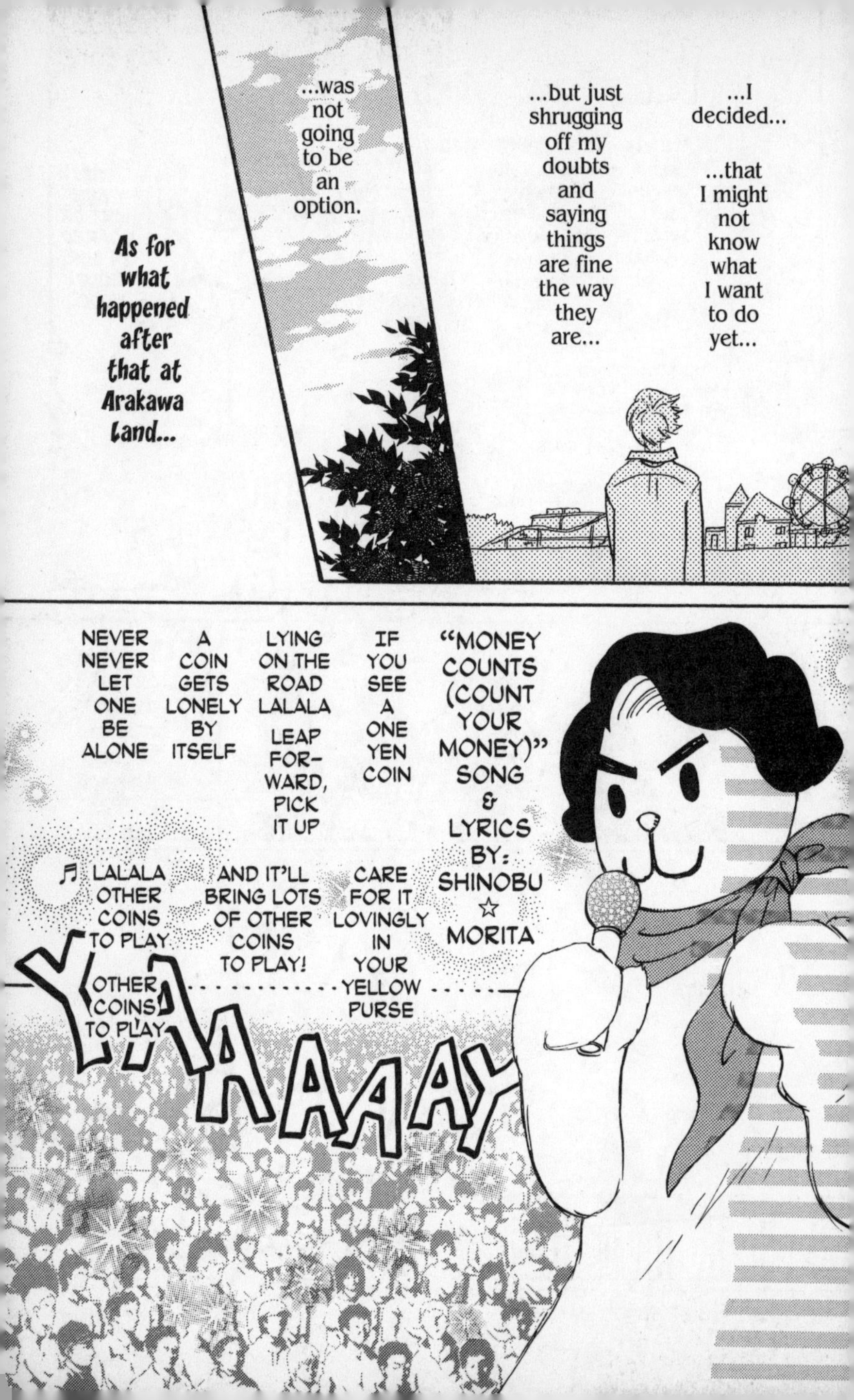
...I decided...
...that I might not know what I want to do yet...
...but just shrugging off my doubts and saying things are fine the way they are...
...was not going to be an option.
As for what happened after that at Arakawa Land...
"MONEY COUNTS (COUNT YOUR MONEY)" SONG & LYRICS BY: SHINOBU ☆ MORITA
IF YOU SEE A ONE YEN COIN
LYING ON THE ROAD LALALA
LEAP FOR-WARD, PICK IT UP
A COIN GETS LONELY BY ITSELF
NEVER NEVER LET ONE BE ALONE
CARE FOR IT LOVINGLY IN YOUR YELLOW PURSE
AND IT'LL BRING LOTS OF OTHER COINS TO PLAY!
♫ LALALA OTHER COINS TO PLAY
OTHER COINS TO PLAY
YAAAAY

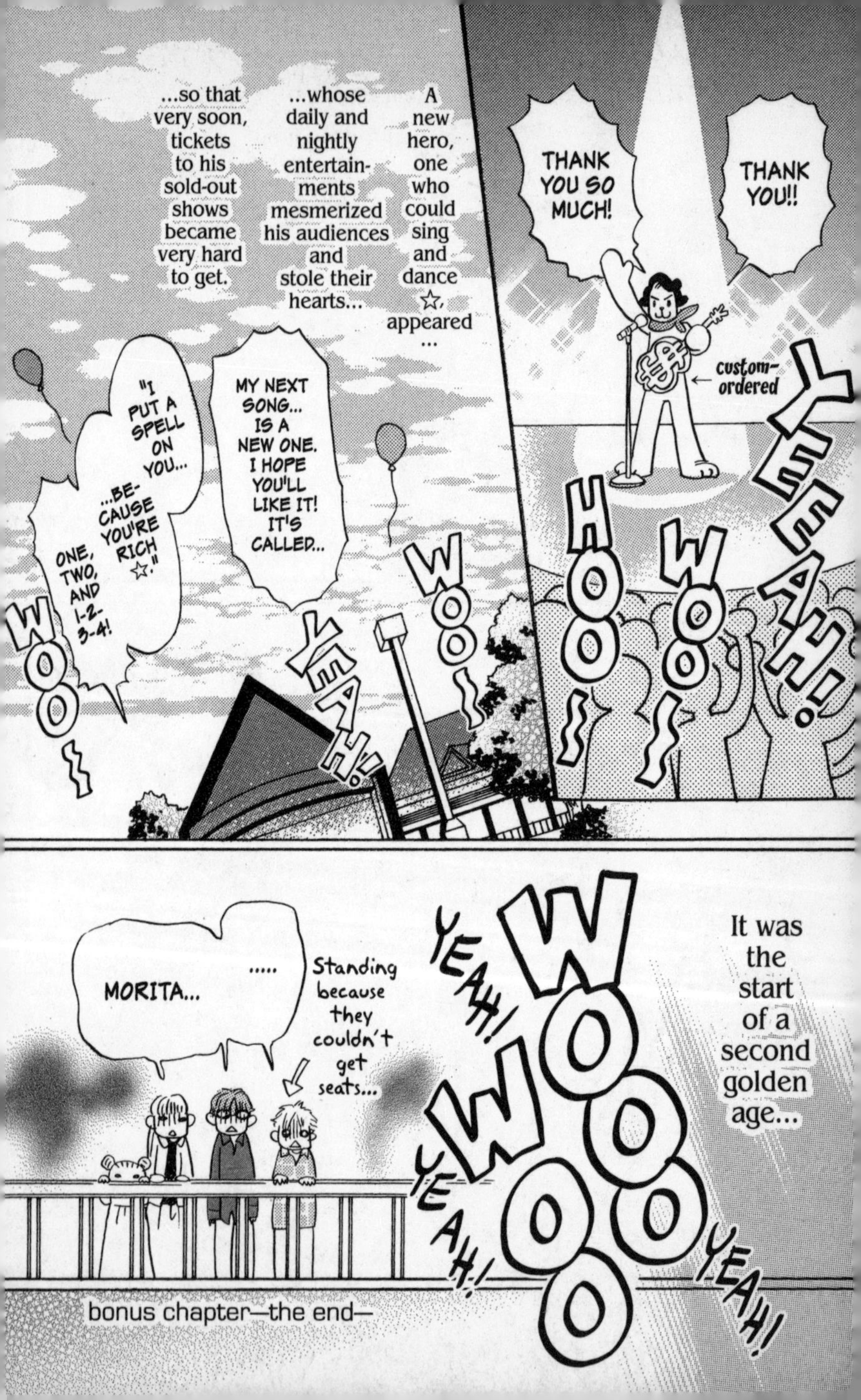
THANK YOU!!
THANK YOU SO MUCH!
custom-ordered
YEAH!
WOO~
HOO~
A new hero, one who could sing and dance ☆, appeared...
...whose daily and nightly entertainments mesmerized his audiences and stole their hearts...
...so that very soon, tickets to his sold-out shows became very hard to get.
WOO~
YEAH!
MY NEXT SONG... IS A NEW ONE. I HOPE YOU'LL LIKE IT! IT'S CALLED...
"I PUT A SPELL ON YOU... ...BECAUSE YOU'RE RICH ☆."
ONE, TWO, AND 1-2-3-4!
WOO~
It was the start of a second golden age...
YEAH!
WOOOOOO
YEAH!
YEAH!
Standing because they couldn't get seats...
.....
MORITA...
bonus chapter—the end—

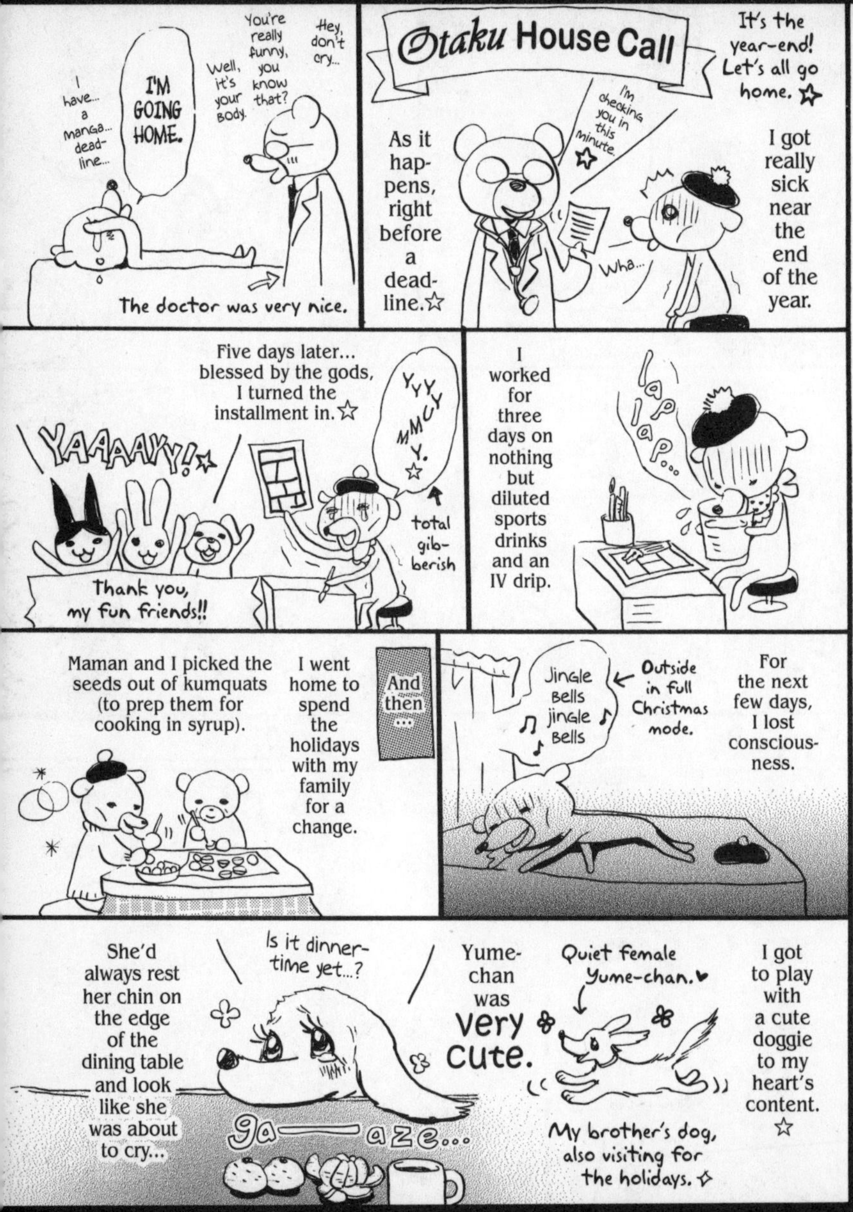
Otaku House Call
It's the year-end! Let's all go home.
I got really sick near the end of the year.
I'm checking you in this minute.
Wha...
As it happens, right before a deadline.
Hey, don't cry...
You're really funny, you know that?
Well, it's your body.
I'M GOING HOME.
I have... a manga... deadline...
The doctor was very nice.
I worked for three days on nothing but diluted sports drinks and an IV drip.
lap lap...
Five days later... blessed by the gods, I turned the installment in.
YYYY MMUY Y.
total gibberish
YAAAAAY!
Thank you, my fun friends!!
For the next few days, I lost consciousness.
Outside in full Christmas mode.
Jingle Bells jingle Bells
And then...
I went home to spend the holidays with my family for a change.
Maman and I picked the seeds out of kumquats (to prep them for cooking in syrup).
I got to play with a cute doggie to my heart's content.
Quiet female Yume-chan.
Yume-chan was very cute.
My brother's dog, also visiting for the holidays.
Is it dinner-time yet...?
She'd always rest her chin on the edge of the dining table and look like she was about to cry...
ga—aze...

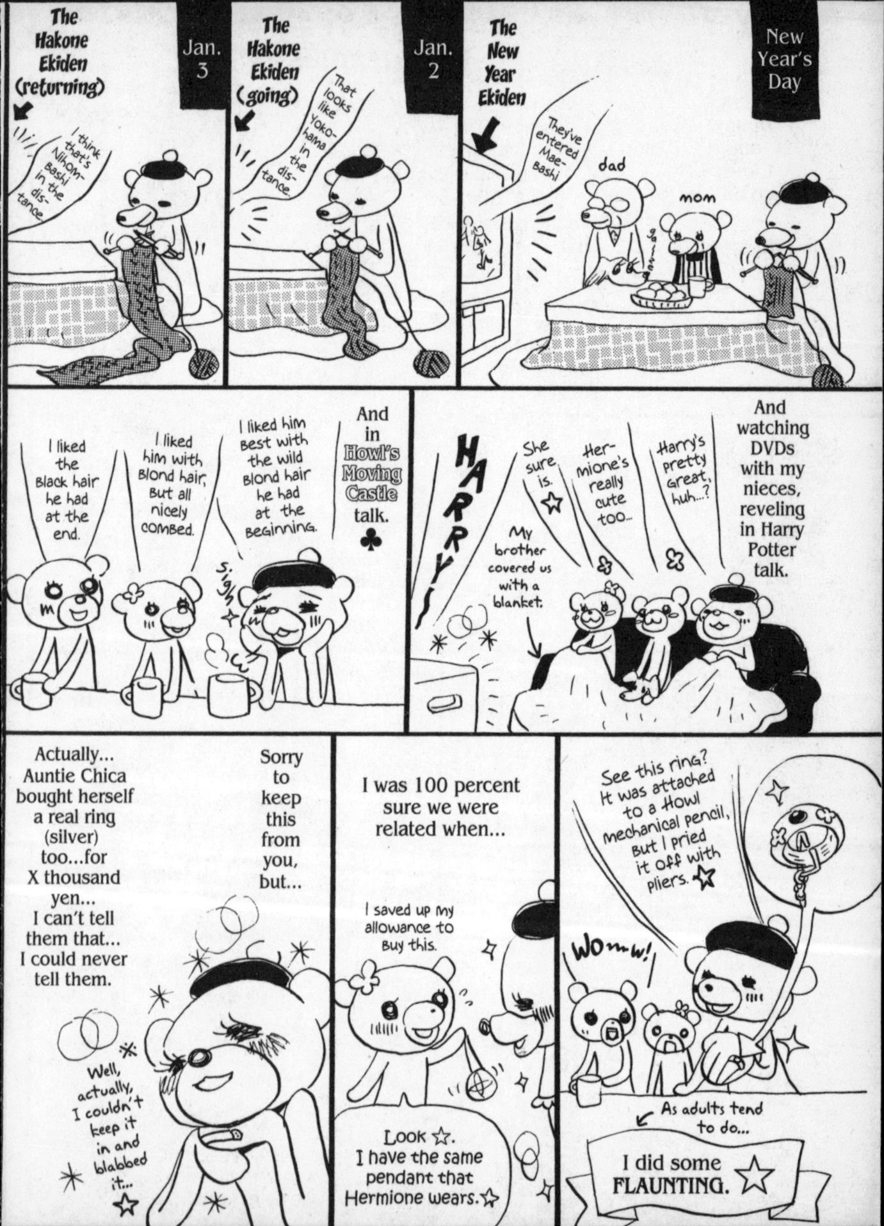
New Year's Day
The New Year Ekiden
They've entered Mae-Bashi
dad
mom
Jan. 2
The Hakone Ekiden (going)
That looks like Yoko-hama in the dis-tance.
Jan. 3
The Hakone Ekiden (returning)
I think that's Nihom-Bashi in the dis-tance.
And watching DVDs with my nieces, reveling in Harry Potter talk.
Harry's pretty great, huh...?
Her-mione's really cute too...
She sure is. ☆
HARRY!
My brother covered us with a blanket.
And in Howl's Moving Castle talk. ♣
I liked him best with the wild blond hair he had at the beginning.
I liked him with blond hair, but all nicely combed.
I liked the black hair he had at the end.
sigh
See this ring? It was attached to a Howl mechanical pencil, but I pried it off with pliers. ☆
WOmw!
As adults tend to do...
I did some FLAUNTING. ☆
I was 100 percent sure we were related when...
I saved up my allowance to buy this.
Look ☆. I have the same pendant that Hermione wears. ☆
Sorry to keep this from you, but...
Actually... Auntie Chica bought herself a real ring (silver) too...for X thousand yen... I can't tell them that... I could never tell them.
Well, actually, I couldn't keep it in and blabbed it... ☆

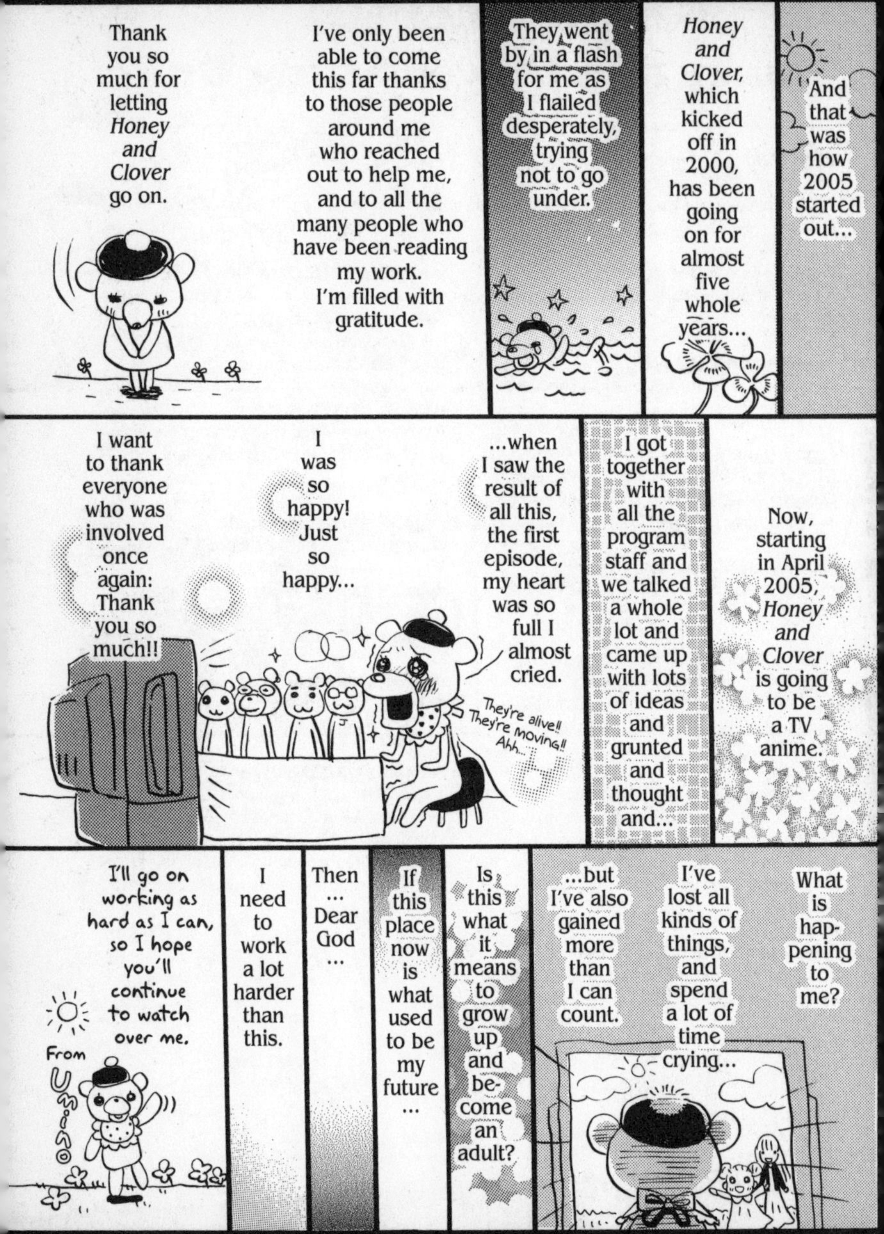
And that was how 2005 started out...
Honey and Clover, which kicked off in 2000, has been going on for almost five whole years...
They went by in a flash for me as I flailed desperately, trying not to go under.
I've only been able to come this far thanks to those people around me who reached out to help me, and to all the many people who have been reading my work. I'm filled with gratitude.
Thank you so much for letting Honey and Clover go on.
Now, starting in April 2005, Honey and Clover is going to be a TV anime.
I got together with all the program staff and we talked a whole lot and came up with lots of ideas and grunted and thought and...
...when I saw the result of all this, the first episode, my heart was so full I almost cried.
They're alive!! They're moving!! Ahh...
I was so happy! Just so happy...
I want to thank everyone who was involved once again: Thank you so much!!
What is hap-pening to me?
I've lost all kinds of things, and spend a lot of time crying...
...but I've also gained more than I can count.
Is this what it means to grow up and become an adult?
If this place now is what used to be my future...
Then... Dear God...
I need to work a lot harder than this.
I'll go on working as hard as I can, so I hope you'll continue to watch over me.
From Umino

To be continued ★

I'm keeping a rental diary.
http://www2.diary.ne.jp/user/162279/

Honey and Clover Study Guide

Page 6, panel 2: Hamabi
This is the short name for Hamadayama Bijutsu Daigaku, the Hamadayama Art Institute.

Page 7, panel 1: O Matsushima
A poem attributed to either Matsuo Bashô or Tawarabo.

Page 7, panel 5: Hatoya
The Hatoya is a hotel in Ito City in Shizuoka Prefecture.

Page 7, panel 5: Matsushima no sayo…
A traditional folk song called "Saitara Bushi." The lyrics basically mean "No temple is so great as Matsushima's Zuiganji."

Page 7, panel 5: Takasaki
A city fifty minutes north of Tokyo by bullet train.

Page 7, panel 5: Bon Odori
A type of dance performed during Obon, the Japanese festival to honor the deceased. Each region has its own style of dancing and music for the Bon Odori.

Page 8, panel 2: Zuiganji Temple
A Buddhist temple that was founded in 828 CE. The current buildings were completed in 1609 by the shogun Date Masamune. The caves and grottos on the temple grounds were carved out by the monks.

Page 8, panel 4: Shôrin-zan Darumaji
A Buddhist temple in Takasaki. Among other things, it is known for hosting the Daruma-ichi, the largest and most well-known daruma market in Japan.

Page 16, panel 2: Sendai
A city one hour and forty minutes north of Tokyo by bullet train. It is on the same latitude as Washington, D.C..

page 35, panel 5: Oarai Shinkin
Shinkin means "credit union." Many Japanese companies, like banks and newspapers, give people towels or other small gifts for being members.

page 36, panel 2: Nattô
A type of fermented soybean considered an acquired taste due to its strong smell and slimy texture.

Page 36, panel 4: Rice scoop
In Japanese, this is called *shamoji* (しゃもじ).

Page 37, panel 1: Sylgard
A type of plaster or clay commonly used in building construction.

Page 38, panel 1: Kiriboshi daikon
Kiriboshi daikon are strips of dried daikon radish that are soaked in water before use.

Page 55, Panel 2: Omiyage (souvenirs)
It's customary to buy regional foodstuffs for your office and friends when you travel. Mayama couldn't decide what to buy, so he bought more than enough. The packages include *purin* (similar to flan), cakes, and *manju* (Japanese sweets).

Page 58, panel 4: Katsu curry
Japanese-style curry made with *katsu*, breaded and deep-fried pork cutlet.

Page 70, panel 3: Nama yatsuhashi
A Kyoto specialty made from rice flour, sugar, and cinnamon. *Nama yatsuhashi* has a soft texture, and when wrapped around bean paste, it is called *otabe*. Cooked *yatsuhashi* becomes cracker-like.

Page 75, panel 5: Omikuji
It literally means "sacred lots," and they are drawn at shrines and temples. There are usually five grades of fortune, although seven grades and beyond can be found. The five grades are *daikichi* (big luck), *kichi* (luck), *chûkichi* (medium luck), *shôkichi* (small luck), and *kyô* (bad luck).

Page 92: Hokkaido
The northernmost and second largest of the Japanese islands. It is also the least developed and coldest of the islands.

Page 92, panel 2: Wakkanai
The northernmost city in Japan. Cape Soya, the northernmost point, is located in Wakkanai, and from it you can see Russia (or at least a Russian island).

Page 92, panel 4: Haramaki
Thick bands of fabric, usually wool or cotton, worn around the belly to help a person keep warm. Recently they have started to become more fashionable in Japan and have even made it over to America.

Page 96, panel 5: Enoshima
An island at the mouth of Katase River, near Fujisawa in Kanagawa Prefecture. It is part of a resort area known for its natural beauty.

Page 96, panel 5: Yuigahama beach
A beach near Kamakura, in Kanagawa Prefecture.

Page 110, panel 5: Kenji Miyazawa
A beloved Japanese children's author from the early 20th century (1896-1933). Some of his works have been translated into English, including *Night on the Milky Way Railroad*, *Matasaburo the Wind Imp*, and *Once and Forever: the Tales of Kenji Miyazawa*.

Page 119: The Big Dipper
It is *Hokutosei* (北斗星) in Japanese, which literally means "big dipper." It is a sleeper train that runs from Ueno to Sapporo in about 16 and a half hours.

Page 151, panel 5: Namahage
A Japanese bogeyman in Akita Prefecture, of the type used to scare misbehaving children.

Page 156, panel 4: Omiki
Sacred sake offered to the gods at Shinto altars like the *mikoshi*.

Page 156, panel 4: Mikoshi
A portable Shinto shrine. During festivals, people carry the mikoshi around on their shoulders using long poles.

Page 174, panel 2: Project X, Taguchi Tomorowo
A weekly show on NHK that tells the story of some big challenge faced by a group of people, usually a Japanese company in its early days (but not always) by mixing interviews, documentary footage, and reenactments. The narrator Taguchi Tomorowo has a very distinctive style of speaking, which Mayama is mimicking.

Honey and Clover will be an anime starting this April. Just the other day, I got to see all of the characters moving, for the first time... I almost cried. They were so boisterously alive in the light of springtime. It made me so happy. So very happy.

-Chica Umino

Chica Umino was born in Tokyo and started out as a product designer and illustrator. Her beloved *Honey and Clover* debuted in 2000 and received the Kodansha Manga Award in 2003. *Honey and Clover* was also nominated for the Tezuka Culture Prize and an award from the Japan Media Arts Festival.

HONEY AND CLOVER
VOL. 7
The Shojo Beat Manga Edition

This manga volume contains material that was originally published in English in *Shojo Beat* magazine, #47-49. Artwork in the magazine may have been slightly altered from that presented here.

STORY AND ART BY CHICA UMINO

English Translation & Adaptation/Akemi Wegmuller
Touch-up Art & Lettering/Sabrina Heep
Design/Yukiko Whitley
Editor/Pancha Diaz

VP, Production/Alvin Lu
VP, Publishing Licensing/Rika Inouye
VP, Sales & Product Marketing/Gonzalo Ferreyra
VP, Creative/Linda Espinosa
Publisher/Hyoe Narita

Printed in Canada

Published by VIZ Media, LLC
P.O. Box 77010
San Francisco, CA 94107

www.viz.com

Shojo Beat Manga Edition
10 9 8 7 6 5 4 3 2 1
First printing, September 2009

RATED T+ FOR OLDER TEEN

PARENTAL ADVISORY
HONEY AND CLOVER is rated T+ for Older Teen and is recommended for ages 16 and up. This volume contains adult situations.

ratings.viz.com

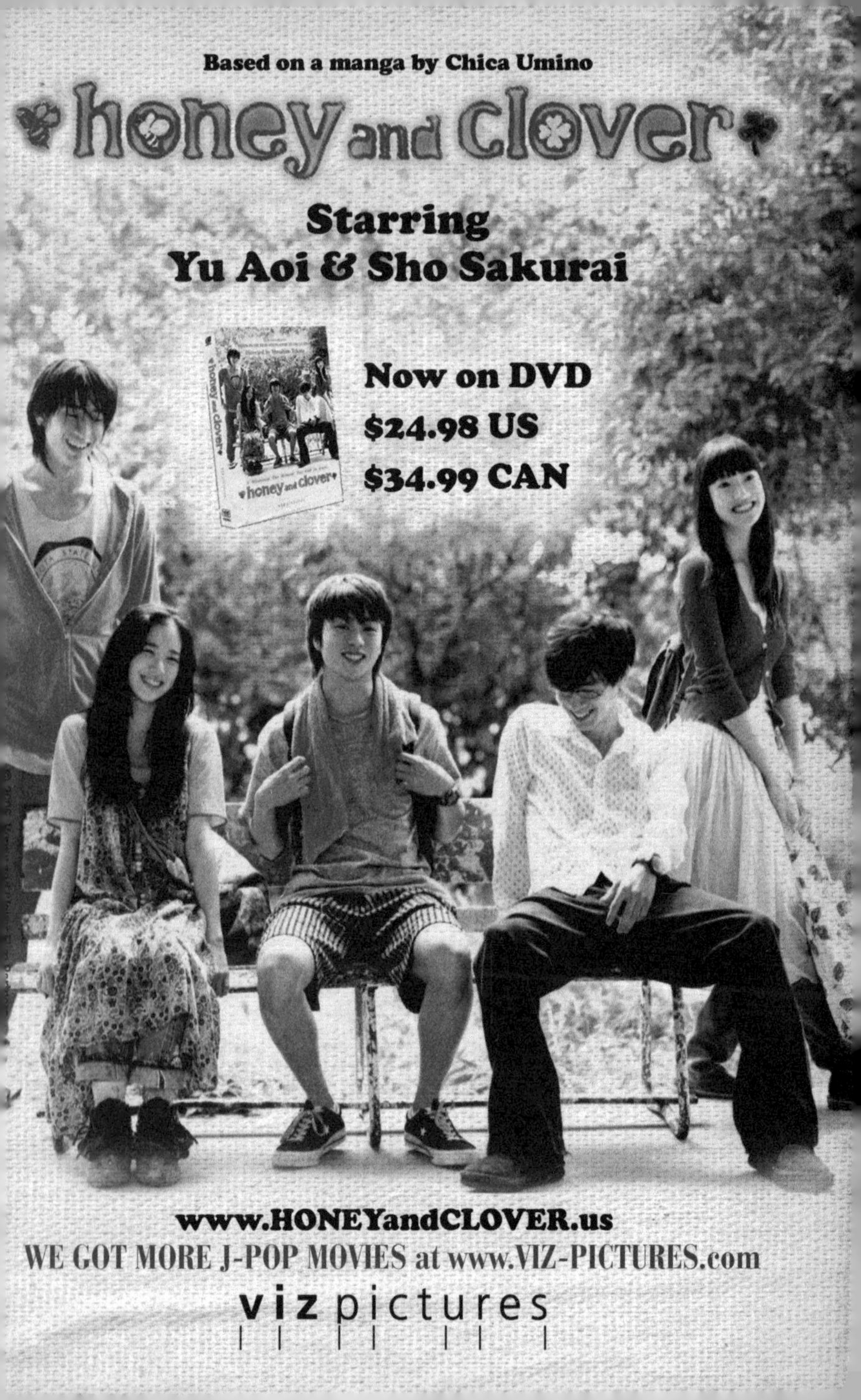
Based on a manga by Chica Umino
honey and clover
Starring
Yu Aoi & Sho Sakurai
Now on DVD
$24.98 US
$34.99 CAN
www.HONEYandCLOVER.us
WE GOT MORE J-POP MOVIES at www.VIZ-PICTURES.com
viz pictures

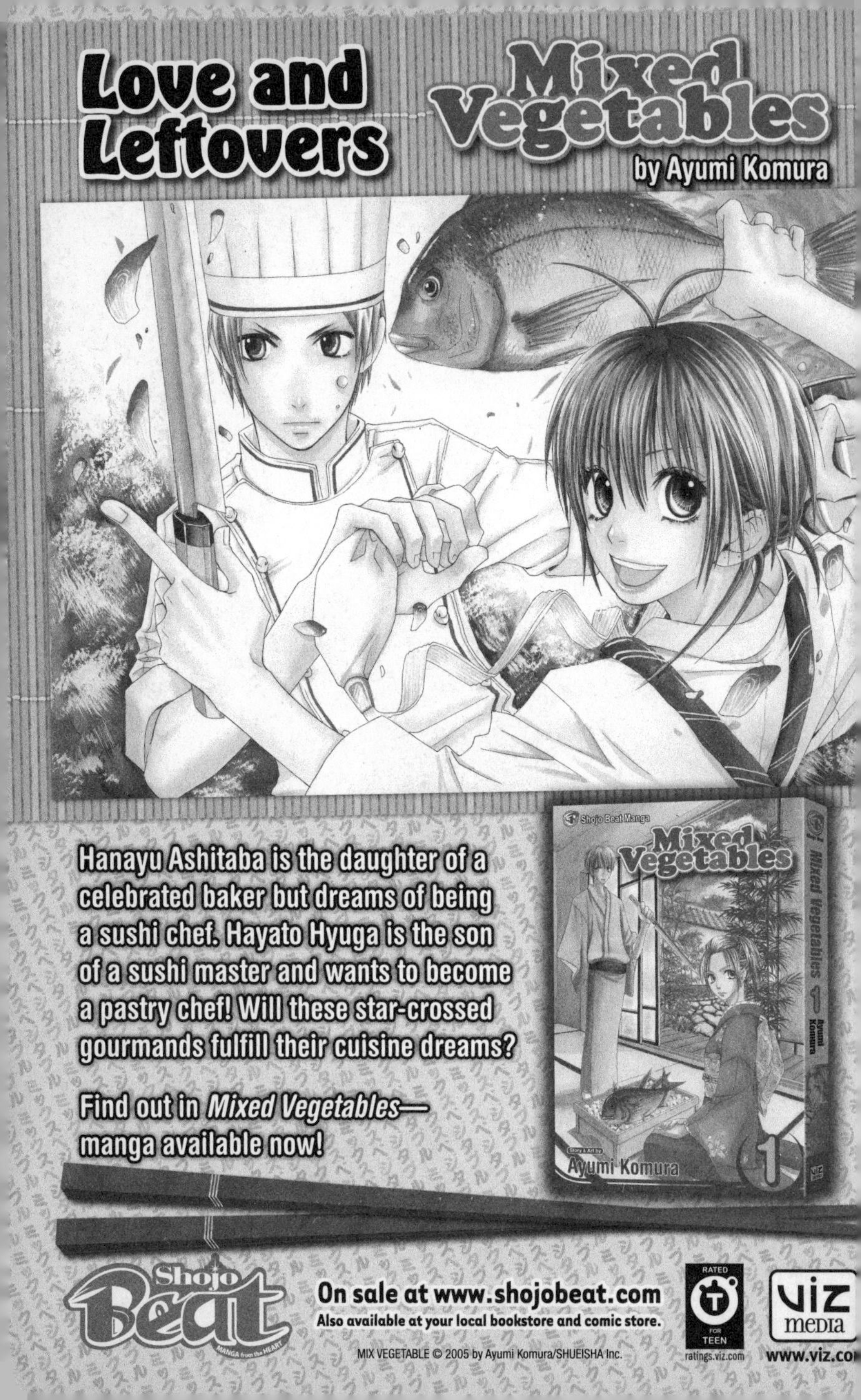

Love and Leftovers
Mixed Vegetables
by Ayumi Komura
Shojo Beat Manga
Mixed Vegetables
Ayumi Komura
1
Hanayu Ashitaba is the daughter of a celebrated baker but dreams of being a sushi chef. Hayato Hyuga is the son of a sushi master and wants to become a pastry chef! Will these star-crossed gourmands fulfill their cuisine dreams?
Find out in *Mixed Vegetables*—manga available now!
Shojo Beat
MANGA from the HEART
On sale at www.shojobeat.com
Also available at your local bookstore and comic store.
MIX VEGETABLE © 2005 by Ayumi Komura/SHUEISHA Inc.
RATED T FOR TEEN
ratings.viz.com
VIZ media
www.viz.com

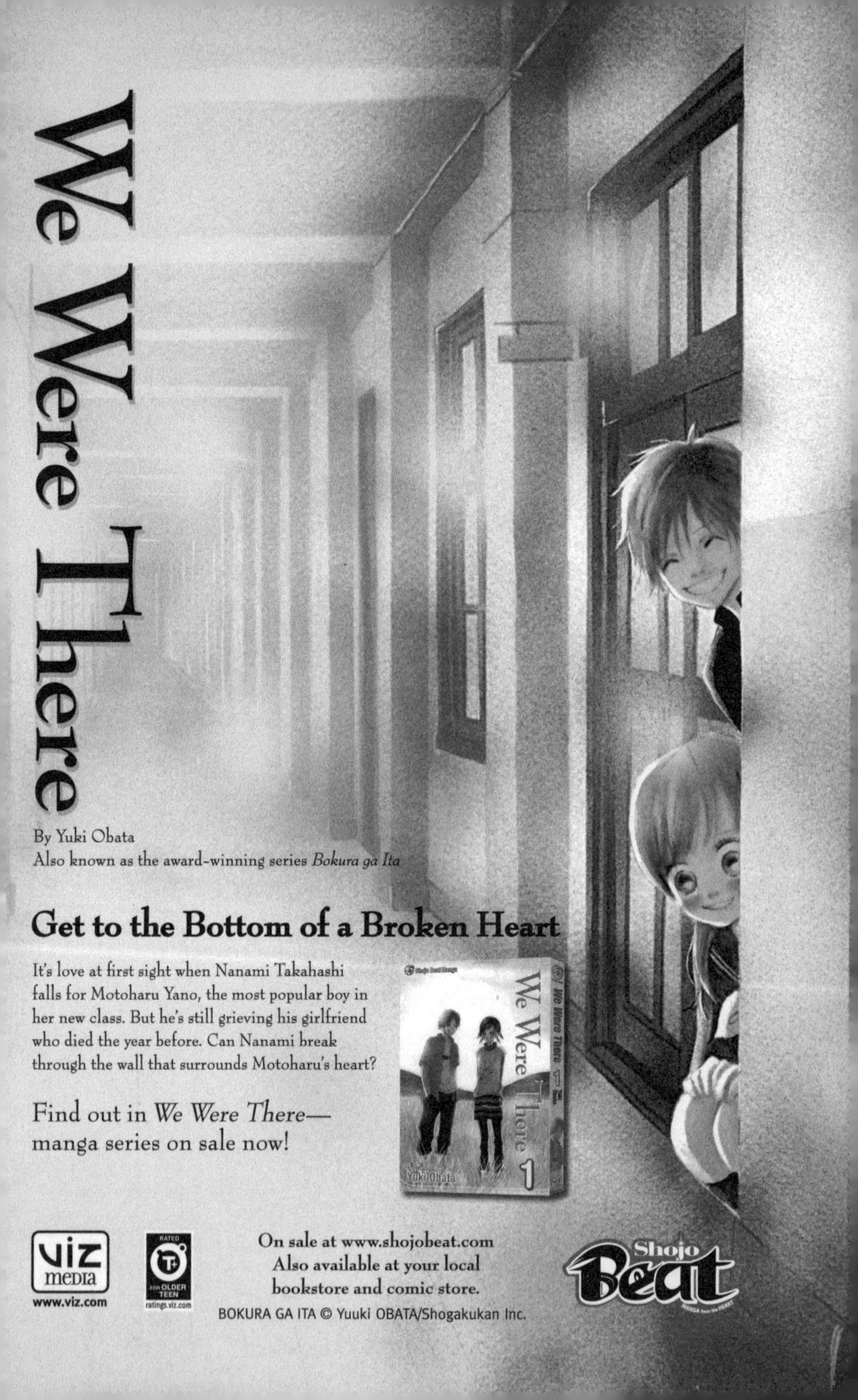

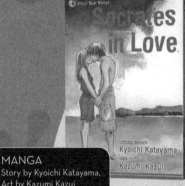